# STEPHEN ROACH ON
# THE NEXT
# ASIA

*Opportunities and Challenges for
a New Globalization*

### STEPHEN S. ROACH

*For Ed Yardeni —
We've had great
fun over the years.
Think Asia!
Be happy —
Best
6/11*

WILEY

John Wiley & Sons, Inc.

Published by John Wiley & Sons, Inc., Hoboken, New Jersey.
Published simultaneously in Canada.

For general information on our other products and services or for technical support, please contact our Customer Care Department within the United States at (800) 762-2974, outside the United States at (317) 572-3993 or fax (317) 572-4002.

Wiley also publishes its books in a variety of electronic formats. Some content that appears in print may not be available in electronic books. For more information about Wiley products, visit our web site at www.wiley.com.

*Library of Congress Cataloging-in-Publication Data:*

Roach, Stephen, 1945–
    Stephen Roach on the next Asia : opportunities and challenges for a new globalization / Stephen Roach.
       p.   cm.
    Includes index.
    ISBN 978-0-470-44699-7 (cloth)
    ISBN 978-0-470-64604-5 (paper)
       1. Investments—Asia.   2. United States—Foreign economic relations—Asia.   3. Asia—Foreign economic relations—Asia.   I. Title.
    HG5702.R63 2009
    332.67'3095—dc22                                                    2009023131

Printed in the United States of America
10  9 8 7 6 5 4 3 2 1

*For the 1.8 billion who remain on the outside looking in:*

*There can't be a Next Asia without you.*

# ■ Contents ■

# CHAPTER 4   PAN-ASIAN CHALLENGES                        261

# CHAPTER 5   U.S.-CHINA TENSIONS                          327

# ■ *Acknowledgments* ■

This effort is an outgrowth of the journey that I have been on over the past quarter century plus. There are countless souls who have touched me along the way—offering guidance, encouragement, feedback, and pushback at each and every fork in the road. In the interest of space, I single out those who have been instrumental in guiding me in my explorations of Asia and in getting me to put pen to paper in finishing this project—apologies to those who may have been left out.

My friends and colleagues at Morgan Stanley are at the top of the list. From John Mack, who came up with the hare-brained scheme to kick me upstairs and ship me off to Asia full time, to my partners in the region—Wei Christianson, Shane Zhang, Owen Thomas, Vincent Chui, Charlie Mak, Kate Richdale, Gokul Laroia, Will McLane, Aisha De Sequeira, Chetan Ahya, Ridham Desai, Qing Wang, Matthew Ginsburg, Che-Ning Liu, Gary Kuo, Ho Yang, and Jon Kindred—thanks to all of you and your teams for your unfailing support, curiosity, incredibly hard work, and for never failing to respond to my middle-of-the-night salvos. Your passion for Asia is infectious. It gave me the same bug.

The value of this journey is underscored by the friends I've made and the relationships that I have been privileged to build literally all over Asia—individuals who have added immeasurably to my own thinking and analysis of this extraordinary region. Special mention is due to my good friends in China—especially Zhu Min, Guo Shuqing, Lou Jiwei, Gao Xiqing, Jianxi Wang, Yang Yuanqing, Zhou Xiaochuan, Hu Xiaolian, Liu Minkang, Lu Mai, Levin Zhu, Liu Andong, Justin Lin, Fan Gang and Xiang Huaichen. Elsewhere in Asia, I have immense gratitude and respect for the insights of my friends in India—especially Mukesh

Ambani, Deepak Parekh, Montek Singh Ahluwalia, Rajiv Lall, and Pramod Bhasin—and in Singapore—especially Lee Kuan Yew, Lee Hsien Loong, Ho Ching, Ng Kok Song, and Heng Swee Keat. And this book has benefited immeasurably from my special friends in Hong Kong—in particular, Donald Tsang, K-S Li, Charley Song, Lawrence Lau, Frank Sixt, Solina Chau, Laura Cha, Ronnie Chan, Joseph Yam, and Shan Weijian. Finally, there is a cottage industry of Asian experts living outside the region, whose counsel and inspiration have been critical in shaping my impressions over the years. In that vein, I am particularly grateful to David Loevinger, David Ho, Pedro Nueno, Nick Lardy, Morris Goldstein, Laura Tyson, Jack Wadsworth, and Chip Kaye.

It took a lot of blocking and tackling to pull this effort together. My Morgan Stanley support team was awesome in that respect—especially the indefatigable Stefanie Fischer who shepherded this project along at each and every stage—but also Noel Cheung, Susanna Ip, Katherine Tai, and Denise Yam. My gratitude also to the editorial team at Wiley, especially Bill Falloon, Stacey Fischkelta, and Meg Freeborn.

Finally, my family. How they put up with my wanderlust, long absences, nocturnal work habits, and chronic jet lag, I'll never know. For my special partner, Katie—and our six wonderful girls—"Thanks" doesn't exactly cut it. But it will have to suffice for now—and it comes from the bottom of my heart.

# ■ *Introduction* ■

As the most dynamic and rapidly growing region in the world over the past decade, Developing Asia has attained a new level of prosperity. From China to India, the region's per capita income has more than doubled since the wrenching Asian financial crisis of 1997–1998. Since 1990, over 400 million fewer Asians are living at poverty levels defined by incomes of less than $2 per day. On the surface, the region has much to celebrate on the long and arduous road to economic development. Many believe the Asia Century is now at hand.

Such celebration may be premature. As 2008 came to an end, every economy in the region had either slowed sharply or tumbled into outright recession. Far from having the autonomous capacity to decouple from weakness elsewhere in the world, export-led Developing Asia had become even more tightly tethered to foreign markets than was the case a decade earlier. The export share of panregional gross domestic product (GDP) hit a record 47 percent in 2007, fully 10 percentage points higher than the portion in the late 1990s. With approximately 50 percent of those exports earmarked for the rich countries of the developed world, a rare and sharp synchronous downturn in the United States, Europe, and Japan undermined an increasingly important source of Asia's seemingly invincible growth dynamic. Far from celebrating a newfound resilience, the region was reeling from a severe external shock. Like it or not, Asia's newfound ascendancy remains precarious.

Ironically, this very outcome was predicted by China's Premier, Wen Jiabao. In a statement following the conclusion of the National People's Congress in March 2007, Premier Wen acknowledged that the Chinese economy looked extremely strong on the surface, especially in terms of

GDP and employment growth. Yet, beneath the surface, he cautioned, such strength was far more questionable. In the case of China, he warned of an economy that was increasingly, "unbalanced, unstable, uncoordinated, and unsustainable." Little did he realize at the time how those "four uns," as they were later to become known, would pose an immediate and tough challenge to China's growth imperatives. Nor did he or other Asian leaders appreciate the broader implications of those insights for the region as a whole.

In warning of the precarious state of the Chinese economy, Premier Wen Jiabao was expressing concerns about the nation's very risky macro bet. With nearly 80 percent of its GDP going to exports and fixed investment, China had become overly reliant on cross-border exports and on the investments required to support the logistics and capacity of its increasingly powerful export machine. In the boom, that structure worked spectacularly. With world exports moving up from 25 percent to a record 34 percent of global GDP trade over the 2000–2008 period, export-led economies had nothing but upside. They were in the right place at the right time, perfectly positioned to reap major windfalls in an era of unfettered globalization. But with the global boom now having gone bust, the imbalances of Asia's export-led growth strategy have played out to the downside with a vengeance. The region was overly reliant on exports at precisely the moment when external demand collapsed. Not only has China slowed dramatically—with export growth turning sharply negative in late 2008 and industrial output growth slipping into the low-single-digit zone—but the rest of an increasingly China-centric Asian economy has been quick to follow.

China's export dependency went far beyond the unbalanced structure of its real economy. Its financial and currency policies were also aimed at deriving maximum support from external demand. A closed capital account and an undervalued renminbi (RMB) were icing on the cake for China's powerful strain of export-led growth. Moreover, to the extent that its currency management objectives required ongoing recycling of a massive reservoir of foreign exchange reserves into U.S. dollar-based assets, such capital inflows helped keep longer-term U.S. interest rates at exceptionally low levels. In effect, China's implicit interest rate subsidy ended up becoming a key prop to bubble-prone U.S. asset markets and, ultimately, for the asset-dependent American consumer.

The linkage between Asian growth and the American consumer bears special mention. The U.S. consumer is still the dominant consumer in the global economy. Although America accounts for only about 4.5 percent of the world's population, its consumers spent about $10 trillion in 2008. By contrast, although China and India collectively account for nearly 40 percent of the world's population, their combined consumption was only about $2.5 trillion in 2008. Moreover, within the large economies of the developed world, America's trend growth of nearly 4 percent in real consumer demand over the past decade and a half was fully three times the pace of underlying consumption growth in Europe and Japan. During the boom, China and the rest of Asia reaped enormous benefits from a mercantilist growth model that was tied increasingly to the voracious appetite of the American consumer. As private U.S. consumption eventually surged to a record 72 percent of real GDP in early 2007, it was a virtuous cycle that seemed to have no end. Yet, as is now painfully evident, that boom became a bubble that has now burst.

In the end, nothing was more important to export-led economies—not just in Asia but elsewhere in the world—than the staying power of the American consumer. Unfortunately, Asia did not do a good job in hedging that bet. Once the asset-dependent American consumer went from boom to bust in the aftermath of the subprime crisis, export-led China and the rest of Asia quickly found itself with nowhere to hide. To the extent that the United States is now only in the early stages of a multiyear consumption retrenchment—a strong possibility, in my view—the problems of an unbalanced Asian economy may be even more acute.

But that's not the only challenge that Asia faces. Significantly, Premier Wen Jiabao's warning was not just about the imbalances of an economic and financial structure that had become overly reliant on exports. By raising concerns over instability, he was also cautioning of the perils of overreliance on energy, industrial materials, and base metals. In an era of booming global growth, the threat of the so-called commodity supercycle and its ever higher price structure was a crushing burden on resource-intensive developing nations. The Premier urged China to focus more on what he called a "scientific development" strategy that would be based on improved efficiencies of resource consumption. Similarly, by warning of the lack of coordination, Wen was highlighting the fragmentation of the Chinese system—not just its banks and companies but also a system of governance that was still heavily dominated by power blocs at the provincial and local level. And his concerns over sustainability were specifically aimed at pollution and environmental degradation—unmistakably negative externalities of China's fixation on open-ended manufacturing-led economic growth.

To the extent that the Chinese experience is a microcosm of the broader Asian development model, Premier Wen Jiabao's "four uns" are very much a blueprint of what it will take to realize the aspirations of the Asian Century. The *Next Asia* defines the daunting character of that transition. It won't be easy—nor will it happen over night. Despite the extraordinary successes of the past decade, Asia now faces a new set of formidable challenges. Just as the financial crisis of the late 1990s was a wake-up call for the region to put its financial house in order, the global crisis and recession of 2008–2009 is a strong signal for Asia to refocus the basic structure of its economic development model.

From a macroeconomic point of view, better balance is Asia's most urgent priority. Central to that rebalancing will be the long-awaited emergence of the Asian consumer. For a region steeped in a culture of saving, this will not be an easy transformation. Here again, China undoubtedly holds the key. Its legendary excesses of precautionary savings are traceable to two major developments—massive layoffs associated with over 15 years of state-owned enterprise (SOE) reforms and the lack of an institutionalized social safety net. With SOE reforms likely to be ongoing—albeit probably at a slower pace in the years ahead—China needs to redouble its efforts on the welfare front. This includes more aggressive initiatives in the areas of social security, pensions, medical care, and unemployment insurance. China's 11th Five-Year Plan that was launched in early 2006, highlighted all of these areas as urgent priorities for a transformation to more of a consumer-led growth framework. Yet for reasons that remain unclear, the government has failed to deliver on these counts. That needs to change if China is to lead the way in the structural transformation that is at the heart of the *Next Asia*.

The same is true of other key dimensions of Asia's challenge. Heightened efforts in the area of resource efficiency are an urgent priority in dealing with the unstable characteristics of its growth experience. A shift from manufacturing-led export growth to more of a services-based consumption model will relieve some of the inherent biases of energy- and resource-intensive growth. But Asia must also do more in the way of investing in alternative energy technologies, retrofitting existing production platforms, and moving to lighter construction and production techniques. A key challenge in this regard is to stay the course of resource efficiency in the downturn of the global commodity cycle. In an era of soaring commodity prices, reductions in the commodity content of economic growth become an obvious and urgent imperative. When the cycle swings the other way, however—as is very much the case for a world in recession—there is always the temptation to put off the heavy lifting for that proverbial another day. For the *Next Asia,* that temptation must be avoided at all costs.

So, too, should be the related case for environmental remediation and greener growth—central to the region's sustainability problems. Air and water pollution have become endemic to Asia's hypergrowth. That's especially true in China, home to seven of the ten most polluted cities in the world and whose level of organic water pollutants is, by far, the worst in the world—more than more three times the emissions rate of the number two polluter, the United States. Asia has attempted to explain away its environmental problem in per capita terms—arguing that when scaled by its enormous population, its pollution problem still falls well short of that in less populated developed countries. Asian leaders have also argued that since economic development, itself, is a resource-burning and pollution-intensive endeavor, the delayed onset of the region's economic takeoff casts it unfairly as the villain in an era of global warming. Although both of these claims, have considerable merit, unfortunately, a damaged planet has little sympathy for the Asian excuse. On an absolute basis, Asia now makes the largest contribution to total growth in global pollutants—a trend that must be arrested, regardless of the size of its population or the state of its economic development.

The *Next Asia* will also have to come to grips with its inherent lack of coordination by exerting greater control over its fragmented economies, markets, and political systems. Premier Wen Jiabao's concerns over the lack of coordination in China reflect a system that has long been known for a diffusion of localized power bases. China's four largest banks, for example, still have over 50,000 branches between them—branches that in many cases function autonomously with respect to deposit gathering and lending policies. Such a fragmented banking system has long been a major complication for China's central bank and its execution of a coherent monetary policy. Asia's rural-urban dichotomy also creates a natural fragmentation to its social and economic fabric—underscoring ever-widening income and educational disparities that remain a major source of instability in the region. Widespread corruption further complicates the macro implementation of Asia's development imperatives. The more the region matures and makes further progress on the road to economic development, the greater the need for improved macro coordination.

Premier Wen Jiabao's "four uns" largely offer inward-looking prescriptions. But the *Next Asia* still has much to gain from its external linkages—especially by focusing more on the benefits of cross-border economic integration. Perhaps the greatest opportunity in that regard could come from closer ties between the two greatest powers in the region—Japan and China. Despite a long and difficult history between them, these two nations are natural complements in many key respects. Japan, with its declining population and high-cost work force, has much to gain from Chinese outsourcing and efficiency solutions. China, with its need for new technologies and pollution abatement, has just as much to gain from Japan's leadership position in both areas. And the rest of an increasingly integrated Asian economy would be well positioned to realize the benefits of supply-chain externalities that could be important by-products of greater integration between China and Japan.

Change and growth have been the mantra for Asia for the past quarter century. But the endgame of sustained economic development and rising prosperity continues to be a moving target. Developing Asia has enjoyed spectacular success in the decade after the wrenching financial crisis of the late 1990s. But, as they say in the investment business, a track record of success is no guarantee of future performance. The current global recession is an important wake-up call for Asia—in effect, a challenge to the old way, and a not-so-subtle hint to find a new recipe for its growth model. The *Next Asia* that emerges from this transition will need to be all about a shift in focus from the quantity to the quality dimension of the growth experience. Although the quality of economic growth is something of an amorphous construct, its attributes are undoubtedly steeped in better balance, stability, coordination, sustainability, and integration. This is the essence of a critical transformation that could well usher in more of a proconsumption, lighter, and greener Asian economy than is the case today. The *Next Asia* will need to measure its success increasingly on those counts.

This collection of essays addresses the challenges and opportunities, as well as the stresses and strains, that await the *Next Asia*. It is both a journal and a framework. In the first sense, it is a creature of the debate that embroiled financial markets and policy circles during the critical period of 2006–2008—a debate that I was actively engaged in, initially as Morgan

Stanley's Chief Economist and then as the Chairman of the firm's Asian businesses. These three years saw the world at both its highs and its lows—an unbalanced global economy lurching toward the final stages of an unsustainable boom followed by the sickening implosion of a bust of unimaginable proportions. It was a period that not only marked a critical turning point for the global economy but also one that underscores the risks and rewards that await the *Next Asia*.

The framework is organized around five building blocks that I believe will be key in driving the coming transition of Developing Asia: the wake-up call of the global crisis, Asia's critical role in the globalization debate, the rebalancing imperatives of the Chinese economy, a new pan-regional framework of integration and competition, and a frank discussion of the risks of trade frictions and protectionism.

This latter risk cannot be minimized. As the biggest beneficiary of globalization, Asia stands much to lose if the rich countries of the developed world—especially the United States—start to use trade policy to shield hard-pressed middle-class workers from the angst of the global labor arbitrage. In a period of deepening recession and rising unemployment, pressures on labor can only intensify—increasing the temptations and perils of China bashing and other forms of scapegoating. As responsible stewards of globalization, both the West and the East will need to be steadfast in forestalling such an outcome. Yet as the pendulum of political power has swung from capital to labor, there is a growing risk those noble principles could be compromised. In that case, the consequences would be dire for all of us, especially for an externally dependent Asian economy.

Needless to say, the *Next Asia* has a full plate as it now faces a most daunting transition. Although predicting the future is always problematic, one thing is absolutely certain: For Asia, inertia is not an option. It is, of course, always tempting to take the path of least resistance and avoid the wrenching changes that a consumer-led, lighter, and greener Asia now requires. But that is a path to nowhere—one that will ultimately stymie the region's ambitious development objectives.

Change is never easy—especially on a scale that the *Next Asia* requires. But change has been at the core of all the Asian miracles of the post–World War II era. Once again, circumstances require this dynamic region to look inside itself and reinvent the model that will take it to the next phase of its remarkable journey. I remain confident that Asia will be able to pull it off. At the same time, I don't underestimate the risks that the

*Next Asia* will face as it once again moves out of its comfort zone. That's something we all have in common in looking to the postcrisis era.

In order to preserve the flow of the extraordinary chain of events of the past several years, the essays in each chapter are presented largely in sequential order. Facts and conclusions prevailing at the time of writing have not been altered to fit the events that have since transpired. Instead, they are left largely in their raw initial form—providing a real-time impression of what it's like to try to crack the code of one of the most challenging periods in modern economic history. Although some of the data points presented in this fashion have been altered by the rush of subsequent events, the broad sweep of the analytics and conclusions have withstood the test of time reasonably well—at least, so far. But there are no guarantees for a world in crisis—or even for a megatrend as compelling as the *Next Asia*. Stay tuned.

# Chapter 1

# A World in Crisis

## Introduction

As the greatest beneficiary of globalization, Asia continues to take an important cue from the broader global environment. With the world economy in its most wrenching crisis in 75 years, that cue is more daunting than ever before.

The origins of this crisis will long be debated. As the world still grapples with the wrenching aftershocks of what was initially billed as America's subprime crisis, it is entirely premature to render a definitive verdict on the how's and why's of this mess. Suffice it say, the financial crisis that began in earnest in 2008 was the outgrowth of a confluence of failures, including massive risk management mistakes on Wall Street, egregious errors by rating agencies, staggering lapses of regulatory oversight, a politicization of the home-ownership and mortgage boom, and the search for returns by yield-hungry investors on Main Street.The most serious failure, in my view, was that of central banks.That's especially the case with America's ideologically driven Federal Reserve, led by market libertarians who condoned an insidious succession of asset bubbles and ignored its regulatory responsibility in an era of unprecedented financial engineering and excess leverage.

The main thesis of this chapter is that this is not just a financial crisis. The excesses in the financial markets were so extreme they ended up infecting the real side of the global economy. Nowhere was that more evident than in the United States, where asset-dependent consumers drew extraordinary support from the confluence of property and credit bubbles. In the second half of 2008—in the aftermath of the bursting of those twin bubbles—the American consumer pulled back more severely than at any point in the post-World War II era. Yet that correction left the consumption share of GDP at a still elevated 71 percent in late 2008—down only 1 percentage point from its record 72 percent high in early 2007 and 4 percentage points above the prebubble norm of 67 percent that prevailed from 1975–2000. With personal debt ratios still excessive and saving rates far too low, there is good reason to believe that there is more to come in what looks to be a multiyear adjustment for the U.S. consumer. If mean reversion is in the offing for a postbubble U.S. consumer, and if that mean is close to the prebubble norm of the consumption share of U.S. GDP, then only about 20 percent of the correction has occurred.

As America has entered a major postbubble shakeout, so, too, has the rest of an interconnected world. It's not just the cross-border linkages of trade flows that have been shocked by the capitulation of the world's largest consumer. Liquidity-driven asset bubbles have burst everywhere— from emerging market equities to most segments of the global commodity market.The pitfalls of a postbubble world are especially daunting for an externally led Asian economy.

Lacking dynamism from its main source of external demand—the U.S. consumer—Asia faces two distinct possibilities: slower growth or the imperatives of uncovering new sources of growth. Since the latter option takes time to implement, I conclude that the Asian growth dynamic is likely to be a good deal slower in the years ahead than the

7 percent growth pace that has been realized since the turn of the century. For now, I would pencil in about 5 percent growth in panregional GDP for Developing Asia over the next three to five years.

A similar downshift is likely to be in the offing for the global economy. Notwithstanding the massive policy stimulus that has been injected into the system, America's multiyear consumer retrenchment will provide stiff headwinds to global growth for quite some time. In that important respect, policy stimulus will be "pushing on a string"—leading to something resembling a Japanese-like outcome for a postbubble world economy. There will be no V-shaped recovery from this global recession. When it comes in earnest—probably at some point in 2010—the rebound in world economic growth is likely to be unusually anemic.

Meanwhile, it's important not to get too far ahead of this story—a postcrisis world still has to pick up the pieces from a wrenching global recession. This is a profound challenge to policy makers, regulators, and politicians—to say nothing of posing a challenge to the free-enterprise system of market capitalism. To date, the policy response has been very short-term oriented. In effect, it has marshaled the heavy artillery of fiscal and monetary policy, together with government-sponsored capital injections and bailouts, toward rescuing and restarting a damaged and dysfunctional financial system.

Although this short-term focus is understandable in light of the extraordinarily dangerous freezing up of global credit markets, there are deeper longer-term issues that policy makers must also confront. At the top of the list are the daunting imperatives for a postbubble world to come up with nothing short of a new recipe for economic growth. In effect, the unbalanced global growth model of the past decade—dominated by America's excess consumption and Asia's excess saving—needs to be turned inside out. The United States needs to save more and consume less while Asia needs to save less and consume more. Policies need to be directed toward those twin objectives with an aim toward fostering the long-awaited rebalancing of a postbubble world. The crisis that began in 2008 is a wake-up call that global rebalancing can no longer be deferred to that proverbial another day.

The problem is not with capitalism but with its system of governance. As such, this crisis is a wake-up call to central banks, regulators, and their political overseers—the authorities who are charged with being the ultimate whistle-blowers in an era of excess. Sadly, that didn't happen as a bubble-prone world lurched headlong toward disaster. Central banks were especially derelict in their responsibilities. Although the monetary authorities did a terrific job in winning the war against the Great Inflation of the 1970s and early 1980s, they failed in their efforts to manage the peace of the postinflation global economy. Blinded by ideology, monetary policy makers paid little or no attention to the imperatives of financial stability. Instead, they believed incorrectly that the world was learning to live with its imbalances. Needless to say, the postbubble world is paying a horrific price for this dereliction of duty. That leaves the body politic with little choice other than to alter the policy mandate of central banks to incorporate an explicit focus on financial stability. A crisis like this must never be allowed to happen again.

# A Subprime Outlook for the Global Economy

*October 18, 2007*

Atter nearly five fat years, the global economy is headed for serious trouble. This will come as a surprise to policy makers and investors, alike—most of whom were counting on boom times to continue.

At work is yet another postbubble adjustment in the world's largest economy—this time, the bursting of America's massive property bubble. The subprime fiasco is the tip of a much larger iceberg—an asset-dependent American consumer who has gone on the biggest spending binge in the modern history of the global economy. At the turn of the century, the bursting of the dot-com bubble triggered a collapse in business capital spending that took the United States and global economy into a mild recession. This time, postbubble adjustments seem likely to hit U.S. consumption, which, at 72 percent of GDP, is more than five times the share the capital spending sector was seven years ago. This is a much bigger problem—one that could have much graver consequences for the United States and the rest of the world.

There is far more to this story than a potential downturn in the global business cycle. Another postbubble shakeout poses a serious challenge to the timeworn inflation-targeting approach of central banks. It also challenges the body politic's acceptance of a new strain of asset-dependent global economic growth. Subprime spillovers have only just begun to play out, as has the debate this crisis has spawned.

## Game Over for the American Consumer

The American consumer has been the dominant engine on the demand side of the global economy for the past 11 years. With real consumption growth averaging nearly 4 percent over the 1996–2006 interval, U.S. consumption expenditures totaled over $9.6 trillion in 2007, or 19 percent of world GDP (at market exchange rates).

Growth in U.S. consumer demand is typically powered by two forces—income and wealth (see Figure 1.1). Since the mid-1990s, income support has lagged while wealth effects have emerged as increasingly powerful drivers of U.S. consumption. That has been especially the case in the current

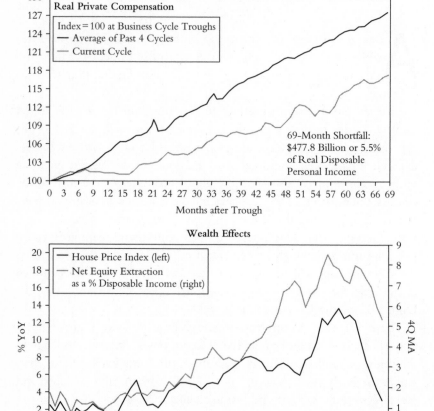

**Figure 1.1**   The Macro Drivers of U.S. Consumption

*Source:* Office of Federal Housing Enterprise Oversight (OFHEO), Federal Reserve, U.S. Bureau of Economic Analysis, Morgan Stanley Research.

economic expansion, which has faced the combined headwinds of subpar employment growth and relatively stagnant real wages. As a result, over the first 69 months of the now-ended expansion, private-sector compensation—the broadest measure of earned labor income in the U.S. economy—increased only 17 percent in real, or inflation-adjusted, terms. That was nearly $480 billion short of the 28-percent increase that had occurred, on average, over comparable periods of the past four U.S. business cycle expansions.

Lacking in support from labor income, U.S. consumers turned to wealth effects from rapidly appreciating assets—principally residential property—to fuel booming consumption. By Federal Reserve estimates, net equity extraction from residential property surged from 3 percent of disposable personal income in 2001 to nearly 9 percent by 2005—more than sufficient to offset the shortfall in labor income generation and keep consumption on a rapid growth path. There was no stopping the asset-dependent American consumer.

That was then. Both income and wealth effects have come under increasingly intense pressure—leaving consumers with little choice other than to rein in excessive demand. The persistently subpar trend in labor income growth is about to be squeezed further by the pressures of a cyclical adjustment in production and employment. In August and September 2007, private sector nonfarm payrolls expanded, on average, by only 52,000 per month—literally one-third the average pace of 157,000 of the preceding 24 months. Moreover, this dramatic slowdown in the organic job-creating capacity of the U.S. economy is likely to be exacerbated by a sharp fall in residential-construction-sector employment in the months ahead. Jobs in the homebuilding sector are currently down only about 5 percent from peak levels, despite a 40 percent fall in housing starts; it is only a matter of time before jobs and activity move into closer alignment in this highly cyclical—and now very depressed—sector.

Moreover, the bursting of the property bubble has left the consumer wealth effect in tatters. After peaking at 13.6 percent in mid-2005, nationwide house price appreciation slowed precipitously to 3.2 percent by mid-2007. Given the outsize overhang of excess supply of unsold homes, I suspect that overall U.S. home prices could actually decline in both 2008 and 2009—an unprecedented development in the modern-day experience of the U.S. economy. Mirroring this trend, net equity extraction has already tumbled—falling to less than 5.5 percent of disposable personal income in the second quarter of 2007 and retracing more than

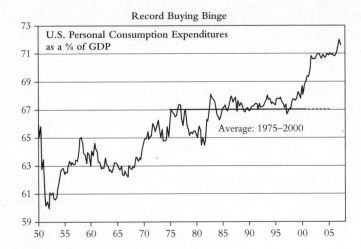

**Figure 1.2**   The Overextended American Consumer
*Source:* U.S. Bureau of Economic Analysis, Morgan Stanley Research.

half the run-up that began in 2001. Subprime contagion can only reinforce this trend—putting pressure on home mortgage refinancing and
thereby further inhibiting equity extraction by U.S. home owners.

With both income and wealth effects under pressure, it will be exceedingly difficult for savings-short, overly indebted American consumers to
maintain excessive consumption growth. For a U.S. economy that has
drawn disproportionate support from a record 72 percent share of personal consumption (see Figure 1.2), a consumer-led capitulation spells
high and rising recession risk. Unfortunately, the same prognosis is likely
for a still U.S.-centric global economy.

## Don't Count on Global Decoupling

A capitulation of the American consumer spells considerable difficulty
for the global economy. This conclusion is, of course, very much at odds
with the notion of "global decoupling"—an increasingly popular belief
that depicts a world economy that has finally weaned itself from the ups
and downs of the U.S. economy.

The global decoupling thesis is premised on a major contradiction:
In an increasingly globalized world, cross-border linkages have become
ever more important—making globalization and decoupling inherently

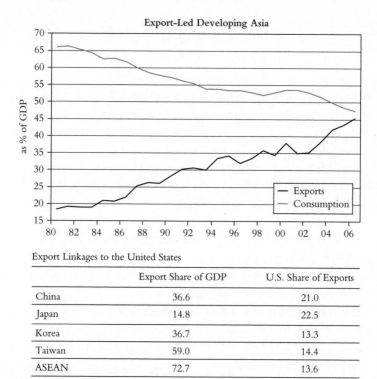

**Figure 1.3** The Myth of an Asian Decoupling

*Source:* International Monetary Fund, Asian Development Bank, Morgan Stanley Research.

inconsistent. True, the recent data flow raises some questions about this contention. After all, the world seems to have held up reasonably well in the face of the initial slowing of U.S. GDP growth that has unfolded over the past year. However, that's because the downshift in U.S. growth has been almost exclusively concentrated in residential building activity—one of the least global sectors of the U.S. economy. If I am right, and consumption now starts to slow, such a downshift will affect one of the most global sectors of the United States. I fully suspect a downshift in America's most global sector will have considerably greater repercussions for the world at large than has been the case so far.

That's an especially likely outcome in Asia—the world's most rapidly growing region and one widely suspected to be a leading candidate for global decoupling. However, as Figure 1.3 clearly indicates, the macrostructure of Developing Asia remains very much skewed toward an export-led growth dynamic. For the region as a whole, the export share has more than doubled over the past 25 years—surging from less than 20 percent in 1980 to more than 45 percent today. Similarly, the share going to internal private consumption—the sector that would have to drive Asian decoupling—has fallen from 67 percent to less than 50 percent over the same period.

Nor can there be any mistake about the dominant external market for export-led Asian economies. The United States wins the race hands down—underscored by a 21 percent share of Chinese exports currently going to America. Yes, there has been a sharp acceleration of intraregional trade in recent years, adding to the hopes and dreams of Asian decoupling. But a good portion of that integration reflects the development of a China-centric pan-Asian supply chain that continues to be focused on sourcing end-market demand for American consumers. That means if the U.S. consumer now slows, as I suspect, Asia will be hit hard—with cross-border supply-chain linkages exposing a long-standing vulnerability that will draw the global decoupling thesis into serious question.

A downshift of U.S. consumption growth will affect Asia unevenly. A rapidly growing Chinese economy has an ample cushion to withstand such a blow. Chinese GDP growth might slow from 11 percent to around 8 percent—hardly a disaster for any economy and actually consistent with what Beijing has tried to accomplish with its cooling-off campaign of the past several years. Other Asian economies, however, lack the hyper-growth cushion that China enjoys. As such, a U.S.-led slowdown of external demand could hurt them a good deal more. That's especially the case for Japan, whose 2 percent growth economy could be in serious trouble in the event of a U.S.-demand shock that also takes a toll on Japanese exports into the Chinese supply chain. Although less vulnerable than Japan, Taiwan and South Korea could also be squeezed by the double whammy of U.S. and China slowdowns. For the rest of Asia—especially India and the ASEAN economies—underlying growth appears strong enough to withstand a shortfall in U.S. consumer demand. But there can be no mistaking the end-game: Contrary to the widespread optimism of investors and policy makers, the Asian growth dynamic is actually quite vulnerable to a meaningful slowdown in U.S. consumption growth.

## The Great Failure of Central Banking

The recent chain of events is not an isolated development. In fact, for the second time in seven years, the bursting of a major asset bubble has inflicted great damage on world financial markets. In both cases—the equity bubble in 2000 and the credit bubble in 2007—central banks were asleep at the switch. The lack of monetary discipline has become a hallmark of an unfettered globalization. Central banks have failed to provide a stable underpinning to world financial markets and to an increasingly asset-dependent global economy.

This sorry state of affairs can be traced to developments that all started a decade ago. Basking in the warm glow of a successful battle against inflation, central banks decided that easy money was the world's just reward.

America's IT-enabled productivity resurgence in the late 1990s was the siren song for the Greenspan-led Federal Reserve—convincing the U.S. central bank that it need not stand in the way of either rapid economic growth or excess liquidity creation. In retrospect, that was the "original sin" of bubble-world—a Fed that condoned the equity bubble of the late 1990s and the asset-dependent U.S. economy it spawned. That set in motion a chain of events that has allowed one bubble to beget another—from equities to housing to credit—as the Fed countered each postbubble aftershock by an aggressive monetary easing that set the stage for the next bubble.

There is one basic problem with all asset bubbles—they always burst. And when that happened to the equity bubble in 2000, the Federal Reserve threw all caution to the wind and injected massive liquidity into world financial markets in order to avoid a dangerous deflation. With globalization restraining inflation and real economies recovering only sluggishly in the early 2000s, that excess liquidity went directly into asset markets.

Aided and abetted by the explosion of new financial instruments—especially what is now over $440 trillion of derivatives worldwide—the world embraced a new culture of debt and leverage. Yield-hungry investors, fixated on the retirement imperatives of aging households, acted as if they had nothing to fear. Risk was not a concern in an era of open-ended monetary accommodation cushioned by what was mistakenly believed to be a profusion of derivatives-based shock absorbers.

As always, the cycle of risk and greed went to excess. Just as dot-com was the canary in the coalmine seven years ago, subprime was the warning shot this time. Denial in both cases has eerie similarities—as do the spillovers that inevitably occur when major asset bubbles pop. When the dot-com bubble burst in early 2000, the optimists said not to worry—after all, Internet stocks accounted for only about 6 percent of total U.S. equity market capitalization at the end of 1999. Unfortunately, the broad S&P 500 index tumbled some 49 percent over the ensuing two-and-a-half years, and an overextended Corporate America led the U.S. and global economy into recession.

Similarly, today's optimists are preaching the same gospel: Why worry, they say, if subprime is only about 14 percent of total U.S. securitized mortgage debt? Yet the unwinding of the far-broader credit cycle, to say nothing of the extraordinary freezing up of key short-term financing markets, gives good reason to worry—especially for overextended American consumers and a still U.S.-centric global economy.

Central banks have now been forced into making emergency liquidity injections. The jury is out about whether these efforts will succeed in stemming the current rout in still overvalued credit markets. Although tactically expedient, these actions may be strategically flawed because they fail to address the moral hazard dilemma that continues to underpin asset-dependent economies. Is this any way to run a modern-day world economy?

The answer is an unequivocal "no." As always, politicians are quick to grandstand and blame financial fiduciaries for problems afflicting uneducated, unqualified borrowers. Yet the markets are being painfully effective in punishing these parties. Instead, the body politic needs to take a look in the mirror—especially at the behavior of its policy-making proxies and regulators, the world's major central banks.

It is high time for monetary authorities to adopt new procedures— namely, taking the state of asset markets into explicit consideration when framing policy options. Like it or not, we now live in an asset-dependent world. As the increasing prevalence of bubbles indicates, a failure to recognize the interplay between the state of asset markets and the real economy is an egregious policy error.

That doesn't mean central banks should target asset markets. It does mean, however, that they need to break their one-dimensional fixation on CPI-based inflation and also pay careful consideration to the extremes of asset values. This is not that difficult a task. When equity markets go to excess and distort asset-dependent economies as they did in the late 1990s, central banks should run tighter monetary policies than a narrow inflation target would dictate. Similarly, when housing markets go to excess, when subprime borrowers join the fray, or when corporate credit becomes freely available at ridiculously low "spreads," central banks should lean against the wind.

The current financial crisis is a wake-up call for modern-day central banking. The world can't afford to keep lurching from one bubble to another.

The cost of neglect is an ever-mounting systemic risk that could pose a grave threat to an increasingly integrated global economy. It could also spur the imprudent intervention of politicians, undermining the all-important political independence of central banks. The art and science of central banking is in desperate need of a major overhaul.

## The Political Economy of Asset Bubbles

There may be a deeper meaning to all this. It is far-fetched to argue that central banks have consciously opted to inflate a series of asset bubbles—and then simply deal with the aftershocks once they burst. At work, instead, are the unintended consequences of a new and powerful asset-led global growth dynamic that is very much an outgrowth of the political economy of growth and prosperity.

This outcome reflects the confluence of three megatrends—globalization, the IT revolution, and the provision of retirement income for aging workers. Globalization has injected a powerful new impetus to the disinflation of the past quarter century, facilitating a cross-border arbitrage of costs and prices that has put unrelenting pressure on the pricing of goods and many services, alike. At the same time, IT-enabled productivity enhancement—initially in the United States but now increasingly evident in other economies—has convinced central banks that there has been a meaningful increase in the noninflationary growth potential in their respective economies. Finally, rapidly aging populations in Japan, Europe, and the United States are putting pressure on plan sponsors—public and private, alike—to boost investment yields in order to fund a growing profusion of unfunded pension and retirement schemes.

A key result of the interplay between the first two of these megatrends—the globalization of disinflation and IT-enabled productivity enhancement—has been a sharp reduction in nominal interest rates on sovereign fixed-income instruments for short- and long-term maturities, alike. Lacking in the yield to fund retirement programs from such riskless assets, investors and their fiduciaries have ventured into increasingly riskier assets to square the circle. That, in conjunction with the ample provision of liquidity from inflation-relaxed central banks, has driven down yield spreads in a variety of risky assets—from emerging-market and high-yield corporate debt to mortgage-backed securities and a host of other complex structured products. In an era of spread compression and search for yield, the rising tide of ample liquidity covered up a profusion of jagged and dangerous rocks. As the tide now goes out, the rocks now get uncovered. The subprime crisis is a classic example of what can be unmasked at low tide.

The same set of forces has had an equally profound impact on the investment strategies of individual investors. Lacking in traditional yield from saving deposits and government bonds, families have opted, instead, to seek enhanced investment income from equities and, more recently, from residential property. This has created a natural demand for these asset classes that then took on a life of its own—with price increases begetting more price increases and speculative bubbles arising as a result. As long as inflation-targeting central banks remained fixated on their well-behaved narrow CPIs, there was little to stand in the way of a powerful liquidity cycle that gave rise to a multibubble syndrome.

In the end, it is up to the body politic to judge the wisdom of this arrangement—essentially, whether the inherent instability of increasingly asset-dependent and bubble-prone economies is worth the risk. Lacking a clear feedback mechanism to render such a verdict, it falls to the world's central banks—the stewards of economic and financial stability—to act as proxies in resolving this problem. This is where the problem gets particularly thorny. It takes a truly independent central bank to take a principled stand against the systemic risks that may arise from the progrowth mindset of the body politic and act to "take the punchbowl away just when the party is getting good"—to paraphrase the sage advice of one of America's legendary central bankers, William McChesney Martin. Yet as recently retired Fed Chairman Alan Greenspan concedes, "I regret to say that Federal Reserve independence is not set in stone."[1]

Greenspan's confession underscores the important distinction between two models of the central banker—those who are truly politically independent and those who are more politically compliant. The United States has had both types. I would certainly put Paul Volcker in the former category; amid howls of protest, his determined assault against the ravages of double-digit inflation was conducted at great political risk. In the end, he held to a monetary policy that was fiercely independent of political pressures. By contrast, Arthur Burns, who I worked for in the 1970s, was highly politicized in his decisions to avoid the wrenching monetary tightening that a cure for inflation would eventually require. The market-friendly stance of Alan Greenspan—and the asset-dependent

---

1. See Alan Greenspan, *The Age of Turbulence: Adventures in a New World,* New York: The Penguin Press, 2007.

U.S. economy it spawned—was more consistent with the model of the complaint central banker who was very much in sync with the pro-growth mindset of the body politic. Greenspan's memoirs are as much about politics as economics—underscoring his much stronger sense of the interplay between these two forces than a more independent central banker might otherwise perceive.

However, Greenspan's basic point is well taken: It is not easy for any central banker to do unpopular things—especially if he happens to be a political animal operating in a highly charged political climate. But that's where I would draw the line. With all due respect to Alan Greenspan, the truly independent central banker was never supposed to win political popularity contests. I would be the first to concede, however, that it will take great political courage to forge the new approach toward monetary policy that I am advocating, but it can be done—as exemplified by the legacy of Paul Volcker.

In the end, it will undoubtedly take a crisis to provide central banks with the political cover they believe they need to broaden out their mandate from the narrow dictums of consumer price index (CPI)-based price stability. With the credit cycle unwinding at the same time that Washington might be tempted by protectionism, and with the overly indebted American consumer in trouble, the wisdom of condoning asset-dependent, bubble-prone economies may finally be drawn into serious question.

## A Subprime Prognosis

How all this plays out in the global economy in the years immediately ahead is anyone's guess. I have long framed the tensions shaping the outlook in the context of global rebalancing—the need for a lopsided world economy to wean itself from a US.-centric growth dynamic. A partial rebalancing now appears to be at hand—likely to be led by the coming consolidation of the American consumer. That is painful but good news for those of us who have long worried about the destabilizing risks of a massive U.S. current-account deficit. But a more complete global rebalancing is a shared responsibility—one that must also be accompanied by an increase in domestic demand from surplus-saving economies elsewhere in the world. To the extent that doesn't happen—and, as underscored earlier, that remains my view—then an asymmetrical rebalancing dominated by slowdown in U.S. consumer demand should take a meaningful toll on global growth.

For a world economy that has been on a close to 5 percent growth path for nearly five years, that points to nothing but downside over the next few years. It's always hard to pinpoint the magnitude of such a shortfall with any precision, but I would not be surprised to see world GDP growth slow to a virtual standstill at some point in 2008. Such an outcome could prove especially troublesome for the earnings optimism still embedded in global equity markets. The silver lining of such a prognosis likely would be cyclical relief on the inflation front—providing support for sovereign bonds.

But, as I have attempted to underscore earlier, the issues shaping the medium-term prognosis for the global economy go far beyond a standard call on the business cycle. America's asset-dependent growth paradigm is finally at risk. And with those risks comes the potential for collateral damage elsewhere in a still U.S.-centric global economy. Dollar risks are especially problematic but so, too, is the collective wisdom—or lack thereof—of central bankers and politicians who have allowed the world to come to this precarious point. Policy making and politics remain driven purely by local considerations. Yet the stresses and strains of a globalized world demand a much broader perspective. A new approach is needed—before it's too late.

# Save the Day

*September 25, 2007*

C urrencies are first and foremost relative prices—in essence, they are measures of the intrinsic value of one economy versus another. On that basis, the world has had no compunction in writing down the value of the United States over the past several years. The dollar, relative to the currencies of most of America's trading partners, had fallen by about 20 percent from its early 2002 peak. Recently it has hit new lows against the euro and a high-flying Canadian currency, likely a harbinger of more weakness to come.

Sadly, none of this is surprising. Because Americans haven't been saving in sufficient amounts, the United States must import surplus savings from abroad in order to grow. And it has to run record balance of payments and trade deficits in order to attract that foreign capital. The United States current account deficit—the broadest gauge of America's imbalance in relation to the rest of the world—hit a record 6.2 percent of GDP in 2006 before the pressures of the business cycle triggered a temporary reduction in 2008. Even so, savings-short America must still attract some $3 billion of foreign capital each business day in order to keep its economy growing.

Economic science is very clear on the implications of such huge imbalances: Foreign lenders need to be compensated for sending scarce capital to any country with a deficit. The bigger the deficit, the greater the compensation. The currency of the deficit nation usually bears the brunt of that compensation. As long as the United States fails to address its saving problem, its large balance of payments deficit will persist and the dollar will eventually resume its decline.

The only silver lining so far has been that these adjustments to the currency have been orderly—declines in the broad dollar index averaging a little less than 4 percent per year since early 2002. Now, however, the possibility of a disorderly correction is rising—with potentially grave consequences for the American and global economy.

A key reason is the mounting risk of a recession in America. The bursting of the subprime mortgage bubble—strikingly reminiscent of the dot-com excesses of the 1990s—could well be a tipping point. In both cases, financial markets and policy makers were steeped in denial over the risks. But the lessons of postbubble adjustments are clear. Just ask economically stagnant Japan. And of course, the United States lapsed into its own postbubble recession in 2000 and 2001.

Sadly, the endgame could be considerably more treacherous for the United States than it was seven years ago. In large part, that's because the American consumer is now at risk. In early 2007, consumption expenditures peaked at a record 72 percent of the GDP—a number unmatched in the annals of modern history for any nation.

This buying binge has been increasingly supported by housing and lending bubbles. Yet home prices are now headed lower—probably for years—and the fallout from the subprime crisis has seriously crimped home mortgage refinancing. With weaker employment growth also putting pressure on income, the days of open-ended American consumption are finally coming to an end. This makes it all but impossible to avoid a recession.

Fearful of that outcome, foreign investors are becoming increasingly skittish over buying dollar-based assets. The spillover effects of the subprime crisis into other asset markets—especially mortgage-backed securities and asset-backed commercial paper—underscore these concerns. Foreign appetite for U. S. financial instruments is likely to be sharply reduced for years to come. That would choke off an important avenue of capital inflows, putting more downward pressure on the dollar.

The political winds are also blowing against the dollar. In Washington, China-bashing is the bipartisan sport *du jour*. New legislation is likely, which would impose trade sanctions on China unless China makes a major adjustment in its currency. Not only would this be an egregious policy blunder—attempting to fix a multilateral deficit with nearly 100 nations by forcing an exchange rate adjustment with one country—but it would also amount to Washington taxing one of America's major foreign lenders.

That would undoubtedly reduce China's desire for U. S. assets, and unless another foreign buyer stepped up, the dollar would come under even more pressure. Moreover, the more the Fed under Ben Bernanke follows the easy-money Alan Greenspan script, the greater the risk to the dollar.

Why worry about a weaker dollar? The United States imported $2.2 trillion of goods and services in 2006. A sharp drop in the dollar makes those items considerably more expensive—the functional equivalent of a tax hike on consumers. It could also stoke fears of inflation—driving up long-term interest rates and putting more pressure on financial markets and the economy, exacerbating recession risks. Optimists may draw comfort from the vision of an export-led renewal arising from a more competitive dollar. Yet history is clear: No nation has ever devalued its way into prosperity.

So far, the dollar's weakness has not been a big deal. That may now be about to change. Relative to the rest of the world, the United States looks painfully subprime. So does its currency.

# Coping with a Different Recession

## January 17, 2008

This is not a garden-variety recession. The U.S. economy has slipped into its second postbubble downturn in seven years. Just as the bursting of the dot-com bubble triggered a recession in 2001–2002, the simultaneous popping of housing and credit bubbles are doing the same right now. This recession will be deeper than the shallow contraction earlier in this decade. Back then, the dot-com-led downturn was sparked by a collapse in business capital spending—a sector that at its peak in 2000 accounted for only 13 percent of U.S. GDP. The current recession is all about the coming capitulation of the American consumer—a sector that amounts to a record 72 percent of GDP, or over five times the share of the capital-spending sector that triggered the postbubble recession seven years ago.

For asset-dependent U.S. consumers, retrenchment is all but inevitable. With income growth lagging, the spending binge of the past six years was reinforced by a surge of housing-led wealth creation. That bonanza is now over. Home prices fell for the nation as a whole in 2008—the first such occurrence since 1933. And that is not exactly a comforting comparison. Moreover, access to home equity credit lines and mortgage refinancing—the means by which home owners have borrowed against their property—has been impaired by the aftershocks of the subprime crisis. As a result, consumers now have to resort to spending and saving the old-fashioned way—drawing the bulk of their support from income rather than assets. In what is likely to be an increasingly sluggish income climate, that spells a meaningful pullback of consumer expenditures. For that reason, alone, it was all but impossible for the United States to avoid outright recession.

## Global Implications

This is a very big deal for the broader global economy. Initially, the world has held up relatively well in the face of a prerecession downshift in the U.S. economy. But that quickly changed when America's recession shifted from homebuilding activity—its least global sector—to consumer demand, its most global sector. For the rest of the world, this transition came as a rude awakening. Many have been banking on a "global decoupling"—in essence, resilience elsewhere in the world in the face of a U.S.-demand shock. In particular, there was hope that young consumers from rapidly growing developing economies could fill the void left by weakness in U.S. consumers.

That hope was misplaced. The U.S. consumer is, by far, the biggest consumer in the world. Americans spent over $9.5 trillion in 2007, whereas the Chinese consumer spent around $1 trillion and Indians another $650 billion. Given the huge scale of U.S. consumption, it is almost mathematically impossible for Chinese and Indians to fill the void left by a meaningful pullback of the American consumer. For export-led developing economies in Asia, as well as for Japan, a weakening of U.S. consumption represents a softening in one of their biggest destinations of end-market demand. Lacking in vigor from its internal private consumption, the likelihood of growth slowdowns in externally dependent Asian economies is quite high.

A recent softening of Chinese export growth may well be the leading edge of this development. In December 2007, growth in Chinese exports to the United States slowed to a 6.8 percent year-over-year rate—only about one-fourth the 26 percent surge in 2006. Reflecting this pullback, the growth in overall Chinese exports slowed to 22 percent—down about 5 percentage points from the 27 percent gain of 2006. With exports accounting for nearly 40 percent of Chinese GDP and the biggest source of global consumption now on the wane, downside risks to the Chinese economy can hardly be ignored. And courtesy of supply-chain linkages, the rest of an increasingly China-centric Asia should now be quick to follow.

The Canadian economy, where exports to the United States account for about 25 percent of its GDP, is also starting to falter, as evidenced by an unexpected decline in Canadian employment in December 2007. For Mexico, where NAFTA-related linkages to the United States are comparable to those of Canada, there are also early signs of a slowdown. Even Europe, one of the brighter spots in the developed world over the past year, will not be immune to a global slowdown made in America. Germany, long the engine of the European economy, still derives a significant source of its growth from exports. That means the impacts of an external shock made in America, in conjunction with the lagged effects of an appreciating euro, can hardly be minimized. The bottom line for the global economy: When the United States sneezes, the rest of the world can still catch a cold. That's precisely what follows from the cross-border linkages of an increasingly globalized and interconnected world. It makes no sense to preach the gospel of decoupling in an era of globalization.

## Perils of Asset-Dependent Economies

At the core of this recession is a distinctly different set of forces from those of the past: It is an outgrowth of one of the most insidious characteristics of an asset-dependent U.S. economy—a chronic shortfall in domestic saving. With America's net national saving averaging a mere 1.4 percent of national income over the past five years, the United States has had to import surplus saving from abroad to keep growing. That means it must run massive current account and trade deficits to attract the foreign capital. This had been a key factor behind an outbreak of mounting global imbalances—an unmistakable by-product of the stresses and strains of America's savings-short economy.

America's aversion toward saving did not appear out of thin air. Waves of asset appreciation—first equities and, more recently, residential property—convinced U.S. citizens that a new era was at hand. Reinforced by a monstrous bubble of cheap credit, there was little perceived need to save out of income. Assets became the preferred vehicle of choice.

With one bubble begetting another, imbalances reached epic proportions in America's savings-short economy. Despite generally subpar income generation, private consumption soared to a record 72 percent real GDP in early 2007. Household debt hit a record 133 percent of disposable personal income. Moreover, income-based measures of personal saving moved back into negative territory in late 2007. And the current account deficit soared to a record $811 billion in 2006.

None of these trends were sustainable. Many have known this all along. As the imbalances reached rarified territory, it ultimately boiled down to two simple questions: When would they give way and what would it take to spark a long overdue rebalancing? In large part, that's what the current recession is all about.

## Asset-Led Rebalancing

A sharp decline in asset prices is necessary to rebalance an increasingly unstable asset-dependent U.S. economy. It is the only realistic hope to shift the mix of saving away from asset appreciation back to that supported by income generation. That could entail as much as a 20- to 30-percent decline in overall U.S. housing prices and a related deflating of the bubble of cheap and easy credit.

Those trends are now under way. Reflecting an outsize imbalance between supply and demand for new homes, residential property prices fell 6 percent in the year ending October 2007 for 20 major metropolitan areas in the United States, according to the S&P Case-Shiller Index. This decline was a harbinger of a broader downturn in nationwide home prices in 2008 that has continued into 2009. Meanwhile, courtesy of the subprime crisis, the credit bubble has popped—ending the cut-rate funding that fuelled the housing bubble.

As home prices move into a protracted period of decline, consumers have finally recognized the perils of bubble-distorted spending and saving strategies. Financially battered households are now responding by rebuilding income-based saving balances. That means the consumption share of GDP will fall, making recession unavoidable.

America's shift back to income-supported saving will be a pivotal development for the rest of the world. As consumption slows and household saving rises in the United States, the need to import surplus saving from abroad will diminish. Demand for foreign capital will recede—leading to a reduction of both the U.S. current-account and trade deficits. The global economy will emerge bruised, but hopefully much better balanced.

## The Policy Conundrum

Washington policy makers and politicians need to allow this adjustment to run its course. Policy decisions should not be framed with an eye toward the recessions of yesteryear. The policy options of 2008 must, instead, be considered in the context of America's dual problems of asset bubbles and subpar saving. Unfortunately, that does not appear to be the case. The U.S. body politic is now panicking in response to a likely recession—underwriting massive liquidity injections that could produce another asset bubble and proposing fiscal pump-priming that would depress domestic saving even further. The risk, in my view, is that such actions could backfire—essentially compounding the very problems that got America into this mess in the first place.

That's especially the case for monetary policy. For the Federal Reserve, the current recession is a critical wake-up call. America's central bank has been asleep at the switch for far too long. Ever since the equity bubble began forming in the late 1990s, the Federal Reserve has been ignoring, if not condoning, excesses in asset markets. The Fed has argued that it is best to clean up the postbubble mess rather than prevent an asset class from inflating in the first place. Unfortunately, that approach has allowed the United States to lurch from bubble to bubble. Predictably, the bubbles have gotten bigger, as have the segments of the real economy they have infected. Fixated on targeting a narrow "core CPI," which excludes the necessities of food and energy, the Federal Reserve has ignored at great peril the new and powerful linkages that have developed between economic activity and increasingly risky financial markets.

One key message from the recession of 2008 is that the Federal Reserve needs to rethink its reckless bubble-prone policy before it's too late. The last thing America needs is another asset bubble. And yet that's exactly what another round of aggressive monetary easing might produce. Low nominal interest rates are the sustenance of the excess liquidity that inflates asset bubbles. To escape the trap of multiasset bubbles in a low interest rate climate, counter-cyclical monetary easing needs to be more limited than otherwise might be the case. This could well require more of a Volckeresque discipline of tough money rather than the market-friendly actions of the Greenspan-Bernanke approach. The same goes for the Fed's seemingly open-ended support of unfettered and unregulated financial innovation—a derivatives-based revolution that turned out to have been a good deal riskier than the Greenspan libertarian mantra ever presumed. That's the painful and obvious lesson of the subprime crisis and the lethal contagion into credit markets it has spawned.

## Fiscal Policy Constraints

A savings-short U.S. economy also needs to take special care in framing any fiscal-policy response to the current recession. Lacking in domestic funding capacity, I would be in favor of a temporary and targeted fiscal stimulus. The centerpiece of any such package should be expanded unemployment insurance benefits for middle-income workers who lose their jobs—the same workers whose real wages have been stagnant for the better part of a decade. Lacking in saving, a temporary fiscal stimulus is all that the United States can afford. I would categorically rule out any

permanent tax cuts unless they are "revenue neutral"—funded by spending cuts and/or tax increases directed at the upper end of the income and
wealth distribution. This is the wrong time to increase America's still-
large structural budget deficit.

Such a targeted fiscal stimulus would have the advantage of injecting a
limited increment of purchasing power into the most distressed portion
of the income distribution—the innocent victims of yet another postbubble shakeout. Such a fiscal boost, however, should not be designed
with an aim toward propping up personal consumption at unrealisti-
cally high and unsustainable levels. That is the last thing a savings-short
U.S. economy needs. America needs to reduce excess consumption—not
support it. Politics could well complicate a strategy that requires prudence and discipline. And with politicians in both parties now falling
all over themselves to come up with the most alluring counter-cyclical
remedies, this is a very real concern. But recessions are a time of hardship
that require support for those least prepared to cope with cyclical distress.
A targeted package is appropriate under these circumstances.

The daunting constraints of America's unprecedented savings shortfall
raise some very tough questions: Who will fund the incremental fiscal
stimulus that a savings-short U.S. economy cannot finance on its own? If
Washington once again turns to foreign lenders to pick up the tab, will
pricing concessions, in terms of the dollar and real long-term interest
rates, be required to attract the foreign capital? Foreign investors—both
governments and private asset allocators—are now increasingly wary of
adding to their overweight dollar positions. Washington's fiscal spigot
should not be opened once again without taking these key risks into
serious account. And yet, in its characteristic rush to come up with the
miraculous quick fix, neither Congress nor the White House appears
to be paying attention to these potentially dire consequences. Further
downside risks to the dollar and upward pressure on long-term interest
rates cannot be ruled out in such a climate—developments that could
well offset all or part of any fiscal stimulus.

## The Role of the Dollar

Nor should the currency option be viewed as an antidote to a U.S. recession or as a remedy to the global imbalances stemming from America's
asset-led consumption boom. Notwithstanding the rhetorical flourishes
of America's strong-dollar mantra, Washington has actually accepted the

view that a weaker U.S. dollar is now in the nation's best interest. In large part, so has the rest of the world. After all, at its peak in 2006, America's massive current account deficit absorbed about 75 percent of the world's surplus saving, implying that the United States has been the main culprit behind the destabilizing global imbalances of recent years. It follows, goes the argument, that a weaker dollar should be just the shift in relative prices that an unbalanced U.S. and global economy needs.

Yet there is good reason to doubt this view. I have long been negative on prospects for the dollar, but that's mainly been a market call. In fact, there are severe limits as to what can be expected from a depreciation in the greenback. After all, through early 2008 a broad measure of the U.S. dollar had declined 23 percent since February 2002 in real terms, with only minimal impact on America's gaping external imbalance. Dollar bears argue that more currency depreciation is needed. Moreover, protectionists insist that China—which has the largest bilateral trade imbalance with the United States—should bear a disproportionate share of the next down leg in the U.S. dollar.

This is yet another of Washington's potential policy pitfalls. America's current account deficit is due more to a shortage in saving stemming from bubbles in asset prices than from a misaligned dollar. As a consequence, a lasting resolution of the saving and current account problem will require more of a correction in asset prices than a further depreciation of the dollar. Rebalancing via asset prices is likely to be far more effective in solving America's macroeconomic problems than misplaced emphasis on currency depreciation.

## Protectionist Perils

The growing chorus of China-bashers in the U.S. Congress also needs to stand down. America does not have a China problem—it has a multilateral trade deficit with 100 countries. The Chinese bilateral imbalance may be the biggest contributor to the overall U.S. trade imbalance, but, in large part, this is a result of supply-chain decisions by U.S. multinationals. Moreover, the non-Chinese piece of the U.S. trade deficit averaged nearly $600 billion in 2006–2007—almost two-and-a-half times the size of the Chinese piece. As noted above, America's multilateral trade problem is a key outgrowth of the chronic savings shortfall of an asset-dependent economy. It is simply ludicrous—and increasingly dangerous—to pin the blame on China for America's aversion toward saving.

By focusing incorrectly on the dollar and putting pressure on the Chinese currency, Congress would only shift China's portion of the U.S. trade deficit elsewhere—most likely to a higher-cost producer. That would be the functional equivalent of a tax hike on American workers. If the United States returns to income-based saving in the aftermath of the bursting of housing and credit bubbles, its multilateral trade deficit will narrow and the Chinese bilateral imbalance will shrink. If instead, the Congress opts to use trade sanctions to address U.S. trade problems— a very real possibility in today's climate—the risk of a backlash from America's foreign lenders, like the Chinese, could well intensify. In the event of a pullback in China's demand for dollar-based assets, there could be severe consequences for the U.S. currency and long-term real interest rates. Those are key perils on the slippery slope of trade protectionism—a path that must be avoided at all costs.

## Breaking the Daisy Chain

Again, it is important to stress that this is not a garden-variety recession. This downturn is, instead, a painful outgrowth of a savings-short, asset-dependent U.S. economy that has gone to excess. There have been policy and regulatory lapses along the way that have taken the world's largest most powerful economy to this worrisome juncture. But it would be the height of folly to try and address these problems by turning to the same recipes that created the distortions and imbalances in the first place— namely, bubble-prone monetary accommodation and saving-absorbing fiscal stimulus. The cure, instead, must be tailor-made to fit the unique features of the current climate—namely, addressing the excesses of an asset-dependent U.S. economy.

It is going to be a very painful process to break America's addiction to asset-dependent economic behavior—and end the world's addiction to America's asset-led boom. No one wants recessions, asset deflation, and rising unemployment. But this has always been the potential endgame of a bubble-prone, savings-short U.S. economy. And it also has been the greatest flaw of America's excess consumption myth—a scenario that never made sense in an era of subpar income generation. That has long been the message from a gaping current account deficit, a collapse in domestic saving, and record levels of household-sector indebtedness. It was only a question of when the fantasy of an artificial consumption boom would finally come to an end.

The longer the United States puts off this reckoning, the steeper the ultimate price of adjustment. Tough as it is, the only sensible way out is to let markets lead the way. That is what the long overdue bursting of America's asset and credit bubbles is all about. Policy can temporarily cushion the blow for those who will suffer the most, but there is no easy panacea for America's reckless macromanagement of the past decade.

# Davos Diary: 2008

## January 26, 2008

During the 2008 Annual Meeting of the World Economic Forum in Davos Switzerland, I was invited by the *Financial Times* to contribute to their Davos blog. I filed the following five dispatches, all of which elicited vigorous feedback during a most eventful period.

### Will the Fed Rate Cut Work?

JANUARY 22, 2008

Timing is everything, I guess. No sooner had I arrived in Davos, when my Blackberry started chirping with alarms over an emergency 75 basis point Fed rate cut. No new news on the state of the U.S. economy was evident. The only breaking development was a swoon in global equity markets that was likely to be reflected in the form of a similar plunge in the United States. And so the Fed jumped into action. Borrowing a page from the market-friendly script of the Greenspan Fed, Bernanke & Co. offered up a market-friendly action of its own.

Will it work? That's undoubtedly the question that will be hotly debated this year in Davos—a question that I certainly plan to tackle at the opening session on the global economy tomorrow morning. The answer lies in the unique character of this recession. There are two triggers—a bursting of the U.S. house price bubble and a bursting of the credit bubble. I do not believe that aggressive Fed rate cuts will resolve the extreme imbalance between supply and demand in the U.S. property market that will be pushing housing prices lower for some time. Nor do I believe that recent Fed actions will restore the functioning of credit markets to their precrisis state. As a result, pressures are likely to remain intense on housing- and credit-dependent U.S. consumers—a sector that accounts for a record 72 percent of U.S. real GDP.

In essence, the Fed is "pushing on a string" here—unable to stop the recessionary dynamic now unfolding. But there will be consequences in the next recovery: Unfortunately, the U.S. central bank can't seem to break out of the market-friendly trap it fell into nearly a decade ago Panicking over the possibility that yet another bubble is bursting, the Fed is once again injecting liquidity into an asset-dependent U.S. economy. That won't arrest the recessionary dynamic now unfolding, but it could well set the stage for the next asset bubble in America's bubble-prone economy. Have we learned anything from the mess of the past seven years?

## Decoupling or Globalization—But Not Both
JANUARY 23, 2008

Dreams of decoupling danced in the air on this first official day of meetings at Davos. Decoupling, of course, is the latest macro fad—a scenario where the world no longer sneezes when the United States catches a cold. The decoupling enthusiasts were out in full force at the kick-off session on the global economy on Wednesday morning. As a long-standing panelist in this session—with the exception of last year, when only optimists were invited—I didn't offer much support for this view.

My case is relatively simple. Developing Asia—where the growth dynamic is the strongest and the hopes of resilience are the deepest—remains very much an externally dependent economy. For the region as a whole, exports hit a record high of 47 percent of GDP in 2007—more than double the 19 percent share of 1980. At the same time, private consumption fell to a record low of 48 percent of panregional GDP in 2007—down sharply from the 66 percent reading in 1980. If the fast growing economies of East Asia were truly decoupled, these trends would be the opposite: Export shares would be falling and domestic consumption would be rising.

The decoupling crowd also dreams of alternative sources of global consumption arising from Asia's two new giants—China and India—that would be more than sufficient to offset a shortfall in U.S. consumption. Don't count on it. The United States consumed over $9.5 trillion in 2007—fully six times the combined consumption totals for China ($1 trillion) and India ($650 billion). It would be almost mathematically impossible for "Chindia" to fill the void that is likely to be left by a consolidation of the American consumer. For externally led Developing Asia, the proverbial sneeze in the face of a U.S. cold is more likely than not.

Maybe that's what the recent sharp correction in Asian equity markets is all about.

In the Q & A part of the session, howls of protest came from representatives of Latin America, Central Europe, and even Asia. The European decoupling advocates accosted me in the halls outside the session. Yet globalization, long the mantra of Davos, is all about increased integration of the global economy through trade and capital flows. As I said to one of the more hopeful, "You either believe in decoupling or globalization—but not both."

## Being Right on the Economy—At Last
JANUARY 24, 2008

At the end of a long first day in Davos, one phrase is ringing in my ears: "Well, you're finally right." The subtext, of course, is a thinly veiled critique of my long-standing bearish view on the U.S. economy—an economy that I have characterized repeatedly as unbalanced, income-short, overly indebted, saving deficient, bubble prone, and all those other lovely attributes of a nation that I believe has long been living beyond its means.

Of course, the jury is still out on whether this is that proverbial moment of reckoning. It certainly feels like the Great Moderation is now giving way to the Great Unraveling. But I've been through enough of these situations over the years to know that you can never underestimate the inherent resilience of a Teflon-like U.S. economy. America has dodged tough bullets before and it could certainly happen again. But in the aftermath of the simultaneous bursting of monstrous housing and credit bubbles, my macro framework is finally flashing something darn close to a breaking point.

Small consolation, some might say. After all, for traders and short-term-oriented investors, being early is often judged as the functional equivalent of being wrong. On that basis, I would be the first to concede that my bearish call on the United States has been lacking in one critical respect: While the events that are now unfolding suggest that my basic macro framework appears to have been correct, I have hardly distinguished myself in getting the timing right.

Confession time. At the risk of sounding overly defensive, my own experience is testament to one of the greatest flaws of macro—the timing dimension of any call. Let's face it, with few exceptions, we macro folk are not good traders. My approach has always been grounded in analytics—focusing more on the tensions that arise from economies in disequilibrium. My basic supposition is that these tensions eventually reach a breaking point, triggering corrections that return an economy to a more sustainable equilibrium. The how's and why's of that breaking point, or trigger, are invariably the stuff of exogenous shocks—the bolt from the blue that I find almost impossible to predict with any accuracy.

The key for me is the framework and the tensions. Get those right and you stand a much better chance of nailing the big macro calls. The risk is that you're always early. But when the turn finally comes, you are in a much better position to understand it and to be prepared for the consequences. Being finally right has its benefits, too.

## Sovereign Wealth Funds: Can Beggars Really Afford to Be Choosey?
JANUARY 25, 2008

Why all the fuss about Sovereign Wealth Funds (SWFs)? This is one of the thorniest issues being debated in Davos this year. And there was plenty of tension in the air in a packed session on Thursday morning, when representatives from several leading SWFs came face-to-face with an anxious West.

It's not so much the scale of this new class of investors—with SWF assets under management currently estimated at around U.S. $2.9 trillion and estimated by some to climb to U.S. $12 trillion by 2015. It's simply the fear of foreign ownership posed by this increasingly powerful group of state-controlled asset managers. Sadly, it boils down to nothing more than a thinly veiled manifestation of financial protectionism.

The pushback on SWFs from the United States is especially disconcerting. A savings-short U.S economy is the world's largest external borrower—still requiring roughly U.S. $3 billion of foreign capital inflows per business day to fund a massive current account deficit. Traditionally, those inflows have been lodged primarily in low-yielding U.S. Treasuries. But America's foreign lenders—largely poor developing countries—have become rightfully convinced in recent years that they need higher yields on their investments. And, so, following the basic precepts of modern portfolio theory, diversification into higher-yielding assets is now under way.

This is the red flag for protectionists. The experiences of the ill-fated foreign acquisition attempts of American assets by China's CNOC and

Dubai Ports World still ring in the air of an increasingly xenophobic body politic in the United States. Such concerns are a great mystery. In fact, there is not one shred of evidence of an SWF recently deploying its capital for strategic or geopolitical purposes. Their interests are largely in minority, nonvoting stakes that provide relatively high and safe rates of return. As one representative of a leading SWF from the Middle East protested, "These fears are based purely on assumption." Fair point.

Some Western politicians are demanding that, at a minimum, SWFs agree to a new code of conduct that establishes their collective commitment to basic principles of transparency, potential conflicts, and other dimensions of corporate governance. Rather interesting that the same demands have not been made on hedge funds and private equity investors. But an even deeper question emerges for savings-short Washington who seems quite willing to dictate both the terms and the form of capital that is received from America's foreign lenders: Can beggars really afford to be so choosey?

## You Can't Keep a Good Optimist Down
JANUARY 26, 2008

It's hard to keep a good optimist down. And they didn't stay down for long. Over the course of this year's World Economic Forum, there was a distinct mood change. As I read the Davos crowd, the sentiment seemed to shift from despair on Wednesday to guarded optimism by Friday.

I have to confess that I don't always trust myself as an objective barometer in reading the collective mindset at such a large gathering. So I checked out my assessment with a few trustworthy and objective observers, and they corroborated my observation.

As one of the kick-off speakers on Wednesday, I guess I played a role in setting a rather dour tone at the beginning of this year's events. For a few hours, I encountered no pushback whatsoever from those passing in the halls. But then the crowd started to get more aggressive in challenging my case.

The main reason behind this mood swing was trust in the authorities. The combination of a shockingly aggressive Fed easing, together with quick U.S. congressional agreement on a $150 billion fiscal stimulus package, left the Davos crowd feeling that not all was lost on prospects for the U.S. economy after all. Suddenly, the recession call that seemed so convincing on Wednesday seemed far more unlikely on Friday. And if the United States is able to avoid a downturn, went the argument, then the global decoupling debate was suddenly irrelevant.

I was quick to counter. Arresting the recessionary dynamic now under way in the United States is not like stopping a washing machine in mid-cycle, I argued.

The two most powerful forces now at work—the bursting of property and credit bubbles—are not likely to be arrested by aggressive monetary and fiscal easing. As the support from asset markets and easy credit wanes, housing-dependent American consumers still seem likely to bring consumption into closer alignment with income generation. This rebalancing should, in turn, lead to a meaningful reduction in the record 72 percent of U.S. real GDP that is currently earmarked for personal consumption—the critical ingredient in the recession of 2008.

In part because of lags, Washington's policy package should have more of an impact on the next recovery. And there are no guarantees that such impacts will be quite the ray of sunshine the Davos crowd was starting to envision.

Aggressive monetary easing sets the stage for yet another bubble-led recovery. And fiscal stimulus for a savings-short U.S. economy puts the onus, once again, on foreign lenders to pick up the tab. In short, it's "same old, same old" in Washington—hardly a comforting sign that U.S. authorities have learned much of anything from another bubble-induced implosion.

As I was leaving the Congress Centre in Davos for the final time this year, one of my oldest central banker friends pulled me aside. "You were too hard on Ben (Bernanke)," he said. "He really had no choice other than to act in support of the markets. I would have done the same." Around the world, market-friendly central bankers stand shoulder to shoulder in their penchant to keep the magic alive for an asset-dependent world. Time to get out of Davos.

# Double Bubble Trouble
## March 5, 2008

Amid increasingly turbulent credit markets and ever-weaker reports on the economy, the Federal Reserve has been unusually swift and determined in its lowering of the overnight lending rate. The White House and Congress have moved quickly as well, approving rebates for families and tax breaks for businesses. And more monetary easing from the Fed could well be on the way.

The central question for the economy is this: Will this medicine work? The same question was asked repeatedly in Japan during its "lost decade" of the 1990s. Unfortunately, as was the case in Japan, the answer may be, "No."

If the American economy were entering a standard cyclical downturn, there would be good reason to believe that a timely countercyclical stimulus like that devised by Washington would be effective. But this is not a standard cyclical downturn. It is a postbubble recession.

The United States is now going through its second postbubble downturn in seven years. Yet this one stands in sharp contrast to the postbubble shakeout in the stock market during 2000 and 2001. Back then, there was a collapse in business capital spending, a sector that peaked at only 13 percent of real GDP.

The current recession has been set off by the simultaneous bursting of property and credit bubbles. The unwinding of these excesses is likely to exact a lasting toll on both homebuilders and American consumers. Those two economic sectors collectively peaked at 78 percent of GDP, or fully six times the share of the sector that pushed the country into recession seven years ago.

For asset-dependent, bubble-prone economies, a vigorous cyclical recovery—even when assisted by aggressive monetary and fiscal accommodation—isn't a given. Over the six years ending in mid-2007, income-short consumers made up for the weak increases in their paychecks by extracting equity from the housing bubble through cut-rate borrowing that was subsidized by the credit bubble. That game is now over.

Washington policy makers may not be able to arrest this postbubble downturn. Interest rate cuts are unlikely to halt the decline in nationwide home prices. Given the outsize imbalance between supply and demand for new homes, housing prices may need to fall an additional 20 percent to clear the market.

Nor have aggressive interest rate cuts done much to contain the lethal contagion spreading in credit and capital markets. Now that their houses are worth less and loans are harder to come by, hard-pressed consumers are unlikely to be helped by lower interest rates.

Japan's experience demonstrates how difficult it may be for traditional policies to ignite recovery after a bubble. In the early 1990s, Japan's property and stock market bubbles burst. That implosion was worsened by a banking crisis and excess corporate debt. Nearly 20 years later, Japan is still struggling.

There are eerie similarities between the United States now and Japan then. The Bank of Japan ran an excessively accommodative monetary policy for most of the 1980s. In the United States, the Federal Reserve did the same thing beginning in the late 1990s. In both cases, loose money fueled liquidity booms that led to major bubbles.

Moreover, Japan's central bank initially denied the perils caused by the bubbles. Similarly, it's hard to forget the Fed's blasé approach to the asset bubbles of the past decade, especially as the subprime mortgage crisis imploded last August.

In Japan, a banking crisis constricted lending for years. In the United States, a full-blown credit crisis seems to be doing the same.

The unwinding of excessive corporate indebtedness in Japan and a "keiretsu" culture of companies buying one another's equity shares put extraordinary pressures on business spending. In America, an excess of household indebtedness could put equally serious and lasting restrictions on consumer spending.

Like their counterparts in Japan in the 1990s, American authorities may be deluding themselves into believing they can forestall the end-game of postbubble adjustments. Government support is being aimed, mistakenly, at maintaining unsustainably high rates of personal consumption. Yet that's precisely what got the United States into this mess in the first place—pushing down the savings rate, fostering a huge trade deficit, and stretching consumers to take on an untenable amount of debt.

A more effective strategy would be to try to tilt the economy away from consumption and toward exports and long-needed investments in infrastructure. That won't be easy to achieve. Such a shift in the mix of the economy will require export-friendly measures like a weaker dollar and increased consumption by the rest of the world, which would strengthen demand for American-made goods. Fiscal initiatives should be directed at laying the groundwork for future growth, especially by upgrading the nation's antiquated highways, bridges, and ports.

That's not to say Washington shouldn't help the innocent victims of the bubble's aftermath—especially lower- and middle-income families. But the emphasis should be on providing income support for those who have been blindsided by this credit crisis rather than on rekindling excess spending by overextended consumers.

By focusing on exports and on infrastructure spending, we might be able to limit the recession. Such an approach might also set the stage for a more balanced and sustainable economic upturn in the next cycle. A stimulus package aimed at exports and infrastructure investment would be an important step in that direction.

The toughest, and potentially most relevant, lesson to take from Japan's economy in the 1990s was that the interplay between financial and real economic bubbles causes serious damage. An equally lethal interplay between the bursting of housing and credit bubbles is now at work in the United States.

American authorities, especially Federal Reserve officials, harbor the mistaken belief that swift action can forestall a Japan-like collapse. The greater imperative is to avoid toxic asset bubbles in the first place. Steeped in denial and engulfed by election-year myopia, Washington remains oblivious of the dangers ahead.

# Even When the Worst Is Over—Watch Out for Aftershocks

*April 15, 2008*

E very financial crisis is different, but at some point, they all end. It is hard to know if the end of this one is at hand, but there are grounds to believe the worst of the firestorm may be burning itself out.

Among the reasons: liquidity injections by central banks, especially the U.S. Federal Reserve, have erred on the side of overkill. Moreover, some of the actions have been unconventional, especially the opening of the Fed's discount window to investment banks for the first time since the 1930s.

Also, the failure of Bear Stearns is reminiscent of similar catharses that have marked the bottom of earlier crises, from the failure of Herstadt Bank in 1974 to the demise of Long-Term Capital Management in 1998.

However, there is far more to the macro endgame. This crisis has been big enough to have triggered a host of feedback effects that should endure long after financial markets begin to heal.

First and foremost, there is the impact on the real economy. This is particularly true of the United States, where income-deficient, housing-dependent consumers are caught in a vice between a cyclical erosion of labor income and the bursting of housing and credit bubbles. Add to that a steep recession of homebuilding activity, and risks have tipped decidedly to the downside for fully 78 percent of the U.S. economy. As a result, corporate profits should fall well below expectations, especially for the nonfinancial component of the S&P 500. As indicated by the recent earnings shortfall at General Electric, such optimism, in the face of recession, points to especially painful feedback effects for the stock market.

Second, there are lagged impacts on the broader global economy. In an era of globalization, the world economy has become tightly linked through cross-border flows of trade, financial capital, information, and labor. Export-led Developing Asia has been a big beneficiary of the surge in global demand and world trade over the past five-and-a-half years. Now that the global business cycle has turned, Asia will have a very hard time decoupling itself from a consolidation of the U.S. consumer.

Third, it seems quite likely that bruised and battered financial institutions will have to contend with an additional round of pressures. Until now, financial intermediaries have been hit mainly by crisis-related disruptions on the credit front. But as is typically the case with erosion on the demand side of the real economy, a cyclical deterioration in loan quality for households and businesses is coming.

Fourth, feedback effects could also hit commodity markets—the sole surviving bubble in an increasingly bubble-prone world. By now, most are convinced that commodities are in a permanent "super cycle," with the limited expansion of supply failing to keep up with a growing appetite on the demand side of the equation sparked by commodity-intensive economies such as China and India. However, with global GDP growth in 2008–2009 likely to fall well short of the near 5 percent average pace of the past five years, a cyclical correction in the economically sensitive prices of oil, base metals, and other nonfood commodities seems likely.

Fifth, a political backlash to this crisis is likely to lead to a new wave of re-regulation. Just as the bursting of the dot-com bubble and an outbreak of corporate accounting scandals led to passage of Sarbanes-Oxley Act of 2002, U.S. politicians now seem equally committed to a recasting of the regulatory framework governing financial markets. The U.S. Treasury has already fired an opening salvo in what is likely to be an intense and drawn-out debate. As an added twist, look for the U.S. Congress to rewrite the Fed's policy mandate to make the central bank more accountable for avoiding destabilizing asset bubbles in the future.

Financial markets have breathed a sigh of relief that the worst may now be over. Maybe that is the case for the crisis, itself.

But do not confuse that possibility with an all-clear sign for the real economy, stock markets, or the political cycle. As the United States slips into recession, a chain of increasingly powerful feedback effects is likely to follow. The after-shocks of this crisis will shape the landscape for years to come.

*Postscript: Obviously, the worst was far from over with the demise of Bear Stearns. The failure of Lehman Brothers—some six months later—now stands as the most prominent monument of a failed industry. Hopefully, that precedent will not be surpassed—although one of the key lessons of this crisis is, never say never. Even so, the basic premise described above still stands—the macro impacts of this crisis have now shifted from financial services firms to the real side of the U.S. and global economy. These feedback effects will likely endure for years to come.*

# Pitfalls in a Postbubble World

*August 1, 2008*

A year ago, there was barely an inkling of what was about to transpire in world financial markets and the global economy. There were some early warning signs that all was not well in the subprime slice of the U.S. mortgage market. But as was the case of the dot-com bubble in early 2000, subprime was widely judged to be of little consequence for the macro story. The broad consensus of consumers, business people, policy makers, and politicians ignored simmering problems on the subprime front and believed that the global boom of the preceding five years was very much intact.

Alas, similar to circumstances in 2000, the bloom is now off the rose—the postbubble global business cycle has turned. World GDP growth, which averaged close to 5 percent annually over the 2004–2007 period—the strongest four consecutive years of global growth since the early 1970s—now seems headed back down into the 2 percent range for the next three years. Such a growth pace would fall far short of the 45-year trend of 3.7 percent in world GDP growth. And it would mark a stunning deceleration for a world that had become convinced in the permanence of the new global growth boom.

The interplay between financial markets and the real economy undoubtedly holds the key to the global macro outlook over the next few years. I have found it helpful to break down the prognosis into three stages:

The credit crisis is the first stage. Sparked by the subprime meltdown in the Summer of 2007, an unprecedented cross-product contagion quickly spread to asset-backed commercial paper, mortgage-backed securities, structured investment vehicles (SIVs), interbank offshore (LIBOR) financing, leveraged lending markets, auction rate securities, so-called monoline insurers, and a number of other opaque products and structures. Unlike the Asian financial crisis 10 years earlier, which was a powerful cross-border contagion, the "originate and distribute" characteristics of today's complex instruments and structures ended up infecting offshore investors as well. That puts the current crisis in the rarefied breed of being both cross-product and cross-border. United States financial institutions generally have been aggressive in marking down the value of distressed securities. Largely for that reason, I believe that this first phase is about 60 percent complete—more behind the United States than ahead of it but still a good deal more to come as the business cycle now kicks in and produces yet another round of earnings impairment for financial intermediaries.

The second stage reflects the impacts of the credit and housing implosions on the real side of the U.S. economy. The main event here is the likely capitulation of the overextended, savings-short, overly-indebted American consumer. For nearly a decade-and-a-half, real U.S. consumption growth averaged close to 4 percent per year. As asset-dependent consumers now move to rebuild income-based saving and prune outsize debt burdens, a multiyear downshift in consumer demand is likely. Over the next two to three years, I expect trend consumption growth rate to be around 1.5 percent. There will be quarters when consumer spending falls short of that bogey and the U.S. economy remains mired in recession. There will undoubtedly also be quarters when consumption growth is faster than the 2 percent norm and it will appear that a recovery is under way. Such rebounds, unfortunately, should prove short lived for postbubble American consumers. This aspect of the macro-adjustment scenario has only just begun—suggesting that Phase II is only about 20 percent complete.

The third stage is a global phase—underscored by the linkages between the U.S. consumer and the rest of the world. Due to cross-border trade lags, those linkages are only now just beginning to play out. Early impacts are already evident in China, where GDP growth slowed to 10.1 percent in the second quarter of 2008 on the back of a compression of export growth to the United States. As Japan and Europe now weaken—collectively accounting for about 30 percent of China's total exports—heretofore-resilient pieces of Chinese external demand will also begin to falter, possibly prompting another down leg in Chinese GDP growth from 10 percent to 8 percent within the next six months. A similar story is likely for Japan. Overall Japanese export volume growth went negative in June 2008 ($-1.6$ percent year-over-year) for the first time in 16 months. At work was emerging sluggishness in Japanese exports to Europe and elsewhere in Asia—once resilient markets that previously had been masking emerging weakness to the United States.

China and Japan are at the opposite ends of Asia's external vulnerability chain. China has a huge cushion—nearly 12 percent growth over the past two years—to ward off the blow of an external shock. Japan, by contrast has been only a 2 percent growth economy in recent years and has no such cushion. In a weaker external demand climate, the downside to Chinese economic growth appears to be around 8 percent. For Japan, the downside is probably closer to zero—underscoring the distinct possibility of a recessionary relapse in Asia's largest economy. Phase III currently appears to be only about 10 percent complete.

In short, this macro crisis is far from over. As the United States now adjusts to much tougher postbubble realities, the rest of an interdependent world should follow. Moreover, there are undoubtedly feedback effects between the three stages—especially between the credit cycle and debt-dependent economies in the United States and around the world. All in all, macro adjustments should last well into 2009 and probably spill over into 2010.

## Financial Market Implications

The events of the past year have certainly not been lost on financial markets. As forward looking discounting mechanisms, much of the macro adjustments that have unfolded are now discounted in the price of major asset classes. But denial remains deep about the full extent of the adjustments. To the extent that there is more to come in the global economy, the same can be said for financial markets. Four broad conclusions in that regard:

With equity markets now in bear-market territory in most parts of the world, it is tempting to conclude that the worst is over. I am suspicious of that prognosis. The trick is to resist the temptation to view equity markets as a homogenous asset class. The distinction between financials and nonfinancials is critical. The former have certainly been beaten down. That is not the case for nonfinancials, however. For example, consensus earnings expectations for the nonfinancials component of the S&P 500 are still centered on prospects of close to 25 percent earnings growth over 2007–2008. As U.S. economic growth falters, however, I expect earnings risks to tip to the downside for nonfinancials—underscoring the distinct possibility of yet another important down leg in global equity markets. The equity bear market is likely to shift from financials to nonfinancials.

For bonds, the prognosis centers on the interplay between inflation and growth risks—and the implications such a tradeoff has for the policy stance of central banks. As inflation fears have mounted recently, yields on sovereign government bonds rose as market participants started to discount a return to more aggressive monetary policy stances of major central banks. In a faltering growth climate, I suspect cyclical inflation fears will end up being overblown and monetary authorities will become fearful of overkill. Over the near term, major bond markets could rally somewhat on the heels of a rethinking of the aggressive central bank tightening scenario. Over the medium term, I concede that the jury is still out on stagflation risks, especially in inflation-prone developing economies. The bond market prognosis is more uncertain over that time horizon.

For currencies, the dollar remains center stage. I have been a dollar bear for over six years for one reason—America's massive current account deficit. While the U.S. external shortfall has been reduced somewhat over the past year-and-a-half—largely for cyclical reasons—at 5 percent of GDP, it is still far too large. And so I remain fundamentally bearish on the dollar. At the same time, it appears that the dollar has overshot on the downside over the past year on the fear that subprime is mainly a U.S. problem. As the global repercussions of the macro crisis now spread, I believe that investors will rethink the belief that they can seek refuge in euro- and yen-denominated assets. As a result, I could envision the dollar actually stabilizing or possibly even rallying into year-end 2008 before resuming its current-account induced decline in 2009.

The commodity market outlook is especially topical these days. A year from now, I believe that economically sensitive commodity prices—oil, base metals, and other industrial materials—will be a good deal lower than they are today. Two reasons—a marked deceleration in global growth leading to an improvement in the supply-demand imbalance, as well as a pullback in commodity buying by return-seeking financial investors. At work in this latter instance are mainly long-only, real-money institutional investors such as global pension funds—all of whom have been advised by their consultants to increase their asset allocations into commodities as an asset class. Such herding behavior of institutional investors invariably turns out to be wrong—underscoring the possibility of an investor pullback from this asset class that would reinforce shifting economic fundamentals. Soft commodities—mainly agricultural products—as well as precious metals could well be exceptions to a likely cyclical softening in economically sensitive commodity markets.

## Perpetuating the Madness?

The current financial crisis is hardly lacking in superlatives. Whether it is truly the worst debacle since the Great Depression, as many have argued, remains to be seen. But it is certainly a watershed event—especially since it draws into sharp question the fundamental underpinnings of a U.S. economy that has long ignored its imbalances and excesses. Sadly, America's body politic seems both unwilling and unable to fathom the magnitude of the problems that have come to a head in this crisis.

Tax policy is a case in point. Rebates to overextended American consumers have been the first line of defense, and there is new talk in Washington of a second round of such stimulus measures. Yet with personal consumer spending hitting a world record 72 percent of real GDP in 2007, the government's injections of spendable income are aimed at perpetuating the biggest consumption binge in modern history. For a nation that desperately needs to save more and spend less—and thereby pay down debt and reduce its massive current account deficit—politically expedient personal tax cuts are the wrong medicine at the wrong time.

Washington's response to the housing crisis is equally problematic. The Congress has made foreclosure containment a centerpiece of the fix. This is consistent with a philosophy that has long stressed ever-rising rates of home ownership as a key objective of U.S. public policy. Yet an obvious and painful lesson of the subprime crisis is that there are some Americans who simply cannot afford to purchase a home. Foreclosure is a tragic, but ultimately necessary, consequence of misguided home buying. For low-income victims of the housing bubble, assistance should be directed at income support rather than at perpetuating uneconomic home ownership. By opting for the latter, Congress is inhibiting the requisite decline in home prices that ultimately will be necessary to clear the market and bring the housing crisis to an end.

Nor have the financial authorities distinguished themselves in this crisis. Once again, Washington is condoning undisciplined risk taking through actions that temper the consequences of the bursting of the risk bubble. In effect, the authorities are shielding irresponsible risk takers and thereby enabling the moral hazard that has become increasingly ingrained in today's financial culture. At the same time, a Federal Reserve that continues to ignore the perils of asset bubbles in the setting of monetary policy is guilty of reckless endangerment to the financial markets and to an increasingly asset-dependent U.S. economy.

In short, Washington has responded to this financial crisis with a politically driven, reactive approach. This does little to change bad behavior. Far from heeding the tough lessons of an economy in crisis, Washington is doing little to break the daisy chain of excesses that got America into this mess in the first place.

More than anything, America now needs tough love—a new course that owns up to years of excess and accepts the remedies those excesses now require. It is not that difficult to fathom the broad outlines of what that new approach might entail—more saving, as well as more investment in both people and infrastructure. An energy policy might be nice as well—as would be more prudent stewardship of the financial system. This program won't win any popularity contests, but in the end, it is America's only hope for a sustainable postbubble prosperity.

## Lessons

It didn't have to be this way. America went to excess, and the rest of an export-dependent world was more than happy to go along for the ride. Policy makers and regulators—the stewards of the global economy—looked the other way and allowed the system to veer out of control. Investors, businesspeople, financial institutions, and consumers were all active participants in the Era of Excess.

The key question going forward is whether an adaptive and increasingly interrelated global system learns the tough lessons of this macro upheaval. At the heart of this self-appraisal must be a greater awareness of the consequences of striving for open-ended economic growth. The United States could not hit its growth target the old fashioned way by relying on internal income generation, so it turned to a new asset- and debt-dependent growth model. For its part, export-dependent Developing Asia took its saving-led growth model to excess: Unwilling or unable to stimulate internal private consumption, surplus capital was recycled into infrastructure and dollar-based assets—in effect, forcing super-competitive currencies and exports to become the sustenance of a new development recipe.

This crisis is a strong signal that these strategies are not sustainable. They have led to multiple layers of excess—underscored by a precarious interplay between internal and external imbalances within and between the world's largest economies. It took unsustainable credit and risk bubbles to hold this system together in an unstable equilibrium. But now those bubbles have burst, unmasking a worrisome disequilibrium that demands a new approach to policy and an important shift in behavior by households, businesses, and financial-market participants.

Financial and economic crises often define some of history's greatest turning points. They can be the ultimate in painful learning experiences. But if all the authorities can do is opt for the politically expedient quick fix, a globalized world will have squandered a critical opportunity to put its house in order. That would be the ultimate tragedy. If this crisis demonstrates anything, it is that it only gets tougher and tougher to pick up the pieces in a postbubble world.

# Panic of 2008:
## Enough Scapegoating

*October 1, 2008*

I n my more than 35 years as a professional economist, I have endured five recessions and about a dozen financial crises. Yet never has one hit this close to home. That makes the experience personal, which runs the added risk of coloring the judgment of the cold calculating analyst that I like to think I am. But here's a shot, in any case.

While we have been in a credit crisis for more than 14 months, there can be no mistaking the telltale signs of the panic phase of this crisis that first became evident in the week of September 15, 2008. We are in the midst of what the academic Charles Kindleberger called the "revulsion stage" of a crisis—indiscriminate and contagious selling of distressed assets that leads "banks to stop lending on the collateral of such assets."[2] When such fear grips the markets, investors (and speculators) are quick to generalize—punishing many for the sins of few. That's the most dangerous phase of any crisis—when market implosions start to take on a self-reinforcing life of their own.

The most important thing I can say about financial panics is that they are all temporary—they either die of exhaustion or are overwhelmed by the heavy artillery of government policies. That raises the most important question of all: What will it take to bring this panic to an end? Kindleberger, again, lays it out very clearly. He argued that financial panics tend to feed on themselves until one or more of three things happen: (1) prices fall to depths that bring investors back into distressed assets; (2) exchanges are closed; (3) central banks spring into action. Right now, progress is not encouraging on any of those counts.

---

2. See Charles Kindleberger, *Of Manias, Panics, and Crashes: A History of Financial Crises.* Hoboken, NJ: John Wiley & Sons, 2005.

That's particularly true of the liquidity injections proposed by U.S. fiscal authorities—the so-called Emergency Economic Stabilization Act of 2008 that was surprisingly rejected by the U.S. House of Representatives on September 29. With financial markets melting down in the aftermath of Congress' politicization of this crisis, I have a sneaking suspicion that U.S. politicians will now quickly change their minds and vote to approve this plan in the next few days. And that will most assuredly benefit the most illiquid portions of increasingly dysfunctional credit markets.

Unfortunately, the so-called Congressional fix is deficient in several key respects. That's especially the case with respect to the scope of the package. The original Paulson Plan was set at $700 billion. Yet the congressional version proposed a down payment of only $250 billion and offered up the remainder in two separate tranches—one tied to presidential approval and the other dependent on a new congressional authorization. During times of crisis and panic, the policy response should err on the side of overkill. This approach erred on the side of underkill.

Furthermore, a policy response should also be unmistakably direct in its focus to arrest markets in disarray. The original Paulson plan of three-and-a-half pages erred with its lack of specificity. But at least it was unmistakably clear in taking dead aim on dysfunctional mortgage and credit markets. Congress responded with 110 pages of legislation, complete with added stipulations on equity warrants for participating institutions, restrictions on executive compensation, a supplementary insurance scheme, and four new bureaucratic oversight functions. This dilutes the thrust of the policy response and blunts its impact on market angst.

With the fiscal package falling short on those counts, the burden for a crisis fix is now likely to fall more acutely on monetary policy. In times of extreme crisis—and that is most assuredly the case today—the central bank needs to make a strong and unequivocal statement that it is prepared to do everything in its power as a lender of last resort.

Specifically, I think the Fed needs to borrow a page from the Greenspan script of the Crash of 1987 and send a direct and simple message of open-ended liquidity support to markets in crisis. At the same time, it should make a strong symbolic move by cutting its policy rate by 50 basis points immediately to let the markets know it takes this matter very seriously. And the Fed should enlist other major central banks to join in a rare coordinated policy action.

I am convinced that such a powerful monetary policy response, in the face of a suboptimal fiscal response, would go a long way in stopping the madness that is now gripping financial markets. Such actions would also go a long way in tempering the collateral damage that is now being inflicted on the U.S. and broader global economy. Fed Chairman Ben Bernanke is supposedly one of the most renowned living experts on the Great Depression. He knows better than anyone that the most important lesson of all from that earlier period was a series of major policy blunders by America's central bank. That knowledge now needs to be put to work.

Today's Fed is hardly an innocent bystander to this mess, especially in light of the role it played in condoning the excesses of the past decade. Is it doomed to stay that course, as well as repeat the errors of the 1930s? My bet is a resounding "No"—but it's high time for Bernanke to dispel any doubts once and for all. And, it's high time for the U.S. Congress to put aside the politics of scapegoating and get on with the heavy lifting of crisis containment. The alternative is simply unacceptable.

# Global Fix for a Global Crisis
## October 9, 2008

There is no longer any middle ground. An ever-deepening crisis spells one of two things—the distinct possibility of a wrenching downturn in the global economy or an opportunity for healing and recovery. The ball is in the court of the authorities.

The rare coordinated easing by the world's leading central banks on October 8, 2008—50 basis point rate cuts by the Fed, the ECB, and central banks in Canada, England, Sweden, and Switzerland—was an important step in the right direction. The risk is that it may not have been enough.

This crisis is so grave and so threatening that it is critical that policy err on the side of overkill, not underkill. That is true of both monetary and fiscal policy alike.

I would have preferred to have seen rate cuts of twice the magnitude that were announced on that Wednesday—leaving no mistake about the power of the weapons being deployed as well as the collective resolve of the stewards of the global economy.

I would also have preferred that a blanket statement had been issued by the world's leading central banks, saying that they are collectively prepared to backstop global liquidity in the broadest sense. This endorsement should also include the cash (but not derivatives) markets of counterparty risk.

But central banks can't do the job alone. Follow-up efforts are needed. Specifically, I would also like to see a coordinated initiative endorsed by the world's leading fiscal authorities announced this coming weekend at the G-7/IMF/World Bank meetings in Washington. Such an initiative should include a commitment to recapitalize a seriously weakened global banking system. It should also offer public sector support to mortgage holders with negative equity positions as well as propose a sweeping review of mandates for regulatory policy, monetary policy, and global risk management practices.

There would be enormous benefits from such a combined monetary and fiscal fix. It would be the functional equivalent of a massive tax cut for a crisis-torn global economy. It would unclog the clogged arteries in credit markets. It would put financial institutions on sounder footing. It would provide some visibility to the bottom of the global business cycle. And it would usher in a new era of transparency, improved disclosure, improved underwriting standards, and enhanced oversight. It would also provide a new focus on financial stability and greater accountability and discipline in an all-too-reckless world.

Notwithstanding my long-standing bearishness on the global economy and world financial markets, I am now actually hopeful that the world is at a critical turning point. We have gone to the edge of an abyss that few thought was ever possible. Having stared into the darkness, the authorities hopefully have a better appreciation of what is truly at stake. It is not too late. If the world now pulls together, we can avoid the Armageddon endgame.

We didn't have to come this close to disaster. Steeped in denial, policy makers around the world were operating largely in an ad hoc mindset—coping with asset- and institution-specific issues as they arose on a case-by-case basis. That may have worked in crises of the past—but not this time. The reactive and incremental approach has to be replaced by one that is proactive and powerful—in essence, deploying all of the firepower in the policy arsenal. This is definitely not a time to keep ammunition in reserve.

In the end, this is not just a crisis of markets, financial institutions, risk management, and regulators. It is a crisis of leadership. Looking to the upcoming G-7 meeting, the authorities who gather in Washington this weekend should be locked in a room until they come up with a true global fix for this mother of all global crises. Incrementalism is not an option. If world leaders follow such a course, there is legitimate hope for a new global healing and eventual recovery. It is premature to bank on such an optimistic outcome. But if that turns out to be the case, the world must also be mindful of the pitfalls of any postbubble recovery—avoiding at all costs the enduring excesses of liquidity and risk appetite that finally brought the system to its knees. There will be no second chance.

# Changing the Fed's Policy Mandate

*October 28, 2008*

A regulatory backlash is now under way as the U.S. body politic comes to grips with the financial crisis. Wall Street—or what is left of it—is first in the line of fire. But the era of excess was as much about policy blunders and regulatory negligence as about mistakes by financial institutions. As Washington creates a new system, it must also redefine the role of the Federal Reserve.

Specifically, the U.S. Congress needs to alter the Fed's policy mandate to include an explicit reference to financial stability. The addition of those two words would force the Fed not only to aim at tempering the damage from asset bubbles but also to use its regulatory authority to promote sounder risk management practices. Such reforms are critical for a postbubble, crisis-torn U.S. economy.

This is not the first time the U.S. Congress has needed to refine the Fed's mandate. After the great inflation of the 1970s, the so-called Humphrey-Hawkins Act of 1978 was enacted. That required the Fed to add price stability to its original post–World War II policy target of full employment. In the late 1970s, Congress felt the Fed needed the full force of the law to tackle a corrosive inflation problem. This legislative change empowered Paul Volcker, a later Fed chairman, in his courageous assault on double-digit inflation.

By focusing on financial stability, the Fed will need to adjust its tactics in two ways. Firstly, monetary policy will need to shift from the Greenspan-Bernanke reactive, postbubble clean-up approach toward preemptive bubble avoidance. Second, the U.S. central bank will need to be tougher in enforcing its neglected regulatory oversight capacity.

By adding financial stability to the Fed's policy mandate, I am mindful of the pitfalls of multiple policy targets. However, single-dimensional policy targeting does not cut it in a complex world. As such, the Fed will need to be creative in achieving its mandated goals—using monetary policy, regulatory oversight and enforcement, and moral persuasion. Just as the Fed has been reasonably successful in its twin quests for price stability and full employment, I am confident it can rise to the occasion with the addition of financial stability to its mandate.

I am not suggesting the Fed develop numerical targets for asset markets. It should have discretion about how it interprets the new mandate. Yes, it is tricky to judge when an asset class is in danger of forming a bubble. But hindsight offers little doubt of the bubbles that developed over the past decade—equities, residential property, credit, and other risky assets. The Fed wrongly dismissed these developments, harboring the illusion it could clean up any mess later. Today's problems are a repudiation of that approach.

There is no room in a new financial stability mandate for bubble denialists such as Alan Greenspan, the former Fed chairman. He argued that equities were surging because of a new economy; that housing forms local not national bubbles, and that the credit explosion was a by-product of the American genius of financial innovation. In retrospect, while there was a kernel of truth to all of those observations, they should not have been decisive in shaping Fed policy. Under a financial stability mandate, the Fed will need to replace its ideological convictions with common sense. When investors buy assets in anticipation of future price increases, the Fed will need to err on the side of caution and presume that a bubble is forming that could threaten financial stability.

The new mandate would also encourage the Fed to deal with excesses by striking the right balance between deploying its policy interest rate and other tools. In times of asset-market froth, I favor the leaning-against-the-wind approach with regard to interest rates—pushing the Federal funds rate higher than a narrow CPI-inflation target might suggest. But there are other Fed tools that can be directed at financial excesses—margin requirements for equity lending as well as controls on the issuance of exotic mortgage instruments (zero-interest rate products come to mind). In addition, the Fed should not be bashful about using the bully pulpit of moral persuasion to warn against the impending dangers of asset and credit bubbles.

Of equal importance is the need for the Fed to develop a clearer understanding of the linkage between financial stability and the open-ended explosion of derivatives and structured products. Over the past decade, an ideologically driven Fed failed to make the distinction between financial engineering and innovation. It understood neither the products nor their scale, even as the notional value of global derivatives hit $516,000bn in mid-2007 on the eve of the subprime crisis—up 2.3 times over the preceding three years to a level that was 10 times the size of world GDP. The view in U.S. central banking circles was that an innovations-based explosion of new financial instruments was a huge plus for market efficiency. Unfortunately, that view turned out to be dead wrong.

Driven by its ideological convictions, the Fed flew blind on the derivatives front. On the one hand, this was hardly surprising because these are largely private, over-the-counter transactions. What is surprising is that the authorities failed to develop metrics that would have helped them understand the breadth, depth, and complexity of the derivatives explosion. This trust in ideology over objective metrics was a fatal mistake. Like all crises, this one is a wake-up call. The Fed made policy blunders of historic proportions that must be avoided in the future. Adding financial stability to its mandate is vital to preventing such errors again.

# An Early Leadership Opportunity for Barack Obama

*November 6, 2008*

For President-elect Barack Obama, the campaign mantra of "change and hope" will meet a very quick reality test. Courtesy of a wrenching economic and financial crisis, his leadership skills could, in fact, be tested even before he assumes office. Not only would it be appropriate for him to weigh in on the mid-November 2008 G-20 summit in Washington, but his views could well be decisive in shaping the post-election efforts of the U.S. Congress to craft another economic stimulus package. In these troubled times, the new leader of the free world can hardly afford to remain silent.

Leadership and national image building go hand in hand. If he rises quickly to the occasion, President-elect Obama will be off to an excellent start in recasting America's image to the world. Three principles should guide him in this urgent task.

First, his core strategy should be to foster a long overdue rebalancing of the U.S. economy. A dysfunctional growth model must be guided away from the asset- and debt-dependent consumption binge of the past dozen years toward a significant increase in long depressed domestic saving. Only then can the United States achieve a sustained reduction of its massive current account deficit, necessary to fund sorely needed investments in infrastructure and human capital.

Second, Barack Obama needs to move quickly in restoring America's commitment to globalization. That means repudiating the politically inspired scapegoating of China and other saber rattling on the trade front. To do that, the president-elect needs to tackle a daunting middle-class real-wage stagnation problem—the source of economic anxiety that has been the political foil for Washington's increasingly worrisome protectionist tilt.

Third, the newly elected president must provide leadership to the regulatory reform of America's bruised and battered financial system. There is a very real risk in today's highly charged political climate that a regulatory backlash could go too far and end up impeding the efficiency of America's market-based system of capital allocation. Reregulation must be even-handed, aimed not only at Wall Street but also at the rating agencies, a bubble-prone Federal Reserve, and other regulatory authorities.

If President-elect Obama can push early for a principled and judicious approach to financial sector reforms, there is good reason to hope that the new system will be a major improvement from the old one, ushering in an era of transparency, improved disclosure, better underwriting standards, and enhanced oversight. America's financial markets and institutions would then be grounded in a new sense of discipline, accountability, and stability, capable of providing just the anchor that an all too unstable and reckless world sorely needs.

If Barack Obama can demonstrate early leadership in these three areas—saving, trade, and financial reform—the U.S. and global economy will be in much better shape than it is today, and the United States of America will have taken a giant step in reshaping its image in an increasingly troubled world.

# Dying of Consumption
## November 28, 2008

I t's game over for the American consumer. Inflation-adjusted personal consumption expenditures are on track for rare back-to-back quarterly declines in the second half of 2008 at nearly a 4 percent average annual rate. There are only four other instances since 1950 when real consumer demand has fallen for two quarters in a row. This is the first occasion when declines in both quarters will have exceeded 3 percent. The current consumption plunge is without precedent in the modern era.

The good news is that lines should be short for today's first shopping day of the 2008 holiday season. The bad news is more daunting: rising unemployment, weakening incomes, falling home values, a declining stock market, record household debt, and a horrific credit crunch. But there is a deeper, potentially positive, meaning to all this: Consumers are now abandoning the asset-dependent spending and saving strategies they embraced during the bubbles of the past dozen years and moving back to more prudent income-based lifestyles.

This is a painful but necessary adjustment. Since the mid-1990s, vigorous growth in American consumption has consistently outstripped subpar gains in household income. This led to a steady decline in personal saving. As a share of disposable income, the personal saving rate fell from 5.7 percent in early 1995 to nearly zero from 2005 to 2007.

In the days of frothy asset markets, American consumers had no compunction about squandering their savings and spending beyond their incomes. Appreciation of assets—equity portfolios and, especially, homes—was widely thought to be more than sufficient to make up the difference. But with most asset bubbles bursting, America's 77 million baby boomers are suddenly facing a savings-short retirement.

Worse, millions of home owners used their residences as collateral to take out home equity loans. According to Federal Reserve calculations, net equity extractions from U.S. homes rose from about 3 percent of disposable personal income in 2000 to nearly 9 percent in 2006. This newfound source of purchasing power was a key prop to the American consumption binge.

As a result, household debt hit a record 133 percent of disposable personal income by the end of 2007—an enormous leap from average debt loads of 90 percent just a decade earlier.

In an era of open-ended house price appreciation and extremely cheap credit, few doubted the wisdom of borrowing against one's home. But in today's climate of falling home prices, frozen credit markets, mounting layoffs and weakening incomes, that approach has backfired. It should hardly be surprising that consumption has faltered so sharply.

A decade of excess consumption pushed consumer spending in the United States up to 72 percent of gross domestic product in 2007, a record for any large economy in the modern history of the world. With such a huge portion of the economy now shrinking, a deep and protracted recession is inevitable. Consumption growth, which averaged close to 4 percent annually over the past 14 years, could slow into the 1 percent to 2 percent range for the next three to five years.

The United States needs a very different set of policies to cope with its postbubble economy. It would be a serious mistake to enact tax cuts aimed at increasing already excessive consumption. Americans need to save. They don't need another flat-screen TV made in China.

The Obama administration needs to encourage the sort of saving that will put consumers on sounder financial footing and free up resources that could be directed at long overdue investments in transportation infrastructure, alternative energy, technologies, education, worker training, and the like. This strategy would not only create jobs but would also cut America's dependence on foreign saving and imports. That would help reduce the current account deficit and the heavy foreign borrowing such an imbalance entails.

We don't need to reinvent the wheel to come up with effective saving policies. The money has to come out of Americans' paychecks. This can be either incentive driven—expanded 401(k) and IRA programs—or mandatory, like increased Social Security contributions. As long as the economy stays in recession, any tax increases associated with mandatory saving initiatives should be off the table. (When times improve, however, that may be worth reconsidering.)

Fiscal policy must also be aimed at providing income support for newly unemployed middle-class workers—particularly expanded unemployment insurance and retraining programs. A critical distinction must be made between providing assistance for the innocent victims of recession and misplaced policies aimed at perpetuating an unsustainable consumption binge.

Crises are the ultimate in painful learning experiences. The United States cannot afford to squander this opportunity. Runaway consumption must now give way to a renewal of saving and investment. That's the best hope for economic recovery and for America's longer-term economic prosperity.

# Uncomfortable Truths about Our World after the Bubble

*December 3, 2008*

The textbooks have little to say about postbubble economies. That makes the current prognosis all the more problematic. A profusion of asset bubbles has burst around the world—from property and credit to commodities and emerging market equities. That's an especially rude awakening for a global economy that has become dependent on the very bubbles that are now imploding. It is as if the world has suddenly been turned inside out.

The American consumer is a case in point. Real personal consumption expenditures are on track for rare back-to-back quarterly declines in the second half of 2008, at close to a 4 percent average annual rate. Never before has there been such an extraordinary capitulation of the American consumer.

Similar extremes are evident elsewhere. Europe and Japan have joined the United States in the first synchronous G3 recession of the post–World War II era. Nor has the developing world been spared. While most big developing economies should avoid outright contractions in overall output, sharp deceleration is evident in China, India, and Russia. Hong Kong and Singapore—Asia's two prosperous city states—are both in recession. Moreover, reminiscent of the Asian financial crisis of 1997–1998, the currencies of South Korea, Indonesia, and India are under severe pressure. As the commodity bubble implodes, a similar boom-bust pattern is unfolding in Australia, New Zealand, Canada, and the Middle East.

Crises invariably trigger finger-pointing. This one is no exception. Global observers have been quick to blame the United States, arguing that it's all about the excesses of Wall Street and America's subprime fiasco. Some would take it even further and condemn the freewheeling model of market-based capitalism. Let the record show, however, that while the United States certainly made its fair share of mistakes, the rest of the world was more than happy to go along for the ride.

That's especially the case in Asia, where China and other producers upped the ante on their export-led impetus to economic growth. By 2007, the export share of Developing Asia's gross domestic product exceeded 45 percent—fully 10 percentage points higher than the share prevailing during the Asian financial crisis of the late 1990s. Moreover, the Chinese led the way in recycling a disproportionate share of their massive reservoir of foreign exchange reserves back into dollar-based assets. That kept their currency, the renminbi, highly competitive, as any export-led economy likes, but also prevented U.S. interest rates from rising, keeping the magic alive for bubble-dependent American consumers. In effect, the world's bubbles fed off each other.

Nor did anyone force the German Landesbanken and the Swiss universal banks to invest heavily in toxic assets. And the new mega-cities of the Gulf region—Dubai, Doha, Riyadh, and Abu Dhabi—owe their very existence to the oil bubble. Now all of these bubbles have burst, leaving a bubble-dependent world in the lurch.

A postbubble shakeout is likely to be the defining feature of the global economic outlook over the next few years. Three conclusions on the postbubble prognosis are most apparent:

One, do not analyze a postbubble recession as a normal business cycle. As economies that levered their asset bubbles to excess—especially the United States—come to grips with tough postbubble realities, a powerful deleveraging will ensue. That could prolong the duration of the downturn, as well as inhibit the vigor of the subsequent recovery.

Two, on the demand side of the global economy, focus on the American consumer—the biggest and most overextended consumer in the world. With personal saving rates still close to zero and debt loads remaining at all-time highs, U.S. consumption is heading for a Japanese-style multiyear adjustment. After 14 years of nearly 4 percent average growth in U.S. real consumer spending, gains could slow to 1 to 2 percent over the next three to five years. And no other consumer in the world is capable of stepping up and filling the void.

Three, on the supply side of the global economy, focus on China. Industrial production growth has been cut in half in China, rising at just

8 percent year-on-year in October 2008 following five years of average gains of about 16.5 percent. With the global economy in recession, this outcome should hardly come as a surprise for a Chinese economy that has seen its export share of total gross domestic product nearly double from about 20 percent to almost 40 percent over the past seven years. China is paying a steep price for its own imbalances, especially a lack of support from internal private consumption.

In short, look for a postbubble world to remain in recession throughout 2009, followed by an anemic recovery, at best, in 2010. In an era of globalization, we became intoxicated with what cross-border linkages were able to deliver on the upside of a boom. But as that boom went to excess and spawned a lethal globalization of asset bubbles, the inevitable bust now promises an exceedingly tough hangover.

# A Postbubble Global Business Cycle

*January 7, 2009*

There will be no V-shaped recovery for a world economy that has just entered its most severe recession of the post–World War II era. While the worst of the global downturn may run its course by late 2009, the risk is that any rebound in 2010 will be anemic and fragile. After nearly 5 percent average annual growth in world GDP in the four-and-a-half years preceding the so-called subprime crisis, global growth seems likely to average only about 2 percent over the next three years—well below the 3.7 percent trend of the past 40 years.

At work is a powerful postbubble shakeout for an unbalanced global economy. Headwinds are likely to be especially stiff on the demand side, long dominated by an unsustainable U.S. consumer-spending binge. With a notable lack of dynamism from private consumption elsewhere in the world, the external demand underpinnings of export-led economies will be impaired. Commodity producers will also suffer collateral damage from a U.S.-led slowdown in global demand. In short, the movie of the past decade is about to run in reverse.

The retrenchment of the American consumer is likely to be the pivotal development for the global economic prognosis. Unfortunately, U.S. consumers have long been ripe for the fall. With vigorous consumption gains consistently outstripping a subpar pace of income generation over the past 14 years, savings-short, overly indebted households drew freely on the combination of property and credit bubbles to take consumer spending up to a record 72 percent of real GDP in late 2006 and early 2007. But now, with those twin bubbles having burst, U.S. consumption has fallen sharply at close to a 4 percent average annual rate in the second half of 2008. Although that's a record rate of decline for two consecutive quarters, this adjustment has been sufficient to reduce the consumption share of real GDP by only one percentage point to a still excessive 71 percent.

In light of the extreme pressures still bearing down on U.S. consumers— not just record debt and low saving, but also wealth destruction to homes and 401K plans as well as income losses associated with sharply rising unemployment—there is good reason to believe that a consumer-led rebalancing of the U.S. economy has only just begun. That portends a further decline of the U.S. consumption share of GDP—possibly down to the 67 percent prebubble norm that prevailed in the final 25 years of the 20th century. To the extent such a mean reversion is likely—a reasonable deduction, in my view—that means only about 20 percent of the U.S. consumption adjustment has been completed.

That poses a major problem for the global economy. The United States remains the world's dominant consumer. While America accounts for only about 4.5 percent of the world's total population, its consumers spent about $9.7 trillion in 2007—almost five times the combined consumption of only about $2 trillion coming from the nearly 40 percent of the world's population that lives in China and India. Nor do any of the world's other big consumers—notably those of Europe and Japan—have a growth dynamic on a par with the American consumer; private consumption growth in these two economies has been closer to 1 percent per annum over the past decade—less than one-third the pace of that in the United Sates. In short, prospects for a multiyear compression in U.S. consumer demand pose a major problem for an unbalanced global economy.

That's particularly true for export-led Developing Asia, the most rapidly growing region in the world. In 2007, the export share of Developing Asia's GDP hit a record high of 47 percent—up about 10 percentage points from the portion prevailing a decade earlier. By contrast, the private consumption portion of the region's GDP fell to a record low of 47 percent in 2007—down from close to 55 percent prevailing 10 years ago. Lacking an offset from internal consumer demand, Developing Asia is extremely vulnerable to an external demand shock. And that is exactly what is now unfolding. It's not just prospects for a multiyear weakening in U.S. consumer demand but also the onset of a rare synchronous G-3 recession—with simultaneous contractions in the United States, Europe, and Japan. Little wonder that every economy in export-led Developing Asia is now either slowing or already in recession. The hopes and dreams of decoupling—an overly optimistic scenario that envisioned emerging market economies having the wherewithal to stand on their own in an otherwise weakening world—are in tatters.

All this underscores a striking asymmetry to the global rebalancing that is now unfolding. The excesses on the demand side are being tempered by a dramatic consolidation of the American consumer. Although this adjustment has just begun, the pressures are so severe that there is good reason to believe that U.S. consumption growth will remain quite weak for years to come. Conversely, there are few signs of a spontaneous acceleration in private consumption growth elsewhere in the world. Lacking in institutionalized safety nets—especially social security systems and pension regimes—consumers in developing economies remain predisposed more toward precautionary saving than discretionary spending.

That's especially the case for transitional economies such as China, where state-owned enterprise reforms have spawned massive job losses affecting over 60 million workers during the past 15 years. This has led to a heightened sense of employment and income insecurity—triggering a powerful outbreak of precautionary saving. As a result, the Chinese consumption share of GDP fell to a record low of nearly 35 percent in 2007, leaving China more dependent than ever before on exports and investment to maintain economic growth at a fast enough pace to prevent a serious increase in unemployment and social instability. Long the greatest beneficiary of globalization, an unbalanced Chinese economy stands much to lose in the face of a massive external demand shock.

The asymmetries of global rebalancing could well be decisive in shaping the contour of any recovery in the global economy. As always, it will take a vigorous rebound in consumer demand to spark a classic V-shaped upturn. Notwithstanding Washington's massive policy stimulus, the overextended American consumer is not about to deliver that spark. Without a new global consumer, any recovery in the world economy is likely to remain disappointingly weak.

# America's Japan Syndrome
*January 13, 2009*

No one in his or her right mind thinks that the United States could fall victim to a Japanese-like lost decade. After all, goes the argument, even if there were similarities between prebubble conditions in both economies, U.S. policy makers have the advantage in knowing what their counterparts in Japan did wrong. Out of those lessons comes a game plan that is widely presumed to prevent America from falling into a Japanese-style quagmire.

If it were only that simple! For starters, the parallels between the crises in Japan and the U.S. are striking. Both economies suffered from the bursting of two major bubbles—property and equity in the case of Japan and property and credit in the United States. Both had broken financial systems stemming from egregious risk management blunders. Both were victimized by a reckless lack of oversight—regulatory failures, misdirected rating agencies, and central banks that ignored asset bubbles. The *coup de grâce* was the lethal macro impacts of the twin bubbles on the real side of both economies—the corporate sector in the case of Japan and the consumer sector in the United States.

So much for history. How relevant are Japan-U.S. comparisons in gauging the future? Can America's policy makers avoid the postbubble pitfalls that left Japan mired in a decade of stagnation and deflation?

Those in charge in the United States—especially the Federal Reserve—believe that America is different, possessing both the wisdom and the conviction to avoid Japanese-like outcome. The Fed laid the groundwork for this assertion back in 2002, when the United States was reeling from the dot-com-induced bursting of the equity bubble. A landmark paper co-authored by 13 Fed staff economists concluded that the speed and vigor of the monetary policy response were key in avoiding a replay of the Japan syndrome.[3] The Bank of Japan, they argued, was too slow to grasp the enormity of postbubble risks. It follows, in this view, that a quicker and bolder policy reaction would have made a critical difference.

And so the script was written for America's central bank: Bubbles come and go—not much you can do about that, the Fed has long maintained. However, if the monetary authority is speedy in riding to the rescue of a postbubble economy, a Japanese style trap can be avoided. This approach appeared to pass an important reality check in the aftermath of the bursting of the U.S. equity bubble in 2000. The Fed was quick to slash the federal funds rate by 550 basis points to 1 percent and the U.S. economy eventually recovered. Alan Greenspan, in a celebrated mission-accomplished speech, boasted that ". . . our strategy of addressing the bubble's consequences rather than the bubble itself has been successful . . ."[4]

That experience gave the Federal Reserve license to prescribe the same medicine to subsequent postbubble shakeouts. Unfortunately, those tactics backfired. There is good reason to believe that the Fed's clean-up campaign after the bursting of the equity bubble in 2000 was, in fact, a one-off success—it provided a short-term fix at the cost of creating a long-term disaster. By following the anti-Japan script and pushing the policy rate down to rock-bottom levels and holding it there, the Fed ended up inflating the biggest bubbles of them all—property and credit.

Fear not, claim the optimists. America has been much quicker than Japan to write down bad loans, inject new capital into its banks, embrace a large fiscal stimulus, and adopt the so-called quantitative easing tactics of monetary policy. Noble as these efforts are, they may not be enough. That's because they do not arrest the most powerful force at work in the postbubble U.S. economy: Excess consumption now has to be tempered no matter what. The overextended, savings-short, asset-dependent American consumer has only just begun what appears to be a multiyear retrenchment. That means the authorities in Japan and the United States may have something else in common—limited policy traction and the related frustration of pushing on that proverbial string.

All this raises the distinct possibility that the U.S. central bank may have drawn the wrong lessons from Japan's lost decade. The correct

---

3. See Alan Ahearne, et. al., "Preventing Deflation: Lessons from Japan's Experience in the 1990s," Federal Reserve International Financial Discussion Paper 729, June 2002.
4. See Alan Greenspan, "Risk and Uncertainty in Monetary Policy," January 3, 2004.

policy prescription may have less to do with the speed and scope of postbubble clean-up tactics and more to do with avoiding major asset bubbles in the first place. Just as the Bank of Japan failed on that score, so, too, did the Fed. The new and critically important lesson: Central banks can no longer afford to address asset bubbles after the fact.

Yet there is an ominous distinction between the United States and Japan—the impacts of bubbles on their respective real economies. At more than 70 percent of U.S. GDP, the bubble-infected American consumer actually poses a much greater risk to today's U.S. economy than that imparted by Japan's bubble-induced capital-spending boom, which accounted for only about 17 percent of Japanese GDP at its peak in the late 1980s. Moreover, since the U.S. consumer is, by far, the biggest and, up until recently, the most dynamic of the large consumers in the world, the global implications of America's postbubble shakeout are likely to be far more severe than those imparted by Japan.

So what can the United States do to avoid becoming another Japan? Quite frankly, not much. In many critical respects, the die is already cast. By focusing on investments in infrastructure, alternative energy technologies, and human capital, the Obama Administration is correct in attempting to contain the recession and initiate a long overdue rebalancing of the U.S. economy. However, these actions will not cure the postbubble hangover of the overextended consumer. Most of all, that will take time but it will also require income support for the innocent victims of recession and a new prosaving mentality that encourages American families to live within their means.

Like Japan of the 1990s, the United States faces stiff headwinds for the foreseeable future. And until the rest of the world uncovers a new consumer—not a likely outcome during the next few years—a protracted global slowdown is a distinct possibility.

# Whither Capitalism?

## *February 23, 2009*

Rare is the crisis that doesn't shake fundamental beliefs and values. And the world's most wrenching financial crisis in 75 years has certainly done all that and more. Significantly, it has prompted many to question that most cherished of institutions, market-based capitalism. With governments around the world intervening on a seemingly massive scale, those concerns are hardly groundless.

In one sense, this is nothing new. The history of capitalism is very much a continuum of tough tests. Financial panics, periodic recessions, and even the Great Depression are all part of the stress testing that has long shaped the rough and tumble evolution of market-based capitalism. The core premise of capitalism rests on the simple notion that free markets and the free-enterprise system they promote are the optimal and most efficient means by which any society can allocate its scarce resources of labor, capital, and land. The magic of capitalism is the manner by which this allocation occurs—tasks that are ultimately executed by the "invisible hand" of Adam Smith.

That's not to say capitalism doesn't allow the State to play an important role in providing public goods like defense, internal protection, retirement security, and certain utilities such as water, transportation networks, and power. Yet private enterprise is the lifeblood of the capitalist model of income generation, wealth creation, and sustained economic growth. The enduring successes of the United States stand in sharp contrast to the failure of the central planning approach of the former Soviet Union. The stunning record of Chinese economic development is an explicit endorsement of capitalism—a development model that hinges critically on the ownership transition from state-owned enterprises to privately held companies.

But now the U.S. economy—the poster child of capitalism—is in the midst of its most wrenching financial crisis and recession since the 1930s. Many of the once-proud icons of Corporate America stand at the brink of failure and collapse. The full force of U.S. government policy is being directed at arresting this potentially lethal implosion. Under the too-big-to-fail doctrine, the lessons of the Great Depression have been central in framing a massive campaign of state-directed intervention into critical segments of once sacrosanct private industries and markets.

Such emergency government investments in privately held companies—capital injections as well as backstop financing—have become an all-too-frequent outgrowth of what started out as a mere subprime crisis. At the same time, compensation caps, home mortgage foreclosure mitigation efforts, and politically engineered consumer lending programs all smack of a quasi-socialization of American finance. Add to that, Washington's newfound aggression on trade policy—"buy America" government procurement policies, along with Chinese currency bashing—and it seems as if the U.S. strain of capitalism is being turned inside out.

## Bailouts in Context

Notwithstanding the claims of a sensationalist media, the scale of state-directed intervention in America's privately held corporations remains relatively small. That shows up under careful examination of the two industries that have been the focus of such efforts—finance and autos. According to U.S. Commerce Department statistics, the value added by banks, securities firms, and other financial intermediaries collectively accounted for 6.2 percent of the private sector's GDP in 2007; the insurance sector made up another 2.8 percent, whereas the share going to motor vehicles manufacturers was just 0.8 percent. Private employment shares of these newly protected industries are even smaller—5.3 percent for finance and insurance and just 0.7 percent for motor vehicles.

To be sure, recent government interventions have been targeted at a subset of specific companies within these industries rather than at the entire industry, itself; for example, capital injections under the so-called TARP (Troubled-Asset Relief Program) framework were initially directed at just nine financial institutions whereas emergency bridge financing was extended to two of Detroit's Big Three. Clearly, there are important behavioral spillovers between companies that have been direct recipients of government funds and those that have not received such assistance but are wary that they could be next. Combining the direct and indirect effects in these two industries provides an outside estimate of the U.S. government's recent "intervention share" of around 6 to 10 percent in the private economy.

That means, of course, that more that 90 percent of the private sector in the United States is still operating largely as a free-enterprise system. That is not exactly consistent with the widely popularized image of a "bail-out nation" that has been offered up to depict a U.S. economy in chaos and a market-based system on the brink of collapse.

## Postcrisis Endgame

I would be the first to concede that for a crisis of the severity that is currently under way it is certainly possible that the government's recent interventionist actions could end up being only the first of many such efforts to come. Should recent actions beget more interventions in the future, the current angst over the crisis of capitalism would only grow.

Two key concerns are relevant in assessing such a possibility—that the need for intervention will spread and that the emergency pallia-tives of temporary support will eventually become permanent. The first concern depends critically on the depth and duration of the current U.S. recession. In my view, the main factor that will shape this outcome will be the coming adjustments of the bubble-dependent American consumer—currently still more than 70 percent of the U.S. economy. As the consumer goes, so goes the endgame of this most extraordinary business cycle.

Recent trends are hardly encouraging in this regard. Real consump-tion fell by nearly 4 percent (at an annual rate) in both of the final two quarters of 2008—the steepest back-to-back declines of the post-World War II era. If the retrenchment of U.S. consumption continues at such an unprecedentedly rapid pace, then an increasingly deeper recession is a distinct possibility—an outcome that could trigger considerably more distress in private sector businesses and concomitant efforts by the gov-ernment to avoid failures in an increasingly broader swath of U.S. industry. I don't think it is a coincidence that Washington-directed interventions accelerated dramatically in the final three-and-a-half months of 2008—when a veritable implosion of the financial system led to a precipitous deterioration in business and consumer sentiment. Should that firestorm persist, fears over the crisis of capitalism will only deepen.

Despite my long-standing concerns over the prospects for postbubble U.S. consumption, I do not believe such a macrocollapse scenario is the most likely outcome. While I expect that a good deal more consolidation lies ahead for the American consumer, an historical stickiness of U.S. consumption habits argues for a more gradual—albeit prolonged—normalization of consumer demand. Moreover, to the extent Washington's recently enacted $787 billion fiscal stimulus package limits the contraction in aggregate demand and puts a floor on the depth of this recession, there is reason to be encouraged that the retrenchment of the American consumer will proceed at a less disruptive pace than was the case in late 2008. Time will obviously tell, but if that prognosis turns out to be correct, a sharp increase in the scope of interventions and bailouts is less likely than otherwise might be the case.

The second concern—that of the exit strategy from the recent sharp step-up in U.S. government support—is more problematic. The debate over fiscal policy is now being framed in the context of an era of trillion dollar budget deficits rather than in a climate in need of a temporary fiscal stimulus. President Obama's recent emphasis on the eventual restoration of a postcrisis fiscal discipline is encouraging, but this could well be his toughest political battle on economic policy. At the same time, the Federal Reserve now speaks of an enduring regime of extraordinary monetary accommodation and liquidity injections into dysfunctional markets and beleaguered financial institutions. In short, it's hard to have much confidence in the case for a prompt postcrisis normalization of U.S. fiscal and monetary policies, especially since the authorities have no experience whatsoever in pulling off such a Great Escape.

An increasingly intractable exit strategy is, unfortunately, the rule and not the exception for relapse-prone economies that have suffered from the bursting of major asset and credit bubbles. As Japan's experience shows with painful clarity, once a postbubble economy needs to go on the life-support of extraordinary fiscal and monetary stimulus, it is extremely difficult to wean the chronically ill patient from this medicine. Nearly 20 years after the bursting of the Japanese equity bubble, the nation's public-sector debt stands at 148 percent of GDP; moreover, the Bank of Japan is now celebrating the tenth anniversary of its zero-interest rate policy. The same can be said of halfway measures on the road to nationalization for insolvent industries. The longer the ultimate solution is avoided for zombie-like companies, the more elusive the postbubble exit strategy and the more dependent a weakened business sector becomes on ongoing government intervention and support. All in all, as long as a decisive and transparent exit strategy from the policies of crisis containment is lacking, there is good reason to suspect that the debate over the efficacy of market-based capitalism will continue.

## Shared Responsibility

In the end, the true test of capitalism will most likely come from its ideological roots—in particular, from the ability of the body politic to endure the often-harsh verdict of free markets and their all too frequent penchant for creative destruction. In crisis and recession, the tolerance for such pain is invariably subjected to its sternest test—a trial under duress that often turns into a destructive blame game. The search for scapegoats can become an obsession—in effect, a lightning rod for national angst. But scapegoating can play an even more destructive role—it can bias and eventually undermine the reregulatory fix that invariably follows any crisis.

Therein lies one of the greatest potential pitfalls in the postcrisis backlash of 2009. Wall Street has been singled out as the villain in this crisis. On one level, this is understandable. Financial service firms did make many serious and regretful mistakes—from faulty risk management models and perverse incentive systems to misguided business strategies and momentum-driven capital deployment. But they were hardly alone. The modern U.S. financial system has long been under the purview of an institutionalized network of checks and balances, controlled by regulators, a politically independent central bank, and congressional oversight. Rating agencies were empowered as the arbiters of risk assessment. Yet every single one of those safeguards failed to temper the systemic problems that were building for years in the Era of Excess. The question is, why?

The answer is not particularly pleasant—it goes to the heart of a greed-driven capitalism. Booms—artificial or real—distort incentives. Booms also warp values and blind the United States to downside risks. And denial—that most powerful of human defenses—leads the United States to dismiss the tough questions that might draw the staying power of a boom into question. In this boom, there was everything to gain from keeping the magic alive and much to lose by drawing it all into question. In short, the American body politic—from Wall Street to Main Street to Washington—was consumed by the hopes and dreams of the boom and desperate for the good times to continue. And so, by the way, was the rest of the world—especially export-led developing economies whose new-found prosperity was built on selling anything and everything to overextended American consumers. Literally, no one wanted this party to end.

But now the party is over—and painfully so for a world in recession and for markets in chaos. The task ahead is to pick up the pieces, learn the lessons of this crisis, and take actions to ensure these types of problems never occur again. The postcrisis fix can succeed only if it is grounded in the premise of shared responsibility. A targeted politicized fix is not a solution to a systemic problem. Fix the system that gave rise to the crisis—not just the banks that have defined ground zero of a wrenching credit crunch. The piecemeal prescription of the blame game virtually guarantees there will be a next time—an even bigger crisis that deals an even tougher blow to market-based capitalism.

## Rethinking Governance

The dangers of a politically driven postcrisis vendetta cannot be minimized. The current mess is deeply rooted in an ideological approach to economic governance—namely, America's libertarian penchant for self-regulation. Alan Greenspan, the high priest of this approach, framed most of the Federal Reserve's critical policy choices in the context of this ideology. As seen through this lens, asset bubbles were not judged to represent a dangerous build-up of speculative excesses—instead, they were repeatedly perceived as outgrowths of America's thriving free enterprise system. The equity bubble of the late 1990s was justified by the breathtaking acclaim accorded to IT-enabled productivity-led advances of a New Economy. Property bubbles were presumed to be local, not national—especially in an era of rising home ownership at the lower (or subprime) end of the income distribution. And the credit bubble, together with the risk bubble it spawned, was offered as testament to the genius of financial innovation and American creativity. Market libertarians simply looked the other way as the United States lurched recklessly from bubble to bubble.

Bubbles, of course, are always based on a shred of truth. But the post-bubble wreckage of the U.S. economy begs for a very different interpretation than the one that became conventional wisdom over the past decade. So, too, does the Fed's blatant abrogation of its regulatory responsibilities during the Greenspan years. Nowhere was that more apparent than in the central bank's failure to make the distinction between financial engineering and financial innovation. Far from playing the widely popularized role as the ultimate shock absorber, the "originate and distribute" hallmark of the derivatives explosion became a lethal transmission mechanism of cross-border and cross-product shocks. Ideology blinded America's central bank, as well as its political overseers, to the imperatives of discipline—and let an unregulated and increasingly unstable free-enterprise system veer unnecessarily out of control.

Over time, I suspect that this crisis will be seen more as a failure of governance rather than as an inherent flaw in the free-market system, itself. The postcrisis fix will, indeed, turn Wall Street inside out. But the new regime must also include a revamped code of governance—not just regulatory streamlining and reform but also the hardwiring of financial stability into the policy mandates of central banks. Independent central banks that operate apolitically and free of ideology could well be the most important stewards of a postcrisis capitalism. But they can't do it alone. Only through better discipline and more effective governance of regulators, rating agencies, and the political oversight function, can the invisible hand start to work its magic once again.

Capitalism has come a long way since Adam Smith wrote *The Wealth of Nations* more than 230 years ago. Markets and the instruments they trade have become exceedingly complex and interrelated. Today's globalized world is tightly linked through cross-border flows in trade, financial capital, labor, and information. The risks of this new connectivity have been amplified by increasingly complex financial instruments. At the same time, the pendulum of political ideology and control swung toward market libertarianism and self-regulation. In the end, this was an extremely dangerous combination—it allowed complexity to morph into instability. Self-regulation of an unstable system was a disaster waiting to happen. We are living today in the midst of just such a disaster—a crisis of epic proportions.

Yet the demise of capitalism is greatly exaggerated. As the free-enterprise system survived the Great Depression of the 1930s, I have little doubt it will reinvent itself and endure the current crisis. We can and must do much better in making market-based capitalism a safer, more stable, and sustainable system. There has been a major systemic failure of the model that has held the world together since the 1930s. Governance, or the lack thereof—both within the private sector as well as by those charged with regulation and oversight—proved to be the weak link in the chain. Fix that, and capitalism will be just fine.

# After the Era of Excess
## March 5, 2009

The world stopped in 2008—and it was a full stop for the era of excess. Belatedly, the authorities have been extraordinarily aggressive in coming to the rescue of a system in crisis. But as in the case of Humpty Dumpty, they will not be able to put all the pieces back together again. The next era will be very different from the one we have just left behind.

In large part, that is because this is a profoundly different crisis. It stands in sharp contrast to earlier disruptions, such as the Latin debt crisis of the 1980s, the Asian financial crisis of 1997–1998, or the bursting of the dot-com bubble at the turn of the century. In those instances, the pressures were confined largely to a region or an asset class, while the rest of the world benefited from insulation and resilience. This time, there is no place to hide. An unbalanced and interconnected world is now in the midst of a painful but necessary rebalancing.

Steeped in denial during the days of froth, policy makers, financial markets, the business community, and Main Street all reached the same erroneous conclusion—that an increasingly sophisticated and globalized world had learned to live with its imbalances. Some called this the Bretton Woods II era, cemented by a new symbiotic relationship between China (the saver and producer) and America (the borrower and consumer). Under this arrangement, most observers came to believe, unprecedented saving and current-account disparities could be finessed indefinitely, as could record debt burdens and currency misalignments. Someday, went the argument, the world would have to face up to its imbalances, but the day of reckoning was always assumed to be in some far-off, distant future. That was the fatal mistake made by a world in denial. The day of rebalancing is now at hand.

The implosion of 2008 was very much an outgrowth of the unique character of the world's imbalances, which visibly manifested themselves in a succession of ever-larger asset bubbles. The United States lies at the root of this phenomenon. Starting with the dot-com bubble of the late 1990s, the country went down a path littered by a succession of asset bubbles—from equities to property to credit. Bubbles are bad enough in and of themselves. They become all the more treacherous when they infect the real economy. That, indeed, was the most dangerous and destabilizing aspect of the era of excess (see Figure 1.4 on page 80).

In the end, the U.S. consumer was engulfed by the biggest bubble of them all. United States consumption reached an astonishing 72 percent of GDP in 2007, a record for the United States and, for that matter, any major economy in modern history. This consumption spike was fully five percentage points above the 67 percent share that prevailed for 25 years in the prebubble era, from 1975 to 2000. Significantly, the consumption binge was not supported by the economy's internal income-generating capacity; labor compensation—the income forthcoming from current production—fell in late 2008 to a level of more than $800 billion (in real terms) below the trajectory of previous cycles.

Instead, America's consumption binge drew support from two major asset bubbles—property and credit. Courtesy of cheap and freely available credit, in conjunction with record housing price appreciation, consumers tripled the rate of net equity extraction from their homes, from 3 percent of disposable personal income in 2001 to 9 percent in 2006. Only by leveraging increasingly overvalued homes could Americans go on the biggest consumption binge in modern history. And now those twin bubbles—property and credit—have burst, and so has the U.S. consumption bubble: Real consumer spending fell at nearly an unprecedented 4 percent average annual rate in the two final quarters of 2008.

While the original excesses were made in America, the rest of the world was delighted to go along for the ride. With the United States lacking in internal saving, it had to import surplus savings from abroad in order to grow—and ran massive current-account and trade deficits to attract that capital. This fit perfectly with the macroimbalances of the export-led developing countries of Asia, whose exports exceeded a record 45 percent of regional GDP in 2007—fully 10 percentage points higher than their share 10 years earlier, in the depths of the Asian financial crisis. China led the charge, taking its exports from 20 percent, to nearly

40 percent of its GDP over the past 7 years alone. The export-led growth in Developing Asia could well be described as a second-order bubble—in effect, a derivative of the one in U.S. consumption.

Sure, there are destinations for end-market demand other than the United States, an observation that mistakenly led many to believe that Asian exporters were insulated by an increasingly diversified mix of external demand. That was wishful thinking. Once again, China is an important case in point. Yes, the United States now accounts for only about 20 percent of total Chinese exports. Shipments to Europe and Japan collectively account for another 30 percent, while the bulk of the remainder shows up in the form of sharply growing intraregional Asian trade. But there is a serious problem with the notion that China or any other major economy has successfully weaned itself—or decoupled—from overreliance on U.S. markets. Whether it is Europe, Japan, or developing countries of Asia other than China, all have one critical characteristic in common: insufficient internal private consumption and an overreliance on exports as a major and increasing source of growth. Intraregional trade has expanded sharply in Developing Asia, but with internal consumption as a share of GDP continuing to fall, these economies remain hugely dependent on end-market demand in the developed world.

As a result, there can be no mistaking the bottom line of this global recession. When the world's dominant consumer—the United States—enjoys an extraordinary boom, so do the world's major exporters. But when the U.S. boom goes bust, export-led economies around the world are in serious trouble. That's precisely the nature of the adjustment now bearing down so acutely on Japan; Developing Asia; Germany; and America's NAFTA partners, Canada and Mexico. All of these export-led economies are either decelerating sharply or in outright recession.

There's an even more insidious aspect of a bubble-dependent world. The Chinese, of course, led the way in recycling a disproportionate share of their massive foreign-exchange reserves back into dollar-based assets. That kept China's currency highly competitive, as any export-led economy likes, but also prevented U.S. interest rates from rising—thereby keeping the magic alive for bubble-dependent U.S. consumers. In effect, the world's bubbles fed off each other.

That game is now over. With the U.S. consumer most likely in the early stages of a multiyear contraction, the postbubble world is likely to face stiff headwinds for years to come. In large part, that's because

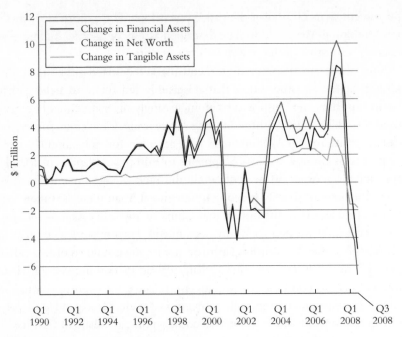

**Figure 1.4**   Change in U.S. Household Assets and Net Worth

*Note:*   Data include nonprofit organizations.

*Source:*   Haver Analytics, McKinsey Global Institute analysis.

there is no other consumer to fill the void. Sluggish growth in consumption has long been the norm in Europe and Japan. The same is the case for developing economies, where consumption is constrained by the imperatives of precautionary saving to compensate for the lack of safety nets such as social security, pensions, and medical and unemployment insurance. In China, the poster child for this problem, consumption as a share of GDP fell to a record low of around 35 percent in 2007— literally half the share in the United States. All in all, a postcrisis global economy is likely to struggle for years in the aftermath of America's consumption boom and in the absence of any dynamism from private consumption elsewhere. This paints a picture of an extremely tepid recovery from the current global recession.

The policy response to this crisis has been disturbing on one critical count: The global body politic is doing its best to resist rebalancing. Near-term tactics are all about containing the crisis, with little appreciation of The strategic implications of these actions. Here as well, America and

China are emblematic of the problem. In the United States, Washington has focused on measures that would sustain excess consumption through tax rebates and other types of income injections. There is also growing support for mortgage foreclosure relief—in effect, perpetuating uneconomic levels of home ownership by many people who simply cannot afford their still-overvalued dwellings. Meanwhile, in China, policy priorities remain focused on providing support for investment, through a massive $585 billion infrastructure program, and on exports, through a shift in currency policy and tax rebates for exporters. By contrast, little is being done to stimulate the Chinese consumer.

Such actions suggest a world that has learned little from a wrenching global rebalancing—a world that believes the answer to recession and crisis is a return to the very same strain of unbalanced economic growth that got the United States into this mess in the first place. Yet in the end, that's the very last thing the world needs. America does not need to perpetuate its unsustainable consumption binge; it needs to save and recycle its savings into investments in infrastructure, alternative-energy technologies, and human capital. China does not need more hypergrowth led by investment and exports; it needs to shift the mix of its economy toward private consumption. Yet both nations seem unwilling, or unable, to make the tough choices that a more strategic policy response requires.

Sadly, this reactive approach reflects a global body politic that always seems to be focused on the quick fix. This time, that reaction has been amplified by the severity of the problem. It's as if the crisis is so threatening that short-term tactics must take precedence over long-term strategy, however noble it may be to promote the structural shifts required to rebalance an unbalanced world. This is where leadership could be decisive in shifting the debate—in having the courage to look beyond the valley.

None of this is to say, of course, that policies shouldn't be acutely sensitive to the plight of the innocent victims of recession and crisis. Unemployed workers need enhanced income support—especially unemployment insurance and retraining programs—and a dysfunctional financial system needs stopgap repairs. However, while the authorities need to backstop a system in acute distress, they must do more. The tactics of crisis containment cannot be the sole focus of the policy response to this wrenching global recession. The world also needs a strategy.

Benefiting from a decisive election victory, Barack Obama has an extraordinary opportunity to provide just that. Early indications pointing to a large public-works spending package—especially for infrastructure and alternative-energy technologies—are very encouraging. But that begs the broader question: Does the rest of the world have the wisdom and the courage to shift the policy debate away from tactics and toward strategy?

This global crisis and recession have a deeper meaning: They give the United States and the rest of the world an opportunity to learn the tough lessons about what went wrong and how to avoid similar mistakes in the future. A failure to heed those lessons and to use the resulting insights in framing new policies would be the biggest tragedy of all.

# Same Old, Same Old
*March 10, 2009*

A crisis-torn world is in no mood for the heavy lifting of global rebalancing. Policies are being framed with an aim toward recreating the very boom that has just gone bust. Washington wants to get credit flowing again to overly indebted American consumers. And exporters around the world—especially in Asia—would like nothing better than a renewal of external demand led by the world's biggest consumer.

This is a recipe for disaster. That's not to say the powerful fiscal and monetary medicine now being administered won't temporarily alleviate the symptoms of a world in distress. But if these policies end up perpetuating the very imbalances that got the global economy into this mess in the first place, the inevitable next crisis will be even worse than this one.

Lest I be accused of fear mongering, it pays to replay the tapes of a decade ago. Then, the Asian financial crisis was widely viewed as the worst crisis since the Great Depression. As contagion spread from Asia to Russia, Brazil, and eventually a large U.S. hedge fund, the ensuing turmoil was dubbed the first crisis of modern globalization. Former Federal Reserve Chairman Alan Greenspan was stunned by what he dubbed an unprecedented "seizing up" of capital markets. Sound familiar?

As appropriate as those superlatives may have seemed in the late 1990s, they ended up depicting a minor squall when compared with the current tsunami. That's just the point: Until an unbalanced world faces up to its chronic imbalances, successive crises are likely to be increasingly destabilizing. Although it's hard to believe that anything could be worse than what's happening today, I can assure you that same feeling was evident in late 1998.

Ironically, the seeds of the current crisis may well have been sown by policies aimed at arresting the Asian financial crisis. Back then, U.S.

authorities did everything they could to ensure that the crisis would not infect the real economy. The Fed's three emergency rate cuts in late 1998 worked like a charm—the U.S. consumer never looked back. The personal consumption share of real GDP soared from 67 percent in the late 1990s to a record 72 percent in the first half of 2007. America's antidote to the Asian financial crisis was the greatest consumption binge in modern history.

Bruised and battered Asia couldn't have asked for more. The binge-buying American consumer was Asia's manna from heaven. It reinforced the region's conviction in its export-led formula for economic development. Developing Asia was quick to up the ante on this approach, pushing the export share of its GDP from 36 percent in 1997–1998 to 47 percent by 2007.

But it didn't stop there. An increasingly integrated Asian economy also discovered the new synergies of a China-centric supply chain. Moreover, commodity producers around the world—especially, in Australia, Russia, Canada, and even Brazil—drew great sustenance from a resource-intensive, export-led Chinese economy.

And so it was in the aftermath of the Asian financial crisis. Imbalances became the rule, not the exception. Yet just as the United States was steeped in denial on the demand side of the global economy, a similar complacency was evident on the supply side. That was true of America's consumption binge—accompanied by record debt burdens, zero saving rates, and a multiplicity of bubbles in asset markets (equity and property) and credit. It was also true of Asia's export boom, which spawned ever-rising current account surpluses, enormous reservoirs of foreign exchange reserves, and a megabubble in commodity markets. Imbalances were a problem for another day. All that mattered back then was the postcrisis fix.

That's precisely the mindset today. To its credit, the Obama stimulus package is framed around the strategic imperatives of investing in infrastructure, alternative energy technologies, and human capital. But the Washington subtext is far more short term, focused mainly on increasingly urgent efforts to jump-start personal consumption. Toward that end, the Fed, the Treasury, and the Congress are all eager to restart borrowing for overextended consumers and prevent foreclosures of overly indebted home owners. The costs of inaction are billed as prohibitive. The U.S. body politic could care less about the debt implications of its stimulus actions.

In Asia, hopes are focused on the mirror image of this tale. The main questions Asians ask these days pertain to the state of the American consumer. Apparently, it's just too hard for Asian policymakers to establish robust social safety nets and stimulate internal private consumption. Unbalanced Asian economies are desperate for unbalanced American consumers to start spending again and spark another postcrisis recovery.

Grow now and ask questions later. That has once again become the mantra for an unbalanced world in crisis. Yet that's the biggest risk of all for global policy. The G-8 failed to embrace the imperatives of global rebalancing after the Asian financial crisis. And the G-20 seems destined to follow the same script at its upcoming summit in early April. What a reckless way to run the world.

# Depression Foil

*April 15, 2009*

D ebate rages over the endgame for the Great Recession. The broad consensus of policy makers, financial-market participants, business leaders, and academics concurs that the world is in the midst of its worst decline since the 1930s. In making that comparison, there is a presumption that another depression is a distinct possibility if immediate steps aren't taken to contain the downward spiral.

This debate misses the point—and dangerously so. Although I have been as bearish as anyone over the past several years, I would still assign a very low probability to a 1930s-style depression for the United States and the broader global economy. Monetary and fiscal authorities have made it quite clear that they are prepared to do everything in their power to avoid such an outcome. Ultimately, I suspect they will get their way.

Yet there is a serious and worrisome risk to this policy strategy. By fixating on the antidepression drill, authorities are failing to address the root cause of the current crisis and recession—the lethal unwinding of unsustainable global imbalances.

As one leading G-7 official put it to me recently, "In the short term, we need to get the world moving again. Then, over the medium term, we will tackle global imbalances." This is the essence of the Depression Foil—a single-minded preoccupation with avoiding a 1930s-style collapse at all costs while putting off the requisite heavy lifting for that proverbial next day.

Unfortunately, the myopia of the political cycle preordains such a policy response. A resumption of economic growth is all that ever seems to matter for poll-driven politicians and their surrogate policy makers. Tough problems are always deferred with a vacuous promise to tackle them in due course. Then that due course always is pushed out further and further in time.

This is precisely the mindset that got the United States into this mess. I well remember the debate over America's current account deficit, one of the most glaring manifestations of an economy built on quicksand.

Some argued that there was nothing to worry about in a world that was now joined in a new "Bretton Woods II" paradigm, where a symbiotic relationship between the creditor (mainly China) and the debtor (the United States) would sustain this imbalance in perpetuity. There were others, such as Alan Greenspan, who worried about the long-term sustainability of America's external shortfall but stressed that such imbalances were likely to persist for much longer than most thought.

The problem with the apologists is that they failed to appreciate the deeper meaning of these imbalances. The U.S. current account deficit didn't emerge out of thin air. It was the outgrowth of an unprecedented shortfall of domestic saving. Saving itself was depressed by the bubble-driven illusions of an asset-dependent U.S. economy and especially by the willingness of consumers to live well beyond their means by extracting equity from overvalued homes.

In short, America's external imbalance was joined at the hip to the toxic interplay between asset and credit bubbles. Moreover, denial was global in scope. Export-led economies were delighted to draw support from bubble-dependent American consumers. And now, that house of cards has collapsed.

Unwittingly, the Depression Foil might well end up recreating this madness. With the risk of a depression viewed as completely unacceptable to the global body politic, the full force of the policy arsenal is being aimed at jump-starting aggregate demand, regardless to the consequences such results might imply for a new build-up of global imbalances.

Once again, the United States. is leading the charge. The Fed wants to get credit flowing again to still overextended American consumers, especially in mortgage markets. The Congress wants to stop the bleeding in the housing market, regardless of the persistent imbalance between supply and demand. And the White House wants consumers to start spending again—to avoid the perceived pitfalls of the "paradox of thrift" brought about by too much saving.

Put it together and it all smacks of a dangerous sense of déjà vu: promoting a false recovery by kick-starting overextended, savings-short American consumers to borrow once again by leveraging their major asset.

Fortunately, the American consumer is smarter than the quick-fix Washington mindset. Shell-shocked families—especially some 77 million

baby boomers for whom retirement planning is an urgent imperative—
know they have no choice other than to save. The personal saving rate
has risen from around 1 percent in the fall of 2008 to more than 4 percent by March 2009, and is on its way to a new postbubble equilibrium
that I would place in the 7.5 percent to 10 percent zone.

Yet policy makers fear such an outcome. It certainly doesn't fit the
script of the Depression Foil. A persistently weak American consumer is
viewed as a worrisome threat to another sickening down leg for a world
in recession.

This is the essence of the macro disconnect that is now shaping postcrisis policies around the world: The global economy has become overly
dependent on one consumer. Yet, like it or not, this source of growth
will be severely impaired for years to come—a necessary and welcome
rebalancing of the U.S. economy. However, this should not be viewed as
a nail in the coffin for a Global Depression scenario.

A retrenchment by the American consumer should be viewed as a wake-
up call for other nations to fill the void by stimulating their own consumers. A globalized world needs to move from one consumer to many.

The Depression Foil blinds policy makers and politicians to the imperatives of global rebalancing. This crisis and the wrenching recession it has
spawned are all about a destabilizing shift in the mix of global saving and
aggregate demand.

That mix needs to be redressed. The excess spenders need to save and
the excess savers need to spend. Policies that encourage such rebalancing
will put the world economy on a more stable and sustainable path and go
a long way in avoiding another crisis like this in the future.

The Depression Foil makes it exceedingly difficult for an unbalanced
world to get its act together. The G-20 summit in April 2009 was notable
for its failure to address this critical challenge. Policy makers and politicians need to move beyond their depression fixation and aim at achieving better balance in the global economy before it is too late.

# Chapter 2

# The Globalization Debate

■ *Introduction* ■ *Open Macro* ■ *The Battleground of Globalization*
■ *The Global Delta* ■ *Beggars Can't Be Choosers* ■ *Perils of a Different Globalization* ■ *Bad Advice and a New Global Architecture*
■ *Doha Doesn't Matter* ■ *Global Speed Trap* ■ *Hitting a BRIC Wall?* ■ *Global Comeback—First Japan, Now Germany* ■ *Labor versus Capital* ■ *Global Lessons* ■ *From Globalization to Localization* ■ *Unprepared for Globalization* ■ *The Currency Foil* ■ *The Shifting Mix of Global Saving* ■

## Introduction

Globalization is one of the most widely used, but least understood, terms of our times. The mechanisms of globalization are fairly clear: In its simplest sense, globalization stems from the integration of the world through cross-border trade flows, capital flows, information flows, and labor flows. The implications of globalization are less clear. The win–win mantra of the globalization advocates does a disservice to the stresses and strains that have emerged over the past decade in an era of unfettered globalization. It presumes, without questioning, that the classic theory of comparative advantage—whereby nations specialize in products they can produce most efficiently—is just as applicable today as it was when it was originally developed by David Ricardo in the early nineteenth century.

Unfortunately, economists, politicians, and policy makers have not done a good job in updating this theory and in explaining and defending globalization to the masses.

This chapter focuses on the tensions of the globalization debate that have recently opened up between the developed and the developing world. As global trade surged to a record 34 percent of world GDP in 2008—well above the 25 percent ratio prevailing at the turn of the century—a powerful cross-border labor arbitrage occurred. Increasingly, companies in the high-cost rich countries of the developed world realized efficiency gains by shifting production to low-cost platforms in the developing world. In executing these efficiency solutions, multinational corporations increasingly substituted well-educated, highly motivated low-wage workers in developing economies for high-wage workers in their home markets. This is a key source of tension in the globalization paradigm. It is undoubtedly one factor that has contributed to a stagnation of real, or inflation-adjusted, wages in many industrial economies. And that, of course, has been a bitter pill to swallow for most workers—especially those in the United States, who have delivered significant productivity improvements since the mid-1990s.

Economics teaches us that workers are eventually rewarded in accordance with their marginal productivity contributions. While that has been the case for low-wage workers in the developing world, it has not been the case for high-wage labor in the developed world as globalization has taken hold over the past decade. In fact, a striking dichotomy has emerged in the distribution of national income in the developed world in recent years. For a broad collection of the world's major industrialized economies, the labor share of national income has fallen to a record low of just 54 percent while the portion going to the owners of capital has soared to a record high of around 16 percent. The problem, again, is that this shift has occurred in an era of unfettered globalization.

This globalization is very different—and in many cases far more destabilizing—than an earlier strain that occurred 100 years ago. Back in the early twentieth century, globalization was concentrated in tradable goods manufacturing activities. As such, it was a globalization that put pressure on blue-collar factory workers—those involved in the production, distribution, and delivery of physical products via the hard infrastructure of ships, rail, and roads.

That was then. Courtesy of the soft infrastructure of the Internet, offshore services platforms in places like India, China, Ireland, and Australia are now perfectly capable of delivering information-based content to desktops anywhere in the world. Consequently, this globalization adds once nontradable services to the equation. And in doing so, it involves white-collar knowledge workers—that segment of the global labor force that has, until now, been sheltered from global competition. This has prompted the angst of globalization to spread from blue to white-collar workers—injecting a new source of tension into the political debate. Moreover, driven by the hyperspeed of IT-enabled connectivity and the rapid penetration of the Internet into the global user community, the globalization of services is proceeding at an extraordinarily rapid clip. Ironically, the developed world has been poorly prepared for both the speed and the breadth of the new competitive challenges that have emerged in the Information Age. It is as if the rich industrial countries have been caught flat-footed by the very globalization they have long championed.

These macro developments have set the stage for the battleground of globalization. As the pendulum of economic power has swung from labor to capital in the developed world, there is now a clear and growing risk that the pendulum of political power could swing from capital back to labor. This, in fact, was a key issue in the 2008 presidential election campaign in the United States. Such a possibility forms the basis of a potential backlash against globalization—a backlash that could well intensify for a world in recession, whose workers feel the mounting pressure of rising unemployment. This raises the distinct possibility that countries could become increasingly driven by the economic nationalism of self-interest, or "localization"—in sharp contrast to the collective interests that have long shaped the support for globalization.

The globalization debate is also central to the rebalancing imperatives of a postcrisis world. While the rich, developed economies need to sort out the distributional tug-of-war between labor and capital, the developing world can't pretend to be disinterested or innocent observers to this problem. As long as low-wage poor countries remain stuck in export-led growth paradigms, they are asking for trouble in an era where middle-class workers in the developed world remain under severe pressure. In order to diffuse the macro tensions of the globalization debate, developing economies need to become consumers—not just producers. In doing so, they offer deep and broad markets to their trading partners in the developed world—underscoring one of the long-standing premises of the proglobalization Ricardian theory of comparative advantage.

Globalization works only if it moves away from the asymmetries of an unbalanced world that currently pit the rich nations against the poor—consumers against producers. Any progress in multilateral trade liberalization, such as the now dormant Doha Round, will remain forever stalled until this key aspect of the globalization debate is resolved. It is in the world's best interest to face up to tensions of the globalization debate as soon as possible. The longer the global body politic ducks this critical issue, the greater the risk of a politically inspired backsliding that could lead to an ominous outbreak of trade frictions or even protectionism.

# Open Macro

*February 21, 2006*

lobalization has forever changed the way the world works. Well,
maybe *forever* is too strong, but there can be no denying the powerful and lasting macro impacts of this megatrend. The cross-border
linkages and spillovers of globalization have reshaped—and in many cases
redefined—the forces that drive inflation, interest rates, wages, profits,
employment, currencies, and economic growth. Yet most of our models—
both economic and financial—are still wedded to the single-country
approach of yesteryear. A new macro is needed that replaces antiquated
closed-economy models with the open models of globalization.

The evidence is too overwhelming to dismiss as happenstance. As of
this writing, the world is in the midst of the strongest four-year spurt
of global growth since the early 1970s, and there has been no meaningful acceleration of inflation. Unemployment rates are dropping and there
has been no appreciable pickup in real wages in the developed world. In
the United States, where productivity growth has been surging and the
unemployment rate is nearing what many judge to be the full-employ-
ment threshold, real-wage stagnation is all the more puzzling. Economics
teaches us that workers ultimately are paid their just reward insofar as
their marginal productivity contribution is concerned. That is no longer
the case in America. Moreover, the world's major central banks have
tightened (the Fed and the ECB) or are contemplating doing so (the
Bank of Japan), and there has been no increase in longer-term interest
rates. At the same time, unprecedented disparities between the world's
current account surpluses and deficits have not resulted in a dramatic
currency realignment. I could go on and on, but suffice it to say, the
macro we all once knew has basically been turned inside out.

Globalization is the main culprit, in my view. As global trade hits new
records each year—it is currently closing in on the 30 percent threshold

as a share of world GDP—some of the most important of the long-standing macro relationships are breaking down. Research conducted by the staff of the Bank of International Settlements (BIS) has carefully documented the sharply diminished correlations between labor costs and inflation for a broad sample of industrial countries over the past decade; similar findings are evident with respect to reduced elasticities between import prices and core inflation.[1] I don't think it's happenstance that these developments have coincided with the onset of an accelerated pace of globalization. The integration of the world economy essentially puts the high-cost developed nations in the same pot with low-cost developing economies. As a result, the sharply increased cross-border flow of goods and the potential for a like trend in services have spawned powerful cross-border arbitrages in labor, capital, and saving. Quiescent inflation, real-wage stagnation, and the great interest rate conundrum could well be outgrowths of this arbitrage.

Why now? After all, globalization has been around for a long time, and the old macro worked reasonably well in the first 50 years after World War II. One new and critically important differentiation is the Internet—the most disruptive technology in modern history. Quite simply, the Internet changes the rules of global engagement. In tradable goods, it revolutionizes the logistics of price discovery and supply-chain management, allowing global producers to keep squeezing costs and pricing—irrespective of resource utilization rates in their home countries. Moreover, in once sheltered services industries, the Internet now connects knowledge workers around the world to desktops anywhere—in effect, converting an increasingly large segment of once nontradable activity into tradables.

A key aspect of this IT-enabled strain of globalization is its speed. The Internet only came into existence about 10 years ago, and yet the user population exceeded 1 billion people in late 2005, with penetration ratios rising to around 60 percent in the developed world, according to Morgan Stanley Internet analyst Mary Meeker. Never before has a major technology reached so many in such a short period of time. Students of technology will tell you that's the norm—that each succeeding wave of technological transformation is accompanied by increasingly rapid rates of dissemination. That was true of railroads, motor vehicles, air conditioning, radio, and TV. The Internet follows that pattern but with

---

1. See Chapter II of the 75th *BIS Annual Report,* June 2005.

an important twist—it rewrites the rules of cross-border connectivity between developing and developed countries, and it takes that connectivity very quickly into the once sacrosanct realm of services.

Yet the journey has only just begun. Not surprisingly, the first wave of the current globalization has been concentrated in the assembly and exchange of manufactured, or tradable, goods. Over the past 15 years, the volume of worldwide trade in goods has increased by 10 percentage points of world GDP—from about 15 percent of global GDP in 1990 to a record of nearly 25 percent in 2006, according to the IMF. By contrast, the globalization of services has lagged. Currently, world trade in services accounts for just 6 percent of global GDP. I firmly believe that services are the new frontier of IT-enabled globalization. In the developed world, services remain the dominant form of economic activity. According to the World Trade Organization (WTO), the value added of the services sector currently accounts for about two-thirds of overall world GDP. On that basis alone, there is plenty of upside to the current 6 percent share of world GDP going to cross-border trade in services. However, given the intrinsic experiential character of services—especially the intangibles that cannot be lifted, or even touched—there are obvious limits to their tradability. The haircut, the string quartet, religious worship, housekeeping, and a broad array of other personal services still require on-site, non-tradable, consumption.

However, for many professional and commercial services, the Internet has opened the door to a much broader world. That's especially true of professional knowledge workers such as software programmers, engineers, designers, doctors, other medical professionals, lawyers, accountants, actuaries, financial analysts, and many business consultants. IT-enabled connectivity brings the output of such knowledge workers from developing economies to desktops literally anywhere in the developed world. Although coming off a low base, such white-collar offshoring is now among the world's most rapidly growing segments of economic activity. The same can be said of commercial services—namely, transportation, travel, communications, construction, insurance, and other financial services. According to the WTO, trade in commercial services has doubled since 1990 to a level that currently accounts for about 20 percent of total world trade in goods and services, combined. As the world shrinks, there is nothing but upside for trade in commercial services.

In my view, the shifting mix of trade from the rich to poor countries is the icing on the cake insofar as the need for an open macro is concerned.

According to IMF statistics, trade volumes in the developing world expanded at a 9.4 percent average annual rate over the 1997 to 2006 period—nearly double the 5.6 percent pace in the developed world over the same period. This divergence stands in sharp contrast with trends over the prior decade, when gains were close to parity in both the developing (6.9 percent per year) and developed (6.7 percent) world. Needless to say, the rapidly growing Chinese trade juggernaut—with exports expanding at a 25 percent clip over the past six years—has played a critical role in driving this trade dynamic. In economics, it is change at the margin that determines the incremental pricing decision. And that's the bottom line for the open macro of globalization: The increasingly dominant role played by the low-cost developing world in driving the rapid growth of global trade in recent years could well be the decisive force shaping the global arbitrage of costs and prices.

Yet policy makers and investors seem stuck in the antiquated, closed-economy constructs of the past. In his first congressional appearance as Fed Chairman, Ben Bernanke stressed the timeworn linkage between U.S inflation risk and slack—or the lack thereof—in domestic labor and product markets. He, of course, is not alone in dwelling on this point. Such short-term Phillips-Curve reasoning remains very much the *raison d'être* of modern-day macro. But this relationship no longer holds in today's increasingly globalized economy. In fact, it hasn't been working for nearly a decade, as pointed out in the BIS research noted above. Again, I don't think that is a coincidence—nor do I think this anomaly is about to fade. If anything, given the upside potential of IT-enabled trade in global services, I think the cross-border arbitrage could well intensify in the years ahead.

Policy makers need to heed the lessons of the past several years very carefully. Fiscal and monetary authorities should consider the implications of their domestic policy actions in the context of open models—rather than just relying on the closed models of yesteryear. Policy stimulus may no longer lead to accelerating inflation in a world awash in excess supply that is constantly arbitraging away excess costs and pricing. Instead, the impacts of such stimulus may show up more in the global liquidity cycle and asset markets. Moreover, the global saving arbitrage has the potential to broaden the amplitude of liquidity cycles. That's especially the case today, with the world's biggest deficit (America's) being funded increasingly by China—an export-dependent growth machine that remains more than willing to provide sustained support to its biggest external market.

As long as inflation remains at bay, the rules of old macro suggest little reason to worry. Yet that may well prove to be the biggest risk of all in today's unbalanced world. Open macro draws attention to the perils of asset bubbles and the excesses of asset-dependent economies. That suggests that this is no time for complacency.

# The Battleground
# of Globalization
## *February 6, 2006*

The global labor market was always destined to be the battleground of globalization. Signs of this conflict are everywhere. At work is an increasingly powerful IT-enabled global labor arbitrage that is reslicing the global pie. For the industrial world, the pendulum of economic returns has swung from labor to capital, whereas for the developing world, the benefits have accrued mainly to labor. The rules of macro engagement are being challenged as never before.

The squeeze on labor in the developed world could well be one of the most important macro developments of our lifetime. In the structurally impaired economies of Europe and Japan, globalization has exacerbated the inherent inefficiencies of rigid labor markets. The result has been a protracted period of historically high unemployment (in Europe) or chronic underemployment (in Japan). In response, Japan is in the process of dismantling its once sacred institution of lifetime employment. Meanwhile, Germany, still the bellwether of Old Europe, has been transforming its workforce increasingly into part-timers and contract temps; the latest stats put such flexi workers at 39 percent of the total German workforce—up sharply from the 29 percent share 10 years ago. At the same time, there has been a marked slowing in the growth of Euro zone compensation per employee—down to 1.5 percent in 2005 (a fractional decline in real terms) versus average gains of 2.4 percent over the 2001–2004 period.

Even in the United States, with supposedly the world's most flexible labor market, workers are feeling unprecedented pressures. The current expansion is notable for the confluence of subpar job growth and relatively stagnant real wages. This has resulted in a significant compression of the share of output remunerated to labor in the developed world. In the United States, for example, the private sector compensation component of personal income has risen only 12 percent in real terms in the 49-month time span of the current expansion. This falls about $365 billion short of the 20 percent increase that would have occurred had the current cycle tracked the average trajectory of the past four expansions. Nor is the United States an outlier. The combined compensation shares of the United States, Europe, and Japan fell to 54.4 percent of gross national income in late 2005—the lowest reading in the 15-year history of this series (see Figure 2.1).

These are the telltale signs of the global labor arbitrage at work. As trade in manufactured goods continues to grab an ever-increasing record share of world GDP—23 percent by IMF estimates in 2005—and as the cross-border exchange of once-nontradable services accelerates, a harmonization of labor costs can be expected. In an increasingly integrated global economy, a failure to rationalize the excesses of bloated cost structures in the high-wage developed economies is tantamount to capitulation of market share.

But there's an important twist to this development. It's one thing for labor's reward to be squeezed in the low-productivity growth economies of Europe and Japan. It's another thing altogether for these same pressures to bear down on the pay of highly productive American workers.

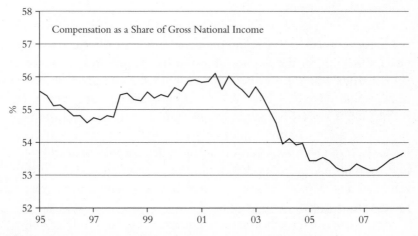

**Figure 2.1**   G-3 Compensation Proxy: US, Europe, and Japan

*Source:* National Sources, Morgan Stanley Research.

This runs against the grain of one of the basic axioms of classic macro—that workers are ultimately paid in accordance with their marginal product. However, that hasn't been the case in the United States for quite some time. Over the 2001–2005 interval, productivity growth averaged 3.3 percent in the nonfarm business sector of the U.S. economy—basically double the 1.6 percent gains in real hourly compensation over the same period. I don't think this is a random development. Only a megaforce like the global labor arbitrage could drive such a wedge between productivity and worker rewards.

The flip side of the pressures on labor in the developed world is accelerating growth of labor input in the developing world. China and India—collectively accounting for nearly 40 percent of the world's population—are obviously the most important cases in point. According to official government statistics, total employment in China is estimated to have hit 752 million in 2004—up 71 million from the job count a decade earlier. In India, total employment rose by 40 million over this same 10-year period, from 323 million in 1995 to 363 million in 2004.

Wage disparities are only one force behind the cross-border arbitrage—Chinese manufacturing wages are less than 10 percent of those in the United States, and India's wages are about half China's. Another dimension comes from the dual benefits of IT-enabled connectivity, providing, on the one hand, a pipeline that links both factory- and knowledge-worker employment in the developing economies directly into integrated global platforms and, on the other hand, a potential for U.S.-style productivity dividends.

Compensating shifts in the return to capital are the mirror image of the impacts on labor. Reflecting the compression of labor costs, corporate profitability in the developed world has surged sharply in recent years. United States profit shares hit a record share of national income in 2005, and there have been sharp earnings gains accruing to a newly restructured Corporate Japan in the past three to four years. In Europe, an outsize surge of nonfinancial corporate net worth in 2004, steady increases in the business sector's gross operating surplus to an eight-year high in 2005, and ongoing declines in the compensation share of Euro zone national income are strong indications of a significant increase in the return on capital in the region.

Meanwhile in China, the tradeoff is going the other way. While Chinese workers are on the leading edge of reaping the benefits of globalization, the owners of Chinese capital are not. At least, that's the message that can be taken from the extraordinary disconnect between booming GDP growth and sagging domestic Chinese stock markets, which declined by about 50 percent over the 2001 to 2006 interval.

The implications of the global labor arbitrage can be broken down into three areas—economics, financial markets, and politics. In terms of economics, labor wins in the developing world but loses in the developed world—at least for the foreseeable future. That puts unrelenting pressure on income generation in the rich economies, raising serious questions about the sustainability of consumer-led growth dynamics. The United States has finessed this possibility—at least for the time being— by extracting equity from asset holdings. This strategy works, however, only for as long as the value of the underlying assets holds up. If the air is coming out of the U.S. housing bubble, as I now suspect, then there is good reason to worry about U.S. leadership on the demand side of the global economy—and equally good reason to worry about who steps up to fill the void.

For financial markets, the biggest risk would be a shortfall in global growth. In early 2006, the broad consensus of investors is looking for the global economy to hold up this year about as well as it did in 2005. If the U.S. consumer falters, goes the argument, other consumers—from China, Japan, or even Europe—are thought to be in the wings and ready to fill the void. Moreover, there is an equally strong view that a seamless transition to capex-led growth is close at hand. I remain highly suspicious of such optimism, and believe that these so-called handovers from one source of global growth to another may be surprisingly difficult to pull off. To the extent I'm right, and the global labor arbitrage tilts the risks to world GDP growth to the downside, equity markets could suffer whereas bonds may find greater support.

The political implications of the global labor arbitrage could well be the most vexing of all. The immediate risks are heightened trade frictions, with an outside chance of protectionism. Why else would Washington-led China-bashing continue to get traction as the U.S. unemployment rate slips below 5 percent? Once jobless, now wageless, the current economic recovery is not going well for many beleaguered middle-class workers in the United States. Nor is this a partisan issue. New York liberal Democrat Sen. Charles Schumer has joined forces with South Carolina conservative Republican Sen. Lindsey Graham to lead the political assault on China. Never mind the weak economics of this argument. The plight of the American worker has become the political *cause célèbre* of globalization.

To his credit, U.S. President George W. Bush took the high road on this issue—arguing in his 2006 State of the Union address that America must resist the dark forces of protectionism and, instead, treat globalization as a competitive challenge. This puts the onus on educational reform, the training of more engineers and scientists, research and development incentives, and innovation. The problem with these proposals is that they offer no instant gratification for a body politic that is used to the quick fix. But that takes us to the biggest challenge of all posed by the global labor arbitrage—it has only just begun.

# The Global Delta

*January 13, 2006*

Growth is great. Every investor knows that, and so do most business leaders, policy makers, and academics. Almost by definition, rapidly growing developing economies like China and India win the global growth sweepstakes, hands down. The clunkers in the developed world—especially Europe and Japan—pale by comparison. On the surface, the verdict is inescapable: If you are looking for growth, it's out with the old industrial countries and in with the new developing economies. Yet that superficial comparison overlooks some critical aspects of the global growth sweepstakes. There's more to the global delta than meets the eye.

Consider the record in 2005: Based on the IMF's latest estimates, China and India were the two most rapidly growing major economies in the world in 2005, having expanded in nominal terms by 15.5 percent and 12.2 percent, respectively. The combined growth rate of these two economies of 14.5 percent in 2005 was more than four times that recorded in Europe (3.5 percent) and fully 2.4 times that in the United States (6.1 percent). Little wonder why China and India get all the attention in an otherwise growth-starved world!

But wait a minute. As rapidly as China and India grew in 2005, their contribution to world growth was dwarfed by that of the more slowly growing U.S. and European economies. As can be seen in Table 2.1, nominal GDP increased in the United States by fully $718 billion in 2005 and by $447 billion in Europe. By contrast, the combined increases in China and India amounted to a relatively paltry $337 billion.

This is exactly what you would expect from the law of large numbers. The United States accounted for 28.4 percent of world GDP in 2005—more than six times the 4.4 percent share of China and more than 16 times the 1.7 percent share of India. As a result, at current levels of activity,

**Table 2.1**  The Global Delta in 2005 (Dollar-Based Nominal GDP at Market Exchange Rates)

|            | Growth, % | Growth, US$ bil. | $ Growth per pctg pt., US$ bil. | Share of World GDP, % |
|------------|-----------|------------------|---------------------------------|-----------------------|
| U.S.       | 6.1       | 718.1            | 117.7                           | 28.4                  |
| Europe     | 3.5       | 446.7            | 127.6                           | 30.3                  |
| Japan      | 0.0       | 1.1              | 46.7*                           | 10.6                  |
| Asia ex-Japan | 12.9   | 541.4            | 42.0                            | 10.8                  |
| China      | 15.5      | 256.0            | 16.5                            | 4.4                   |
| India      | 12.2      | 81.0             | 6.6                             | 1.7                   |
| Emerging Europe | 20.1 | 335.0            | 16.7                            | 4.6                   |
| Latin America | 19.3   | 346.6            | 18.0                            | 4.9                   |

*Japan calculation derived on the basis of hypothetical 1 percent increase in nominal GDP.

*Source:* International Monetary Fund, Morgan Stanley Research.

every one percentage point of growth in the U.S. economy translates into $118 billion—fully seven times the $16.5 billion increment generated by 1 percentage point of nominal Chinese GDP growth and about 18 times the $6.6 billion delta that comes from every 1 percentage point of Indian growth. Similarly, each percentage point of European growth is the equivalent of about 8 percentage points of Chinese growth and 19 points of Indian growth. Moreover, once Japan starts growing again in nominal terms—an outcome that should occur in 2006—a comparable result can be expected. As expressed in dollars, every 1 percentage point of nominal GDP growth in the Japanese economy would be worth nearly three times that of a 1 percentage point gain in China and about seven times a comparable increase in India.

This is pretty basic stuff, but I think it helps put the search for growth in context. Yet these results basically depict the state of play as it exists today. That begs important questions about the future. To answer those questions, we ran some simple 30-year simulations of nominal GDP growth in the G-3 economies (United States, Europe, and Japan) compared with reasonable trajectories in China and India. For each of the economies in question, we made assumptions with respect to long-term potential GDP growth, inflation, and currency movements. In the case of the U.S. economy, nominal GDP growth was held steady at 6 percent

**Table 2.2**   Nominal GDP Growth Deltas: 2005–2035 (Billions of U.S. Dollars)

|               | 2005 | 2010 | 2015 | 2025 | 2035 |
|---------------|------|------|------|------|------|
| United States | 718  | 944  | 1263 | 2262 | 4052 |
| Europe        | 447  | 808  | 1032 | 1680 | 2737 |
| Japan         | 1    | 218  | 265  | 392  | 580  |
| China         | 256  | 426  | 750  | 2331 | 7240 |
| India         | 81   | 109  | 176  | 456  | 1183 |

*Source:* Morgan Stanley Research.

over the 30-year interval—consisting of 3 percent potential real GDP growth and 3 percent inflation. For Europe, the simulation was run off 5 percent nominal GDP growth, comprised of 2 percent potential growth and 3 percent inflation. In Japan, we assumed 4 percent nominal GDP growth, made up of 2 percent potential growth and 2 percent inflation. For China, the simulation was based on 12 percent nominal GDP growth, consisting of 7 percent potential growth, 3 percent inflation, and 2 percent annual currency appreciation. And finally, for India, a 10 percent nominal GDP growth rate was assumed, comprised of 6 percent potential growth, 3 percent inflation, and 1 percent annualized currency appreciation.

Many of these assumptions may seem arbitrary or questionable, but I think they provide a good ballpark approximation of the potential shifts in the growth contributions among the G-3, China, and India. The results of this exercise are summarized in Table 2.2, which shows the dollar-based annual change in each country's nominal GDP—the growth delta—at designated 5- and 10-year intervals.

Not much changes by 2010. Over the next five years, China and India make little progress in closing the "delta gap" with the US and Europe. By 2010, the combined first differences in nominal GDP of these two large developing economies are only 30 percent that of the collective delta of the United States and Europe—virtually identical to that evident in 2005. Nevertheless, our simulations suggest that by 2010, China's GDP delta—the dollar-based change in its nominal GDP—should be nearly double that of Japan.

Thereafter, the mix of the global growth dynamic starts to undergo more significant changes. By 2015, the scale of China's economy should surpass that of Japan. At that point, China's annual dollar-based delta of

$750 billion would amount to about 65 percent of the average deltas in the United States and Europe.

By 2025, these simulations suggest that the pendulum of global growth will have shifted dramatically in China's favor. By then, China's annual delta should be well in excess of Europe's and slightly larger than that of the United States—putting China in first place insofar as its dollar-based incremental contribution to world GDP growth is concerned. Twenty years out, in 2025, the Chinese economy should be essentially twice the size of Japan's and about 60 percent the size of Europe's.

In the final 10 years of our simulation, the ascendancy of China is nearly complete. By 2033, the size of China's economy should surpass that of Europe's, making it the second-largest economy in the world and putting it within shouting distance of the United States. But the real story is on the growth delta front. If, in fact, China is able to maintain a 12 percent dollar-based growth trajectory over the next 30 years, while the United States and Europe hold to 6 percent and 5 percent paths, respectively, then by 2035 China's annual dollar-based growth delta will be larger than that of the United States and Europe, combined. As for India, at the end of this simulation, it comes close to matching the size of the Japanese economy but remains dwarfed by China. By 2035, this simulation places China at five times the size of the Indian economy.

It should be stressed that these are simulations, not forecasts. The results are heavily dependent on the assumptions just laid out. A lot can certainly change over a 30-year period that would bear critically on the validity of these assumptions. From a fundamental standpoint, the key swing factors of this exercise are undoubtedly the relative productivity parameters embedded in the potential GDP growth trends, highlighted by roughly 2 percent per annum in the case of the United States and about 6 percent with respect to China. Europe and Japan should probably lag the United States, whereas Indian productivity seems unlikely to match the Chinese trajectory.

There are, of course, innumerable what-ifs that could drastically alter the outcome along the way. China could stumble. The G–3 could collectively ride the wave of a sustained IT-enabled productivity boom. India could leapfrog over China—adding a powerful manufacturing engine to its already vibrant services-led growth dynamic. Or another country (e.g., Russia) or region (Eastern and Central Europe) could emerge from the pack. Although I can't rule out any of those possibilities, I would give them considerably less credence than the assumptions outlined in the baseline simulation above.

I find this simulation exercise especially useful in that it lays bare the economic assumptions that are embedded in the notion of a China-centric twenty-first century. Right now, the world is only just beginning to sense what lies ahead if China stays the course of reforms and productivity enhancement. Commodity prices are already surging in response—oil and non-oil alike. Trade frictions are building as China leads the way in driving the global labor arbitrage. If our simulations are anywhere close to the mark, the world has a grace period of about five years before it really begins to feel the heat of China's emergence. How the world then copes with China may well be the biggest what-if of all.

# Beggars Can't Be Choosers
## *February 27, 2006*

A merica is at risk of turning protectionist at a time when its need for foreign capital has never been greater. China-bashing is on the rise in Washington once again, and there has been a political firestorm over a proposed—and now deferred—acquisition by Dubai Ports World of a UK operator of five East Coast container terminals in the United States. This backlash reflects a highly combustible mixture of macro and politics. America's savings shortfall has led to a massive trade deficit, which, in conjunction with a protracted stagnation of real wages for middle-class U.S. workers, has triggered a classic political blame game. In response, the drumbeat of protectionism is growing louder and louder. Ever-complacent financial markets could care less.

Notwithstanding legitimate concerns over matters of national security in a post-9/11 world, there is a very simple and extremely powerful macro point that is being overlooked in this debate: America no longer has the internal wherewithal to fund the rapid growth of its economy. Suffering from the greatest domestic savings shortfall in modern history, the United States is increasingly dependent on surplus foreign savings to fill the void. The net national savings rate—the combined saving of individuals, businesses, and the government sector after adjusting for depreciation—fell into negative territory to the tune of $-1.2$ percent of national income in late 2005. That means America doesn't save enough even to cover the replacement of its worn-out capital stock. This is a first for the United States in the modern post–World War II era—and I believe a first for any hegemonic power over a much longer sweep of world history.

Faced with a shortfall of domestic savings, countries basically have two choices—to curtail economic growth or borrow from the rest of the world. The first option just doesn't cut it in the land of abundance. America, in general, and its consumers, in particular, treats rapid economic growth as an entitlement. That leaves the US with little choice other than to pursue the second option—drawing heavily on the global saving pool in order to fund economic growth. Once the United States started down the slippery path of consuming beyond its internal means, it became harder and harder to break the habit. Ironically, it has become more and more difficult to accept the consequences of that habit—a nation that has become beholden to external funding and production. And yet that's exactly how China and Dubai fit into America's macro equation.

That underscores a key attribute of the savings-short, deficit nation: It is forced to run current account deficits in order to attract the requisite foreign capital and saving. And in the case of the United States, where external funding needs are so massive—now closing in on $800 billion per year, or about $3 billion per business day—most of the current account imbalance shows up in the form of a huge trade deficit. In 2005, for example, the trade deficit in goods and services accounted for fully 93 percent of the total current-account gap.

With that external funding imperative comes key geopolitical trade-offs. Thanks to China, America actually cut a rather extraordinary deal for its trade deficit dollar in 2005—a net balance of some $200 billion of low-cost, high-quality Chinese goods that expanded the purchasing power of U.S. consumers. If, however, Washington politicians now choose to close down trade with China by imposing high tariffs or forcing a major Chinese currency revaluation—precisely the intent of a bipartisan coalition headed up by Senators Schumer (D-NY) and Graham (R-SC)—those actions could easily backfire.

Absent the China supply line, the trade deficit for a savings-short U.S. economy wouldn't shrink as the politicians seem to imply. Instead, due to America's savings shortfall and concomitant external funding needs, the overall trade deficit would remain large and merely gravitate to another foreign producer—most likely, one with a higher cost structure. Such a shift in America's external sourcing would amount to the functional equivalent of a tax hike on the American consumer. Similarly, if Washington were eventually to kill the cross-border bid from Dubai, another source of capital inflows would be required to fill the external funding gap. But maybe the next investor would then ask for tougher financing terms.

The current political boil raises a critical question: Can a savings-short United States select its lenders as well as dictate the terms of its external financing needs? The simple answer to the first part of the question is

"Yes"—targeted protectionist actions can, indeed, redirect the sources of external commerce and funding. Through tariffs à la Schumer-Graham, or nontariff restrictions on Dubai-based investors, the United States could attempt to shift the mix of its trade and capital inflows. Such actions would do nothing, however, to address the basic problem. As long as the U.S. economy is locked on a subpar domestic saving path, it is increasingly reliant on the kindness of strangers to provide the sustenance of its economic growth—both in terms of capital as well as goods. Country-specific protectionist actions would succeed only in shifting America's trade deficit and concomitant capital surplus elsewhere in the world.

There's an even darker side to the recent protectionist backlash in the United States—the crass politics of scapegoating. The ongoing angst of middle-class American workers has become a political football—even with the national unemployment rate below 5 percent. It's not hard to figure out why. A U.S. labor market that was once trapped in a jobless recovery is now mired in a wageless recovery—an extraordinary stagnation of real wages even in the face of strong productivity growth. At the same time, the U.S. is suffering from a record trade deficit, whose largest bilateral piece is with China. Bingo—the politicians are quick to point the finger at China as being responsible for the trade-related pressures bearing down on beleaguered U.S. workers. With midterm elections looming in the U.S., I suspect this protectionist posturing could well intensify in the months ahead.

But who is really to blame in all this? At the end of the day, America's saving shortfall—the origin of destabilizing capital and trade flows—is a by-product of conscious choices made by the U.S. body politic. The Federal budget deficit, which has accounted for the bulk of the plunge in national saving over the period of 2000–2006, is made in Washington, not in Beijing. The negative personal saving rate is an outgrowth of pro-consumption tax policies—again, made in Washington. America's elected representatives are the source of resistance to tax reforms, such as a consumption tax, that might address the deficiencies of private saving. Of course, politicians never want to admit that they are the problem. Instead, they prefer to pin the blame on others—in this case, China and Dubai.

Washington needs to be very careful what it wishes for. In effect, the United Arab Emirate (UAE) is being told that it is fine to recycle its petro-dollars into Treasuries—just don't buy American port facilities. China is getting the same message—revalue your currency, curtail your exports to the United States, don't buy Unocal, but don't dare stop gobbling up dollar-based financial assets. Meanwhile, the United States does next to nothing to shoulder its share of the problem—a staggering shortfall of domestic saving. Such political hypocrisy is a recipe for serious trouble, in my view. The longer the United States avoids the heavy lifting of fixing its saving problem and continues to point fingers at others, the greater the risks that America's current-account financing problem will end in tears.

Political, social, ethnic, religious, military, and security considerations have always been important pieces of the Big Puzzle. In today's newly globalized world, these noneconomic factors may be more relevant than in the past. *New York Times* columnist David Brooks argued recently that the role of economics has been relegated to bit-player status in today's increasingly fractured world—going so far as to posit that "Economics . . . is no longer queen of the social sciences."[2] Brooks's point is well taken. Perhaps the greatest irony of the current strain of globalization is that cross-border integration has unmasked cross-cultural frictions. The closer knit the world becomes through trade flows, capital flows, and information flows, the greater the discomfort level that seems to arise within individual segments of the world.

Throughout history, financial markets have served the useful—and at times, painful—purpose of arbitrating the interplay between economic and noneconomic factors. That venting function could take on a very different meaning in today's era of IT-enabled globalization. Moreover, the coming turn in the global liquidity cycle may well amplify the implications of any such venting. Left to its own devices, open macro could perpetuate the disinflationary underpinnings of a bullish financial market climate. The bond market conundrum might endure, as could the resilience of the U.S. dollar. However, the politics of globalization—which are now spinning in an increasingly protectionist direction—raise serious questions about whether open macro ultimately will be left to its own devices. From time to time, economics has its limits in shaping the macro outcome for world financial markets. This feels like one of those times.

In the end, the answer to the question posed about whether open macro ultimately will be left to its own devices is "No." Savings-short America is hardly in a position where it can carefully select its lenders as well as dictate the terms of its massive external financing program. In other words, beggars can't be choosers—nor should they put undue

---

2. See his op-ed piece, "Questions of Culture" in the February 19, 2006 *New York Times*.

pressure on their external support system. The harder the protectionist push from Washington, the greater the risks of a financial market backlash that hits the dollar and U.S. real interest rates. Economics and markets may be increasingly global but politics remain decidedly local. That is globalization's greatest paradox—and, quite possibly, its most daunting challenge. America is a microcosm of that paradox.

# Perils of a Different Globalization

## March 20, 2006

Economics and politics are on a dangerous collision course. As the forces of globalization strengthen, the drumbeat of protectionism is growing louder. Made in France, the European strain of protectionism reflects a newfound nationalism that strikes at the heart of panregional integration. Made in America and exacerbated by fear of China, a different strain of protectionism plays to the angst of middle-class U.S. wage earners.

Whether the threat is perceived to be from the inside (as it is in Europe) or the outside (as in the United States), the responses of increasingly populist politicians are worrisome, to say the least. French Prime Minister Dominique de Villepin is seeking to protect strategic industries from foreign ownership. In the United States, it's not just resistance to foreign takeovers; bipartisan support is also building in the Senate to impose steep tariffs on China. All this harkens back to the demise of an earlier globalization that many date to the enactment of the infamous Smoot-Hawley Tariff Act of 1930—a political blunder that may well have been key in turning a U.S. stock market crash and recession into worldwide depression. Like the circumstances over 75 years ago, the current global trade dynamic has played an increasingly important role in boosting the world economy. Protectionism, and the contraction in global trade it would trigger, puts all that at risk.

Today's world, of course, is very different than it was back then. So, too, is the fabric of a globalization that is causing such a powerful political backlash. In the early part of the twentieth century, the world was brought together by the cross-border exchange of manufactured products. In the early part of the twenty-first century, globalization has swept beyond tradable goods into a very different realm of commerce—information flows, financial capital, and services.

A globalization that moves from tangible tradable goods activity to the more intangible functions of the knowledge economy is not well understood. But the impacts of this shifting character of cross-border integration could well be more powerful than they were in the past. That's because the incidence of the disaffected—the workers who feel the brunt of intensified global competitive pressures—is shifting into a segment of the global labor market that has never really known the meaning of job anxiety and stress. Blue-collar workers in factories have, of course, long been on the front line in facing the ups and downs of business cycles, as well as the intensification of global competitive pressures. By contrast, white-collar workers in services-based enterprises have not. That is now changing. The rules of engagement on the battleground of globalization are being rewritten. The services economy is now on the leading edge of feeling the stresses and strains of an increasingly competitive and open world economy.

This is a truly extraordinary development in the continuum of economic history. Economists have long dubbed services as "nontradables"—underscoring the time-honored proposition that service providers had to reside in close proximity with their customers to offer in-person delivery of expertise, advice, or assistance. In the Internet Age, the boundaries between tradables and nontradables have become blurred. Now, with the click of a mouse, many once-nontradable services can be offered up from anywhere in the world. At work is the globalization of software programming, engineering, design, medicine, accounting, consulting, and a multitude of other professional services. Labor input—and the knowledge-based content of the service it delivers—is now beamed to your desktop on a real-time basis from Bangalore, whether you like it or not. This compresses both the quantity (i.e., headcount) and the price (i.e., real wage) of higher-cost labor input in the developed world—with most of the impact presently showing up in the form of a persistent stagnation of real wages. The result is an IT-enabled globalization that throws long-sheltered knowledge workers into the global competitive arena for the first time ever.

As in the early 1930s, the new strain of globalization has spawned a political backlash. But the pressures are very different as they migrate from manufacturing to services. That's not to say blue-collar workers aren't feeling the heat in today's world. Unfortunately, there just aren't that many of them left. Factory sector workers currently account for only about 15 percent of total employment in the G-7 collection of major industrial countries (the United States, Canada, Japan, France, Italy, Germany, and the UK)—about half the 29 percent share prevailing as recently as 1970. Although there could well be more to come in the attrition of manufacturing employment (the U.S. portion is now close to 10 percent), simple math tells us this aspect of the hollowing has just about run its course.

With the pendulum of global competition now swinging toward services, the resulting white-collar shock has added a new and very destabilizing element to the globalization debate. It has created a deepening sense of anxiety that afflicts workers who have long harbored the belief that they would not have to face pressures from low-wage offshore talent pools. The persistent stagnation of inflation-adjusted wages in the developed world—even in a high-productivity-growth U.S. economy—has shattered that false sense of security. It is an exceedingly painful, but perfectly logical outgrowth of an increasingly powerful IT-enabled global labor arbitrage.

Politicians have been quick to come to the defense of the new warriors of globalization. The numbers leave them with little choice. Unlike the sharply reduced ranks of manufacturing employees in the developed world, services are the dominant source of work, income generation, and political power. In the G-7 countries, services currently account for close to 75 percent of the total workforce—literally five times the share of manufacturing. And yet that's where the current strain of globalization is playing out with greatest intensity and, accordingly, where it meets its greatest resistance from the politicians. Little wonder that services reforms have stalled in Europe, or that the Doha Round of multilateral global trade liberalization has been stymied by a highly contentious debate over services.

Significantly, the new globalization could be far more disruptive than the strain of the early twentieth century. That's due importantly to the extraordinary speed of the transformation now at work. A century ago, the burst of globalization was also spectacular, but the new connectivity of the early twentieth century still faced very real physical constraints— namely, the expansion of shipping capacity and the construction of ports and overland transportation networks. The modern-day strain of globalization does not have to face such daunting physical constraints. The only limiting factors today are growth in IT-enabled connectivity and bandwidth—both of which have continued to expand at explosive rates, long after the law of large numbers might have produced slower growth. The rapid expansion of global Internet usage continued in excess of a 15 percent annual rate in 2005—even though total worldwide penetration pierced the 1 billion threshold toward the end of 2006.

In other words, the infrastructure of today's globalization of intangibles is being installed at a much more rapid pace than was the case in the globalization of tangibles a century ago. In essence, that's because the hurdle rates of disseminating the new technologies of connectivity are much lower today. That key differentiating development, in conjunction with the rapid growth in high-quality offshore knowledge-worker talent pools, has enabled the global labor arbitrage to move much more rapidly up the value chain than was the case in the early twentieth century. Around 2001, when the debate was first joined on white-collar offshoring, the focus was on relatively low-value-added data processing and call centers. Today, the whole gamut of higher-value-added professional services workers is feeling the heat. As a result, the current strain of white-collar shock has the potential to dwarf the impacts of the blue-collar shock of a century ago.

The debate breaks down over what needs to be done. Rich countries are flirting dangerously with protectionism while poor countries continue to bet on export-led growth. Meanwhile, the new competition fostered by IT-enabled globalization hurtles ahead at breakneck speed. At the same time, the global labor arbitrage is forcing a realignment of relative wages in the world economy, with the rich developed world fearing a race to the bottom while the poor developing world is hoping to ride the rising tide. The combination of IT-enabled globalization and real-wage stagnation in the developed world creates an angst that is too tempting for populist politicians to resist. The hyperspeed that drives this disruptive integration of the world risks turning concern into panic, providing a perfect set-up for a protectionist backlash.

Unfortunately, there is no easy resolution of these political and economic tensions. In the end, the competitive profile of any knowledge worker reflects the interplay between skill sets and fully-loaded costs. A nation's stock of human capital is key in shaping the former, whereas the ever-declining price of IT-enabled connectivity adds an important new wrinkle into the cost calculus. Countries that sign up for globalization must meet both aspects of this challenge head on. The hyperspeed by which the rules of a new competition are changing in the Internet Age adds a critical urgency to the politicization of globalization—and to the protectionist pressures it has evoked.

The orthodox prescription is to counsel patience—that the win–win of globalization eventually will raise living standards in the developing world while creating new markets to be tapped by industrial countries. Yet the unprecedented speed of an IT-enabled globalization draws the rewards of that patience into serious question—at least for the foreseeable future. In the end, politicians are usually at their best in counting votes. With workers in services outnumbering those in manufacturing by a factor of five to one, the body politic in the industrial world has cast its ballot in favor of protectionism. Opportunistic politicians are taking the bait—seemingly unconcerned about the tragic lessons of the 1930s. Although globalization is very different today than it was back then, the risks of making an equally tragic mistake on trade policy should not be minimized.

# Bad Advice and a New Global Architecture

*April 24, 2006*

S o China didn't give on the great currency issue after all. After months of increasingly intense expectations, China President Hu Jintao's April 2006 visit to Washington ended pretty much as it began in grappling with the currency issue. The Chinese leadership has rejected the pressure to institute a major revaluation of the renminbi. This flies in the face of the conventional wisdom offered by many—from prominent academics and leading U.S. politicians to the recent G-7 communiqué. Although China could now have to face the wrath of the protectionists as a result, in my view, the Chinese leadership has made the right decision at the right time. The U.S. and G-7 body politic has given China truly terrible advice on this key issue. This, I'm afraid, is emblematic of a much bigger problem: The world has the wrong policy architecture to deal with the new challenges of globalization.

This is not the first time that Washington has tried to browbeat a major U.S. trading partner into submission by using the blunt instrument of currency appreciation as the remedy for a bilateral trade imbalance. Repeatedly during the 1980s, when the United States was in the midst of another external crisis—a current account deficit that peaked at a then-unheard of 3.4 percent share of GDP—Washington pounded on Japan to let the yen rise. After all, the deficit with Japan was the biggest piece of the then-gaping U.S. multilateral trade deficit. The theory was if Japan repriced the currency underpinnings of its unfair competitive advantage, all would be well for an unbalanced United States and for an unbalanced world. Unfortunately, the Japanese heeded this advice, and the yen/dollar cross-rate soared from 254 in early 1985 to an intraday peak of 79 in the spring of 1995. Sadly, Japan's *endaka* (strong yen) was a major factor behind its subsequent undoing—fueling the mother of all asset bubbles in equities and property that ended with a sickening collapse into a protracted postbubble deflation. Twenty years later, America and the G-7 are offering the Chinese the same bad advice that took Japan down a road of unmitigated macro disaster. Fortunately, saner minds have prevailed in Beijing.

It's worth belaboring this comparison a bit further. There are important lessons from the Japan side as well as from the U.S. side that bear critically on China's macro strategy. Japan was already a very wealthy and prosperous nation when it acceded to *endaka* in the 1980s. Then—and now—Japan as the world's second-largest economy, was operating from a position of strength. In 1985, its per capita GDP was about 50 percent that of the United States. It thought—incorrectly, as it turns out—that it could afford to take a gamble with currency appreciation. China, by contrast, is still a very poor economy. Its per capita GDP of $1,700 in 2005 is only 4 percent that of the United States. Moreover, China is at a very delicate point in its reform process, undertaking a truly extraordinary transformation in its system of ownership that has great consequences for both itself and the broader world economy. Unlike the Japan of 20 years ago, China is operating from a position of weakness as it confronts the calls for a sharp RMB revaluation.

The United States is also in a far more vulnerable position today than it was back then. As a share of GDP, its current-account deficit is twice the size of the peak shortfall in 1987—and undoubtedly heading for further deterioration. Despite the 1980s-style trade-bashing rhetoric coming out of Washington, America's external imbalance is hardly China's fault. As I have droned on *ad nauseum*, it is a critical outgrowth of an unprecedented U.S. savings deficiency—a net national savings rate that actually plunged into negative territory in late 2005. By contrast, the U.S. national savings rate was in the 6 percent zone in the mid-1980s, providing much more of a macro cushion than is evident today. With the current shortfall of domestic savings dwarfing that of 20 years ago, it's hardly shocking that the Washington angst factor is far more intense today than it was back then. America is in a much deeper hole in 2006 than it was in 1985.

The tragedy in all this is the lack of urgency in setting a global agenda to deal with global imbalances. Governance of the global economy currently rests in the hands of the two main Bretton Woods institutions—the IMF and the World Bank. Established in the immediate aftermath of World War II, these organizations were both designed for a different world in a very different time. The 11-year-old World Trade Organization (WTO) is the newest kid on the block, but with protectionist risks rising and the Doha Round of trade liberalization going nowhere, this is one of the shakiest elements in the global architecture. There's also the Paris-based Organization for Economic Cooperation and Development (OECD), established in 1961, that tabulates statistics and issues reports on its 30 member countries in the developed world. Finally, there are the infamous and rapidly proliferating Gs—the G-7, G-8, G10, and G-20— groups of large and important nations who come together periodically with great fanfare, yet produce increasingly vacuous, market-following communiqués on the major issues of our times.

Over the years, there have been frequent calls for the reform of the international financial architecture. Another such effort is currently under way—spearheaded by Mervyn King, Governor of the Bank of England, who argued in a speech earlier this year that the IMF was in danger of slipping into obscurity. Others have joined the reform movement, including IMF Managing Director Rodrigo de Rato and U.S. Under-Secretary of Treasury Tim Adams. The wheels of reform turn slowly in the international arena. In their just-completed meetings, both the G-7 and the IMF endorsed the concepts of multilateral surveillance and con-sultations—policy lingo for owning up to the cross-border ramifications of imbalances. Although I was delighted to see this nod toward putting the official seal of approval on the rebalancing movement, a severely unbalanced world needs far more than a new discussion platform.

Quite simply, the institutional pillars of the global financial and economic architecture—the IMF, the World Bank, the WTO, and the OECD—have lost their way. These huge bureaucracies, who collectively employ about 16,000 individuals with administrative expenses that easily total around $2.5 billion per annum, are hopelessly out of step with the new character and unprecedented hyperspeed of today's IT-enabled glo-balization. The composition of the Euro-centric G-7—the centerpiece of the global political power structure—says it all: To exclude China and India but to include four European countries (Germany, France, Italy, and the UK) plus Canada is completely out of step with the new global economy. Europe is one entity, or is at least trying to be; there is no reason for multicountry representation of one economic bloc in modern global institutions. Nor is Canada exactly a dominant player on the global stage. At the same time, China and India, with their combined share of nearly

40 percent of the world's population, remain on the outside looking in. Yet, they are, in many respects, driving the very globalization that is shaking the world's power structure, and are brought into the process only as outsiders or observers. The same can be said for the world's oil producers. The high councils of globalization are effectively missing some of their most important representatives.

There are several steps that can be taken immediately to update the architecture of globalization. I would suggest three principles to guide the process: First, *consolidation*: The world does not need a multitude of institutions charged with dealing with different facets of the same problem. The IMF, World Bank, WTO, and OECD should be merged and radically streamlined. They have become bureaucratic fiefdoms, ripe for turf wars; they work at cross-purposes and dilute the message. Second, a global economy and its requisite steward need a *policy mandate*. Just as central banks have policy rules, so too should the institutions of the global architecture. In my view, this mandate should include objectives with respect to global imbalances, price stability, sustainable growth, full employment, the elimination of poverty, and protection of a fragile environment. Actionable global goals should be updated in the context of this mandate at least one a year.

Third, the new global architecture needs both *accountability* and an *enforcement* mechanism. Why create a new global superstructure if it doesn't have any clout? The groundwork is already being laid in this area—as evidenced by the G-7's and IMF's recent endorsement of the multilateral surveillance and consultation framework noted earlier. But the process needs traction. This could take the form of a clear and coherent statement from a newly created world governing council at least twice a year that identifies the stresses and strains of globalization. The next step will be even trickier. I would propose that the major players of globalization—starting with those at the G-20 level—be required to submit biannual reports on policy compliance with the global mandate just described. These reports should be submitted by each country's central bank and fiscal authority, as well as by those charged with the critical task of foreign exchange reserve management. It would be the global counterpart of the Federal Reserve's biannual report to the U.S. Congress on the state of monetary policy. These steps would take accountability to the global level.

I am hopeful that an increasingly interdependent world is headed in this direction. At the current pace, however, I doubt if I will be around to set foot in the Promised Land. In the meantime, I worry that globalization is occurring at such lightning speed that the world's antiquated policy architecture will be incapable of dealing with the inevitable next strain of global problems. The financial crisis of 1997–1998, with a currency contagion that spread around the world like wildfire, was but a warning shot of what to expect. Unfortunately, as evidenced by the extraordinary compression of emerging market debt spreads, those lessons are now all but forgotten. Meanwhile, China-bashing continues unabated and oil prices are at levels that were unimaginable just a few years ago. At the same time, one nation is running a current account deficit that hit an annual rate of $900 billion in the fourth quarter of 2005—larger than the GDP of all but nine nations in the world today. An unprepared world can only be blindsided by its next crisis. Singling out China underscores the perils of sticking with the old way. This is no way to run the world or to cope with the increasingly complex stresses and strains of globalization.

# Doha Doesn't Matter

*August 4, 2006*

oo much has been made of the apparent failure of the Doha Round of trade liberalization. It does not spell the end of globalization. Nor does it signal an imminent threat to the expansion of cross-border trade. Instead, the lessons of Doha bear more on the trust factor—the unwillingness of the world's body politic to buy into the win-win boosterism of globalization. In the rough and tumble arena of global competition, that may be par for the course—but hardly the disaster that the breakdown of trade talks has been widely made out to be.

The Doha Round was probably doomed from the start. Conceived in the highly emotional aftermath of 9/11 as a politically motivated endorsement of globalization, there was great hope for a major new breakthrough on the world trade front. However, it turns out that a tough macro climate made concessions exceedingly difficult for rich and poor countries, alike. The seemingly intractable battle over agricultural subsidies—always a contentious issue under the best of circumstances—was a foil for much deeper-rooted misgivings. A powerful global labor arbitrage put employment and real wages under intense pressures in the developed world, causing great resistance to a further lowering of trade barriers in the industrial world. And rapidly growing export-led developing countries resented being cast in the role of scapegoats—giving them little incentive to offer concessions of their own. For about a year, the handwriting has been on the wall that this round of trade liberalization was going nowhere. By the time the talks finally collapsed, expectations were so low that not all that much was really lost.

There's nothing like the hype of a well-staged media event centered around a breakthrough in multilateral trade negotiations. But what really counts for the world economy is the power of the global trade dynamic. Despite repeatedly stiff resistance to the Doha agenda for nearly five years, there can be no mistaking the extraordinary gains in world trade that have occurred over that same period. Global trade volumes—calculated as the average of export and import growth—rose by 6.6 percent per annum over the 2002–2005 period; that pace was about 50 percent faster than the 4.3 percent average world GDP growth over the same time frame. As a result, the ratio of exports to world GDP rose by 4.0 percentage points from 24.1 percent in 2001 to 28.1 percent in 2005—the strongest four-year increase since the early 1970s (see Figure 2.2). Putting it another way, the growth in global exports accounted for fully 40 percent of the cumulative increase in world GDP over the four-year period (2002—2006). In the end, that's what matters most. Despite the psychological headwinds of a doomed Doha Round, the strength in global trade went well beyond any vigor that can be attributed to the global business cycle.

What that means is that global trade barriers may already be low enough to have established a breakthrough threshold for accelerating globalization. As noted earlier, I can't help but think that the hyper-speed of an IT-enabled connectivity is an important new catalyst in this equation—providing multinational corporations with new options to cope with increasingly intense competitive pressures. Yes, the Internet has revolutionized the cross-border logistics of price discovery and supply-chain management in manufacturing businesses. But the big story is that it has also transformed the knowledge-based output of once

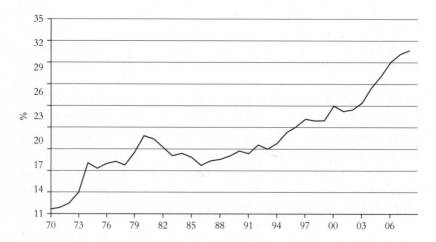

**Figure 2.2**   Global Trade as Percent of World GDP
*Source:* International Monetary Fund, Morgan Stanley Research.

nontradable services into tradable activities; that's increasingly true of high-value added services such as software programming, engineering, design, medical care, legal assistance, accounting, and a broad array of business consulting and financial analysis functions. A Doha breakthrough—especially the watered-down agreement that negotiators were aiming for in the end—would have paled in comparison to these powerful organic developments that are now driving the cross-border trade of both goods and services in an IT-enabled global economy.

All this is not to say there aren't serious problems on the global trade front. Suffering from the twin pressures of job and real-wage insecurity, rich countries feel increasingly threatened by globalization and are pushing back on free and open trade. The rapid growth of white-collar offshoring is a particularly big deal in the current climate. Even though the absolute number of lost jobs has been small so far, the fear of where this trend is going—and what it implies for the globalization of real-wage convergence—are sources of considerable anxiety among long-sheltered knowledge workers in the developed world. "No jobs are safe anymore," is the refrain I hear constantly in the developed world.

The United States and China are lightning rods in this debate. The United States, with its massive trade deficit, feels more exposed than ever. With a $200 billion bilateral imbalance with China having accounted for 25 percent of a record $800 billion multilateral U.S. trade deficit in 2005, Washington has lapsed into the blame game. Over 25 pieces of China-bashing trade legislation have been introduced in the U.S. Congress in the past two years alone. A multilateral breakthrough in the Doha Round would have done little, in my view, to dissuade Washington from taking dead aim on China.

In a narrow sense—namely, from the point of view of hard-pressed workers—the politicization of globalization is understandable. Yet in a broader context, protectionism is entirely misplaced and may well be an inappropriate response to unusual macro characteristics of both the U.S. and Chinese economies. For example, as long as the United States runs a zero net national savings rate, it is forever doomed also to run large current-account and trade deficits. Like it or not, this is an inherent bias of America's wealth-dependent, savings-short economy. By going after China, Washington politicians are unwittingly taking aim at the mix of the U.S. trade deficit, while doing absolutely nothing to address the problems that have given rise to the overall external imbalance.

Similarly, nearly two-thirds of China's export growth over the past dozen years is attributable to foreign-invested enterprises—Chinese subsidiaries of foreign multinational corporations and joint-venture partners. The very existence of these subsidiaries is an outgrowth of conscious decisions made by Western businesses—an important ingredient of new efficiency solutions that are being implemented in the name of competitive survival. This is a very different development than Western-based charges of unfair competition by indigenous Chinese companies. Politicians continue to ignore these macro sources of trade tensions. I guess it's always easier to find a scapegoat than to look in the mirror.

There is a potentially tragic irony to the juxtaposition between the surging global trade and the political backlash against globalization. There are inherent biases to the macro performance of both the United States and China that are setting up these two nations for trade conflicts. If left unattended, these conflicts pose much greater risks to globalization than the failure of trade talks. By fixating on misplaced perceptions of unfair trade, U.S. politicians are avoiding the bigger issues that need addressing. A successful completion of the Doha Round would have done next to nothing to focus Washington politicians on these macro imperatives and defuse mounting bilateral trade tensions between the United States and China.

From the start, Doha was a sideshow to the main event in the global economy. Nearly five years of disappointing progress in multilateral negotiations didn't make a dent in an increasingly powerful world trade dynamic. Barring a major outbreak of protectionism or an abrupt downturn in the global business cycle, it's hard to see a sudden reversal in this trend. The fundamentals of IT-enabled globalization have become far more important than multilateral agreements in driving the global trade cycle. A successful completion of the Doha Round of trade liberalization would have been nice. But the benefits from a heavily watered-down agreement would have been fleeting, at best. There are much bigger fish to fry in an increasingly contentious era of globalization.

# Global Speed Trap

## *September 11, 2006*

The hyperspeed of IT-enabled globalization remains one of the most powerful, but least understood forces at work in today's world economy. It drives accelerated cross-border linkages through trade in goods and now increasingly in services. It also drives a vigorous global labor arbitrage. With this speed come equally potent secondary implications—both for financial markets in the form of inflationary headwinds and for the global body politic in the form of a political backlash and protectionist risks. Those who blindly extol the supposed win-win virtues of globalization risk overlooking the pitfalls of the global speed trap.

As stressed repeatedly in this chapter, this globalization is different. A century ago, the world was also in the midst of a flourishing globalization, a Golden Age of accelerated cross-border capital mobility and rapidly expanding international trade. It was brought to an end by a hugely disruptive confluence of geopolitical and internal shocks: two world wars, the Great Depression, and a virulent protectionism. While the earlier globalization lasted—roughly from 1880 to 1914—the world economy went through a dramatic transformation very reminiscent of what is occurring today. But there are three critical factors that distinguish this globalization from its antecedent of a century ago—its financing, breadth, and speed. Understanding these distinctions is essential if we are to succeed in making the modern strain of globalization work.

The financial dimension of the current globalization is the mirror image of that which occurred 100 years ago. Back then, the great power—Britain—was a lender to the developing world, with current account surpluses that averaged about 4.5 percent of GDP over the 1880–1914 period. By contrast, today's great power—the United States—is a net borrower from the developing world, with a current account deficit that hit a record of nearly 6.5 percent of GDP in 2005. The notion of poor countries saving to support excess consumption of the rich is antithetical to everything we have been taught about the long history of economic development and globalization.

The breadth factor is also very different today than it was in the first globalization. Back then, cross-border integration on the real side of the global economy was concentrated in the exchange of tangible manufactured products. Today, as noted earlier, there is an added and important twist: The current wave of globalization does not just involve the physical exchange of tradable goods but also includes once nontradable intangibles—largely knowledge-based services of white-collar workers.

The speed factor continues to impress me as the most unique characteristic of this globalization. It is an outgrowth of a revolutionary IT-enabled connectivity that has brought the world together as never before. That's certainly true of tradable goods, where IT capabilities have revolutionized global price discovery and the logistics of supply chain management that sit at the center of global manufacturing platforms. Moreover, many knowledge-based services can now be delivered on a real-time basis through IT-enabled pipelines to desktops anywhere in the world. In 2001, such services offshoring was concentrated in the low-value functions of call centers and data processing. Today, it involves much higher-valued functionality in engineering, design, software programming, accounting, medical expertise, legal assistance, financial analysis, as well as a broad array of consulting activities. In essence, the globalization of 100 years ago was a physical integration of the global economy—with cross-border delivery of manufactured products flowing through a costly infrastructure of ships, railroads, and eventually roads. Today's globalization is both physical and knowledge-based—augmented by the new infrastructure of a ubiquitous and relatively inexpensive e-based delivery system.

The speed factor also reflects one of the most extraordinary by-products of this globalization—a dramatic acceleration in the pace of competitive leapfrogging. History tells us that the gestation of competitive prowess is normally a long and drawn-out process. It typically takes a nation considerable time to develop skill-sets, innovation, design, production, and distribution capabilities in globally competitive industries. As such, positions in the competitive sweepstakes have changed glacially over time. That is not the case in the current high-speed globalization, with modern China having rewritten the script of competitive leapfrogging. This can be seen in Figure 2.3, which illustrates the rapidly shifting market shares in global exports of two of the world's

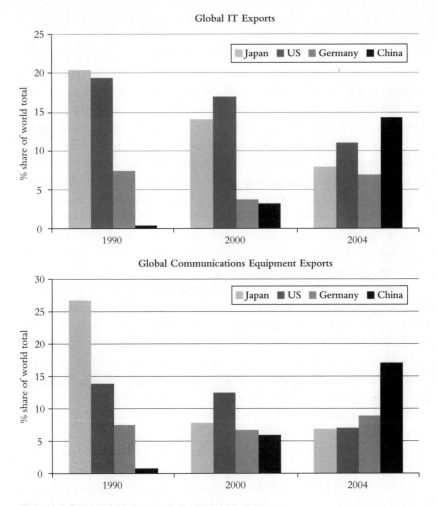

**Figure 2.3**   The Hyper-Speed of Globalization
*Source:* United Nations.

most rapidly growing product lines—information technology hardware
and communications equipment.[3] In both cases, China has come from
virtually nowhere as recently as 1990 to attain positions of global domi-
nance in 2004. The gains have been especially dramatic since 2000, when
China ranked thirteenth in global market share in IT and fifth in

3. See Catherine Mann's *Accelerating the Globalization of America,* Institute for
International Economics, Washington, D.C., 2006.

communications equipment. A scant four years later and China was first in both of these key product lines.

Of course, the flip side of China's rapid ascendancy has been the equally swift decline in global leadership of the former titans, especially Japan and the United States. For IT products, Japan went from first position in 1990 to fifth in 2004. United States market share in IT exports went from 19.3 percent in 1990 to 11.0 percent in 2004. In communications equipment, Japan also went from first in 1990 to fifth in 2004. United States market share in global communications exports was essentially cut in half over the same period—from 13.9 percent in 1990 to 7.0 percent in 2004. Interestingly enough, Germany has held its own in both of these two leading-edge export businesses; its 6.9 percent share in global IT exports in 2004 is only fractionally below that prevailing in 1990, whereas its share of global communications equipment actually inched up from 7.4 percent in 1990 to 8.9 percent in 2004.

The hyperspeed of IT-enabled globalization is not without its equally powerful implications. Rapid competitive leapfrogging is but one of the telltale footprints of this development. So, too, are new sources of disinflation. The speed factor also shows up in the form of an accelerated expansion of world trade—growing close to 9 percent per year over the 2004–2006 period versus earlier trend increases of around 5 percent over the preceding six years. As global trade now closes in on a record 30 percent share of world GDP and low-cost economies such as China and India take an ever-larger slice of tradable goods and services, this puts downward pressure on global price levels. It's no accident that as globalization has intensified, the once domestically dominated price-setting mechanism has broken down in many industrial economies; witness the sharply reduced correlations between inflation and its long-standing determinants, such as labor costs, import prices, and currencies.[4] That doesn't mean inflation can't exhibit periodic cyclical fluctuations in response to shifting conditions in domestic labor and product markets. But it does suggest that any such cyclical pressures are likely to be tempered by the structural, and broader, forces of globalization. If the current inflation scare is put in that context, its upside could be surprisingly limited—a bond-friendly outcome for financial markets.

Equally significant are social and political pressures arising from the speed factor, traceable to the job displacement and real wage compression

---

4. See the 75th *BIS Annual Report,* June 2005.

of an increasingly powerful global labor arbitrage. Globalization is spreading rapidly up the value chain to once-sheltered white-collar workers at the same time that labor compensation shares have fallen to record lows as a share of developed world incomes. The resulting "white-collar shock" has taken the political arena by storm. The United States, with its massive trade deficit, is particularly vulnerable to a political backlash against globalization. As noted earlier, in the fine tradition of scapegoating, Washington has taken the lead in blaming China for this state of affairs, with over 25 bills introduced in the U.S. Congress in the past two years that would impose trade sanctions on the Chinese. Unfortunately, the speed factor and protectionist risks go hand in hand.

In the end, the speed of global economic and financial market integration is a double-edged sword. The rapid growth of IT-enabled connectivity provides exciting new opportunities for the developing world while it instills a new sense of fear and insecurity in workers in the developed world. Yes, courtesy of IT-enabled globalization, the world is coming together more rapidly than ever. But can it avoid an increasingly perilous speed trap? That remains a critical question for world financial markets, as well as for the global economy. The answer to that question could well determine the fate of the current era of globalization.

# Hitting a BRIC Wall?

*September 25, 2006*

It's always risky to paint different pictures with the same brush. That's true of economies as well as financial assets. And it's especially true of the so-called BRICs (Brazil, Russia, India, China) construct that has taken investors by storm in recent years—driven by a fixation on the seemingly open-ended growth potential of Brazil, Russia, India, and China. The danger lies both in generalization and extrapolation. As cyclical risks to the global economy mount, the BRICs might be the first to crack.

For investors, BRICs have been especially alluring in a low-return world. In the year ending September 22, 2006, local currency returns for MSCI equities were 12.8 percent in Brazil, 38.4 percent in Russia, 51.1 percent in India, and 39.1 percent in China. For the BRICs grouping as a whole, year-over-year returns are 30.4 percent—over twice the 13.3 percent returns of equities in the developed markets. Meanwhile, emerging market debt spreads are at near-record tights, and there is widespread conviction that risk is a thing of the past for what historically has been one of the world's riskiest asset classes. On the surface, this outstanding performance seems well justified by equally impressive fundamentals. With the exception of Brazil, economic growth has been rapid and accelerating in the BRICs. And these countries have put their financial houses in order—building up massive reservoirs of foreign exchange reserves, reducing exposure to external indebtedness, turning current account deficits into surpluses, and adopting more flexible currency regimes. Who could ask for more?

Notwithstanding these impressive accomplishments, I suspect over the next couple of years the BRICs story will be one of differentiation rather than generalization. As the global economy now moves into more of a cyclical phase, each of these four developing economies and their respective financial markets is likely to be subjected to very different stresses and strains than has been the case in recent years. Although the four large BRICs economies have a number of things in common, they also have very distinct internal economic structures and financial systems, as well as different channels of external linkages to the rest of the world. In a boom, these differences can be glossed over. But as the boom fades and the tide goes out, the broad-brush approach implied by the BRICs construct may be increasingly less useful to investors and policy makers, alike.

Instead, I suspect each of the BRICs is likely to face some unique challenges in the years immediately ahead. That's especially the case for China—the gorilla of the group, which accounts for fully 58 percent of combined BRICs GDP as measured by the IMF's purchasing power parity metrics. China faces two sets of relatively immediate macro pressures—the internal challenges of cooling off an overheated investment sector and the external pressures likely to bear down on its export potential. The combination of monetary tightening and administrative edicts of the central planners may already be having an impact in arresting the internal pressures. Growth in fixed asset investment slowed to 21 percent year-over-year in August 2006—a significant downshift from the 31 percent gains in the first seven months of 2006. There has also been a marked downshift in Chinese industrial output growth from a 19.5 percent peak comparison in June 2006 to 15.7 percent in August. At the same time, the threat of a U.S.-led protectionist backlash, in conjunction with a likely post-housing bubble deceleration of U.S. consumer demand, could well arrest heretofore open-ended Chinese export growth. Over the past nine months, the world has come increasingly to view China as a perma hypergrowth story. I suspect that conclusion will be challenged in the year ahead.

The coming slowdown in the Chinese and U.S. economies is likely to have very important implications for the two commodity-intensive economies in the BRICs aggregate—Russia and Brazil (see Figure 2.4). Of these four economies, Russia is, by far, the closest to a pure commodity play. The World Bank estimates that nonagricultural commodities account for about 34 percent of Russian GDP. Moreover, energy makes up about 70 percent of Russia's MSCI-based equity market capitalization, with other materials accounting for another 8 percent. Not surprisingly, commodities dominate an export-led Russian economy. Within the BRICs aggregate, Russia's reliance on exports (31.9 percent of its GDP in 2005) is second only to China (an export share of 33.7 percent); moreover,

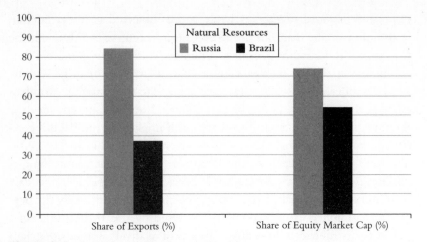

**Figure 2.4**   BRICs and the Commodity Play

*Source:* Morgan Stanley Capital International, Central Bank of Russia, Central Bank of Brazil.

about 85 percent of Russia's total exports are commodities—65 percent energy, 17 percent metals and stones, and 3 percent timber. With China accounting for about 50 percent of the total growth in global demand for energy and industrial materials over the past three years, there is no way a slowdown in the Chinese economy wouldn't take a major toll on the commodity-intensive Russian economy. Russia, which benefited the most from the global commodity boom, could well suffer the most as the commodity cycle turns.

Brazil could also feel the heat in a softer global commodity demand climate. As noted earlier, of all the BRICs, the Brazilian growth dynamic has been by far the weakest—with GDP growth averaging just 2.2 percent per annum over the 2001–2005 period. That's literally one-fourth the 8.9 percent average annual growth rate for the three other BRICs over the same interval—reason enough to question why Brazil even qualifies being lumped together with other BRIC economies. Moreover, within the BRICs universe, Brazil has the thinnest cushion of support from internal demand—private consumption actually declined at a −0.5 percent average annual rate over the 2001–2005 period. Next to India, Brazil is the BRIC that is least reliant on exports. However, in recent years, Brazil's external dependency has risen significantly, with the export share of its GDP more than doubling from 6.2 percent in 1996 to 14.9

percent in 2005. And primary products accounted for fully 34 percent of its total merchandise exports in 2005—driven not just by historically strong linkages to the United States but also by growing dependence on a commodity-short Chinese economy. Over the past five years, China and the United States have collectively accounted for fully 30 percent of Brazil's cumulative growth in merchandise exports. Needless to say, a cyclical slowdown in those two economies could prove especially problematic for a relatively sluggish Brazilian economy.

Of all the BRICs, India is best positioned to withstand the vicissitudes of the global business cycle. It has an ample cushion of internal demand—private consumption of 61 percent of GDP in 2005—and goods exports account for a relatively small share of its economy (12.9 percent of GDP). As such, it is much better insulated than the other BRICs to ward off external pressures from the United States and/or China. India's main problem at this point is more political than economic—with a reform-oriented leadership increasingly stymied by the politics of coalition management. This is less of a cyclical problem and more of a structural issue. Within the BRIC universe, however, India suffers the most from a serious twin deficit problem—an 8.7 percent consolidated government budget deficit and a 1.5 percent current account deficit. So far, these imbalances have not posed a major problem for Indian financial markets and the real economy. However, in the event emerging-market investors embark on a long-overdue shift to risk aversion, India's currency and interest-rate vulnerability cannot be minimized.

The BRICs aggregate is far from a homogeneous group of rapidly growing, large developing economies. In fact, there are sharp contrasts in the macro characteristics of its four components that could well amplify the impacts of a downturn in the global business cycle. The commodity angle is likely to be especially telling in that regard, with one of the BRICs economies dominating growth on the demand side of the equation (China) and two other members playing key roles on the supply side (Russia and Brazil). That means a China slowdown has the clear potential to drive a wedge between these two distinctly different types of BRICs economies. Moreover, lacking in domestic demand—especially private consumption—China, Russia, and Brazil don't have much to fall back on in the event of a cyclical adjustment in the global economy. Russia strikes me as especially vulnerable, while India should be least affected. The Chinese and Brazilian economies probably lie somewhere in between.

The romance of the BRICs is one of the great siren songs of globalization—four large developing economies that collectively account for 27 percent of world GDP (on a purchasing power parity basis) and over 42 percent of the world's population. If their development strategies flourish, the mathematics of extrapolation cast the BRICs in a powerful role in reshaping the world. In the nearly 40 years that I've studied economic development, it's always the "ifs" that seem to get in the way. Brazil, Russia, India, and China each face unique and tough challenges as developing economies. Lumping them together as a seemingly monolithic aggregate conveys a false sense of resilience and dynamism to the current era of globalization. It also glosses over some tough and distinctly different adjustments that could lie ahead for each of these countries in what looks to be an increasingly cyclical climate for the global economy. For investors, that raises serious questions about whether outperformance of the BRICs is about to give way to underperformance.

# Global Comeback—First Japan, Now Germany

## October 2, 2006

At the end of the 1980s, the apparent ascendancy of the Japanese and German economies was one of the more astonishing developments of the modern era. The defeated powers of World War II had literally risen from the ashes, while the victor—the United States—was widely believed to be sinking into a permanent state of decline. Yet nothing could have been further from the truth. Japan's bubble economy was soon to burst, and the combination of German reunification and European integration ushered in a long period of structural malaise in Germany. Meanwhile, America did what it does best; it reinvented itself on the back of an extraordinary renaissance of productivity-led restructuring. I suspect that this debate is about to come full circle: First Japan and now Germany—the world's second and third largest economies—are on the mend, while a savings-short, asset-dependent U.S. economy may struggle to stay the course.

In the rush to embrace the new powers of globalization—especially China and India—we risk losing sight of the old stand-bys. The United States, Japan, and Germany still collectively account for 43 percent of world GDP as measured in dollar-based market exchange rates. In purchasing power parity terms—an IMF-based metric that attempts to adjust for disparities in foreign exchange rates—the combined weighting of the three economies is 30 percent. Either way, there can be no mistaking the dominant role the powerhouses of the industrial world still play in driving the global economy and world financial markets.

Nor do I buy the view that we should forget about Germany and bury it in some amorphous pan-European aggregate. Notwithstanding the advent of the euro, the ECB, and meaningful progress on the road to panregional economic integration, individual European countries still have very distinct economic identities. A high-productivity German economy is a case in point—as is the Italian economy with its steadily declining productivity trend. The just-released Global Competitiveness survey of the World Economic Forum underscores the persistence of important intra-European disparities. German business competitiveness is ranked second only to the United States and well above that of the UK (8) and Japan (9)—to say nothing of France (16), Spain (30), and Italy (38). And Germany still accounts for the dominant share of European GDP—28 percent of the original 12-country euro area as measured on a purchasing power parity (PPP) basis. It may not be fashionable in Europhile circles, but I have no problem still looking at Germany as one of the top three powers in the global economy.

Yet in recent years, I am just as guilty as anyone—if not more so—in turning my attention as a global economist to China and India. Both of these large developing nations are in the midst of stunning transitions that could well remake the global economic order over the course of this century. And China and India are already having major impacts on the mix of world trade, as well as the global pricing of labor and commodities. But they remain far from the pinnacle of prosperity enjoyed in the rich countries of the industrial world: Per capita GDP in China is still only about 5 percent of the combined average in the United States, Japan, and Germany, and India's standard of living is less than half of China's. Compared to the tortoises of the developed world, the developing world's hares seem to be running at lightning speed. But as Aesop reminds us, slow-moving leaders with a massive head start should never be taken for granted.

The leaders aren't exactly standing still either. As I travel the world, I sense something big is brewing in the mix of industrial world economic activity. Four years ago, there were whispers of revival in Japan. They came mainly from the business sector, where a massive restructuring was gathering momentum. Anecdotal at first, these reports turned out to be an accurate portent of a stunning turnaround to come in the Japanese economy. Today, there are similar whispers in Germany. I have been to Germany twice in late September of 2006, and in meetings with a wide range of German business managers, the verdict was nearly unanimous—a powerful restructuring is now bearing fruit. Like the case in Japan a few years earlier, this could well be the start of a reawakening in the world's third-largest economy.

The official data flow has yet to capture the full extent of these turnaround stories. Japanese GDP growth has accelerated to a 2.6 percent average annual rate in the past three years (2003–2006)—double the anemic postbubble trend evident since the early 1990s. But with Japan's CPI expected to increase just 0.2 percent in 2006–2007, it is entirely premature to sound the all-clear on deflation. The German economy is turning in a very good year in 2006—a 2.1 percent increase in real GDP, or nearly double the 1.25 percent average gains of 2004–2005. However, with a large VAT tax hike looming, there is understandable concern of a sharp payback in 2007.

Trends in real GDP growth don't tell the full story. Beneath the surface, something important in Japan and Germany is stirring on the productivity front—for my money, the most important arbiter of sustainable economic progress in any nation. Japanese productivity growth averaged 2.1 percent over the 2003–2005 period—nearly double the 1.2 percent trend over the 1995 to 2002 interval. There has also been a pickup—albeit more recent—in German productivity; output per worker expanded at a 1.7 percent average annual pace in the five quarters ending mid-2006— more than double the anemic 0.7 percent trend from 1998 to 2004. The improvements in Japanese and German productivity pale in comparison to America's productivity renaissance—a 2.8 percent average annual increase over the 1996 to 2005 period, or a doubling of the anemic 1.4 percent trend recorded over the 22-year 1974–1995 interval. But they may be important first steps in the right direction.

Undoubtedly, a portion of the recent improved productivity growth in both Japan and Germany appears traceable to a cyclical, or transitory, acceleration in economic activity. Some of that cyclical impetus will be unwound if, in fact, aggregate economic growth slows in both economies in 2007. Yet this need not be construed as a serious setback. In studying corporate restructuring for now close to 20 years, my experience tells me that once the business sector gets religion in facing up to competitive challenges, cyclical pressures in operating conditions invariably lead to an intensification of cost cutting and other forms of restructuring. The United States is a case in point: Corporate restructuring began in earnest in the first half of the 1980s, but it wasn't until the mild recession of the early 1990s that those efforts intensified and finally bore fruit in the form of a powerful and sustained productivity revival beginning in the mid-1990s.

I think there is a good chance for a similar outcome to German restructuring in 2007. I suspect Corporate Germany will rise to the occasion of a slowdown in 2006 and intensify its cost-cutting efforts in such a climate. Having spoken with a broad cross-section of focused and very determined German business managers over the past few weeks, I am encouraged that the micro anecdotes match up well with the macro imperatives outlined earlier. I also believe that the improved flexibility of still-rigid German labor markets, together with a long-overdue increase in the IT share of corporate Germany's capital stock, will provide important tailwinds to German productivity in a tougher cyclical climate.

And so the story comes full circle. Both Japan and Germany currently seem to be where the United States was in the early 1990s—upping the ante on corporate restructuring, thereby sowing the seeds of an early-stage productivity revival. At the same time, the United States may well have maxed out on its restructuring and productivity story. Capital deepening associated with America's transformation to an IT-enabled production platform is well advanced, and the heavy lifting on corporate cost cutting may be more in the past than in the future. And, of course, the United States, with its massive current account deficit, faces its own set of tough cyclical challenges—especially as savings-short consumers now come to grips with the bursting of America's last asset bubble. There is a certain sense of *déjà vu* in all of this, but this time with a very different twist: America is widely thought to be at the top of its game as the global economic hegemony, while Japan and Germany have long been written off as has-beens. Just as the tables were turned a mere 15 years ago, a similar about-face could well be in the offing in the years ahead.

A repositioning of the Big Three economies has potentially important implications for global rebalancing. A postbubble retrenchment of the American consumer should undoubtedly provide cyclical relief to the United States current account deficit. But the sustainability of any such improvement depends on whether the rest of the world—in this case, Japan and Germany—can convert productivity gains into consumer-led growth dynamics. The jury remains out on that critical count. Without progress on labor market reforms and retirement security, households in Japan and Germany may remain predisposed toward saving. But if those problems can successfully be tackled and non-U.S. consumption support starts to kick in, the outcome could be a huge plus for global rebalancing.

There are many moving parts in a $46 trillion global economy. But an unbalanced world has suffered as the second and third largest economies have sputtered over the past 15 years. Those days could now be over. First, it was Japan—now it is Germany that appears to be on the mend. And this time, unlike the false promises of the late 1980s, there could well be staying power to these important global comeback stories. If only we could say the same for savings-short America.

*Postscript: The global recession of 2008–2009 has hit Japan and Germany extremely hard. Real GDP could plunge by as much as 6 percent in both economies in 2009. As export-led economies, both Japan and Germany have suffered very much from a cyclical collapse in global demand. The analysis above underscores the potential for productivity-led structural improvements in the years ahead. The cyclical dust will have to settle first before this thesis can be tested.*

# Labor versus Capital

## October 23, 2006

W hat do the world's three largest economies have in common? The answer underscores one of the key tensions of globalization—unrelenting pressure on labor income. The corollary of that phenomenon is equally revealing—ever-rising returns to the owners of capital. For a global economy in the midst of its strongest four-year boom since the early 1970s, this tug-of-war between labor and capital is an increasingly serious source of disequilibrium. It has important economic, social, and political implications—all of which could complicate the coming global rebalancing.

A recent trip to Japan was the clincher. As I found in my travels to Germany in September of 2006, and as has been evident in the United States throughout the current upturn, Japanese labor income remains under extraordinary downward pressure. There is no way this is a coincidence. In all three economies, unemployment has been declining in recent years—a 27 percent drop in the U.S. jobless rate since mid-2003, a 21 percent decline in Japan since early 2003, and a 15 percent fall in the German unemployment rate since mid 2004. Yet in none of the three economies has a cyclical tightening in labor markets resulted in a meaningful increase in real wages and/or the labor share of national income. As of September 2006, fully 57 months into the current cyclical upturn, U.S. private sector compensation is still tracking nearly $400 billion (in real terms) below the average trajectory of the past four business cycles. After a glimmer of revival in early 2005, real-wage stagnation is once again evident in Japan. Nor are there any signs of a meaningful upturn in German real wages; to the contrary, inflation-adjusted compensation per worker in the overall business sector has actually declined in four of the past five years (2001–2006).

The case of Europe merits special comment. We continue to cling to the impression that European workers are different—that sheltered by a deeply entrenched social contract, they enjoy great success in getting more than their fair share of the pie. That depiction is no longer accurate. After having spiked up dramatically in the aftermath of German reunification, pan-European real compensation per employee has been basically unchanged since 2001. Nor is this likely to change as an increasingly tight European labor market now approaches its "speed limit." The structural forces are simply far too powerful—namely, globalization, a shift to part-time and temporary employment, and the diminished power of labor unions. The coming wage round in Germany will undoubtedly test this view, but there is little chance for a major breakout. Far from marching to their own beat, German and other European workers are in the same shape as those elsewhere in the industrial world—suffering from the unrelenting pressures of relatively stagnant real wages.

At work are the increasingly powerful forces of globalization—namely, an intensification of cross-border competition that has given rise to an extraordinary productivity push in the high-wage industrial world. The good news, as noted earlier, is that the productivity payback is now at hand. The United States has recorded a decade of 2.8 percent productivity growth—doubling the sluggish 1.4 percent gains recorded from 1974 to 1995. Japanese productivity growth has averaged 2.1 percent over the past three years (2003–2006), nearly double the 1.2 percent trend from 1995 to 2002. Even German productivity has been on the rise—expanding at a 1.7 percent annual rate over the past five quarters, more than double the anemic 0.7 percent trend over the 1998 to 2004 period.

The bad news is that these breakthroughs on the productivity front have not resulted in any meaningful improvement in labor's share of the pie. Therein lies the puzzle: Economics teaches us that real wages ultimately track productivity growth—that workers are rewarded in accordance with their marginal product. Yet that has not been the case in the high-wage economies of the industrial world in recent years. By our estimates, the real compensation share of national income for the so-called G-7 plus (the United States, Japan, the 12-country euro-zone, the UK, and Canada) fell from 56 percent in 2001 to what appears to be a record low of 53.7 percent in 2006. (*Note:* Due to a lack of harmonized euro-zone data prior to 1996, the compensation share cannot be extended before that period; however, based on BIS [Bank for International Settlements] calculations, the slightly narrower construct of the wage share of G-10 national income is currently lower than at any point since 1975).

Of course, it is important to distinguish between the transitory results of the business cycle and the structural interplay between underlying trends in productivity and real wages. It may well be that productivity strategies are dominated by cost cutting; with labor the largest slice of business production expenses, such tactics lead to constant pressure on the compensation share of national income. It may also be that the improvements in labor market conditions are so recent—especially in Japan and Germany—that the real wage lags simply haven't had time to kick in. However, the U.S. experience draws that latter hope into serious question. Fully 10 years into a spectacular productivity revival, real wages remain nearly stagnant and the labor share of U.S. national income continues to move lower. If the flexible American worker can't do it, why should we presume that others in the industrial world would be any more fortunate?

This takes us to what could well be the biggest challenge in this era of globalization—the ability of the high-wage developed world to convert productivity gains into increases in the labor share of national income. In a recent paper, Richard Freeman of Harvard, and long one of the world's most prominent labor economists, underscores the very tough uphill battle that high-wage workers in the rich countries face in this era of globalization.[5] By his calculation, the ascendancy of China, India, and the former Soviet Union has added about 1.5 billion new workers to the global economy, essentially equaling the workforce existing elsewhere in the world. With global trade and production increasingly shifting into the low-wage developing and transitional economies, what I have called the "global labor arbitrage" puts inexorable pressure on real wages in the high-wage industrial world. Some would argue that the worst of the arbitrage is over, as wage inflation now takes off in China and India. Don't count on it. Even after five years of double-digit wage inflation in China, hourly compensation for Chinese manufacturing workers remains at only 3 percent of levels prevailing in the major industrial economies.

While labor gets squeezed, the owners of capital have enjoyed far more flexibility in this climate. As noted earlier, facing extraordinary competitive pressures, corporations have redoubled their efforts on the productivity front. And those efforts have indeed borne fruit for over a decade in the United States and more recently in Japan in Germany. The fruits of those efforts show up in the form of surging corporate profitability

---

5. See his June 2006 paper, "Labor Market Imbalances: Shortages, or Surpluses, or Fish Stories?"

and increased share prices—with commensurate gains accruing to those workers/households that are fortunate enough to hold shares. America, with its growing incidence of share ownership has led the charge in that respect. But this has hardly been a panacea for most U.S. workers. Federal Reserve survey data show that 63 percent of families in the upper decile of the wealth-distribution owned stocks in 2004—nearly four times the average 19 percent ownership share in the remaining 90 percent of the wealth distribution. Moreover, median equity holdings amounted to $110,000 per household in the same upper decile, fully 13 times average holdings of $8,350 in the remainder of the wealth distribution.[6]

Don't get me wrong—this is not intended to be a replay of my ill-fated "worker backlash" call of the early 1990s, when I mistakenly believed that labor would exercise its power and demand a larger slice of the pie. Today, courtesy of a near doubling of the world's work force and an increasingly potent global labor arbitrage, high-wage workers in the industrial world are all but powerless to act. However, their elected representatives are not. Witness the recent surge of protectionist sentiment, especially in the United States but also in Europe. Nor do I suspect this political backlash to globalization will fade in the aftermath of the upcoming midterm election in the United States—especially, as seems likely, the Democrats garner sizable gains in the Congress. Pressures on high-wage workers in the industrial world are likely to endure for years to come, irrespective, or perhaps because of, the push for higher productivity growth. As a result, the angst of labor should remain high on the political agenda for the foreseeable future.

Contrary, to orthodox win-win theory, globalization is a highly asymmetrical phenomenon. Initially, it creates far more producers than consumers. It also results in extraordinary imbalances between nations with current account deficits and surpluses, and it has led to a widening disparity of the returns between labor and capital. Does this mean that globalization is nearing a breaking point? Hopefully not, but it does mean that the most destabilizing phase of this mega-trend could well be close at hand. As seen through surging corporate profitability, the returns to capital have never been greater. Meanwhile the shares of labor income have never been lower. As day follows night, the pendulum will swing the other way, and so will the balance between real wages and business profitability. It's just a question of when—and under what circumstances.

---

6. See "Recent Changes in US Family Finances: Evidence from the 2001 and 2004 Survey of Consumer Finances," published in the *Federal Reserve Bulletin*, 2006.

# Global Lessons

## December 8, 2006

Since late October 2006, I have circled the globe so many times, my body has lost track of time zones. My recent travels have taken me to Japan, South Africa, the Middle East, Singapore, Hong Kong, China, and Australia. Extensive meetings with business executives, investors, policy makers, and senior government officials in all of these countries cast the global debate in a very different light. Several lessons from these travels strike me as most important:

My recent trips to the Middle East have completely changed my perceptions of this region's global role. In less than 35 years, the oil-producing states in the Gulf have gone from being exporters to users of capital. As a consequence, the ramifications of the current oil shock are very different from those of the past. Massive internal development programs—highlighted by spectacular new urban centers in Dubai, Doha, and Bahrain—are examples of how capital is now being put to work at home investing in tangible assets rather than recycled back into dollar-based financial assets. IMF estimates put current account surpluses of the Middle East at around $300 billion per year in 2006–2007—more than double the average $140 billion external balances of 2004–2005. The region's newfound penchant for internal absorption suggests this surge in surplus saving could well have profound consequences for the global economy and world financial markets.

My first trip to South Africa was a real eye-opener. Johannesburg and Cape Town had prosperity written all over them, but, sadly, the rest of this country did not. With the national unemployment rate still in excess of 25 percent, matters of job and income security entered into most of the discussions I had on this leg of my travels. What surprised me the most was the anti-China sentiment I encountered in South Africa. China, of course, has been nurturing a rapidly expanding relationship with Africa in recent years—resulting in a ten-fold increase in cross-border trade over the past decade. China has become an important source of capital and infrastructure for the region, and Africa offers much in the way of natural resources that China so desperately needs. Yet the backlash was focused on the job front—with many South Africans quick to blame low-cost Chinese competition for the decimation of its once-thriving textile industry. In this key respect, the anti-China backlash I encountered in Africa was no different from that which is evident elsewhere in the world these days. What surprised me was that I had thought the resource-for-capital compact between Africa and China might temper that friction. A similar conclusion could be drawn from all the fanfare over the China-Africa summit held in November of 2006 in Beijing—an unprecedented gathering that included leaders from over 40 African countries. Beneath the surface, however, there can be no mistaking the undercurrent of anti-China sentiment evident in job-short South Africa.

In Australia, environmental issues came up at literally every meeting. Most concede that their unique drought-affected circumstances—the culmination of six of the driest years on record—have undoubtedly played a key role in bringing this issue to a head. But maybe that's precisely the point for the rest of us. With concerns over a fragile environment mounting, it doesn't take much for national sentiment to swing. One of the more savvy Australians I met with forcefully argued, "A year ago, post-Katrina America was just one storm away from a similar tipping point." Meanwhile, former U.S. Vice President Al Gore was well received in Australia this September (2006), and his movie on global warming, *An Inconvenient Truth*, apparently struck a very receptive chord. At the same time, there was much debate over the UK's recent contribution to this debate—the *Stern Review*, which dangled the tantalizing, yet highly contentious possibility that if the world moved now, it could avoid a looming environmental catastrophe by investing a mere 1 percent of global GDP annually in measures aimed at reducing greenhouse gas emissions.[7] As I look back on my discussions with global leaders in late October 2006, Australia was hardly alone in voicing concerns over climate change. Similar worries were evident in China, elsewhere in Asia, and in Africa. Because of the country's extreme circumstances, the Aussie voices may have been louder, but they are very much in line with a rising tide of

---

7. See Nicholas Stern, *The Economics of Climate Change: The Stern Review*. Cambridge: Cambridge University Press, 2007.

global concern over the perils of climate change. Sadly, America remains on the outside looking in—at least for now.

Asia's lessons are equally intriguing. It is always risky to paint such a diverse region with one brush, but there are some common threads that emerge from extensive visits to Japan, China, Singapore, and Hong Kong. First, Asia doesn't buy the myth perpetrated in the West that a new generation of consumers is taking the region by storm.[8] Developing Asia knows full well that its export share has risen from around 20 percent to nearly 40 percent of panregional GDP over the past 20 years whereas its private consumption share has fallen from 70 percent to less than 50 percent over the past 30 years. The need for a pro-consumption rebalancing is not only evident in Developing Asia but is also recognized to be of great importance in Japan, where the consumer has largely been missing in action from an otherwise impressive recovery. Second, Asia is in denial over the possibility of a growth accident in the United States. That would obviously deal a serious blow to the Chinese export machine—as well as to the Japans, Koreas, and Taiwans that drive Asia's increasingly China-centric supply chain, which provides many of the components that go into goods that eventually get shipped to America. Finally, Asia ex-Japan is blinded by a very powerful liquidity cycle—the surging flows of low-cost capital that have priced most of the risk out of its stock and bond markets. I remember well the haunting words I heard from a seasoned investor in Hong Kong in late November of 2006, "It hasn't felt this good since 1997."

Notwithstanding the jet-lag and sleep deprivation, there's nothing like the sheer exhilaration of peering into the inner sanctum of globalization. The more I travel the world, the less convinced I am that our cavalier win-win theories do this megatrend justice. Nor do I believe that we should measure progress on the road to globalization by fixating on the quantitative metrics of surging cross-border flows of trade, capital, and information. In the end, globalization is more about the assimilation of shared values of a still very diverse world. A successful globalization requires a global coping mechanism, namely, a world that learns how to resolve the tensions that invariably arise between nations. A failed globalization—precisely what happened in the early twentieth century—is all about a world that succumbs to geopolitical tensions, trade protectionism, and economic and financial instability.

---

8. See, for example, the cover story and leader in the October 19, 2006 issue of *The Economist*. "America drops, Asia shops."

In my multiple spins around the world in the fall of 2006, I was struck by both the successes and failures of the current strain of globalization. But I was also taken with the persistence of localization—nations that remain more caught up in self-interest rather than in the collective benefits of an integrated global economy and world financial markets. It's easy to talk the talk of globalization. It's much harder to walk the walk. That's the lesson that hit me the hardest.

# From Globalization to Localization

*December 14, 2006*

On one level, there seems to be no stopping the powerful forces of globalization. Not only has the world just completed four years of the strongest global growth since the early 1970s, but in 2006, cross-border trade as a share of world GDP pierced the 30 percent threshold for the first time ever—almost three times the portion prevailing during the last global boom over 30 years ago. There can be no greater testament to the stunning successes of globalization!

On another level, however, there are increasingly disquieting signs. That's because of a striking asymmetry in the benefits of globalization. While living standards have improved in many segments of the developing world, a new set of pressures is bearing down on the rich countries of the developed world. Most notably, an extraordinary squeeze on labor incomes has occurred in the industrial world—an outcome that challenges the fundamental premises of the win-win models of globalization. Ricardian comparative advantage tells us that the first win goes to low-wage workers in developing economies who enter the global economy, initially through their involvement in export production and eventually as a new class of consumers. The second win is presumed to benefit the rich nations of the developed world—where consumers can expand their standard of living by buying low-cost, high-quality goods from poor countries and where workers can ultimately gain from being involved in the production of more sophisticated products exported to increasingly prosperous developing economies.

It is a great theory, but it's not working as advertised. The first win is hard to dispute. China has led the way, more than quadrupling its per capita GDP since the early 1990s. Other developing countries have lagged the

Chinese experience but have still made considerable progress in boosting living standards. India's standard of living, for example, has more than doubled during the past 15 years. Moreover, according to IMF statistics, per capita GDP in Eastern and Central Europe is likely to have expanded at a 3.6 percent average annual rate in the decade ending 2007—a dramatic acceleration from the 0.3 percent pace of the prior 10-year period. In the Middle East, a 2.7 percent trend in the growth of per capita output in the decade ending 2007 would be nearly double the 1.5 percent pace of the previous 10 years. Developing Asia stands out from the rest of the pack, with a 6.2 percent average annual increase in per capita GDP estimated over the 1998–2007 period—little changed from the equally vigorous 6.3 percent trend over the 1988–1997 interval. Moreover, the first win hasn't just gone to labor. Four years of extraordinary returns for emerging market stocks and bonds underscore impressive returns to capital, as well.

The problem lies with the second win—the supposed benefits accruing to the rich countries of the developed world. That's where the going has gotten especially tough. In recent years, the benefits of the second win have accrued primarily to the owners of capital at the expense of the providers of labor. At work is a powerful asymmetry in the impacts of globalization and global competition on the world's major industrial economies, namely, record highs in the returns accruing to capital and record lows in the rewards going to labor (see Figure 2.5). The global

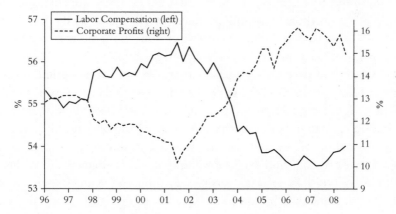

**Figure 2.5**  The Battle Between Capital and Labor (Shares of National Income: G7+Economies)

*Note:* G7+ includes the US, Japan, EMU, UK, and Canada.

*Source:* National Sources, Morgan Stanley Research.

labor arbitrage has put unrelenting pressure on employment and real wages in the high-cost developed world—resulting in a compression of the labor income share down to a record low of 53.7 percent of industrial world national income in mid-2006. With labor costs easily accounting for the largest portion of business expenses, this has proved to be a veritable bonanza for the return to capital—pushing the profits share of national income in the major countries of the industrial world to historical highs of 15.6 percent in the second quarter of 2006.

This asymmetry in the second win is not without very important consequences. In days of yore—when labor and its organized unions actually had bargaining power—the current squeeze on labor income in the developed world would have undoubtedly resulted in some form of a "worker backlash." In today's increasingly globalized world, however, workers have no such power. But their elected political representatives most certainly do. And there can be no mistaking the important shift that has recently occurred in the political alignment of the industrial world—with the voting majority shifting from the procapital right to the prolabor left. Not only is that the case in the United States, but such a tendency is also evident in Germany, France, Italy, Spain, Japan, and possibly even Australia.

The political response in the United States bears special mention. Most importantly, it has not arisen out of thin air—there are important macroanalytic reasons behind this backlash. Unlike Europe and Japan, where relatively stagnant real wages have matched up quite closely with weak or declining productivity, in the United States, real compensation has been going nowhere in a rising productivity climate. Over the five-year, 2001–2005 period, real compensation per hour in the nonfarm business sector expanded at just a 1.4 percent average annual rate—less than half the 3.1 percent pace of trend productivity over this same period. While macro teaches us that, over time, workers are rewarded in accordance with their marginal product, that most assuredly has not been the case during America's newfound productivity renaissance. Moreover, recent research has pointed up the inequity of the so-called productivity dividend that has accrued to U.S. workers. According to Ian Dew-Becker and Robert Gordon of Northwestern University, only those in the top 10 percent of the U.S. income distribution have experienced growth in labor income equal to or above aggregate productivity growth since 1997.[9]

---

9. See "Where Did the Productivity Growth Go," *Brookings Papers on Economic Activity*, 2005.

These issues were not lost in the recent midterm 2006 elections in the United States. Aside from the obvious referendum on Iraq, exit polls suggest that the squeeze on labor income and its distributional ramifications were uppermost in the minds of American voters. And, now, a Democratic Congress is about to find itself center stage in the battle between capital and labor. The old Congress was quite transparent about where it is headed in this regard—having introduced some 27 separate pieces of legislation since early 2005 that would impose some type of punitive actions on trade with China. The new Congress could go further—not just on the trade-frictions front but also in embracing additional elements of a prolabor agenda. In fact, newly elected Democratic leaders already have promised immediate passage of the first increase in the minimum wage in 10 years. In my view, these are just the early warning signs of a U.S. Congress that is likely to be far more sympathetic to the plight of labor than it was in the past.

Nor is America alone in tilting to the prolabor left. In France, the ascendancy of Ségolène Royal offers a modern-day mix of prolabor politics with a protectionist bias. Italy's Prodi is also prolabor, and in Spain, Zapatero is certainly more sympathetic to the plight of labor than Aznar was. In Germany, Merkel has tilted increasingly toward labor after she nearly lost the election running on a pro-market reform agenda. The new Abe government in Japan has teamed up with the center right in support of the "second chance society"—attempting to make certain that the victims in the rough and tumble arena of global competition are given the opportunity to come back. And in Australia, Kevin Rudd, the newly anointed opposition leader, seems set to center his platform on the struggle of the average worker.

This prolabor political tilt is as much an outgrowth of the hyper-speed of IT-enabled globalization as it is traceable to the competitive pressures bearing down on workers in both manufacturing and services. With a sense of economic insecurity moving rapidly up the occupational hierarchy—from software programmers and engineers to medical and legal professionals—a palpable sense of shock is spreading rapidly into the white-collar knowledge-worker occupations that have long been shielded from economic adversity. This has resulted in a serious loss of confidence in the second win of globalization—in effect, shattering the illusion that trade liberalization would be the rising tide that lifts all boats. In response, the pendulum has swung from the theoretical promises of globalization to the self-interest of individual countries—in essence, a localization.

I fully realize it is heresy to challenge the greatest megatrend of our lifetime. So let me state categorically that I am not heralding the demise of globalization. What I suspect is that a partial backtracking is probably now at hand, as a leftward tilt of the body politic in the industrial world voices a strong protest over the extraordinary disparity that has opened up between the returns to capital and the rewards of labor. The extent of any backtracking is a verdict that lies in the hands of the politicians— specifically, how far they are willing to go in legislating efforts to narrow this disparity. History does not treat the record of such political intervention all that well. Unfortunately, that doesn't mean opportunistic politicians will resist the temptations to try.

An era of localization will undoubtedly have some very different characteristics from those of the recent past. The most obvious—wages could go up and corporate profits could come under pressure. But it also seems reasonable to expect prolabor politicians to direct regulatory scrutiny at excess returns on capital, focusing, in particular, on the perceptions of excess returns in financial markets (i.e., hedge funds and private equity) as well as on the inequities of rewards at the upper end of the income distribution (i.e., tax cuts for wealthy citizens and the excesses of executive compensation). Moreover, localization taken to its extreme could also spell heightened risks of protectionism, especially if the global economy slows and unemployment starts to rise in 2007, as seems likely. Under those circumstances, localization could ultimately give rise to accelerating inflation, higher interest rates, greater volatility in financial markets, and a potentially vicious unwinding of an overextended credit cycle. And, of course, the protectionist ramifications of localization could prove equally challenging for the beneficiaries of globalization's first win— dynamic new companies in the developing world and the employment growth they generate.

Don't confuse prognosis with advocacy. Many of these potential developments, especially a drift toward protectionism, are without any redeeming merit, in my view. But this is what happens in free-market systems when trends go to extremes. An era of localization will undoubtedly have more frictions than the unfettered strain of capitalism and globalization that has been so dominant over the past decade. The big question, in my mind, pertains mainly to degree: How far will the pendulum swing from globalization to localization? The answer rests with the body politic. The repercussions lie in economies and financial markets.

# Unprepared for Globalization
*February 2, 2007*

There was a dramatic moment at the 2007 World Economic Forum in Davos that I will long remember. It came during one of the sessions on the global economic outlook, when concerns were being raised about the possibility of a Washington-led political backlash against globalization—a conclusion that I have long warned of. Montek Singh Ahluwalia, Deputy Chairman of India's Planning Commission, was quick to respond along the lines of, "Don't blame us. For years, you in the developed world demanded that we in the developing world get our act together, open up, and reform. And now that we have and the payback is at hand, you don't like it."

I have had the pleasure of getting to know Mr. Ahluwalia over the years and have found him to be deep thinking and most engaging, with a razor-sharp analytical mind. His point is a very important one; it challenges one of the great contradictions of the globalization debate. Yet it begs the question of why: Why is the developed world pushing back so hard against the very process of global integration it has so long espoused? Granted, motives are always open to subjective interpretation. But I suspect that Montek's complaint also touches on one of the most important, but overlooked issues in the current global debate—that the rich countries of the developed world are simply unprepared for the stunning successes of an IT-enabled globalization. Lacking in preparation, the developed world is now on the defensive—and, unfortunately, ripe for a politically driven backlash.

As I have stressed in my own work, a key element in all this is speed (see "Global Speed Trap," p. 127–131). Unlike the slowly evolving pace of the globalization of a century ago, the current strain is unfolding at lightning speed. A major difference is the technology of the distribution system. In Globalization I, it took ships, rail, and eventually motor

vehicles to facilitate the cross-border exchange and delivery of manufactured goods. It also required the time-intensive construction of ports,
rail systems, and roads. Globalization II built on this earlier infrastructure
but then added a new twist of its own—the revolutionary connectivity
of the rapidly growing Internet. Where it took at least 30 years for the
cross-border network to reach a critical mass in the first globalization,
this time around it all came together in less than a decade.

There is, of course, nothing new about the accelerated rate of technology absorption that underpins both globalizations. Over time, each major
wave of innovation has hit its critical mass of penetration considerably
faster than the wave that preceded it. For example, it took 38 years for
radio to reach 50 million U.S. households; similar levels of penetration
for television were hit in 13 years, for cable–TV in 10 years, and for the
Internet in only 5 years.[10] While this is the norm in the long continuum
of technological breakthroughs, it seems to have played an especially critical role in the current build-up of tensions in the global economy. It has
pushed this globalization ahead at hyperspeed—in sharp contrast with
the glacial pace of its antecedent a century earlier.

Nor can there be any doubt of the unusual breadth of the current
globalization. Unlike the first episode, which was all about the cross-
border exchange of tradable manufactured goods, the IT-enabled second
globalization opens up a similar possibility for many once nontradable
services. This was not supposed to happen, according to the two-sector
Ricardian models of economic theory. For high-wage economies, it was
fine to trade away market share in manufactured products. Displaced
workers could then seek refuge in nontradable services—incurring
steep retraining and other transition costs but eventually drawing security from performing knowledge-intensive tasks (such as software programming, engineering, medical advice, and consulting) that played to
the natural endowment of their unique skill-sets. The Internet all but
obliterated that sense of job security in an increasingly knowledge-based
industrial world. With the click of a mouse, the output of a wide range
of knowledge workers residing in low-wage developing countries can
now be exported to desktops on a real-time basis from anywhere in the
world. This has led to an unprecedented wave of white-collar shock, as

10. See *The Internet Report* by Mary Meeker and Chris DuPuy, Morgan Stanley
Research, December 1995.

once sheltered knowledge workers in the rich countries face the tough pressures of international competition for the first time ever.

Both the speed and breadth of this globalization has caught the developed world by surprise. While the world's leading economies have long been preaching the gospel of trade liberalization and international opportunities, they have done little to prepare for the sudden arrival of new competitive threats. But the hyperspeed of an IT-enabled globalization should not be seen as an excuse. In many respects, the rich countries of the developed world took job and income security for granted—failing or unwilling to see the challenge that was rapidly building halfway around the world. That's especially the case on the human capital side of the equation—the essence of competitive advantage in the Information Age. As can be seen in Figure 2.6, back in the pre-Internet days of the early 1990s, the United States, Europe, and Japan were far in the lead in turning out newly minted science and engineering graduates from their colleges and universities. A decade later, China and India had surged to the lead—at precisely the time when IT-enabled connectivity gave these low-wage knowledge workers the opportunity to compete head-on with their high-wage counterparts in the developed world. Lagging educational reform in the industrial world only compounded the problem. Workers in ever-complacent developed economies were, in effect, blindsided by the new globalization.

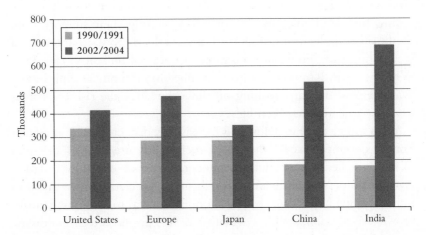

**Figure 2.6**   Global Supply of University Graduates in Science and Engineering
*Note:* Includes first university degrees in S&E. Data is for the latest year available (i.e., 2002 to 2004).

*Source:* U.S. National Science Foundation, NASSCOM, Morgan Stanley Research.

The United States was even more lackadaisical in its approach to dealing with intensified international competition. Drawing down its income-based savings rate to record lows—a net national savings rate that averaged just 0.7 percent of national income over the 2003–2005 period—America became a huge importer of surplus saving from abroad, and had no choice other than to run massive current-account and trade deficits to attract that capital. This bias toward ever-widening trade deficits left the U.S. exposed to the comparative advantage of the main beneficiary of the new globalization—China. Unprepared on two counts—undersaving and underinvesting in human capital—America is feeling the heat from the pressures of international competition as never before.

Unfortunately, all this was a lethal combination—a lack of preparation by the developed world, rapid development in the emerging economies, and a new IT-enabled cross-border connectivity. Out of this lethal combination, a new fear has arisen—job and income security in the developed world. Add in widening disparities in the income distribution and record returns to the owners of capital, the fear becomes all the more palpable for middle-class workers in industrial economies. This angst has now sparked an important shift in the political winds of the rich countries, with the pendulum of power now swinging from the procapital Right to the prolabor Left in the United States, France, Germany, Italy, Spain, Japan, and Australia. Reacting to this shifting sentiment, politicians are now upping the ante on protectionist threats against the developing world—in effect, shifting their support from the broad considerations of globalization to the narrow self-interests of localization (see "From Globalization to Localization" on p. 150–154). With the Doha Round of global trade liberalization on life support and Washington-led China-bashing on the ascendancy, the risk of protectionism can hardly be taken lightly.

What can be done to defuse this increasingly dangerous state of affairs? For the developed world, there is an increasingly urgent need to equip its highly skilled workers with the modern-day tools of the Information Age. The imperatives of education reform and accelerated investment in human capital have never seemed more essential as tools of competitive prowess. In addition, the United States needs to get its act together on the saving front—eliminating what risks becoming an organic bias toward chronic and ever-contentious trade deficits. The developing world, for its part, needs to offer assurances that it is respectful of the core competencies of a new globalization—namely, intellectual property rights.

Clamping down aggressively on the widespread piracy of intellectual property could go a long way in defusing global tensions.

Montek Singh Ahluwalia has an important point—it didn't have to be this way. Globalization is a two-way street. The poor countries of the developing world are finally making extraordinary progress in lifting their standard of living and offering opportunity for hundreds of millions of people to escape the ravages of poverty. It has taken courage and determination on the part of the developing world to push ahead on reforms and open itself to the rest of the world. And yet just when the poor countries begin to reap the benefits of this strategy, an unprepared developed world turns the tables and threatens to put up new walls of its own. Such hypocrisy could be the ultimate tragedy of this globalization. Both rich and poor countries, alike, need to own up to the shared responsibilities of defusing these tensions—before it's too late.

# The Currency Foil

*February 9, 2007*

A ll eyes are on currencies on the eve of another G-7 meeting of
finance ministers and central bankers. Focus on the Chinese renminbi remains intense from the American side, and the Europeans
are increasingly concerned about the weakness of the Japanese yen. In
my view, these concerns are misplaced. In a world where the main misalignments are on the saving-investment axis, currency solutions are not
the remedy. This timeworn fixation on foreign exchange markets detracts
from the heavy lifting of structural change that is required to meet the
competitive challenges of globalization head-on.

The politicization of the Chinese currency issue has been a hallmark
of the US-China debate of the past several years. The logic is straightfor-
ward: Most U.S. workers are feeling enormous pressures about job and
income security—labor's share of national income is back to historical
lows and the gap between the rich and everyone else is getting larger and
larger. Meanwhile, the United States is now suffering from the mother of
all trade deficits—an external imbalance that hit about 7 percent of GDP
in 2006. The key presumptive link in this equation is that workers and
their elected representatives have concluded that this ever-widening trade
deficit is the source of labor's deepening sense of angst. The smoking gun
comes in the form of a Chinese bilateral deficit that now accounts for 29
percent of America's total multilateral trade gap—easily the largest portion of the U.S. external shortfall. Washington views China as the culprit
to all that ails the American worker. It then follows that an adjustment of
an undervalued renminbi is the fix that can assuage the pain.

Europe's yen complaint is of a different ilk. Currently at 157 in
February 2007, the euro-yen cross rate has appreciated dramatically in
recent years—now up over 75 percent from the all-time low in October
2000 to the strongest level in eight and a half years. For a European

economy that is still lacking in vigorous support from internal demand—
especially private consumption—any currency-related pressures on external demand must be viewed with great concern. That's especially the case
with a still high—albeit declining—pan-regional unemployment rate of
7.6 percent and a persistence of relatively stagnant real wages. However,
unlike the U.S. with its massive trade deficit, Europe's overall external
position is nearly in balance—a current account deficit of around −0.3
percent of GDP in 2006–2007. But here's the rub for Europe: Despite a
nice cyclical pop of 2.7 percent real GDP growth in 2006, Europe still
views itself as a 2 to 2.25 percent grower—in essence, lacking the vigor
to provide much further relief for pressures bearing down on labor. For
such a sluggishly growing European economy, any currency-related pressures on its external sources of growth are a much bigger deal than is the
case for the United States, which enjoys much more solid support from
internal consumption. The recent weakness of the yen is perceived as a
worrisome threat in that context.

The question for G-7 policy makers is whether a currency fix—namely,
pushing for a stronger RMB and yen—is in the world's best interest.
This is an interesting intellectual debate but probably misses the subtext
of the real hand-wringing—whether currency realignments will temper
the domestic political concerns now evident in the United States and
Europe. The answer, in my view, is an unequivocal "No." In the case of the
United States, the outsize bilateral imbalance is a symptom of a much bigger problem—an unprecedented shortfall of domestic saving that drove
the net national saving rate to historical lows of just 1 percent over the
three-year 2004–2007 period. For an economy like that of the United
States, where the political constituency for rapid economic growth is very
powerful, savings shortfalls create an inherent bias toward chronic trade
deficits. America is left with no choice other than to import surplus saving
from abroad in order to fuel its appetite for growth. The only way to get
that foreign capital is to run large current account and trade deficits. The
distribution of those deficits then follows along the lines of comparative
advantage. China fits all too nicely into that equation—both as a supplier
of surplus saving and as a source of low-cost, increasingly high-quality
goods. There is little reason to believe that a stronger RMB will force
Americans to save more. The best Washington can hope for if it relies on
such a remedy is to shift the China piece of the U.S. multilateral imbalance somewhere else, most likely to a higher-cost producer, which would
be the functional equivalent of a tax hike on the American consumer.

There's another element of the "RMB fix" that bears noting insofar as the United States is concerned. America's trade problem is primarily one of excess imports—not insufficient exports. As of the fourth quarter of 2006, goods imports were running 73 percent higher than goods exports. The import surge, in my view, is very much an outgrowth of an extraordinary period of excess personal consumption—with the consumer spending share of U.S. GDP rising to 70 percent over the past five-year 2001–2006 period from an average of 67 percent over the 1975–2000 period. With labor income growth unusually weak over the current economic recovery cycle—private sector compensation currently tracking over $425 billion (in real terms) below the norm of previous cycles—U.S. consumers have drawn increasingly from the wealth effects of asset appreciation to finance both consumption and saving. With income-based savings rates having fallen into negative territory for the first time since the early 1930s, the excess consumption and the outsize import surge it has spawned is a major source of America's macro saving imbalance. A stronger RMB-dollar cross rate cannot be expected to temper this imbalance in any way whatsoever. The excesses of asset-driven consumption are best addressed through asset markets themselves—a development that now seems to be under way as the U.S. property bubble bursts. Moreover, given the sheer size of the imbalance between imports and exports, an equilibrating realignment of the dollar would have to be so huge that it would be politically unaccept-able to the rest of the world—not just the Chinese but also the Europeans, the Japanese, and America's other Asian trading partners.

Nor should Europe count on a realignment of the yen to underwrite its growth imperatives. In large part, that's because Japan is not even close to being Europe's major trading partner. As of the third quarter of 2006, Japan accounted for just 2.5 percent of total pan-European merchandise exports, well below shares going to the United States (14 percent), OPEC (5.3 percent), China (3.9 percent), and Latin America (3.9 percent). The same is true on the import side of Europe's trade equation. Japanese-made prod-ucts account for just 4 percent of total European merchandise imports—well behind shares coming from China (10 percent), the United States (9 percent), OPEC (8.9 percent), and Latin America (4.7 percent). Yes, the euro has, indeed, borne the brunt of the yen's recent weakness. And, yes, Germany and Japan compete aggressively in several export markets. But given Japan's relatively small share of overall European trade flows, it is by no means clear that a strengthening of the yen would have a material impact on European economic growth. In short, like America's hand-wringing over the Chinese RMB, Europe's yen fixation appears equally overblown.

The G-7 doesn't have much to do these days. The glory days of the Plaza and Louvre Accords of the 1980s are long gone. After the highly celebrated recognition of the perils of global imbalances in May 2006, the G-7 has retreated back into its ever-hardening shell of irrelevance. Traditionally, this gathering of the world's Wise Men has been an important signaling mechanism for currency markets. And currencies, of course, have long been—and still are—a hot button in political circles. Those concerns are heating up again—especially in the United States with respect to the Chinese RMB and now in Europe with respect to the Japanese yen. But in a global economy, beset by major saving imbalances and structural competitive issues, the impacts of a politically expedient currency fix are likely to ring increasingly hollow. The world needs to do a much better job in coming to grips with the stresses and strains of globalization.

# The Shifting Mix of Global Saving

*June 6, 2007*

C ontrary to widespread beliefs, there is no glut of global saving. Yes, global saving has risen steadily over the past several decades, but contrary to widespread belief, the rise in recent years has been no faster than the expansion of world GDP. In fact, the overall global savings rate stood at about 24 percent of world GDP in 2006–2007, up only slightly from the 23.0 percent reading in 1990 (see Figure 2.7). At the same time, there has been an important shift in the *mix* of global savings, away from the rich countries of the developed world toward the poor countries of the developing world. This development, rather than overall

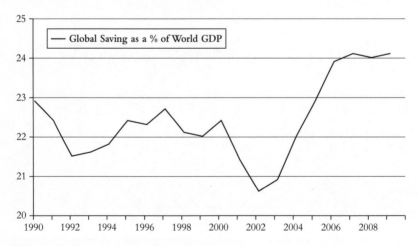

**Figure 2.7** What Global Saving Glut?

*Source:* Internatonal Monetary Fund.

trends in global saving, is likely to remain a critical issue for the world economy and financial markets in the years ahead.

The past decade has witnessed an especially stunning change in the mix of global saving. According to IMF statistics, the rich countries of the developed world—which made up 80 percent of world GDP in 1996—accounted for just 43 percent of the cumulative increase in global saving over the 1996–2006 period. By contrast, the poor countries of the developing world—which made up only 19 percent of world GDP in 1996—accounted for fully 58 percent of the cumulative increase in global saving over the past decade, or approximately three times their weight in the world economy. This wealth transfer from the poor to the rich—the exact opposite of the wealth transfer that occurred in the first globalization of the early twentieth century—is one of the most extraordinary developments in the modern history of the global economy.

The United States stands out for its extreme negligence on the savings front. By 2006, America's gross national saving rate—the combined saving of individuals, businesses, and the government sector—stood at just 13.7 percent. That's down from the 16.5 percent rate of a decade earlier and, by far, the lowest domestic saving rate of any major economy in the developed world. Adjusted for depreciation—a calculation that provides a proxy for the domestic saving that is left over after funding the wear and tear on aging capacity—the U.S. net national savings rate averaged just 1 percent over the past three years (2004–2007), a record low by any standards. Over the 1996–2006 period, the U.S. accounted for a mere 12 percent of the total growth in worldwide saving—less than half its 26 percent share in global economy as of 1996. Elsewhere in the developed world, it has been more of a mixed picture. The Japanese savings rate, while a good deal higher than that of the United States, fell from 30.4 percent in 1996 to 28.0 percent in 2006. By contrast, gross saving in the euro area held steady at around 21.0 percent over the past 10 years.

Trends in the major countries in the developing world stand in sharp contrast to those in the developed world. By now, it is well known that the large and rapidly growing developing economies of Asia have led the way in boosting their saving. Collectively, these economies have taken their gross domestic saving rate from 33 percent in 1996 to 42 percent in 2006—enough to have accounted for 31 percent of the overall gain in global saving over this period, fully four-and-a-half times their combined 7 percent share in the global economy as of 1996.

Nor can there be any mistaking the dominant role played by China in driving saving flows in the region. According to IMF estimates, China's gross domestic savings rate rose from 40.5 percent to 50 percent in 2004. My guess is the Chinese savings ratio probably held near that level over the past two years; if so, that means China accounted for about 23 percent of the growth in global saving over the past decade, or three-fourths of Developing Asia's contribution to the increase in world saving. That also means that China's contribution to the expansion of world saving over the past decade has been double that of the United States—an astonishing development in that the American economy is more than five times the size of China's.

Elsewhere in Asia, the global saving impetus over the past decade has been small; for example, only 3 percent has come from the region's newly industrialized economies (i.e., Korea, Taiwan, Singapore, and Hong Kong). The Middle East is the only other significant source of incremental growth in global saving—accounting for 8 percent of the cumulative gain in world savings over the past decade, or one-third the contribution coming from China.

These trends in the mix of global saving are hardly the statistical aberration that many suspect. Much has been made of the so-called flaws in the U.S. Commerce Department's estimates of the personal saving rate. This criticism, which mainly focuses on the failure of government statistics to capture the capital gains pieces of savings arising from property and portfolio investments, misses a key point: National income-based measures of savings were never designed to measure asset-based savings accruals. Instead, they approximate the saving arising from current economic activity—in effect, measuring the difference between domestic expenditures and the income generated from current production. As such, income-based saving gauges are agnostic over the possible existence of alternative asset-based sources of saving. Should any such windfalls occur to individuals, businesses, or even government entities, there is no reason why there couldn't be a shift in the mix between income- and asset-based saving. That doesn't mean the national-income-based savings construct is wrong—it just suggests that another source of savings may well have entered the equation.

The United States has led the way in reorienting its saving strategies. The most visible manifestation of this is a personal savings rate that moved into negative territory for two years in a row in 2005–2006—the first such development since the early 1930s. Drawing freely from a steady stream of wealth effects from sharply rising asset values—first equities and, more recently, property—U.S. households have, in effect, substituted asset-based savings for that which used to be derived from income generation. These asset effects were hardly inconsequential. During the heyday of the property bubble, net equity extraction from residential property rose from 3 percent of disposable personal income in 2000 to nearly 9 percent in 2005.

As asset-based savings increased, the spending side of the U.S. economy still needed to be funded on a cash-accrual basis. That forced America to run massive current account deficits in order to make up for the difference between asset-driven aggregate demand and production-driven income generation. Unfortunately, in a posthousing bubble climate, the asset effects are now swinging the other way—suggesting that national income-based savings measures are likely to become much more meaningful in shaping U.S. aggregate demand than has been the case in a long time.

Saving is the seed-corn for future economic growth. Without it, nations cannot invest in physical or human capital. There are short-term Band-Aids that allow savings-short nations to make ends meet—mainly by borrowing from others and, from time to time, by unlocking value in under-valued assets. The day will come, however, when surplus nations will begin to shift their focus away from functioning as lenders to others and turn, instead, toward providing support for internal needs. The increasingly popular asset allocation shift into sovereign wealth funds (SWFs) could, in my view, be an early warning sign of just such a change in focus. Poor countries want more than undervalued currency regimes that dictate low returns in their massive portfolios of dollar-based assets. They are increasingly seeking higher returns, which the SWFs are designed to achieve. But they also want internal absorption of surplus saving in the form of increasingly vigorous private consumption. Developing economies like China view this as essential to distribute the benefits of economic growth fairly throughout the income distribution.

From the start, the concept of the global savings glut was very much a U.S.-centric vision.[11] This point of view argues that America is doing the world a huge favor by consuming a large portion of underutilized savings generated largely by poor developing economies. But this is a

---

11. See the March 10, 2005, speech of then-Federal Reserve Board Governor Ben Bernanke, "The Global Saving Glut and the US Current Account Deficit," *op cit.*

very different phenomenon than a glut of worldwide savings that is sloshing around for the asking. The real story, instead, is that of a shifting mix in the composition of global saving—and the tradeoffs associated with the alternative uses of such funds. I suspect those tradeoffs are now in the process of changing—an outcome that is likely to put downward pressure on the U.S. dollar and upward pressure on long-term U.S. real interest rates. If the biggest borrower turns protectionist—one of the stranger potential twists of modern economic history—those pressures could well intensify.

The dramatic shift in the mix of global saving over the past decade is a big deal. It drives the equally unprecedented disparity between current account surpluses and deficits—the crux of the global imbalances debate. It also accounts for the gap between trade deficits and surpluses that is shaping the current protectionist debate in the U.S. Congress. In theory, this shift in the mix of saving also has the potential to shape relative asset prices between debtor and lender nations. Although those impacts have yet to have serious consequences, I continue to suspect the risk of such a possibility is a good deal higher than that envisioned by the broad consensus of global investors. Don't count on the saving glut that never was to forestall such outcomes.

# Chapter 3

## Chinese Rebalancing

### Introduction

China is the modern world's greatest development story. Thirty years of reforms and opening up have transformed the world's most populous nation into a formidable power on both the regional and global stages. Since the early 1990s, its per capita income has increased by more than five-fold. And since the turn of the century, China has contributed about twice as much to world GDP growth as the United States (as measured on a purchasing power parity basis). Can it stay this remarkable course?

Many would answer "No" to this question. This reflects a fairly typical mindset. In fact, most of China's spectacular successes over the past three decades have occurred against a backdrop of doubt and skepticism. Fears of social upheaval, the inevitable banking crisis, or an environmental catastrophe were always at the forefront of vast legions of China doubters. Yet those fears never came to pass. I have been steadfast in my own optimism on the Chinese economic outlook over the past dozen years. In the depths of the Asian financial crisis of 1997–1998, I saw a determination and focus in the eyes of the Chinese leadership that spoke of an extraordinary vision of transformation and growth. In the years that have followed, China has delivered—emerging as the unmistakable leader of the modern Asian economy. But in the rough and tumble arena of economic development, there are, of course, no guarantees that what worked in the past is a recipe for success in the future.

I remain confident that China will play an equally important role in shaping the *Next Asia*. However, as I argue in this chapter, a rebalancing of the Chinese economy is critical if it is to maintain this leadership role. I suspect that is exactly what is in the offing. The coming transformation of the Chinese economy will occur out of both necessity and design. First and foremost, it will entail a shift away from a growth dynamic powered largely by exports and fixed investment—two sectors that collectively account for almost 80 percent of total Chinese GDP. No economy, including China, can sustain a growth formula that is so disproportionately skewed to the supply side. As Chinese economic growth slowed sharply in late 2008 in response to an external demand shock made in America, the imperatives of a rebalancing of China's macro structure became all the more evident.

To its credit, and as articulated by Premier Wen Jiabao well before the onset of the so-called subprime crisis, the Chinese leadership owned up to the view that the lopsided composition of their economy is not sustainable (see "Unstable, Unbalanced, Uncoordinated, and Unsustainable," p. 229–233). The answer for the Next China is unmistakable—a shift from an export- and investment-led impetus to more of a proconsumption growth dynamic. While such a transformation has long been talked about, it has failed to materialize for a number of reasons—the most important being a fear-driven precautionary saving propensity stemming from the legacy effects of massive layoffs and an inadequate social safety net. Although China can be expected to address the latter consideration by moving ahead on social security funding and pensions reform, it cannot be expected to halt the state-owned enterprise reforms that have resulted in outsize layoffs. Nevertheless, I am confident that China will eventually deliver on the consumption front—setting in motion yet another megatrend that has the potential to reshape the global landscape. The only question is when, not if.

This chapter also argues that the shift to more of a consumption-led growth dynamic will help China deal with a number of its other problems. That's especially the case if services become an increasingly important part of the Chinese consumption basket—a logical complement to the development of any consumer culture. With services only about 36 percent of its GDP, China has the smallest services sector of any major economy in the world. There is nothing but upside from that exceedingly low share. An increasingly services-oriented Chinese economy would also be more commodity-lite, less energy-intensive, and help promote a greener GDP. In effect, the coming rebalancing of the Chinese economy will address many of the negative externalities of hypergrowth that have been ignored in the first phase of the dramatic development push over the past 30 years. Moreover, to the extent that China has moved to the fore as a leader of the pan-Asian economy, its rebalancing could also be critical in driving an equally powerful transformation for the rest of the region.

China's rebalancing will not be without major consequences for the rest of the world. In particular, a savings-short U.S. economy could come under significant pressure if one of its largest international lenders has less surplus capital to send its way. Yet that's precisely the implication of a Chinese economy that shifts from saving to consumption. Unless America goes the other way and shifts from excess consumption to saving, Chinese rebalancing could have important implications for the terms on which America conducts its international funding—with ominous consequences for both a lower dollar and higher longer-term U.S. real interest rates.

The China of the next 30 years will be a very different China than it was over the past 30 years. Moreover, given China's increasingly powerful role in the world economy, its rebalancing will occur on a scale that makes it a major global event. There is one serious risk to the coming rebalancing of the Chinese economy—a potential slowing in the pace of reforms. China would suffer seriously if external factors such as the global financial crisis lead to a slowing in financial sector reforms. A similar setback would occur if a cyclical rise in unemployment were to derail further reforms of its state-owned enterprises. China's 30 years of spectacular success reflects its willingness to push ahead on reforms—to take short-term risks in order to achieve long-term gains. As long as China stays that course, the coming rebalancing of the Chinese economy should be another in a long string of watershed events for Asia's most dynamic and successful economy.

# China's Rebalancing Challenge

*April 24, 2006*

C hina's accomplishments on the economic development front are unrivalled over the past quarter of a century. But there is no guarantee that any nation can stay the course. Progress invariably begets new problems, and it is absolutely critical to adjust development strategies in response. China is no exception to that rule. There are now signs that the growth model that has worked so brilliantly since 1979 is in need of a major overhaul. I am confident that China will rise to the occasion. A failure to do so could well lead to a serious setback on the road to reform and development.

The good news is that China is on the same wavelength and is now sending the world a very important message: A critical midcourse correction in its development model is imperative—a shift away from export- and investment-led growth to more of a consumer-driven dynamic. This change will not be abrupt, but it could become an increasingly dominant characteristic of the Chinese growth outcome for years to come. It is aimed, first and foremost, at providing greater stability to the Chinese economy. It could also have profound implications for the global economy and world financial markets. The significance of this development should not be minimized. If it occurs, the coming rebalancing of the Chinese economy could well go down in history as a pivotal moment in the world's most important growth story of the twenty-first century.

This conclusion is consistent with the basic thrust of China's just-enacted 11th Five-Year Plan. The essence of the potential adjustment is actually very simple: For the past 27 years, China's remarkable growth story has been built largely on a foundation of resource mobilization— powered by the recycling of a huge reservoir of domestic savings into export- and investment-led growth. That strategy has now outlived its usefulness. Senior Chinese officials believe the time is right to shift to more of a self-sustaining internal demand model, driven increasingly by private consumption. I concur with that key conclusion. Such rebalancing will not only enable China to deal more effectively with both internal and external imbalances, but it takes the reform process to an entirely different level—providing China with the opportunity to turn its attention away from the sheer quantity of growth toward the critically important quality dimension of the growth experience.

## The Consequences of Inaction

China's rebalancing imperatives are obvious. That's especially the case from a pure macro point of view. The economy has become far too reliant on exports and fixed investment. Depending on the metric chosen, these two sectors now account for between 75 percent and 80 percent of overall Chinese GDP (see Figure 3.1). And they are still expanding collectively at around a 25 percent annual rate. If those trends were to continue, the sustainability of the Chinese growth model would be at risk. Years of rapid export growth have already led to serious trade frictions and heightened risks of protectionism. Those pressures would only intensify if China's exports remained on

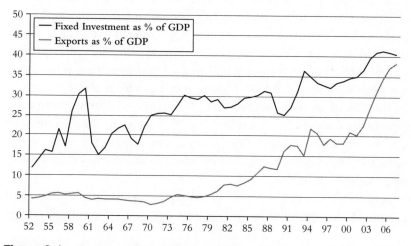

**Figure 3.1**   Ominous Mix of Chinese GDP

*Source:* China National Bureau of Statistics, Morgan Stanley Research.

an open-ended growth path. Recent politically inspired pushback from Washington is only the tip of what could well become a much bigger iceberg.[1]

Moreover, a continuation of soaring investment growth could result in excess capacity and deflation. China is intrinsically a high-investment economy. Given its extraordinary development over the last 27 years and the recent westward push of its growth model, investment should remain well supported by the confluence of infrastructure imperatives, urbanization, and continued industrialization. But on the basis of continued rapid growth in the 25 percent range per annum, the investment share of Chinese GDP, which exceeded 40 percent in 2005, is in danger of crossing the 50 percent threshold. In their earlier heydays of economic development, this ratio never got much above the low-40 percent range in either Japan or Korea. Chinese capacity excesses are already evident in steel, motor vehicles, aluminum, cement, and chemicals. A continuation of open-ended investment would only compound that problem.

The sustainability of China's export- and investment-led model can also be drawn into question from a different, yet equally important, point of view. The negative externalities of an industrial-production-led growth dynamic have become increasingly worrisome—especially over the period of 2002–2006, as industrial output growth powered ahead at close to a 16 percent average annual rate. Open-ended growth in manufacturing activity has led to serious environmental degradation, worker safety problems, and periodic bottlenecks in China's supply chain of strategic materials, especially oil and industrial metals. China's share of global demand in many commodity markets has risen dramatically in recent years—pushing materials prices sharply higher and triggering serious cost pressures for many businesses. These mounting externalities are very visible signs that China is now starting to labor under the stresses and strains of its own success. The acceleration of Chinese economic growth in early 2006 to a blistering 10.2 percent annual rate only underscores that possibility. The faster the growth rate, the more worrisome the externalities. China cannot afford to lose control of its growth juggernaut.

Similarly, the mix between capital-intensive manufacturing (47.3 percent of Chinese GDP in 2005) and services (40.3 percent) reflects yet

---

1. See my March 20, 2006 speech presented in Beijing before the China Development Forum, "Globalization and Mistrust: The U.S.-China Relationship at Risk."

another layer of distortions in China's economy. Services are, by definition, highly labor-intensive activities. As such, they hold great opportunity for China's job creation challenge. But a manufacturing-led growth dynamic is more capital-intensive, taking China down the other road, biasing its growth away from job creation. This is precisely the opposite of what a reform-oriented system requires—especially for China, where state-owned enterprise reforms continue to spur *unrelenting* headcount reductions. China needs labor-intensive—not laborsaving—growth. Services are a much better prescription for achieving that end than manufacturing. Only by a shift in the mix of the economy can China rectify these imbalances and avoid their potentially destabilizing implications.

## The Rebalancing Strategy

The good news is that China's senior leadership appears to get it. The just-enacted 11th Five-Year Plan underscores the ease for a rebalancing of the Chinese economy. Three important aspects of rebalancing are stressed in the plan—the first being a moderation of the overall growth objective. The plan calls for 7.5 percent average real GDP growth through 2010, a marked downshift from the 9.5 percent average pace of the preceding 25 years. This should not be viewed as a worrisome shortfall but instead as more of an effort to raise the quality of Chinese growth. It's not just concerns about the externalities of hypergrowth noted earlier. There are also worries that the blistering 10 percent GDP growth of the past three years (2003–2006) has led to widening income inequalities. These developments heighten the risks of instability, long the biggest threat to reforms. This is where senior Chinese officials draw the line. As Premier Wen stressed recently at the China Development Forum, "China will never backtrack on reforms." A refocusing of growth objectives from quantity to quality should be viewed as an important means to preserve China's commitment to reforms.

The second leg of the stool is the government's intent to rebalance the mix of GDP growth over the next five years (2006–2011). Ma Kai, Chairman of the all-important National Development and Reform Commission, has taken the lead[2] in stressing the need to boost both

---

2. See Ma Kai's March 19, 2006 speech at the China Development Forum, "The 11th Five-Year Plan: Targets, Path and Policy Orientation."

the consumption and services shares of Chinese GDP. He has also underscored the imperatives of an enhanced safety net—not just social security but also rural healthcare and education. This was stressed as necessary to improve income security, thereby reducing the excesses of precautionary savings that continue to inhibit the expansion of private consumption. The likely shift in the mix of Chinese economic activity is consistent with the more moderate GDP growth target over the next five years (2006–2011). That reflects the likelihood that the impetus from rapidly growing exports and investment could fade well before the added support from consumption kicks in.

Financial reforms are a third key aspect of China's rebalancing strategy. The focus, so far, has largely been on banking reforms. But there are equally strong needs for capital markets reforms, especially the development of a corporate bond market. Currency reforms have also been given considerable attention recently, reflecting, in part, the mounting bilateral trade tensions with the United States. China's shift to a new foreign exchange regime in July 2005 was an encouraging first step in that regard. Related to that, senior Chinese financial authorities have expressed concerns over the excessive accumulation of foreign exchange reserves. The rebalancing of the real economy toward increased domestic consumption should lead to more rapid gains in Chinese imports, a related narrowing of its trade surplus, and a reduction in the pace of reserve accumulation. Rebalancing on the real side of the economy thus provides China with more leeway to broaden and deepen the scope of its financial sector reforms.

The bad news is that many outside of China do not get it. Most foreign politicians—especially those in the U.S.—believe that a large and swift currency revaluation should be central to any Chinese rebalancing strategy. Some academics have come to the same conclusion.[3] With financial sector reforms still in the early stages, China has stressed that large currency adjustments could potentially be quite destabilizing—especially insofar as impacts on the banking system and foreign exposure of domestic Chinese corporates are concerned. I think those concerns are well founded. Others have noted that globalization has diminished the macro impacts of currency adjustments over the past decade—suggesting

---

3. See, for example, Olivier J. Blanchard and Francesco Giavazzi, "Rebalancing Growth in China: A Three-Handed Approach," Discussion Paper 5403 from Centre for Economic Policy Research, December 2005.

that China and the world would actually gain little by taking on big risks.[4] Success on the rebalancing front will come as long as China makes progress in tilting the mix of economic growth away from external toward internal demand. The choice of tactics is up to China. Under the circumstances, its long-standing commitment to gradual currency revaluation seems perfectly reasonable and desirable.

## Implications

The implications of Chinese rebalancing are likely to be profound, both for China and the rest of the world. The tilt away from exports and investment toward consumption, along with the moderation of aggregate GDP growth such a rebalancing implies, could well challenge many of the world's perceptions about the so-called China factor. Three potential impacts strike me as most important:

*Commodity markets.* A reduction of investment growth is likely to temper China's impact on the demand side of many industrial commodity markets. In 2007, China, which made up only about 6 percent of world GDP, accounted for around 32 percent of worldwide demand for aluminum and about 40 to 45 percent of global consumption in copper,

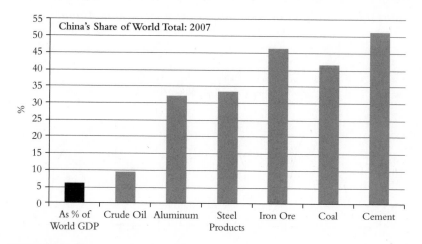

**Figure 3.2**   Surging Chinese Materials Demand
*Source:* Morgan Stanley Research.

---

4. See Chapter 2 of the 75th *BIS Annuaal Report,* June 2005.

iron, steel, and coal (see Figure 3.2). As the pace of Chinese industrial activity slows in the years ahead in accordance with the 11th Five-Year Plan, pressures on the demand side of industrial materials markets should ease. This should underscore the downside risks to commodity inflation at just the time when most business people and investors have concluded that there will be no stopping the upside of a super commodity cycle. China's efforts at energy conservation, as spelled out in the new Five-Year Plan—a targeted 20 percent reduction in energy content per unit of GDP over the next five years—could push prices of oil and refined products lower, as well. Resource-conserving growth has now become an important mantra in Chinese macro circles.

*Currency and trade tensions.* Courtesy of rebalancing, China may be more inclined toward RMB appreciation as a means to promote a shift away from the excesses of export-led growth and provide a stimulus for internal demand. The extent and pace of this appreciation will remain very much dependent on the stability of its financial system. Proconsumption initiatives should also boost Chinese import demand, reducing China's net-export surplus and thereby providing support for its major Asian trading partners such as Japan, Taiwan, and Korea (see Figure 3.3). The combination of further RMB appreciation and reduced external surpluses could play an important role in relieving the anti-China trade tensions now building in the international community.

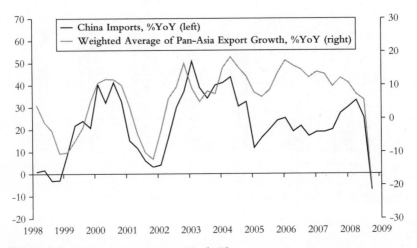

**Figure 3.3**  China–Centric Asian Trade Flows

*Source:* National Sources, International Monetary Fund, Morgan Stanley Research.

*The Chinese consumer.* The Chinese consumer will not spring to life overnight. As noted previously, this is likely to be a major story that evolves over the next three to five years. Chairman Ma of the NDRC stressed that the emphasis will initially be placed on building the infrastructure of consumer markets. This implies a focus on China's labor-intensive tertiary industries involved in distribution and delivery—underscoring not only the opportunities for wholesale, retail, and trans-national shipping but also for e-based retail trade systems. Conditional on the improvement of income security and safety-net support, growth in the Chinese consumer products industry should move rapidly up the value chain from soft to hard goods over the next several years. Significantly, under the terms of WTO accession, foreign multinationals will be allowed increased access to China's domestic retail trade markets within three years.

## The Case for the Chinese Consumer

The consumer story—long China's missing macro link—bears special emphasis in assessing the prospects for Chinese rebalancing. Private consumption fell through the 40 percent threshold of Chinese GDP in 2005, far below the 65 percent norm for most of the world's major economies and the mirror image of the excessive share of the overextended American consumer (see Figure 3.4). To date, modern China hasn't delivered on the

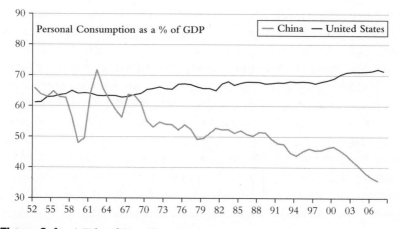

**Figure 3.4**   A Tale of Two Consumers

*Source:* China National Bureau of Statistics, U.S. Bureau of Economic Analysis, Morgan Stanley Research.

consumption story for good reason: The past 27 years have been dominated by an historic transition from a state-owned to a private system. With
that transition has come massive headcount reductions in state-owned
enterprises that have taken a devastating toll on consumer confidence. In
that critical respect, Chinese reforms have had an intrinsic anticonsump-
tion bias. The thrust of the 11th Five-Year Plan suggests there is good
reason to believe that this is now about to change.

Unfortunately, we don't know much about the Chinese consumer.
The data are sketchy and there is little in the way of a meaningful history
of modern-day consumption trends in the world's most populous nation.
In an effort to dig deeper into this issue, I recently came across a study
based on a Gallup Poll of China's consumers.[5] At first, I thought the very
concept of a survey in a nation of 1.3 billion people was unfathomable.
But the Gallup Organization has been in the scientific polling business
for a long time, and they definitely know what they are doing. It turns
out that they have been conducting comprehensive surveys of Chinese
consumer attitudes since 1994. The latest poll is for 2004 and is based on
about 3,600 interviews with urban and rural respondents from around
the country, selected on the basis of what Gallup calls a "rigorous proba-
bility-proportional-to-size sampling design." Another survey is currently
in the field, slated for release this fall.

I found the results fascinating. They go a long way in adding granu-
larity to the saga of the Chinese consumer, but they also shed considerable light on some of the nation's most important macro anomalies.
For starters, the Gallup Poll reveals much about the micro character of
China's emerging consumers—namely, the product-specific shifts in
tastes that are now taking hold. As can be seen in Table 3.1, "Chinese
Consumer Product Ownership," penetration of major household products has increased dramatically over the past decade. Interestingly enough,
Chinese consumption has spread most rapidly into the electronic product
categories—especially televisions, phones (fixed and mobile), and com-
puters. By contrast, with the exception of the microwave oven, increased
penetration of more traditional appliances—washing machines, refrig-
erators, and stereos—has lagged. Putting the Gallup results together with
recent research on broader technology trends, there is good reason to
believe that China will attain the status of having the world's largest

---

5. See W. McEwen, X. Fang, C. Zhang and R. Burkholder, "Inside the Mind of the
Chinese Consumer," *Harvard Business Review*, March 2006.

**Table 3.1**  Chinese Consumer Product Ownership (% of Total Households)

|                      | 1994 | 2004 |
| -------------------- | ---- | ---- |
| Color TV             | 40   | 82   |
| Washing Machine      | 36   | 54   |
| Refrigerator         | 25   | 41   |
| Stereo system        | 13   | 26   |
| Microwave oven       | 3    | 18   |
| Telephone (in home)  | 10   | 63   |
| Mobile telephone     | 2    | 48   |
| Computer             | 2    | 13   |

*Source:* China Survey of the Gallup Organization.

population of wired consumers over the next few years.[6] China, which leapt into second place in the global marketplace for technology, media, and telecom in 2004, could take the lead by 2006; by 2010, most forecasts put China ahead of the United States by a wide margin. This could well be a key differentiating factor of the world's newest consumer.

The micro results of the Gallup Poll also dovetail quite nicely with what we do know about China's macro consumption story. In particular, the tally underscores the well-known bifurcated state of the Chinese consumer—namely, the extraordinary contrasts between those living in urban and rural locations. The income gap is especially notorious—with urban income per household of about $2,950 in 2004 running three times that of rural households at $990.

What surprised me, however, was the answer to Gallup's query to Chinese households on what they felt they needed in order to get by. Urban workers put the average cost of living about 10 percent above annual income. For rural locations, the spread of costs over household income was about 17 percent—underscoring the considerably greater strains on lifestyles for the 57 percent of the Chinese population (or some 745 million people) still residing in the countryside (see Figure 3.5). These results fit quite well with the answer to a related Gallup query on personal savings. Family dissatisfaction is mounting over the amount they are able to set aside each year. In 2004, fully 68 percent of

---

6. See Mary Meeker's "Global TMT Market Sizing," Morgan Stanley Research, March 23, 2006.

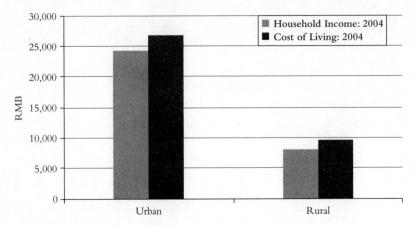

**Figure 3.5**   The Bifurcated Chinese Consumer

*Source:* China Survey of the Gallup Organization.

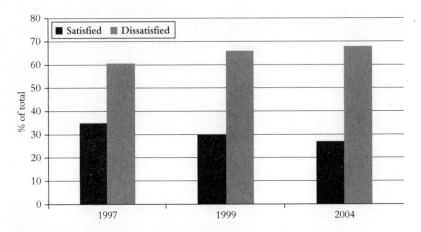

**Figure 3.6**   Chinese Saving Sentiment

*Source:* China Survey of the Gallup Organization.

all Chinese in the Gallup sample were dissatisfied with their ability to save—a meaningful deterioration from the 61 percent reading in 1997 (see Figure 3.6).

One key risk in all this is time; the emergence of the Chinese consumer will undoubtedly unfold very, very slowly. The reason: Generational inertia could make this a long uphill climb. Today's Chinese adults have been subjected to the life-changing shock of state-owned enterprise reform.

The State that once provided the ultimate cradle-to-grave security of the "iron rice bowl" is no longer the backstop of income and lifestyle support. It is quite possible that workers who have lived through this wrenching transition may never have the confidence to reduce precautionary saving. It's very similar to the mindset of a generation of Americans who never again bought stock after having lived through the Great Depression. Instead, it may well take a new generation of Chinese consumers— lacking the memories of reforms—to lead the way. I am very optimistic on the prospects for the coming rebalancing of the Chinese economy and the opportunities that offers for China's consumption dynamic. But I am mindful of the possibility that it may take a good deal longer than I suspect or than China would like.

China has always been the land of many consumers, with a potential that has tantalized the West for centuries. The math of large numbers has always been the most intriguing aspect of the Chinese consumption story. Consider the upside if 1.3 billion people start to buy more of literally anything! It's not just that China has a low consumption content of its own GDP, but it's also that 20 percent of the world's population accounts for only about 3 percent of total global consumption (see Figure 3.7). The potential for the Chinese consumer could well be one of the greatest opportunities for the global economy in the twenty-first century. Unlike earlier false hopes, this one seems for real.

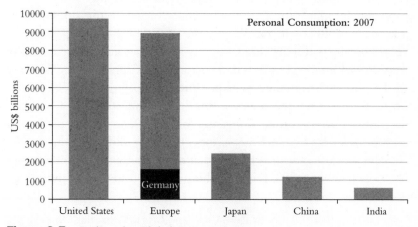

**Figure 3.7**   Scaling the Global Consumer
*Source:* National Sources, Morgan Stanley Research.

## China and the Global Labor Arbitrage

There have, of course, been doubters at virtually every point along the way in the Chinese development story. Yet time and again, China has stayed the course. The latest worry is that China's success will sow the seeds of its own demise—namely, that the land of surplus labor is rapidly running out of workers.[7] If correct, this could lead to excessive wage inflation and a loss of competitiveness, undermining the very job and income security that China so desperately needs in order to sustain economic growth, in general—and consumer demand, in particular. Such concerns, like those of the past, are vastly overblown, in my view.

The anecdotal evidence of rising wages and scattered signs of worker shortages is probably accurate. But the basic conclusion that this portends a broader macro threat—that low-cost Chinese labor is a thing of the past—does not stand up well to careful scrutiny. A recent study published by the U.S. Bureau of Labor Statistics puts the Chinese wage story in context.[8] The analysis is based on comprehensive wage statistics that cover the entire Chinese economy; the only drawback is that this data set stops in 2002. The Bureau of Labor Statistics study does, indeed, find compelling evidence of a brisk acceleration of Chinese wage inflation—a 12 percent annualized clip over the 1999–2002 interval versus average gains of just 2.6 percent over the preceding five years. But this hardly represents the beginning of the end for China. It turns out accelerating Chinese wage inflation has done virtually nothing to close the wage gap with the developed world.

Even after four years of double-digit increases, average hourly compensation for the overall Chinese manufacturing sector amounted to just $0.57 in 2002—literally, 3 percent of the U.S. hourly pay rate of $21.40 during that same year. Contrasts with other nations were equally dramatic. Moreover, hourly compensation for Chinese manufacturing workers in 2002 amounted to 25 percent of the pay rates of Mexico and Brazil, 10 percent of the wages of Asia's newly industrialized economies (i.e., Taiwan, Korea, Hong Kong, and Singapore), and just 3 percent of the norms of Japan and Europe. Sure, there are differences when the Chinese wage aggregate is broken down into pay by urban enterprises ($0.95 per hour in 2002) and by the more rural township and village

---

7. See David Barbosa "Labor Shortage in China May Lead to Trade Shift," *New York Times* April 3, 2006.
8. See Judith Banister "Manufacturing Earnings and Compensation in China," from the August 2005 issue of the *Monthly Labor Review.*

enterprises ($0.41), but that granularity changes nothing. Despite several years of sharply accelerating wage inflation, China still enjoys an extraordinary wage differential when compared with the rest of the world (see Figure 3.8).

It is not all that difficult to extend the Bureau of Labor Statistics study's conclusions through 2005. According to the China Statistical Yearbook, average annual wage payments in China rose 13 percent in 2003 and by another 14 percent in 2004; anecdotal reports suggest that increases in Chinese wage rates apparently continued at close to that clip though 2005. That would suggest that the inflation rate for hourly compensation in China's manufacturing sector over the past three years might have held quite close to the 12 percent pace recorded over the 1999–2002 time frame. If that was the case, then it turns out the level of Chinese hourly compensation remained at 3 percent of that in the U.S. in 2005, doing literally nothing to close the enormous gap in pay rates between the two nations. Nor does a worst-case sensitivity analysis alter the outcome in any material way. Under the alternative assumption that Chinese wage inflation doubled over the past three years—increasing by 25 percent per annum over the 2003–2005 interval versus 12 percent over the 1999–2002 period—the level of Chinese wages would only have moved up to 4 percent of the U.S. norm. The math of small numbers explains the persistence of this outsize differential: Rapid wage inflation from a very low base does little to close the gap with higher-wage economies.

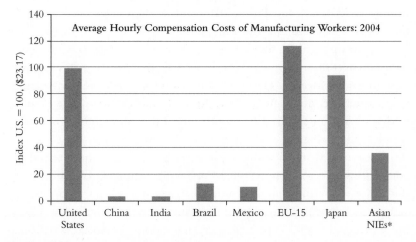

**Figure 3.8** The Global Labor Arbitrage

*Includes Hong Kong, Korea, Singapore, and Taiwan.

*Source:* U.S. Bureau of Labor Statistics, Morgan Stanley Research.

But that's only half the story. Wage increases should never be assessed in isolation. When making judgments about any nation's cost pressures and competitiveness, it is essential to compare wage inflation with productivity gains. It is not good if wage pressures mount while productivity remains stagnant. On the other hand, it is perfectly logical—and in fact desirable—for wages to rise in an economy that is experiencing rapid productivity growth. China fits the latter outcome to a tee. Productivity growth in China's industrial sector—manufacturing, mining, and construction—surged at an average annual rate of nearly 20 percent over the 2000–2004 interval. That's well in excess of the cost pressures implied by 12 percent gains in hourly compensation. That means Chinese unit labor costs remain under excellent control—even in the context of rapid and accelerating wage inflation. That, in turn, would limit any pressures building on either the inflation or the profit margin fronts—doing little to jeopardize China's competitiveness. Upward adjustments of the Chinese currency could certainly alter the international wage comparisons over time. So far, however, the roughly 3.5 percent move in the RMB has done little to alter this calculus. Needless to say, a large currency revaluation—something China continues to resist—could have a more dramatic impact on closing the wage differentials.

Nor do I buy the equally preposterous notion that China is running short of workers, thereby risking a significant loss of market share to some of its equally low-cost Asian neighbors. Over recent years, the industry share of total employment has actually been stagnant or down in India, Indonesia, Malaysia, and Taiwan. By contrast, there have been fractional increases in Thailand and the Philippines. Moreover, it is important to stress again that China's state-owned enterprise sector has reduced headcount by over 60 million workers since 1997, thus creating an enormous pool of unemployed workers that are seeking gainful reemployment in China's new economy. At the same time, as already noted, the Chinese leadership has emphasized the expansion of the labor-intensive services sector as a key element of the just-enacted 11th Five-Year Plan. If China were seriously worried about labor shortages, it would have stayed the course with its capital-intensive, labor-saving manufacturing model. All this is not to say there aren't skill mismatches and other frictional dislocations that arise from time to time in any economy—including China. For example, I continue to hear anecdotal reports of shortages of young women needed for employment in China's rapidly growing textile industry. But these are the exceptions, not the rule, for a nation that continues to have a rural population of some 745 million—by far, the largest pool of surplus labor in the world.

All this underscores the critical role China continues to play in driving the global labor arbitrage—the cross-border migration of production from high-to low-cost labor pools. China's enormous reservoir of low-wage factory workers demonstrates the enduring potential of this arbitrage. A companion study published by the U.S. Bureau of Labor Statistics puts overall manufacturing employment in China at 109 million in 2002—more than double the total factory employment of 53 million for all the G-7 economies of the industrial world, combined.[9] Nor should the arbitrage be viewed as something that just takes place at the low end of the occupational hierarchy. Currently, about 550,000 newly trained engineers and scientists graduate each year from Chinese universities; in India, the count of such graduates is around 700,000 per year. For China and India, combined, this represents a tripling over the past decade in the entry flow into this segment of their high-skilled talent pool, pushing their combined flow of new graduates in engineering and science to about three times that in the United States. Courtesy of IT-enabled offshoring, the global labor arbitrage is now at work in this segment of the occupational hierarchy, as well. In short, China is in little danger of losing the labor-market underpinnings of its powerful growth dynamic. That's unambiguously good news for employment growth and income generation—key pillars of support for the Chinese consumer.

### Risks and Hopes

China's economic progress over the past 27 years has been nothing short of remarkable. But this is no time to bask in the warm glow of success. The Chinese growth model has been pushed to its limit, and a rebalancing is now in order. Such a midcourse correction is not without peril. As always, risks to social stability qualify as the number-one peril, and with the dismantling of state-owned enterprises continuing apace, the risks of rising unemployment remain the biggest threat in that regard. In that vein, a shift away from export- and investment-led support can hardly be taken lightly, especially if it leads to a reduction in economic

---

9. See Judith Banister "Manufacturing Earnings and Compensation in China," from the August 2005 issue of the *Monthly Labor Review*.

growth from the 9.5 percent pace of the past 25 years to the anticipated 7.5 percent trajectory through 2010, as envisioned in the 11th Five-Year Plan. Rapid economic growth has long been viewed as China's most powerful antidote to reform-induced job loss. For an economy that needs about 8 million new jobs each year to keep its urban unemployment rate constant, any growth slowdown is a big deal.

Significantly, China doesn't need 9.5 percent growth to maintain social stability and underwrite its commitment to reforms—7.5 percent will do just fine. There are two reasons why I believe China will be able to cope with the employment implications of slower growth: First, state-owned enterprise reform is now well-advanced and the annualized layoff pace has moderated recently to around 2 million workers—down sharply from earlier losses that were running closer to 7 million per annum. Second, the focus on services in the new 11th Five-Year Plan is especially encouraging in that it directs stimulus to the most labor-intensive segment of economic activity. For both of these reasons, China should be better able to withstand the impacts of an economic rebalancing without compromising its focus on reforms.

China remains the world's greatest growth story. The ownership structure of the economy is in the midst of the most dramatic transition in modern history. But there must be far more to this transition than open-ended growth in industrial activity. The rebalancing envisioned in the 11th Five-Year Plan should make the next stage of the transition more manageable. If all goes according to script, not only will the excesses of the current strain of growth be tempered, but China should also be able to engineer a critical shift in its focus from the quantity to the quality of growth. The result will be more of a consumer-led growth dynamic that provides better balance and sustainability for the Chinese economy.

In the end, China has no choice—it must meet the rebalancing challenge head-on. Over the years, I have learned not to underestimate the vision and determination of China's macro managers, its business leaders, and its people. Time and again, they have made the right moves at the right time. I am equally confident in their collective ability to accomplish the coming rebalancing. The only question is, When?

# A Commodity-Lite China

*June 5, 2006*

No economy has been more important than China in driving global commodity demand in recent years. Many believe this trend will continue indefinitely. But the Chinese leadership has reached a very different conclusion—that this seemingly insatiable demand for industrial materials is not sustainable. As such, it is now making a determined effort to shift to more of a commodity-lite growth model. This could have a dramatic impact on the character of Chinese growth, with important implications for financial markets and the global economy.

There was a major breakthrough in China's impact on global commodity demand in 2005. Not only did it emerge as the world's largest consumer of copper, nickel, and zinc, but China's commodity delta—the growth of its consumption of industrial materials relative to gains elsewhere in the world—literally went off the charts (Figure 3.9).

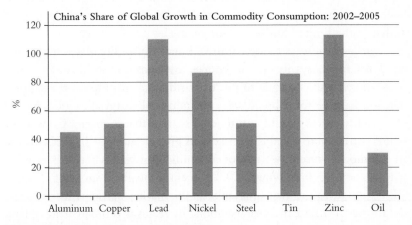

**Figure 3.9**   China's Commodity Delta

*Source:* IEA, World Bureau of Metal Statistics, IMF, Morgan Stanley Research.

For example, in 2005, the growth in Chinese consumption of aluminum accounted for 50 percent of the total global growth in aluminum consumption, 84 percent for iron ore, 108 percent for steel products, 115 percent for cement, 120 percent for zinc, and an astonishing 307 percent of growth in world copper consumption. That's right—for steel products, cement, zinc, copper, and nickel, China's growth in domestic consumption in 2005 stood in sharp contrast to outright declines elsewhere in the world. For a Chinese economy that accounts for only about 4.5 percent of world GDP (current dollars at market exchange rates), the impacts of China's outsize commodity deltas are nothing short of staggering.

At work is a commodity-heavy model of Chinese economic growth. Driven by two sectors—fixed investment and exports, which collectively now account for more than 75 percent of Chinese GDP—the commodity content of Chinese GDP is much higher than would be the case in a more balanced economy. Surging growth in investment and exports has been complemented by an unrelenting push toward urbanization, infrastructure, and industrialization. These are all construction-related activities that have intrinsically high industrial materials content. The residential property boom in coastal China rounds out the picture of this nation's explosive growth in materials consumption. There is an especially tight link between homebuilding and copper. In the United States, for example, the Copper Development Association estimates that 46 percent of total copper usage is earmarked for building construction—with about two-thirds of that total going to the homebuilding sector. While we do not have comparable numbers for China, there is good reason to believe that the copper intensity of its building boom is every bit as great as that in the United States—if not greater.

There are two ways to look at the China commodity play: On the one hand, if China stays its present course, this commodity-heavy development model will continue to put extraordinary pressure on the supply-demand balance for a broad array of industrial materials. Undoubtedly, commodity prices would continue to soar in that scenario. Conversely, China could opt to change the mix of its growth model—in part, because its commodity-intensive strain of economic growth has become prohibitively expensive. Following a 10.3 percent annualized surge of Chinese GDP growth in the first quarter of 2006, market participants endorsed the former scenario; the near-parabolic increases in a broad array of base metals in the early months of 2006 reflected a belief that China would remain locked indefinitely in a commodity-heavy growth formula.

But the Chinese leadership is sending a very different message. Its newly enacted 11th Five-Year Plan is framed around a dramatic rebalancing of the Chinese economy that should result in more of a commodity-lite growth model.

A key feature of the new five-year plan is a shift in the mix of Chinese economic growth away from exports and investment toward private consumption. A number of proconsumption initiatives have been introduced to push China in this direction—income support for rural households, increased minimum wages in Guangdong and other coastal export regions, increased funding of a national social security system, and support for the expansion of labor-intensive services industries such as retail trade, wholesalers, and internal transportation and delivery. At the same time, Chinese planners—namely, the all-important National Development and Reform Commission (NDRC)—have announced a new round of tightening measures aimed at slowing an overheated investment sector. Recent actions are aimed at restricting projects in overinvested industries such as aluminum, cement, ferrous alloys, coal, coking coal, and carbide-based PVC, while penalizing speculative activity in residential property construction. A late-April 2006 monetary tightening by the People's Bank of China augments these administrative measures with a shift in macro policies.

In short, a critical rebalancing of the Chinese economy now appears to be under way. This has two major implications for China's commodity demand: One, China's overall GDP growth rate should slow. Relative to the hypergrowth of an investment- and export-led growth model—two sectors that are still surging at around 30 percent year-over-year—a consumption-led growth dynamic is a good deal slower in any economy. China is unlikely to be an exception. Largely as a result of this shifting mix, the 11th Five-Year Plan calls for a downshift of Chinese GDP to a 7.5 percent average pace in the five years ending 2010—still a vigorous gain by the standards of most economies but a marked slowdown from the 9.5 percent average growth of the past 25 years. Such a slowdown, in conjunction with an important shift in the mix of growth, underscores the distinct likelihood of a reduction in the growth of China's demand for industrial materials in the years immediately ahead.

A second factor likely to be at work are explicit efforts for commodity conservation—in effect, retrofitting China's commodity-guzzling production platform with more commodity-efficient technologies. Oil has been singled out for special attention in this regard. China's newly enacted economic plan contains an explicit target of reducing the energy content of Chinese GDP by 4 percent per year through 2010—or fully 20 percent over the five-year planning horizon. For a nation that currently consumes twice as much oil per unit of GDP as the rest of the world, this goal definitely appears achievable. The Chinese do not have to reinvent the wheel in terms of developing alternative energy technologies. Instead, what China needs to do is to begin replacing its existing production technologies with energy-efficient alternatives already available elsewhere in the world. This is hardly a costless endeavor, but for a nation with the highest savings rate in the world and the largest reservoir of foreign exchange reserves, China can certainly afford to earmark a small portion of those funds toward oil conservation efforts.

Moreover, the Chinese leadership has expressed a strong desire to go well beyond energy conservation in implementing its commodity-lite growth strategy. In the recent words of Ma Kai, China's chief economic planner and Chairman of the NDRC, China's 11th Five-Year Plan also stresses measures aimed at "...transforming economic growth from being driven by large amounts of resources consumption to being driven by the improvement of resources utilization efficiency."[10] This statement is a candid response to what Chairman Ma admits are a number of disturbing problems that arose during the past several years—namely, environmental and ecological degradation, as well as serious resource shortages and bottlenecks. In my view, the implications are unmistakable: One of China's most powerful economic policymakers is essentially pre-announcing a major shift toward a commodity-lite growth model. Meanwhile, China is beginning to exercise its power as the world's dominant player on the demand side of commodity markets—negotiating for broad-based pricing concessions on iron ore and recently announcing sales of excess copper stocks. However, China still has a long way to go in developing effective commodity market strategies.

Don't get me wrong: It is important not to take the image of a commodity-lite China too far. China is hardly going to disappear as a major factor influencing global commodity markets. To the contrary, it remains very much committed to the commodity-intensive endeavors of urbanization, industrialization, and expanded infrastructure. These are all essential to Chinese development aspirations. But China has come to the

---

10. See his March 19, 2006 speech before the China Development Forum.

critical realization that it simply cannot afford to stay the current course. The 11th Five-Year Plan is very careful in stressing that China needs to be far more judicious in managing the quality of its growth dynamic in the years immediately ahead. That means bringing an end to the unbalanced, open-ended growth of its industrial economy. More specifically, that implies China's commodity deltas probably hit their limits in 2005 and could well recede significantly in the years ahead.

As China now comes of age, its focus is shifting away from the quantity to the quality dimension of the growth experience. This is good news for the sustainability of Chinese economic development. It is also good news for the world economy in that it should provide some relief from extreme price pressures in industrial materials markets. It could, however, come as a rude awakening for investors and speculators banking on an open-ended continuation of a China-led super commodity cycle. A commodity-lite China is a very different story than the world has grown accustomed to in recent years.

# Scale and the Chinese Policy Challenge

*June 19, 2006*

T he Chinese economy is overheated for the second time in two years. Yet once again, the Chinese authorities are taking an incremental approach in addressing the problem. This strategy looks increasingly dubious. The bigger China becomes and the further down the road of reform it travels, the tougher it will be to use incremental policy adjustments to steer the economy. China needs a new approach to stabilization policy—before it's too late.

Scale effects now pose a serious challenge to Chinese macro policy strategy. While China still accounts for only about 5 percent of world GDP in 2005 (in dollar-based market exchange rates), its overheated sectors now have a much bigger weight in its own economy as well as in the broader global economy. That's especially the case for China's white-hot fixed investment sector. While China's GDP is only about 18 percent the size of America's, Chinese fixed investment outlays are running at nearly 60 percent of those in the United States. Putting it another way, China's fixed investment surged from over $400 billion in 2000 to $1.1 trillion in 2005—an investment delta of about $680 billion that was nearly 70 percent larger than the delta recorded by the United States (about $400 billion) over the same five-year interval.

Similar comparisons are evident in China's export sector, the other overheated piece of its economy. In 2005, total Chinese manufactured exports hit $762 billion—fully 84 percent of the level of exports goods in the United States, the world's largest trading engine. Here, again, the growth delta is nothing short of astonishing. Over the 2000–2005 period, Chinese export goods have tripled, whereas those from the United States have increased only about 15 percent. That puts China's

$512.9 billion export delta over the most recent five-year period (2001–2006) at 4.2 times that of America ($121.3 billion).

The repercussions of China's investment-and export-led growth surge are global in scope. Significantly, it's not just an export and investment story. It's also a story of increasingly powerful impacts on industrial materials and other commodity markets. As I noted earlier, in 2005 alone, China accounted for 50 percent of total global growth in the consumption of aluminum; for other industrial materials, China's growth contributions were literally off the charts—84 percent for iron ore, 108 percent for steel products, 115 percent for cement, 120 percent for zinc, 307 percent for copper, and well in excess of 307 percent for nickel. I have also argued that with protectionist pressures mounting and the risks of capacity excesses mounting, China must bring its commodity-heavy industrialization phase to an end. Instead, it must embark on a major rebalancing toward consumer-led growth that would lower the commodity content of its GDP. If anything, the investment- and export-led growth blowout in early 2006 makes such a transition all the more urgent.

All this poses an increasingly vexing problem to Chinese policy makers. In a normal market-based economy, fiscal and monetary tools are the primary means by which the authorities temper the excesses of the business cycle. China, however, is far from a normal economy. Despite over a quarter century of impressive reforms, it remains very much a blended economy—a mixture of state- and private-sector-enterprises. The official data suggest that state-owned enterprises still account for about 35 percent of Chinese GDP. However, that share undoubtedly understates the degree of state control in the newly privatized—or "corporatized" in Chinese parlance—segment of the economy. Even after public offerings, the state still maintains sizable majority ownership stakes in most publicly listed, privately owned companies.

Moreover, there can be no mistaking the limited impact that internal market forces have in driving China's two overheated sectors. For example, in 2004, state-owned and collective units still accounted for fully 50 percent of total fixed asset investment in China. In addition, nearly 60 percent of total Chinese exports are generated by foreign-invested enterprises, that is, Chinese subsidiaries of foreign multinationals and joint venture partners. The lingering vestiges of state control, together with the autonomy of foreign sourcing activity, leave little room for the invisible hand of the market to work its magic.

The blended Chinese economy is also supported by a relatively undeveloped financial sector. Despite recent reforms, China is still a long way away from having a fully functioning banking system and capital markets. Two of its big four policy banks are currently listed companies, but the transition to commercially based lending practices is only in its infancy. Nor does China have a well-developed corporate bond market that enables private-sector businesses to secure funding from capital markets. That means the bulk of China's credit allocation continues to rest on the shoulders of a still very fragmented banking system—with decisions made more at the provincial and local level than by head offices in Beijing. As such, monetary policy actions by the central government—namely, recent adjustments in nationwide lending rates and reserve ratios—do little to influence investment spending. Instead, the Chinese authorities have opted for administrative controls to fine-tune investment flows on an industry and geographic basis. As a consequence, the modern-day counterpart of China's central planning bureau—the National Development and Reform Commission—has more to say about the allocation of capital than does the market or its fiscal and monetary authorities.

A big risk for China is that it now gets trapped in the inherent contradictions of its blended economy. The excesses of a domestic and global liquidity cycle compound the problem. Not only have Chinese banks been especially aggressive in pushing out new loans recently—RMB lending in the first five months of 2006 was up 80 percent year-over-year—but China's tightly managed currency float links its money supply to an explosive build-up in foreign exchange (FX) reserves. In 2005, Chinese FX reserve accumulation topped $200 billion, and in 2006, China's stock of such holdings will easily exceed $1 trillion—surpassing Japan as the largest reservoir of FX reserves in the world. The problem for China is that its quasi-pegged currency regime still requires aggressive recycling of these reserves into dollar-based assets. Lacking a well-developed domestic debt market, it is difficult for China to "sterilize" all of those dollar purchases, meaning excess liquidity spills over into domestic economy. Not by coincidence, broad M-2 was surging at a 19.1 percent year-over-year rate in May 2006—fully three percentage points above the central bank's 16 percent target.

Chinese authorities are now scrambling to regain control over a runaway economy. But the response is almost a carbon copy of the approach last used in the overheating of 2004—incremental adjustments in monetary policy and administrative measures aimed at controlling industry-by-industry excesses in investment spending. The basic problem with this approach is that it has been overwhelmed by scale. China's growth dynamic is now so powerful and its economy is so large that incremental policy management can no longer achieve the traction required for effective macro control.

Two overheating alerts in two years underscore the pitfalls of the current approach. The most recent moves to raise bank lending rates by 27 bp (an April 27, 2006 action) and required reserve ratios by 0.5 percentage point (a June 16, 2006 action) may simply not be enough to contain the excesses of China's bank credit cycle. Similarly, a continuation of grudging adjustments to its currency policy may not be enough to contain the globally led excesses of its liquidity cycle, driven importantly by lingering expectations of RMB appreciation. Nor can China count on the micro targeting of administrative adjustments to get the job done. Recent actions aimed at restricting projects in overinvested industries such as aluminum, cement, ferrous alloys, coal, coking coal, and carbide-based PVC, together with measures penalizing speculative activity in residential property construction, are likely to be overwhelmed by the sheer magnitude of the scale problem.

In short, Chinese policy makers need to do more if they are to succeed in containing the excesses of their overheated economy. Scale effects compound the implications of losing control over the economy. In nominal terms, today's economy is fully 35 percent larger than it was in 2004, the last time Chinese authorities were faced with a similar problem. The experience of the past two years—ongoing investment and export excesses, in conjunction with China-led spikes in energy and other industrial commodity prices—underscores the pitfalls of incrementalism in guiding China's blended macro policy strategy. Chinese authorities are caught in the middle, fearful of triggering a boom-bust cycle should policy tighten too much, and concerned about mounting imbalances should policies remain overly accommodative. Either choice is not without risk. But this could well be a pivotal moment when the implications of that choice finally need to be faced.

In my view, the choice is clear-cut: Current circumstances and prospective risks in China argue for a much tighter macro policy stance. Yes, this should result in slower economic growth, a downshift in the growth in commodity demand, and a challenging climate for China's pan-Asian trading partners. But it will also help trigger an increasingly urgent shift from investment- and export-led growth to a consumer-led growth dynamic. These adjustments will not be without dislocations in

China, the rest of Asia, and the broader global economy. But they certainly beat the alternative of letting the economy overheat to a boil.

China still has considerable latitude in how to frame its policy strategy—specifically, how to tilt the mix in its macro policies between fiscal, monetary, and currency adjustments, and how to regulate the speed of reforms. But the longer China avoids a more meaningful shift to macro policy restraint and the longer it leans on investment and exports at the expense of private consumption, the greater the chance of the dreaded hard landing. That's a risk China can no longer afford to take.

# China's Great Contradiction

## July 3, 2006

T he more time I spend in China, the more I am struck by its inherent contradictions. I have made three visits to China in the past twelve weeks (April to July 2006) alone, breaking my own personal record. Over this period, I have spent considerable time in discussions with the Chinese leadership and its top policy officials. I have visited companies—small and large, alike. I have had a glimpse of the future, spending a weekend in Tianjin, the heart of the Binhai New Area, which could well be China's next mega development zone. I have also traveled to the remote reaches of Hainan Island. I gave two lectures at leading Chinese universities, with ample opportunity to engage and debate a broad cross-section of students—by far, the nation's greatest asset. I even dabbled in a now-thriving contemporary Chinese art market. As I sit back and try to pull it altogether, I realize I am asking the impossible. Rich in contrasts and contradictions, China defies generalization.

Yet we in the West remain biased toward looking at China through a very macro lens—focusing on its daunting scale and what that means for us. Ironically, that misses the basic tension that defines Chinese reform and development, a tug-of-war between the micro and the macro. Beijing is the center, the personification of the control mechanism that drives China's macro story. Western impressions of China are formed by pilgrimages of the masses to the power centers of Beijing. It is the Mecca of the China story—but it is not China. An ancient Chinese proverb says it best, "The mountain is high, and the Emperor is far away." In other words, the real China exists at the provincial and local level, far removed from Beijing.

China's image suffers from the "1.3 billion syndrome"—the daunting math of economic development for 20 percent of the world's population. There's not a multinational corporation in the world that hasn't run numbers like this. Nor is there a politician in the developed world who hasn't had to face the concerns of workers and voters that stem from the implications of these calculations. The problem with this perspective is that it portrays China as a monolithic force, driven by the presumption of a relatively seamless transition from a centrally planned economy to a market-based system. In my view, that is the most important contradiction of the new China. While economic control was close to absolute under the old model of the state-owned economy, that is certainly not the case under the increasingly marketized system. Instead, power has gravitated more to the provincial, city, and village levels, making macro control from Beijing exceedingly difficult. There's nothing new, of course, about this phenomenon. There are over 5,000 years of history behind the fragmentation of governance in the Middle Kingdom. But what is new is the juxtaposition between China's persistent fragmentation and an increasingly market-based system—a dissonance that adds considerable complexity to our understanding of recent and prospective trends in the Chinese economy.

The most visible manifestation of this fragmentation shows up in China's runaway investment boom. The macro numbers speak for themselves. Fixed asset investment hit 45 percent of Chinese GDP in 2005 and could exceed the 50 percent threshold in 2006. This is where Chinese macro policy makers could quickly find themselves in a serious bind as they attempt to cool down the economy. Investment activity is driven very much at the local level, funded by a still highly fragmented Chinese banking system. Fixated on social stability and job creation, local communist party officials, through their influence on local bank branches, often have more to say about investment project approval than credit officers in head offices of the big banks in Beijing. The impact of local bank branches dwarfs the role of regulators and central bankers. The implications of this fragmentation effect are not lost on China's senior policy officials. It undermines policy traction at the macro level and raises the risk of a boom-bust response of the investment sector if Chinese officials were to go too far in their tightening efforts. As I noted earlier, the relatively modest moves in the current tightening cycle reflect just such a concern, in my view.

What I find particularly interesting is that Chinese municipalities are now taking it on themselves to issue regulations to cool off their overheated property markets. In other words, it's not enough for Beijing to send the message. It falls to local authorities to get the job done.

Shenzhen has taken the lead with an announcement on June 22, 2006 of ten tightening actions aimed at its property bubble, a pronouncement coming some three weeks after Beijing's so-called administrative edicts. According to press accounts, while there was little response to the national announcements, the Shenzhen residential property market has come to a virtual standstill in response to the local actions. This is an important real-time example of the tension between relatively impotent national tightening measures and the traction achieved through local administrative actions.

In my recent meetings with a broad cross-section of Chinese banks and companies, the tension between local and central control was a recurring theme. Motives are very different in both cases. For local officials, concerns over job creation, income support, and social stability are paramount. In conversations with local businesspersons and bankers, I got the distinct impression that they viewed their mandates and objectives independently of what was going on elsewhere in China. That was especially the case in Tianjin, whose Mayor, Dai Xiang Long, the former governor of China's central bank, certainly knows a great deal about macro policy concerns. Now charged with running this hypergrowth area about 175 km east of Beijing, Mayor Dai sees local growth imperatives in a very different light. He characterized the Beijing view—especially the last shift toward tightening—as being very much at odds with progrowth local objectives. At this point in time, the bankers and businesspersons I met with largely viewed the recent actions of the central government as more of an irritant than a major constraint. Mayor Dai, of course, wore two hats. Over dinner, he conceded that although sustainable growth for the overall Chinese economy was probably much closer to 7 percent than the current 10 percent pace, for Tianjin, he felt the sustainable growth trajectory was closer to 20 percent.

In the end, Jonathan Spence, Yale's great Sinologist, probably had it right, arguing that most Western observers have long wanted to see China in the same light they see themselves.[11] Dating back to Marco Polo's thirteenth-century accounts of his travels through China and going up to the Kissinger/Nixon impressions of the 1970s, Professor Spence deploys his well-honed tools of forensic history to demonstrate how the outside

---

11. See Jonathan D. Spence, *The Chan's Great Continent: China in Western Minds*, W.W. Norton & Company, New York, 1998.

world has failed repeatedly to grasp the "inside China." Well, as best I can tell, we're doing it again. The ascendancy of China onto the world stage has spawned a cottage industry of instant China experts in the West who are using a very traditional Western macro framework to depict the opportunities, as well as the stresses and strains of the Chinese economy. But there is an interesting twist at work today: To some extent, Modern China has played along with this ruse—reinforcing our misimpressions of the Chinese economy. The risk is we've all got it wrong.

On the surface, China presents itself as a very tidy macro package. It has a well-constructed national statistical system that conforms to international standards. It releases a full gamut of economic statistics on a regular basis. It has a central bank that was reorganized in 1998 along the lines of America's Federal Reserve System. Its fiscal policy stance is conveyed annually to the National People's Congress in the form of the Premier's "Work Report." China regularly attends G-7 meetings, weighing in as an outside observer on a broad range of macro issues—from global imbalances and world growth issues to trade policies and currency matters. And as the Chinese economy has come of age over the past 15 years, it has had increasingly important impacts on the rest of the world—especially with respect to inflation trends, global trade and capital flows, commodity markets, and the cross-border arbitrage of jobs and real wages.

With China now having such a Western appearance as well as a major impact on the global economy, we in the West want to believe we can examine the Chinese economy in the same fashion we look at any other macro system. That way, when things go wrong and it looks like China can be implicated in the problem, we can open the macro playbook and come up with a textbook prescription of orthodox remedies. Such is the case with respect to America's gaping trade deficit. Since the bilateral imbalance with China accounts for the largest piece of the multilateral U.S. trade deficit—some 25 percent in 2005—the conventional Washington and academic view has been to recommend a sharp appreciation of the renminbi relative to the dollar. I've never bought that because I view the U.S. trade deficit as a multilateral problem traceable to America's unprecedented shortfall of domestic saving. To deal with the Chinese piece of the problem would simply mean diverting the U.S. trade imbalance elsewhere. But even if China truly were the source of this problem, the currency solution may not make any sense. It requires a well-developed market system to redirect quantities (i.e., trade flows) through changes in relative prices (i.e., foreign exchange rates). Yet China is still very much a blended economy—only partly marketized with a still-large state-owned sector and a relatively undeveloped financial system. It's very difficult for the market-based invisible hand to operate effectively in such a context.

China still appears to be a long way away from a fully functioning macro system. As I crisscrossed this extraordinary country over the past 12 weeks, I was struck more than ever by the tension between the micro and the macro. Macro China has hit a critical sustainability impasse—the economy is far too reliant on investment and exports. And yet Micro China continues to power ahead—driven by autonomous development imperatives at the local level. In the end, fragmentation seriously complicates well-intended policy initiatives of macro control. Until China can resolve this contradiction, effective management of its rapidly growing economy is likely to remain elusive, and the risk of a boom-bust endgame cannot be ruled out.

# Soft Landing Made in China?

## August 21, 2006

With a second interest rate hike in four months, China has upped the ante in an effort to contain its overheated economy. The outcome of this operation transcends the direct impacts on the Chinese economy. It bears critically on China's ever-expanding global supply chain—especially commodity producers, the energy complex, and Asian component manufacturers. Moreover, China's tightening actions could reinforce the normalization campaigns of major central banks in the developed world, thereby buttressing the case for a global soft landing. Can China pull it off?

There can be little doubt that senior Chinese leaders are taking the overheating problem seriously. Both President Hu Jintao and Premier Wen Jiabao have used the bully pulpit repeatedly in urging a shift to slower growth. In terms of policy, the People's Bank of China has led the way. Interest rates and bank reserve ratios have been increased two times in the past four months—twice the degree of monetary tightening that was imposed in 2004, the last time the economy was overheated. On other counts, Chinese policy actions have been relatively limited. Although currency managers have tolerated greater volatility of the renminbi versus the dollar in recent days, there has been little movement in the central tendency of China's foreign exchange rate. Similarly, although some administrative actions have been announced in recent months aimed at containing investment projects in selected overheated sectors, the scope of such measures still appears relatively narrow. In that same vein, little has been heard recently from Chairman Ma Kai of the National Development and Reform Commission (NDRC)—China's chief economic planner and the key point person on the administrative side of its policy equation.

Inasmuch as China remains very much a blended economy, that is, a combination of a state-owned and market-directed system, the verdict on its current tightening campaign is far from clear cut. Significantly, a shift in monetary policy achieves traction only when the banking system and financial markets are fully developed, something that is still very much lacking in China today. A decentralized banking system—dominated by independent local branches of nationwide banks, as well as by largely autonomous regional banks—remains a critical stumbling block to effective macro control of the Chinese economy. The blunt instruments of monetary policy achieve traction only if branch lending is tied to deposit growth and funding costs of the parent bank. Moreover, increases in bank reserve ratios, such as the two that have been announced in the past four months, do nothing to limit bank lending capacity for a system whose major banks have long maintained an excess reserve position.

Largely for these reasons, overall RMB-based bank-lending growth continued to surge at a 16 percent year-over-year rate in July 2006—well in excess of the central bank's targeted lending path. In fact, over the first seven months of 2006, overall loan creation amounted to fully 94 percent of the bank lending targeted for the entire year. In other words, the People's Bank of China has very little to show for a tightening campaign that began in late April.

At the same time, state-owned enterprises (SOEs)—which continue to account for between 30–40 percent of the Chinese economy—behave very differently than private and publicly owned businesses. Since SOEs are not creatures of the markets, they are not heavily influenced by policy actions designed to impact markets. This gets to what could well be a major glitch in the current tightening campaign: As noted earlier, fragmentation of the financial system and real economy could well complicate any Beijing-directed cooling-off initiatives (see "China's Great Contradiction," p. 199–203).

The fragmentation factor is underscored by Figure 3.10, which highlights the dichotomy between hypergrowth in eight of China's 31 provinces and the rest of the country. These regions, which collectively contain about 40 percent of China's total population, have accounted for 72 percent of total Chinese GDP growth since 2000. I have been to many of China's hypergrowth areas myself and witnessed firsthand their explosive growth in infrastructure, urbanization, and capital investment in new plant and equipment. I have also spoken directly with regional leaders in many of these provinces—governors, mayors, and bankers who preach the mantra of open-ended growth for years to come, regardless of cycles in the national economy. Beijing's macro policy adjustments

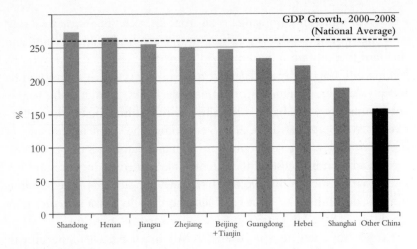

**Figure 3.10**  China's Control Problem: Regional vs. Macro Tensions
*Source:* China National Bureau of Statistics, Morgan Stanley Research.

have done little to arrest the micro sources of overheating. Press reports have highlighted recent punitive actions taken against Inner Mongolian officials for allowing excess investment. But these actions have not done much of anything to temper a runaway growth problem that is still heavily concentrated in coastal China.

In fact, there really aren't any convincing signs of a slowing in China's investment boom. Gains in total fixed asset investment—a sector that rose to fully 45 percent of Chinese GDP in 2005—held at an astonishing 31 percent year-over-year rate in July 2006. The same fragmentation phenomenon is at work here as well—augmented by special tax incentives offered for foreign direct investment. Such foreign commitment to outsourcing has gone hand-in-hand with China's export bonanza. Chinese subsidiaries of multinational corporations and foreign-invested joint ventures—so-called foreign-invested enterprises—have accounted for fully 65 percent of cumulative growth in total exports over the past 12 years. In short, by conscious design, China has become a well-oiled export- and investment-led growth machine driven by powerful micro forces operating at the regional level. The macro tightening initiatives announced by Beijing, which focus mainly on the national price of credit, do not address this key aspect of a regionally driven overheating problem.

Left to its own devices, China's white-hot economy could veer dangerously out of control, culminating in a wrenching boom-bust cycle. In my view, the stakes are simply too high for the Chinese leadership to sit back and allow such a devastating endgame to unfold. I look for a three-pronged cooling-off strategy to address this problem: One, an expansion of administrative edicts aimed at controlling excess investment is likely. So far, restraints have been imposed on just a few industries—namely, aluminum, cement, ferrous alloys, coal, coking coal, carbide-based PVC, and speculative activity in residential property construction. I expect the NDRC to expand this list shortly. Two, the pace of banking-system reform must accelerate if China is to have any hope of achieving traction for monetary policy. The public listing of state-owned policy banks is only the beginning of this process. Banking reform must also entail centralization of a far-flung network of local branches. Three, further macro restraint is needed for both monetary and currency policies: Monetary tightening is the functional equivalent of a rhetorical straightjacket for an undisciplined banking system, while currency reforms could be used to temper foreign political pressures and defuse protectionist risks.

Success for China will likely be measured in two ways: a slowing of industrial output growth below the 15 percent threshold, and a rebalancing of the mix of Chinese GDP growth away from exports and fixed investment toward private consumption. Only if those conditions are satisfied, can the sustainability of Chinese reform and development be assured. Under the presumption that such a slowdown comes to pass, there can be no mistaking the implications for the rest of the world. The energy and commodity-producing complex will be on the leading edge of feeling the impacts, as the mix of China's economic growth should shift toward more of a commodity-efficient growth dynamic driven by private consumer demand (see "A Commodity-Lite China," p. 189–193). China's regional trading partners—especially Japan, Korea, and Taiwan—will also be effected by a slowdown in Chinese output growth that sparks concomitant reductions in demand for manufactured components by Asia's increasingly China-centric supply chain.

The big risk in all of this is that Beijing refuses to bite the bullet and, instead, delays restraint. Concerns over social stability—long the most worrisome repercussion of reforms—could well tempt risk-averse Chinese leaders to let the economy run hotter for longer. Yet this could be a recipe for eventual disaster, triggering a lethal combination of runaway investment morphing into excess capacity, runaway exports triggering protectionism, and runaway excess liquidity leading to asset bubbles. Reining in the excesses of China's overheated economy is an increasingly urgent challenge that senior Chinese leaders must address sooner rather than later. It will take a good deal more in the way of restraint to pull off a Chinese soft landing. However, without such moderation, the case for a global soft landing could be drawn into question. Fortunately, time and again over the past 10 years, China's reformers have risen to the occasion. I am hopeful that will be the case this time as well.

# The Great Chinese Profits Debate

*October 6, 2006*

The profitability of Chinese businesses has suddenly become a *cause célèbre*. One group—led by the World Bank—argues that enterprise profitability has soared in recent years, playing an increasingly important role in boosting China's already high national saving rate and current account surplus. The other side—spearheaded by Weijian Shan of TPG Newbridge and long one of Asia's most successful investors—maintains that China's national income accounts bias conventional measures of profitability to the upside, masking a decidedly subpar return on equity and a serious bank-directed misallocation of capital. The debate is technical and it takes forensic analytics to wade through it, but it has very important implications for investors, China's macro policies, and the Chinese economy.

In a series of recent research papers, World Bank economists came to the very important conclusion that a significant portion of China's sharply elevated national saving rate—estimated to be close to 50 percent of GDP in 2005—is due to sharply rising levels of enterprise saving and profitability. If correct, the resulting windfall of retained earnings implies that China's investment boom has been increasingly self-financed—drawing into serious question the widespread presumption that investment projects have, instead, been funded more by directed lending of a highly fragmented Chinese banking system. Specifically, World Bank economists estimate that after-tax enterprise saving from retained earnings rose to more than 20 percent of GDP in 2005, leading them to conclude that Chinese banks funded only about one-third of enterprise fixed investment while more than 50 percent of the financing came from internally generated profits. The World Bank's findings, which were based on one of the first analyses of China's so-called flow of funds accounts, portray China's business sector as surprisingly sound and robust—increasingly capable of standing on its own in providing the sustenance for future expansion.[12]

In the other corner is Weijian Shan of TPG Newbridge, a former Wharton professor and principal in some of Asia's most important investment transactions of the past decade. In a recent article, Shan took the World Bank economists to task, arguing that their analysis was based on a flawed interpretation and analysis of aggregate data.[13] Basically, Shan underscores the critical distinction between national income-based measures of saving and business profitability and metrics used by businesses and investors. He not only makes the point that national income accounts often go astray in estimating profits, but he also argues that, in the case of China, the World Bank calculations fail to net out income taxes and government subsidies. He goes further to derive the leverage and return characteristics of the Chinese economy that can be imputed from the World Bank scenario, namely that debt-to-equity ratios would need to be declining steadily over time and that return on equity would have to be increasing sharply. As an investor and businessman who has evaluated countless potential transactions in China, Shan speaks from a micro experience that is completely at odds with the macro imputations of the World Bank.

There are three reasons why this debate is such a big deal. First, China is having a serious problem controlling an overheated investment sector. It makes a huge difference if investments are funded internally through surging profits and retained earnings, as the World Bank argues, or if this is a bank-sponsored investment binge. In the former instance, an investment slowdown can best be engineered by policies that crimp internal funding. Alternatively, if runaway bank lending were the culprit, monetary tightening and/or administrative edicts would be more appropriate. Interestingly enough, the World Bank's conclusions appear to have found sympathy in some quarters of official China: recently, a proposal

12. See Louis Kuijs, "Investment and Saving in China," World Bank Policy Research Working paper 3633, June 2005, and an unpublished September 2006 note by Bert Hoffman and Louis Kuijs of the World Bank Office Beijing, "Profits and Investment of China's Enterprises."
13. See Weijian Shan's, "The World Bank's China Delusions," *Far Eastern Economic Review*, September 2006.

was floated for the State to begin collecting dividends from state-owned holding companies—an action designed to crimp an internally funded investment binge. Second, rate of return results are obviously of critical importance to investors in Chinese securities markets—both onshore and offshore. "Profitless prosperity" has long been a major concern of equity investors with respect to Chinese companies. If the World Bank calculations are correct, those fears may be overblown. Third, Chinese banking reform is at the top of the nation's policy agenda—in part, because of the understandable fear of a serious and growing nonperforming loan problem. To the extent that the World Bank is correct, the current Chinese investment boom poses less of a threat to the banks than would be the case under the Shan scenario.

Where do I come out on this? Long ago, I realized that there is never a clear winner in these statistical debates. The numbers can invariably be sliced and diced in a variety of ways to validate a wide range of alternative hypotheses. In the case of China, there's an added twist—the statistics are a good deal shakier than in most other countries. That may especially be the case with respect to its newly constructed flow-of-funds accounts—an elaborate matrix of cross-sector financial transactions that interfaces with the national income accounts. China has long been plagued with measurement problems in its macroeconomic data. Appending a flow-of-funds system to the national income accounts could well compound the problems. To the extent that the World Bank findings rest on these data, I would be even more suspicious. Nor have I ever been all that comfortable in using national income accounts data to assess business sector profitability. Even in countries like the United States, with well-developed statistical systems, the profits estimates have typically been the weakest link in the chain—subject to large revisions, to say nothing of frequent discrepancies with micro data gathered at the company level. Quite frankly, I have to say that I am astonished that the World Bank is leaning so hard on a literal interpretation of what could well be the least reliable piece of Chinese macro data.

Shan's approach stresses the inherent implausibility of the World Bank's findings. If the World Bank's upbeat conclusions on profitability are valid, he points out that several time-honored aspects of the China story need to be re-cast—namely trends in aggregate debt-to-equity ratios as well as return on investment. In the World Bank depiction, these ratios would paint a picture of an increasingly vibrant Chinese business sector that miraculously has repudiated the profitless heritage of state ownership.

Yet with material costs surging and wage pressures mounting, I have a hard time accepting that characterization in the current climate. At the same time, I have long been struck by one of the greatest contradictions of Chinese GDP growth: With fixed investment now fully 50 percent of Chinese GDP and still increasing at close to 30 percent per annum, it is actually quite astonishing that the overall economy hasn't been growing a good deal faster than the 10 percent average over the past decade. By way of comparison, during Japan's high growth era in the early 1960s, which on a GDP basis was quite comparable to the current Chinese experience, its capex-to-GDP ratio peaked out at 28 percent, or more than 20 percentage points below the current Chinese rate. This underscores the inefficiency of aggregate investment in today's Chinese economy—both in absolute terms and in a relative sense when compared with the Japanese experience. This is consistent with Shan's critique and very much against the grain of the World Bank's conclusions.

Martin Wolf, in a recent column in the *Financial Times*, sides with the World Bank—endorsing the notion that Chinese macro policy should be directed at forcing enterprises to reduce surplus saving by paying out dividends.[14] He readily accepts his own depiction of the counterintuitive premise that ". . . the lumbering state-owned sector is making large profits." Wolf argues that, if Chinese business profits aren't strong, then at least one of the following four assertions must be wrong: the current account surplus is overstated, government saving is understated, the investment share of Chinese GDP is lower than estimated, or the personal saving rate is much higher than reported. Since he presumes that none of these possibilities is likely, *post hoc ergo propter hoc*, profits must indeed be booming.

The flaw in this logic could well lie with the personal saving rate. The combination of massive layoffs—headcount reductions by state-owned enterprises exceeding 60 million since 1997—and the lack of a safety net is a classic recipe for a surge in precautionary saving. As noted earlier, a recent Gallup Poll of Chinese consumers is, in fact, quite consistent with such a possibility, finding that the level of dissatisfaction over household saving positions has risen steadily over the 1997–2004 interval (see p. 179–183). Moreover, the private consumption share of Chinese GDP fell to a record low of 38 percent in 2005 and has undoubtedly fallen

---

14. See his October 4, 2006 comment, "Why Beijing Should Dip into China's Corporate Piggy Bank."

further in 2006. In other words, it may well be that the official statistics have distorted the mix of China's domestic saving—allocating too much to the business sector and not enough to households.

When it comes to China, I have been an eternal optimist. My conviction is grounded in the nation's unrelenting commitment to reforms and in the related push toward a market-based system. State-owned enterprise reforms remain central to this daunting transition. This has been a wrenching process—in many cases creating companies from an agglomeration of former government bureaucracies. It takes time for these efforts to bear fruit. A burst of newfound profitability from the Chinese business sector seems highly unlikely at this overheated point in the development cycle.

# China Goes for Quality

## December 4, 2006

The Chinese are getting serious about wanting to shift the focus of their extraordinary economic development from quantity to quality. This transition has been actively discussed in China for over three years, but in extensive meetings in Beijing in late November 2006, I sensed that the quality debate has finally come to a head. This could have very important implications for China's trade policies, commodity demand, environmental considerations, banking reform, and its capital allocation process. It is a very big deal.

Western perceptions of the Chinese economy are formed largely on the basis of the quantity dimension of its remarkable transformation. This is perfectly understandable, because the nation's GDP per capita has more than quadrupled over the past 15 years, taking China from the world's tenth largest economy in 1991 to the fourth largest in 2006. With a population of 1.3 billion people, a 10 percent growth trajectory puts the scale effects of Chinese economic development in an entirely different league than the world has ever experienced. Given the daunting transition from state to private ownership, China needed such hypergrowth to offset the massive job losses stemming from the reforms of its state-owned enterprises (SOE)—cumulative headcount reductions of more than 60 million workers since 1997, alone. The Chinese feel they had no choice other than to focus on the quantity of growth in the face of such extraordinary job loss. The strategy was critical in order to maintain social stability, by far the single greatest concern in this first phase of China's reform experience.

But now the most disruptive phase of SOE reforms is in the past. That eases China's dependence on the quantity imperatives of economic growth and allows reformers the opportunity to focus on the long-neglected quality dimension of its transformation and development. This shift in the character of economic growth couldn't come at a better time. The "negative externalities" of the quantity fixation are starting to loom increasingly formidable. Long dominated by exceptionally rapid gains in export-led industrial activity, the Chinese growth model has been characterized by open-ended investment spending, undisciplined bank funding, environmental degradation, nearly insatiable demand for oil and other industrial materials, and mounting trade frictions. With industrial output, which makes up about 50 percent of Chinese GDP, accelerating to a roughly 17 percent average annual growth rate over the four years ending in 2006, those externalities have become increasingly serious. By shifting its focus from quantity to quality, China is, in effect, acknowledging an increasingly urgent need to address head-on the negative repercussions of hyper growth.

Trade policy is the most immediate item on the quality agenda. The first meeting of the newly established strategic economic dialog with the United States is now less than two weeks away—set for December 14–15 of 2006 in Beijing. Led by U.S. Treasury Secretary Hank Paulson, a high-level U.S. delegation will not want to go away empty-handed when it comes to coping with a large and ever-widening bilateral trade deficit with China—estimated at $202 billion in 2005 and at least $225 billion in 2006, and equal to fully 25 percent of America's record multilateral trade deficit. Paulson has already set the stage for a very important shift in the U.S.-China bilateral trade discussions—attempting to broaden out the debate from a single-minded fixation on the currency issue. That's not to say the U.S. delegation won't put pressure on China to accelerate the pace of renminbi revaluation, but it will also push for more Chinese progress on the equally important matters of financial sector reforms and protection of intellectual property rights (IPR).

What I found in late November 2006 in Beijing is that the Chinese may be willing to move more aggressively on the IPR issue than has been the case in the past. There is a key reason for this shift: Inasmuch as China's economic prowess has moved rapidly up the value chain in recent years—from low-value-added items such as toys and textiles to increasingly high-value-added technology products—there is a growing consensus forming within the Chinese leadership that IPR protection is now in China's best interest, as well. As one senior official put it best to me in late November 2006, "Since the China of tomorrow will be more about innovation, knowledge-based breakthroughs, and brands, we will need to protect our own IPR." This speaks of a China that is now putting increasing value on the quality of its intellectual capital rather than on the quantity potential of its mass-production platform. OECD (Organization for Economic Cooperation and Development) data underscore how far China has come in investing in the basic research underpinnings of intellectual property: In 2006, it overtook Japan and stood second only to the United States in the global research and development spending sweepstakes. Little wonder China now wants to protect its own proprietary knowledge base. There appears to be a great opportunity for a breakthrough on the all-important and long-contentious IPR issue at the upcoming U.S.-China strategic economic dialog—an outcome that could pull the rug out from under the increasingly vocal protectionists in the U.S. Congress.

I also found China more willing to focus on upgrading the quality of its manufacturing technology. The degradation of the Chinese environment has now reached a serious threshold: Fully 7 of the 10 most polluted cities in the world are in China, according to World Bank statistics. Moreover, China leads the world in water pollution by a wide margin, emitting three times as many organic water pollutants as the number two polluter, the United States, whose economy is five-and-a-half times the size of China's. At the same time, Chinese production is woefully inefficient when it comes to reliance on energy and other raw materials. For example, China currently requires about twice as much oil per unit of GDP as the rest of the world, according to the International Energy Association.

The recently enacted 11th Five-Year Plan has a stated target of reducing China's oil per unit of GDP by 4 percent a year, or 20 percent over the 2006–2010 period. At the same time, the government wants to move away from a commodity-heavy growth model that gobbles up outsize portions of base metals and other raw materials. Chinese leaders—especially those at the National Development and Reform Commission, who still guide the national planning process—feel this can best be accomplished by shifting away from rapidly growing commodity-intensive fixed investment toward more of a commodity-lite growth model centered increasingly on private consumption. Whether it's curtailing pollution or cutting back a voracious appetite for energy and other industrial materials, I sensed a heightened awareness in official Beijing to tackle this important aspect of the quality problem.

I noticed a similar approach toward the quality of Chinese bank lending. Interestingly enough, there is a clear consensus among Chinese banking regulators as well as senior banking officials that another round of nonperforming loans is inevitable once the economy slows. Both China's regulators and bankers felt that the excesses of the current investment boom—with fixed investment climbing toward the unheard of and worrisome 50 percent threshold—have become a breeding ground for new NPLs. China very much needs to increase the quality of its capital allocation process. Reforms, according to the Chinese I met with last week, are the only means to accomplish this—especially reforms that inject greater discipline into the investment and loan approval process. The recent imposition of administrative edicts curtailing fixed investment in a number of overheated sectors is helpful in this regard, as is a new effort aimed at increasing the selectivity of foreign direct investment. In both cases, however, the administrative policies are only Band-Aids until the establishment of a robust market-driven system of capital allocation. Equally encouraging are recent public listings of the large Chinese banks, which should inject market-driven incentives into an increasingly commercialized bank lending business. In the end, however, the centralization of a still highly fragmented Chinese banking system is essential in order to instill a rigorous, commercially viable lending culture. With a China slowdown likely to come sooner rather than later, I sensed a new urgency in Beijing in dealing with this critical aspect of the quality problem.

Finally, I picked up a subtle, but important, shift in China's overall attitude toward reform. In the spring of 2006, there were visible signs of a worrisome pushback against one key element of the reform process—the opportunity for foreign multinational corporations to take strategic stakes in Chinese enterprises. There was a gathering concern in some quarters that foreigners were buying precious State assets on the cheap especially because a surging Chinese stock market was quick to inflate the market value of foreign-acquired stakes. According to insiders involved in China's financial sector reforms, those fears have since subsided, as the proreform faction in the senior Chinese leadership recently appears to have won out in a struggle with Party conservatives. A potentially worrisome dilution in the quality of reforms has been avoided as a result.

In the end, the quality of the growth experience is the ultimate arbiter of its sustainability. China has elected to go for quantity since the onset of the current reforms back in 1978. It has had remarkable success in staying that course. But as China now comes of age, it is only natural that such an approach change, with greater attention placed on the quality dimension of the economic growth outcome. There is undoubtedly an important tradeoff between these two characteristics of the growth experience. A new emphasis on quality probably means that China will have to compromise on the quantity front. The good news is that, as a 10 percent growth machine—and recently even faster than that—this is a luxury China can well afford. Contrary to widespread perceptions, China doesn't need 10 to 11 percent economic growth to ensure social stability. Its newly enacted Five-Year Plan, which is tilted toward meaningful improvement on the quality front, calls for just 7.5 percent average GDP growth through 2010.

A major external shock is the only real stumbling block I see in this potential realignment in the Chinese growth model. A U.S.-led shortfall of global growth or a politically inspired outbreak of Washington-led protectionism are the biggest risks in that regard—the former providing a temporary setback and the latter a more worrisome systemic risk. But barring those possibilities, the China I saw in late November in 2006 seems more than willing to pay the price of somewhat slower growth and opt increasingly for quality over quantity. That's outstanding news for China and for the rest of the world.

# Heavy Lifting

## March 5, 2007

The rebalancing of any economy is never easy. Nor is there a boiler-plate recipe for such a daunting transformation. For a state-directed Chinese economy, the challenges are very different from those in a market-based economy like the United States. China is now taking an important step on the road to rebalancing, moving to rein in the excesses of an investment boom and a stock market bubble. A key question for the national People's Congress as it now gathers in Beijing: What comes next?

Most believe the answer lies with the Chinese consumer. The numbers are compelling: Private consumption in the world's most populous nation currently accounts for only about 35 percent of its GDP—half the elevated share in the United States, well below portions elsewhere in the developing world, and quite possibly the lowest consumption share of any major economy in modern history. There's obviously nothing but upside to the case for the Chinese consumer. This is widely billed as one of the great hopes and opportunities of China's rebalancing—able to fill the void left by any slowing in investment or exports.

I wish it were that easy. Centrally planned or not, China can't simply push a button to bring its vast consumer sector immediately into play. Consumer cultures, in many respects, are the DNA of market-based capitalism. China has taken only small steps in that direction. With over 60 million layoffs traceable to the state-owned enterprise reforms of the past decade, job and income insecurity is rife amongst the Chinese workforce. The lack of a nationwide social safety net—especially social security, pensions, medical care, and unemployment insurance—only compounds that problem. As such, Chinese households, motivated by fear of uncertain economic prospects, are predisposed toward an inordinate amount of precautionary saving. Reflecting this penchant for personal thrift, China's national savings rate is now close to 50 percent, the highest for any major economy in the world and a major stumbling block to the development of a more vibrant consumer culture.

The just-released results of the 2006 Gallup Poll of China underscore three key obstacles that the consumer still presents to a rebalancing of the Chinese economy: (1) Fully 65 percent of Chinese households remain dissatisfied with their saving positions, up from a 61 percent dissatisfaction reading in 1997. Consistent with a powerful precautionary saving motive, the Gallup Poll found that worries about an adequate safety net were the major reasons behind such dissatisfaction—especially in the areas of retirement funding, healthcare, and children's education. (2) Widening income disparities are also inhibiting the expansion of a broader base to Chinese consumption. This is evident in both urban and rural areas, where the Gallup tally shows that the difference between the upper and lower quintiles of household incomes increased by about 40 percent in 2006 relative to 2004; this is the largest increase in income inequality in the 10-year history of Gallup's China Poll. (3) The lifestyle benefits of urbanization are concentrated in China's "Top 10" cities; by contrast, citizens in Middle China—medium-size urban centers—remain on the outside looking in. With income disparities increasing much more in medium-size cities than in large ones, China's urban consumption base remains disappointingly narrow.

These findings are not lost on Chinese policymakers. They remain very focused on a proconsumption rebalancing of the Chinese economy. The 11th Five-Year Plan enacted by the National People's Congress a year ago in March 2006 addressed two of these issues head-on: the need for a national safety net and the imperatives of tempering rising income inequalities. Greater priority was placed on support for the woefully underfunded National Social Security Fund, which currently holds just RMB 300 billion, or roughly $30 per capita. Emphasis was also directed at rural income support, especially tax incentives and improved medical and educational allowances. In addition, the latest Five-Year Plan is quite explicit in identifying China's relatively undeveloped service sector as a new and important source of job creation in the future. Chinese leaders recognize the need to draw increased support from labor-intensive tertiary industries, especially those involved in distribution and delivery, like wholesale and retail trade, as well as transnational shipping. On balance, the 11th Five-Year Plan is probably the most proconsumer effort ever put forth by the Chinese leadership. It underscores how far China needs to go in removing the obstacles that currently inhibit the development of a flourishing nationwide consumer culture—a challenge I expect will be actively debated at the 2007 National People's Congress.

Equally serious constraints are evident in China's saving and capital allocation mechanism—and in the financial-sector reforms that any such breakthroughs would require. China has made major progress in the areas of banking and capital markets reforms in the past five years, but these initiatives have effectively started from ground zero. The public listing of three of China's largest banks was a very important step in the creation of a new financial system, especially in instilling a shareholder-value culture that will ultimately drive profitability and discourage lax lending practices. But, here as well, this is a long and arduous road for China—especially the transformation of legions of former government bureaucrats into discriminating bank lending officers. In the end, the integrity of a prudential lending function is the essence of a market-based credit culture for any economy. Through strategic alliances with several major foreign banks, China is making progress in this area, but the heavy lifting in the personnel, internal control systems, and risk management areas of Chinese banking reforms has only just begun.

Two other obstacles compound the capital allocation problem in China: the currency regime and a lack of progress on broader capital market reforms. I don't buy the notion that China's currency policy is a threat to global trade. I feel, instead, that many in the developed world—especially the savings-short United States—are treating RMB-related issues as scapegoats for their own macro shortcomings. I worry more about China's quasi-fixed currency regime as a source of its own domestic instability—largely in fostering massive speculative capital inflows and a build-up of foreign exchange reserves. China's currency policy requires these inflows to be recycled into dollar-based assets and neutralized through a massive sterilization exercise. To the extent that China's undeveloped domestic debt market makes such sterilization difficult, excess liquidity undoubtedly spills over into its banking system. The latest trends in bank lending underscore this problem: Despite a series of recent hikes in bank reserve ratios, RMB loan growth accelerated from 13 percent year-over-year in June 2006 to 16 percent in December 2006. With China's policymakers trying to clamp down on excessive investment, curtail an equity bubble, and limit a new wave of nonperforming bank loans, the persistent excesses of bank lending growth complicates the macro control problem.

An equally glaring shortcoming is China's lack of capital market development, especially the low level of activity in its corporate bond market. In 2006, China's domestic capital markets—equity and bonds, combined—accounted for only about 18 percent of total funds raised by the business sector; equities made up the bulk of that total, whereas corporate bond issuance was only about 3 percent of overall funding. By contrast, banks accounted for fully 82 percent of total credit intermediation. That underscores yet another obstacle on the road to rebalancing: China's still fragmented banking system has long been tied to the funding of a vast network of inefficient and largely unprofitable state-owned enterprises. In the past, this has led to a massive surge of nonperforming loans, a problem that could well resurface once the dust settles on the current bank-funded investment boom. Overreliance on still inefficient banks, in conjunction with a lack of capital-markets-based discipline, underscore the serious risks of a misallocation of Chinese saving and investment.

China is at a critical juncture. Over the past 15 years, its powerful investment- and export-led growth model has been driven by bank-directed recycling of a massive pool of domestic saving. Coupled with aggressive and unprecedented reforms of its state-owned enterprises, China's transition to "market-based socialism" has been nothing short of spectacular. But this strategy is now in danger of outliving its usefulness. The investment sector has gone to excess and the export dynamic is at risk of triggering a protectionist backlash. The lack of a vibrant consumer sector, in conjunction with the legacy effects of state- and bank-directed capital allocation, are critical obstacles that must be overcome if the Chinese economy is to move to the next level.

China's unbalanced macro structure also presents its leadership with major cyclical control problems. Lacking in well-developed market-based systems, China recently upped the ante in opting for administrative controls to cope with its mounting imbalances. The latest such actions—state-directed equity selling and a clampdown of short-term foreign borrowing by domestic Chinese banks—may well have played a key role in sparking a worldwide equity market correction in late February of 2007. In my view, they were not one-off developments. Based on Premier Wen Jiabao's opening speech to the 2007 National People's Congress, these actions may only be the first salvo in a broader tightening campaign. Yet this approach is not without its own shortcomings. Administrative actions not only underscore the state-dominated mindset that still pervades the

China model, but they are mainly stopgap measures that circumvent more robust market-driven solutions. In my view, the only viable answer is an acceleration of reforms, focusing both on the nascent consumer as well as on an embryonic financial system. A successful rebalancing of the Chinese economy is essential to avoid the boom-bust cycles that were so prevalent in the past. Yet until the obstacles to any such rebalancing are removed, China's overheated investment sector and overextended export machine pose increasingly serious risks to sustainable and stable growth.

Brilliant as its success has been since the early 1990s, China can no longer afford to stay the same course. A new direction is essential—and the sooner the better. As the National People's Congress now meets in Beijing, the obstacles to Chinese rebalancing—and the tactics needed to overcome these obstacles—could well be at the top of its agenda.

# Two Birds with One Stone
*March 12, 2007*

Pollution is invariably one of the first impressions visitors form of China. From bicycles to cars in 25 years, urban China rarely sees much in the way of blue sky anymore. Rapid and large-scale industrialization only compounds the problem. The Chinese government knows full well it must take prompt and forceful actions to avoid an environmental crisis. There are encouraging signs that it is now rising to the occasion. Can China pull it off while staying the course of its remarkable economic development strategy?

On a per capita basis, China's pollution problem hardly jumps off the page. Its ratio of carbon emissions per person is less than half the global average and less than one-tenth that of the world's biggest polluter, the United States. China's enormous population, of course, distorts those comparisons. On an absolute basis, it's a different story altogether. In 2006, China's total carbon emissions were more than double those of Japan and Russia, fractionally behind the European Union, and a little more than half those of the United States. The essence of the Chinese environmental degradation problem is both its scale and growth. Over the 1992–2002 period, carbon-dioxide emissions in China have expanded at a 3.7 percent average annual rate, more than two and a half times the global average of 1.4 percent. At that rate, according to a recent report issued by the International Energy Agency, China will surpass the United States as the global leader in carbon emissions by 2009.

In terms of sulfur dioxide, China's current rate of discharge is already double its so-called environmental capacity, and it is responsible for an acid rain that now covers about one-third of China's total land mass. According to sulfur dioxide-based measure of air pollution, seven of the ten most polluted cities in the world are in China (see Table 3.2). With respect to emissions of organic water pollutants, China leads the world by more than three times the number two polluter, the United States (see Table 3.3). Moreover, fully 90 percent of China's urban rivers are polluted, and 90 percent of its grassland has been degraded.[15]

China's environmental moment of truth is now at hand. The problem is twofold: It is not just an issue of moving from dirty to clean technologies, but also a matter of shifting the macro structure of the Chinese economy from a pollution-intensive to an environmentally friendly mix. This latter point is a key and often overlooked aspect of China's environmental challenge. It is also a crucial element of the rebalancing challenge that shapes China's macro debate. This issue, in a nutshell, is that the Chinese economy is heavily skewed toward exports and fixed investment, which now collectively make up over 80 percent of China's GDP. This concentration represents the most lopsided mix of a major economy in modern history. It is not sustainable from a macro point of view because it threatens to produce the twin possibilities of a deflationary overhang of excess capacity and a protectionist backlash to open-ended exports. And it is not sustainable from an environmental point of view because the industrial-production-dominated growth model has a natural bias toward excessive carbon emissions.

**Table 3.2**   Environmental Degradation: Air Pollution Rankings, Sulfur Dioxide (mcg/m³)

| | |
|---|---|
| 1.  Guiyang, China | 424 |
| 2.  Chongqing, China | 340 |
| 3.  Taiyuan, China | 211 |
| 4.  Tehran, Iran | 209 |
| 5.  Zibo, China | 198 |
| 6.  Qingdao, China | 190 |
| 7.  Jihan, China | 132 |
| 8.  Rio de Janeiro, Brazil | 129 |
| 9.  Istanbul, Turkey | 120 |
| 10.  Anshow, China | 115 |

*Source:* World Bank.

---

15. Data cited are from Al Gore's *An Inconvenient Truth,* 2006; Nicholas Stern's *The Economics of Climate Change,"* 2007; and a recent paper prepared by the Development Research Center of China's State Council, "China: Accelerating Structural Adjustment and Growth Pattern Change," 2007.

**Table 3.3**  Emissions of Organic Water Pollutants
(kg/day, million units)

| | |
|---|---|
| 1. China | 6.09 |
| 2. United States | 1.90 |
| 3. Russia | 1.52 |
| 4. India | 1.52 |
| 5. Japan | 1.28 |
| 6. Germany | 1.02 |
| 7. Indonesia | 0.72 |
| 8. Brazil | 0.63 |
| 9. UK | 0.61 |
| 10. Italy | 0.50 |

*Source:* World Bank.

The paucity of data on the carbon intensity of the various sectors of the Chinese economy makes it difficult to quantify the environmental implications of the mix of its GDP. The carbon intensity of the UK experience illustrates what China is up against. Not surprisingly, according to the *Stern Review*, services are at the low end of the UK spectrum, averaging around 0.3 on the carbon intensity scale; for manufacturing industries, the range is wide—motor vehicles (0.5) and sporting goods/toys (0.8) are at the low end while the paper (2.4) and steel (2.7) industries are at the high end. A comparable dispersion is evident in the energy share of UK business costs, with nontransportation services at the low end of the spectrum and manufacturing at the high end.[16]

OK, China is not exactly England. But I strongly suspect that the relative dispersion of the carbon- and energy-intensity of the major sectors of the Chinese economy is comparable to that of the UK. Under that presumption, consider the following: The latest data put China's industrial sector at around 52 percent of its GDP, well in excess of the 32 percent share of the average developed economy and considerably higher than the 37 percent average of the low- and middle-income countries of the developing world. As a result, China's manufacturing-intensive economy is highly skewed toward a pollution- and energy-intensive model of economic activity.

In the case of China, there is an added complication—it is the heaviest consumer of coal of all the major economies in the world today.

---

16. See Nicholas Stern, *The Economics of Climate Change: The Stern Review,* 2007, *op cit.*

According to China's Development Research Center, coal-driven power accounted for fully 79 percent of total electricity generated in 2003, 8 percentage points higher than in 1990 and essentially double the 40 percent share of coal-powered electricity for the world as a whole. The adverse environmental implications of coal power are well known; according to the *Stern Review,* the carbon dioxide emissions of coal per unit of energy generation are twice as much as those associated with natural gas and about 50 percent more than those generated by oil-burning technologies. Inasmuch as UK coal consumption—fueling 34 percent of the country's total energy generation—is less than half the share of China, there is good reason to believe that the pollution implications for the Chinese economy per unit of GDP would be a good deal worse than those implied by the British results just cited.

The India comparison is also interesting. India's per capita carbon emissions are only about half those in China and its total emissions are about one-third those of the Chinese. But the 4.3 percent average annual growth rate of Indian carbon dioxide emissions over the 1992–2002 period is more than 15 percent faster than the rapid growth in China, suggesting that if India stays its current course, its environmental threats will also quickly get out of hand. Even so, the structure of Indian GDP—a much smaller industrial portion (28 percent) than China (52 percent) and a much larger services share (53 percent) than China (34 percent)—is biased toward less pollution- and energy-intensive growth. That's not to let India off the hook, but only to stress that, in terms of environmental risks, China is very much in a league of its own.

The bottom line for China is a GDP that is far more predisposed toward environmental degradation than any other major economy in the world today. For an economy that is growing at 10 percent per year, that spells an endgame of environmental crisis—sooner rather than later—if it stays its present course. And for the planet, even though China currently lags behind the big polluters of the developed world, it could well hold the key to the perils of global climate change. The principles of global remediation, as put forth in international agreements such as the Kyoto Protocol, have always recognized a progressivity of burden sharing—that rich developed economies should fund a greater share of the mitigation than poor developing economies. Yet the Chinese environment is now nearing a critical tipping point that demands urgent action on its own merits rather than special dispensation because of its status as a large, low-income developing country.

China has a rare and important opportunity to kill two birds with one stone. A successful rebalancing of the Chinese economy—moving away from excess reliance on investment and exports and embracing more of a proconsumption growth model—would be a huge plus in dealing with two key issues: On the one hand, it would enable China to avoid the capacity excesses and protectionist risks that might arise from a continued expansion of a severely unbalanced real economy. But it would also tilt the mix of Chinese output away from pollution- and energy-intensive growth. Don't get me wrong: Macro rebalancing should not be seen as a substitute for major environmental policy initiatives—the development and implementation of new technologies and incentives that would lead to a cleaner GDP. But rebalancing could well be an important down payment. By shifting the mix of economic growth away from emissions-intensive manufacturing activities, China would not only avoid serious macro imbalances but it would also buy some important time on the environmental front.

The latest statements from official Beijing are quite encouraging in addressing this conjoined problem. Premier Wen Jiabao's 5 March of 2007 "Work Report" to the National People's Congress strongly endorsed a strategy of macro rebalancing, energy conservation, and environmental remediation. But the time for talk is over. Just as China has had the will and determination to deliver on the reform front over the past 28 years, I am hopeful that it will rise to the occasion and finally deliver on the rebalancing front. In the end, there is no other choice. Time is growing short—for China and for the planet.

# Unstable, Unbalanced, Uncoordinated, and Unsustainable

*March 19, 2007*

Those were not my words—at least not when I heard them firsthand in Beijing last Friday, March 16, 2007. In uncharacteristically blunt language, China's Premier, Wen Jiabao, used the occasion of his annual press conference following the conclusion of the National People's Congress to send a very clear message about the state of the Chinese economy. On the surface, he commended the economy's macro performance in terms of overall GDP and employment growth. However, beneath the surface, he warned that macro conditions were increasingly "unstable, unbalanced, uncoordinated, and unsustainable." I have never known a senior policy maker or political leader anywhere to leave it like that without rising to meet his own self-imposed challenge. Premier Wen has put his reputation firmly on the line. This underscores China's formidable agenda in the years ahead. The statement also has important implications for the near-term policy outlook. China, in my view, now has no choice but to continue tightening as it attempts to bring its rapidly growing and unbalanced economy under control.

The ink was barely dry on the Premier's observations when China's central bank followed the very next day with a rare Saturday announcement of a monetary tightening—the third interest rate hike in 11 months, which reinforces five increases in bank reserve ratios implemented over the last nine months. The latest 27 basis-point hike in the policy lending rate came only a day after Zhou Xiaochuan, Governor of the People's Bank of China, sent a crystal-clear warning, ". . . From a macro perspective, after serious study, we decided to place further controls." In central banking circles, it doesn't get any more direct than that. Suddenly, China's once opaque policy authorities are amazingly transparent—owning up to the seriousness of their macro control problems and setting in motion what I believe will ultimately be a much more determined shift to policy restraint than has been evident a long time.

To some extent, this shift has been data driven. Although China's January–February statistics are always hard to read because of Lunar New Year distortions, there can be no mistaking the reacceleration of economic and financial activity in early 2007. There were marked over-shoots of exports, industrial output, bank lending, while the long-awaited investment slowdown failed to materialize. Moreover, on the heels of the spike in export growth, the trade surplus ballooned to nearly $24 billion in February—fully nine times the levels hit a year earlier, which signals what most senior Beijing officials believe to be a very rapid accumulation of foreign exchange reserves in early 2007. That only further complicates China's already daunting liquidity management challenge.

In short, the data flow in early 2007 depicts a Chinese economy that is once again defying the efforts of a three-year tightening campaign. Beijing has long talked tough on the macro control front, but this talk has not achieved satisfactory results. Persistent excess liquidity, in conjunction with a still highly fragmented banking system and an investment decision-making process that is driven mainly by provincial and local considerations, has undermined policy traction. As Premier Wen Jiabao also indicated at the conclusion of the National People's Congress on March 15, 2007, this is a major challenge to the Chinese leadership. He stressed, this is ". . . not the time for complacency with respect to the economy."

These concerns were very much the focus of the just-completed China Development Forum—an annual gathering in Beijing that follows imme-diately on the heels of the National People's Congress and provides official China with an opportunity to clarify and expand its message. I have been privileged to attend all but one of these Forums since their inception in 2000 and find them to be invaluable in getting a read on the Beijing agenda. The theme in 2007 said it all—"China: Towards New Models of Economic Growth." It is a clear recognition by the State Council (China's cabinet), whose Development Research Center is the official sponsor of the event, that the Chinese economy is at a critical juncture. The Old Model, dominated by a recycling of massive domestic saving into an equally mas-sive investment boom that then supports an all-powerful export machine, has outlived its usefulness. Official China is not only worried about the twin perils of excess capacity and a protectionist backlash to open-ended exports, but is also concerned about the negative externalities of the current model, namely, excess resource consumption, environmental degradation, and widening income disparities.

The Beijing consensus is clear on the broad outlines of the New Model. As underscored by the 11th Five-Year Plan enacted in 2006, the goal is a more balanced economy that draws increasing support from private consumption and a more rational market-based allocation of saving and investment (see "China's Rebalancing Challenge" on p. 172–188). The emphasis on the shift from the quantity to the quality of the growth experience permeated the discussions at the 2007 China Development Forum. Resource conservation and environmental concerns were at the top of the agenda as defining characteristics of the coming regime change. Senior Chinese officials were quite open in expressing major disappointment over the failure to hit the energy conservation and emission-reduction targets that were announced with great fanfare in 2006. This was ascribed to what the Chinese leadership now refers to as "structural pollution," that is, the environmental degradation that is a painfully natural outgrowth of the structural disequilibrium of the old manufacturing-intensive growth model (see "Two Birds with One Stone" on p. 224–228, which reaches a similar conclusion).

The give and take with senior Chinese policy makers is always the highlight of the China Development Forum. Minister Ma Kai, Chairman of the National Development and Reform Commission (NDRC) and the nation's leading macro manager, acknowledged in response to a question that I raised that Premier Wen has ". . . increased our awareness of China's problems." Although he hinted at more administrative measures to come—underscoring likely increases in the area of land control and higher project-approval hurdle rates with respect to environmental impacts and energy consumption requirements—he did not pound the table in favor of restraint. His confident, but generally relaxed, demeanor over the state of the Chinese economy stood in sharp contrast with the far more determined tone expressed by China's Premier. I suspect Minister Ma is about to change his tune. To the extent Chinese authorities are likely to up the ante on tightening, and to the extent that monetary policy traction remains very much in doubt, the burden of restraint should fall increasingly on the central planners at the NDRC.

This conclusion became all the more evident at the closing session of the China Development Forum—the annual audience with the Premier.

I have watched Wen Jiabao grow into his job over the past four years. Today, he speaks with much greater conviction and confidence than he did several years ago in framing the China macro debate. It's not just the way he states the problems, but it is also a new sense of command over the challenge and solutions. He welcomed the opportunity to elaborate on warnings he had just conveyed on the state of the Chinese economy a few days earlier: By *unstable*, he was referring to overheated investment, excess liquidity, and a sharply widening current-account surplus. By *unbalanced*, he was voicing concerns over urban-rural and east-west disparities. By *uncoordinated*, he was drawing attention to the regional fragmentation of the macro economy, to the sharp contrasts between excess manufacturing and an undeveloped services sector, and to the disparities between excess investment and deficient consumption. And by *unsustainable*, he was highlighting the twin perils of environmental degradation and excess resource absorption, as well as persistent tensions in the income distribution. Collectively, the "four uns"—as they became known in our discussions this week in Beijing—made a compelling case for the growth-model change that was the theme of the 2007 China Development Forum. As Columbia Professor and Nobel Laureate Joseph Stiglitz put it in our discussions, "China always adopts new models at key transition points in its development journey. This is one of those times."

As I sit back and reflect over the message from the 2007 Forum and try to benchmark the discussions to those I have heard in each of the previous six years (2000–2006), I am struck by one major shift: There seems to be a much greater determination than ever to get on with the transition to the new model. There is a clear sense that time is growing short. Official China's frank admission of failure in hitting its energy conservation and environmental remediation objectives in 2006 only underscores the sense of urgency. So does the renewed spurt of rapid growth in early 2007. Premier Wen left no room to mistake the significance of this new focus. He went out of his way to stress, "This is a strategic shift for China." It doesn't get much clearer than that.

For those of us in the West, this is a strong signal that we need to update our perceptions of China. Think less of open-ended unbalanced growth and more of a somewhat slower and better-balanced expansion. Think less of an industrial-production dominated model with increasingly destabilizing implications for natural resource consumption and the environment. Think more of a shift to consumption, services, and greener growth. Think also of macro stabilization policies—not just those of the central bank, but especially those of the central planners at the NDRC—that will be used increasingly to up the ante on the tightening required to achieve these objectives. But don't think for a moment that China will back down on the reforms that have driven nearly three decades of its extraordinary transformation.

Time and again, China has used the reform process to spark key transitions in its development journey. I suspect a similar transition is now at hand. In the end, Premier Wen Jiabao said it all as he brought the 2007 China Development Forum to a close, "Our plan is in place. What is needed is action." And I suspect that is exactly what will happen over the course of 2007.

# China's Global Challenge

## March 22, 2008

C hina has rewritten both the theory and history of economic development. In just 30 years, the world's most populous nation has
gone from the brink of economic collapse to the cusp of a newfound prosperity. Driven by the transition away from state-owned system,
bold reforms have spawned an increasingly market-based economy. The
results are nothing short of extraordinary. Following nearly three decades
of 9.5 percent average growth in real GDP, per capita income in China
now exceeds \$2,000—up more than five-fold since the early 1990s. For a
vast nation of 1.3 billion citizens, such an explosive increase in aggregate
living standards is all the more astonishing.

China owes much of its remarkable success to an outward-looking development model that is heavily dependent on foreign trade and on concomitant increases in investments in infrastructure and industrialization that
support its all-powerful export platform. Fortunately, for China, its commitment to such an externally led strain of economic growth coincided
with the flourishing of a new era of globalization and a boom in the global
economy. This serendipitous combination has left China in the enviable
position as perhaps the greatest beneficiary of modern-day globalization.

With those benefits, of course, also come risks and responsibilities. And
China now faces plenty of both as it peers into the immediate future.
The export-led growth model needs rebalancing. The Chinese leadership is the first to admit that it now needs greater focus on the development of autonomous support from internal demand—especially private
consumption. The export-led growth model also leaves China overly
exposed to cyclical developments in the global economy. And after riding
a wave of nearly five years of the strongest growth in global activity since
the early 1970s, there is now good reason for China to worry about a
U.S.-led slowing in world GDP growth. China's export-led development

model has also put the world's most populous nation in the crosshairs of a worrisome antiglobalization backlash. As a responsible global citizen, China must now address those concerns head-on. All in all, as the most open development model in modern history, China now faces a daunting global challenge.

## China's Outward Tilt

Export-led growth models have long been the mainstay of economic development. Yet China has taken this approach to an entirely new level. As can be seen in Figure 3.11, China's share of world trade has risen nearly eight-fold since its economic take-off in 1982, according to estimates by the IMF. This is well in excess of the norm experienced by other Asian economies over comparable periods of their economic development. Closest to China are Asia's newly industrialized economies (NIEs) of Korea, Taiwan, Hong Kong, and Singapore. For this group as a whole—which includes two tiny city-states—the share of world trade share increased five-fold in the first 25 years after their collective economic take-off. While that's an impressive performance, it pales

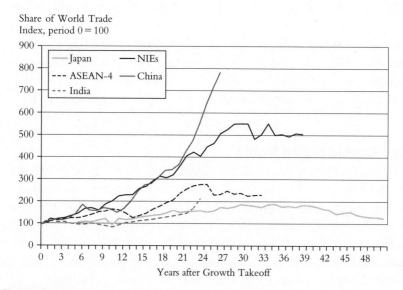

**Figure 3.11**  Globalization's Greatest Beneficiary

*Source:* International Monetary Fund.

in comparison to that experienced by China. For the rapidly growing ASEAN-4—Indonesia, Malaysia, the Philippines, and Thailand—world trade shares were up only a little more than two-fold over a comparable 25-year time period.

The comparison with Japan, Asia's largest and long most dominant economy, is particularly impressive. Dating Japan's post-World War II take-off in 1955, the Japanese share of world trade rose only 1.7 times in the ensuing 25 years, or only about 20 percent the gain experienced by China in a comparable quarter century interval after its takeoff. Although long known for its trading prowess, Japan's external push pales in comparison to that realized by China. The same is the case with respect to India, whose world trade share has only doubled since its take-off in 1990. Asia has, by far, enjoyed the most outward-looking, trade-oriented strain of development in modern history. Yet China stands out from the rest of Asia by a wide margin.

There has been an especially dramatic increase in China's outward tilt since 2000. China's share of world trade has basically doubled in that relatively short period of time. For China, this accelerated push in its outward focus came at just the right point in time. It coincided with an especially powerful wave of world GDP growth, with the 5 percent average global growth pace over the 2003–2007 period the strongest five-year interval of global growth since the early 1970s. For an externally driven Chinese economy this was the functional equivalent of manna from heaven—a sharply increased share of world trade coming at precisely the time when the global growth dynamic was experiencing its most powerful acceleration in a generation. For that reason, alone, China could well be the greatest beneficiary of the modern wave of globalization.

## The Double-Edged Sword

What globalization giveth, it can also taketh. That is true of the global business cycle. It is also true of the world's collective commitment to the architecture of globalization. No economy has benefited more than China from increasingly unencumbered cross-border flows of trade, capital, information, and labor. And, now, those tailwinds could well turn into headwinds. For China, the double-edged sword of globalization is both its greatest opportunity as well as its most vexing challenge.

The upside of the global business cycle has smiled very kindly on China in recent years. With world GDP growth surging at roughly a 5 percent average pace over the 2003–2007 period, China's increasingly powerful export machine couldn't have asked for more. Chinese export growth averaged 30 percent over that same five-year interval—nearly four times the 8 percent average gains in world trade for the world as a whole.

But now the smile of the global business cycle is about to turn into a frown. A U.S.-led global downshift is very much in the cards, as America feels the full force of a bursting of its enormous property bubble. The so-called subprime crisis is but one symptom of this postbubble shakeout. But it is not the endgame. The biggest risk is the staying power of the U.S. consumer. Courtesy of ever-rising home prices, in conjunction with easy and relatively costless access to home equity borrowing programs, American consumers turned into asset-dependent spending machines over the past six years. Net equity extraction from residential property holdings rose from 3 percent to nearly 9 percent of disposable personal income over the 2000–2005 period—more than sufficient to offset a seemingly chronic shortfall of labor income generation (Figure 3.12).

In an income-short, asset-dependent era, America's macro support was turned inside out. The income-based personal-savings rate plunged toward zero and the overall U.S. net domestic savings rate fell to a record low of just 1.4 percent of national income over the 2003–2007 period. Lacking in income-based saving, the United States has had to import surplus saving in order to keep growing—and run massive current account and trade deficits with China and others in order to attract the foreign capital. Consequently, not only were asset-dependent American consumers overextended when the housing bubble burst, but the United States had also gotten itself into a serious and equally unsustainable international financing deficit.

That movie is about to run in reverse. With the income-short American consumer now losing support from both the housing and credit bubbles—an outgrowth of a rare decline in nationwide house prices as well as a vicious subprime contagion that has crimped home equity borrowing—consumption support to the aggregate U.S. economy is likely to turn negative. With personal consumption expenditures having accounted for a record 72 percent of real GDP in 2007, as the twin housing and credit bubbles now burst, it will be very difficult for a housing-dependent U.S. economy to avoid outright recession in 2008. The silver lining of America's second postbubble recession in seven years is a likely narrowing of the U.S. current account deficit. As consumers prune spending in order to rebuild income-based savings rates in a post-housing-bubble climate, America will be able to reduce its demand for

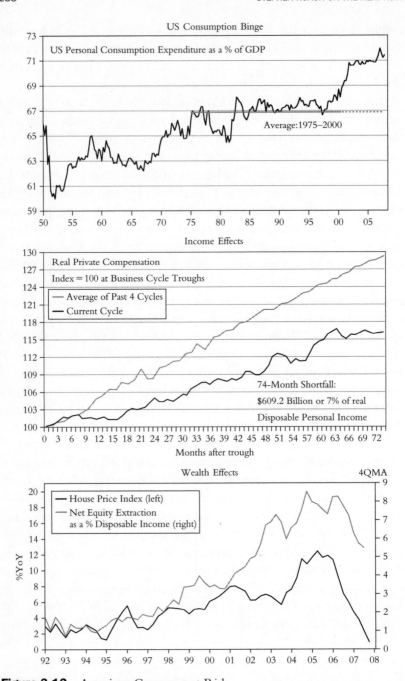

**Figure 3.12**   American Consumer at Risk

*Source:* U.S. Bureau of Economic Analysis, Federal Reserve, OFHEO, Morgan Stanley Research.

saving from abroad—an important and long-awaited step on the road to global rebalancing.

Alas, the rest of the world, including China, must pay a price for the likelihood of sharply diminished support from the American consumer and the U.S. economy. While many are enamored of the possibility of a global decoupling—a classic rosy scenario whereby the world is miraculously shielded from a U.S. downshift—such an outcome is highly unlikely in an increasingly globalized world. Externally oriented Developing Asia is not exactly an ideal candidate for global decoupling (see Figure 3.13).

Nor does an export-led Chinese economy seem like it would be granted special dispensation from a likely shortfall in U.S. consumption. Lacking in autonomous support from internal demand—with China's domestic private consumption only about 36 percent of GDP in 2006—the external shock of a U.S. recession will most certainly put some downward pressure on a torrid Chinese growth rate (see Figure 3.14). With exports nearly 40 percent of Chinese GDP and fully 21 percent of them going to the United States, it's hard to imagine otherwise. For export-led China—the greatest beneficiary of globalization, which draws heavy export support from end-market demand in the United States—there can be no decoupling from America. That's especially likely as the U.S. recession now shifts from homebuilding activity—America's least global sector—to personal consumption, America's most global sector.

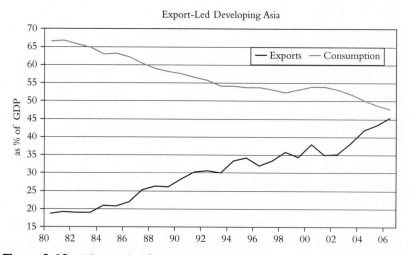

**Figure 3.13**   The Myth of Asian Decoupling

*Source:* Asian Development Bank, Morgan Stanley Research.

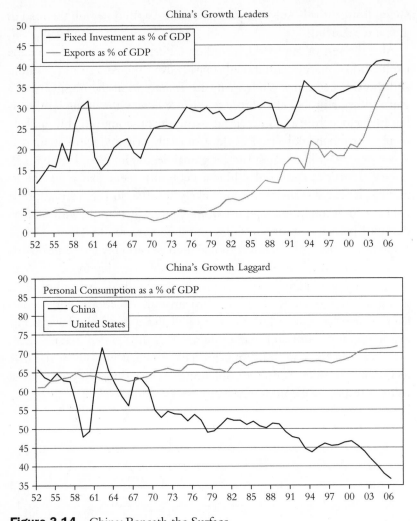

**Figure 3.14**   China: Beneath the Surface

*Source:* China National Bureau of Statistics, U.S. Bureau of Economic Analysis, Morgan Stanley Research.

The first signs of such an adjustment are now evident in early 2008. In January and February, overall Chinese export growth slowed to a +16.8 percent average year-over-year rate—down appreciably from the +25.7 percent increase in 2007. Although these figures may be distorted by the combination of the Lunar New Year celebration and the impact of this year's severe winter storms in China, there can be no mistaking the most powerful force at work—a sharp reversal of Chinese shipments to the United States. In February 2008, Chinese exports to the United States fell to a level that was −5.2 percent below the pace of the year-earlier month; averaging over the first two months of the year, Chinese exports to the United States were essentially unchanged—a dramatic deceleration from the +14.4 percent increase in 2007. Reflecting this important loss of export momentum, industrial output growth has also slowed in early 2008 to a +15.4 percent average rate in January and February—a significant shortfall from the 17 percent growth pace of recent years. As the U.S. recession now takes hold, further downward adjustments to the all-powerful Chinese export machine can be expected. China is far from immune to a global downturn made in America.

That is not necessarily bad news for an increasingly inflation-prone Chinese economy. With the CPI surging at an 8.7 percent year-over-year rate in February 2008, Chinese authorities have underscored the need for slower growth to cool an overheated economy. Despite repeated efforts by the People's Bank of China to use monetary tightening to slow the pace of Chinese economic activity, policy traction has not been evident. Ironically, it may well be that a slowdown in external demand may be a more effective means of achieving this important objective. Given China's serious inflation problem, the resulting cooling off could be an important silver lining of a U.S. recession.

## Backsliding on Globalization

Equally disconcerting for an externally oriented Chinese economy are growing signs of a backlash against globalization. That has shown up most acutely in the form of an increasingly protectionist U.S. Congress. Over the past three years (2005–2007), some 45 separate legislative measures have been introduced on Capitol Hill that would impose some type of trade sanctions on China. Unlike previous years, two of these measures actually passed the key Senate Finance and Banking Committees in 2007—both by overwhelming bipartisan majorities. For now, the subprime crisis seems to have diverted congressional attention away from this line of attack. That limits the likelihood of imminent action. But if I am right and the United States slips into recession in 2008, unemployment will rise sharply—putting even more pressure on the protectionist remedy as a new administration assumes power in Washington in 2009.

In the meantime, a weaker dollar has only increased the decibel level of the protectionist drumbeat. Since the onset of the subprime crisis last August, a broad trade-weighted index of the U.S. dollar has fallen about 7 percent in real terms (through early March 2008), bringing the cumulative depreciation to 24 percent over the six years since February 2002. With the Chinese currency still tightly aligned with the dollar, Washington politicians haven't exactly gotten the RMB break they were looking for. Moreover, with the dollar's latest downturn especially severe against the euro, European politicians have now jumped on the anti-China, RMB-appreciation bandwagon. China, the greatest beneficiary of globalization, is now facing an increasingly broad-based assault by American and European politicians, alike.

However misplaced, the political backlash against globalization has not occurred in a vacuum. As can be seen in Figure 3.15, the rich countries of the developed world have experienced a dramatic and disturbing bifurcation in their income distribution. For G-7 type economies, the labor share of national income is at a record low, whereas the share accruing to the owners of capital in the form of corporate profits is at a record high. This problem is particularly vexing in the United States, where more than a decade of surging productivity growth has been accompanied by near stagnation in real hourly compensation for the median American worker. This is a sharp contradiction of one of the basic premises of

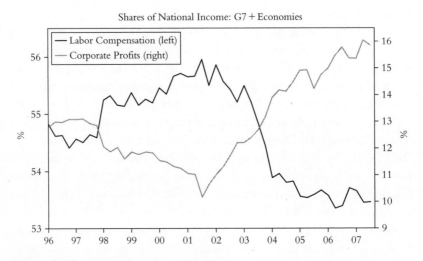

**Figure 3.15** Backlash against Globalization

*Note:* G7+ includes the United States, Japan, EMU, UK, and Canada

*Source:* National Sources, Morgan Stanley Research.

economics—that workers are ultimately paid their just reward in accordance with their marginal productivity contribution.

The resulting middle-class angst, in the context of a massive U.S. trade deficit whose largest bilateral piece is with China, has triggered an outbreak of China-bashing that could well get worse if America now slips into recession as I suspect. As I found in testifying three times in front of the U.S. Congress in early 2007, it does little good to argue against this temptation on either theoretical or empirical terms. The politics of scapegoating have taken Washington by storm. And the anti-China voices in Europe are now getting louder as well. Unfortunately, China—the greatest beneficiary of globalization—is now bearing the brunt of a major geopolitical backlash. Courtesy of recession, it could well get worse in the years immediately ahead.

## Only a Cycle

It is important to put these developments in perspective. The world is hardly coming to an end. At work are the time-honored forces of the business cycle—driven in this case by the U.S. recession that should inevitably be followed by recovery. All cycles are different, and it may well be that this one is much tougher than the shallow downturns of the recent past—especially since it entails a major round of deleveraging and a rare but significant pullback of the American consumer, long the dominant engine on the demand side of the global economy. But it is still only a cycle—whose depth, duration, and character of recovery now become subjects of active debate.

However painful, cyclical adjustments are also an opportunity. In this case, there are important opportunities for China, the United States, and the broader global economy. For China, recent and prospective developments in its external markets underscore the imperative of shifting its growth impetus to private consumption. With the all-important U.S. piece of China's external demand equation about to soften, the need for an offset from internal consumer demand is all the more important. China cannot count on instant gratification on this front. Lacking a safety net—namely, private pensions, social security, unemployment insurance, and medical care—Chinese households are likely to remain very focused on precautionary saving. But to the extent that China's leadership responds to a shortfall in external demand by accelerating the construction of a safety net, the transition to a consumer-led economy could well occur sooner rather than later.

For the United States, there is an equally important opportunity to break the vicious and increasingly destabilizing strain of asset-dependent growth. With each successive asset bubble, the daisy chain of leverage and the excesses of asset-based growth have become far too precarious. America has an opportunity to return to income-driven spending and saving—thereby lowering its massive and increasingly destabilizing current account deficit. And in doing so, the United States can also put a floor under the dollar—tempering one of the most destabilizing forces in world financial markets. As such, this cycle is also an important opportunity for global rebalancing—a reduction of the tensions that have opened up between the world's current account deficit and surplus nations.

No one wants a cyclical downturn. That's especially the case in China, where recessions have long been the ultimate threat for a leadership that is desperate to maintain social stability. The good news is that China has an enormous growth cushion heading into a likely downshift in the global business cycle. Even if its GDP growth rate slows from 12 percent to around 6 to 8 percent on a worst-case basis in the face of a U.S. demand shock, that would hardly be a disaster. The bad news would be if either China—or the United States, for that matter—were to dig in its heels and squander the opportunity for rebalancing that arises when the business cycle turns.

I am hopeful that China will seize the moment and redouble its focus on reforms, especially those that provide support for a long-needed strain of consumer-led growth. Time and again over the past 30 years, China has taken advantage of cyclical downturns to get its macro house in order. I suspect this will be another one of those times. As the world's greatest beneficiary of globalization, an externally oriented Chinese economy now has another opportunity to seize the moment—responding to a downshift in the world business cycle by facing its global challenges head on.

# Consumer-Led Growth
# for China

*February 19, 2009*

No nation has been spared the impact of the worst financial crisis since the 1930s. That includes China—long the most resilient economy in an otherwise weakened world. But now even that premise is being tested. This current crisis poses a major challenge to China's heretofore-brilliant growth strategy.

The challenge arises because of the unbalanced state of the Chinese economy. In recent years, those imbalances actually worked in China's favor. Over the 2001–2007 period, the Chinese export share of its GDP nearly doubled from 20 percent to 36 percent whereas the global export share of world GDP rose from 24 percent to 31 percent. In short, China upped the ante on its export dependence at precisely the moment when global trade enjoyed its most spectacular growth. That effectively turbocharged China's benefits from the strongest global boom since the early 1970s.

That was then. As evidenced by a rare synchronous recession in the United States, Europe and Japan, the world trade boom has now gone bust. And Chinese exports, which had been surging at a 25 percent year-over-year rate as recently as mid-2008, reversed course with a vengeance, ending the year in a mode of outright contraction, before plunging by 17.5 percent in January 2009.

With exports such a large and rapidly expanding slice of the Chinese economy, it is little wonder measures of aggregate activity slowed in an equally dramatic fashion. China's industrial output increased only

5.7 percent in December—one-third the average 16.5 percent growth pace of the preceding five years. And real GDP growth ended the year at just 6.8 percent, in sharp contrast to the 12 percent average pace of the past three years.

China's growth compression as reported on a year-over-year basis masks the severity of its recent downshift. A translation of these figures into sequential quarterly changes, such as those reported by the United States, suggests that Chinese GDP and industrial output growth were in the flat to slightly postive territory as 2008 came to an end. As seen from this real-time perspective, the Chinese economy hit a wall late last year. Such an abrupt downshift implies it will be extremely difficult for China to achieve the government's 8 percent GDP growth target for 2009. An outcome closer to 6 percent is a distinct possibility.

It didn't have to be this way. Two years ago, Premier Wen Jiabao warned of just such a scenario in expressing concerns that the Chinese economy was "unstable, unbalanced, uncoordinated, and unsustainable" (see p. 229–233)." Similar vulnerabilities were anticipated in the 11th Five-Year Plan enacted in 2006, which stressed China's need to embark on a major structural transformation from export- to consumer-led growth.

But the government's execution of this aspect of its plan was lacking. In particular, it failed to build out an institutionalized safety net, that is, the support system necessary to temper the fear-driven precautionary saving that inhibits the development of a more dynamic consumer culture. As a result, the consumption share of Chinese GDP fell to a record low of 36 percent in 2007, underscoring the dark side of China's macro imbalances that is so problematic in this global crisis. A severe external demand shock found an unbalanced Chinese economy without a back-up plan.

A proconsumption rebalancing is the only sustainable answer for China. Proactive fiscal stimulus measures, such as the recently announced RMB4 trillion infrastructure-led investment initiative, can help temporarily. Such efforts borrow a page from China's counter-cyclical script deployed in the Asian financial crisis in the late 1990s and again in the mild global recession of 2000–2001. But these actions are not enough to compensate for the structural vulnerabilities that China's externally dependent growth model now face as American consumers begin a multiyear retrenchment.

China needs to be bold and aggressive in framing proconsumption policies. It should start by announcing major initiatives on the safety net front. Specifically, China should sharply expand the funding of its national social security fund, which currently has only a little over $80 billion in assets under management—not even enough to provide $100 of per capita lifetime retirement income for an aging Chinese population. China also needs to move quickly in establishing a private-pensions scheme, as well as in broadening its support to nationwide health and unemployment insurance. The recent passage of an RMB850 billion three-year medical reform plan is an encouraging, but small, step in that direction.

It is equally important to underscore what China should not do. First and foremost, Chinese policymakers must not be overly optimistic in counting on the old external demand model to start working again. A multiyear weakening of the U.S. consumer is tantamount to a global consumption shock that will impart a protracted drag on any export-led economy. Nor should China be tempted to use the currency lever or other subsidies to bolster its export sector. In an era of rising unemployment and mounting concerns in the developed world over the benefits of globalization, such efforts could be a recipe for anti-China trade sanctions. Those actions might then prompt China to reconsider its role as one of America's most important overseas lenders. And suddenly, the two nations could find themselves on a very treacherous and slippery slope.

History tells us that China is at its best when it faces adversity. That was certainly the case 30 years ago, when a dramatic opening up was required to save a dysfunctional Chinese economy teetering on the brink of disaster. While today's circumstances are certainly not as dire, China should view this crisis as an important wake-up call.

An unbalanced Chinese economy must be rebalanced. The export-led growth formula, which served the nation well for three decades, must now give way to the internal impetus of consumer-led growth. For China, the imperatives of such a rebalancing have never been greater. For the rest of Asia—to say nothing of an unbalanced global economy—China's post-crisis economic leadership role hinges on this critical rebalancing.

# China's Macro Imperatives

*March 22, 2009*

The world is in the midst of its most wrenching crisis and economic downturn since the 1930s. These circumstances have profound implications for all major economies. China is no exception. I would like to underscore three aspects of the Chinese economic outlook that could bear critically on the nation's development and reform in the midst of this severe global crisis. I will focus on strategy, execution, and credibility.

First, on *strategy*, I worry that China does not fully appreciate its vulnerability to a massive external demand shock. China's export sector has nearly doubled since the turn of the century, rising from 20 percent of GDP in 2001 to 36 percent in 2007. That means, of course, that China is heavily dependent on external demand as a major source of economic growth. Unfortunately, the world is in the midst of a severe demand shock that will not end quickly. In large part, that is because the postbubble American consumer—by far, the biggest and long the most dynamic of the large consumers in the world—is still in the early stages of what I believe will end up being a major multiyear compression of consumer demand. Moreover, China's unbalanced growth structure is rigid and can't be changed over night. This makes it even more exposed to a protracted global slowdown.

Most importantly, China must recognize that this disruption of the global environment is not like the circumstances in 1997–1998 and again in 2000–2001. During those periods, China was very successful in embracing proactive fiscal stimulus strategies that bought time until external demand kicked back in. This time, external demand is not coming back as it did in these two earlier episodes. That means the time-honored strategy of the past will not work in the years immediately ahead. If China is counting on that, I think it will be in for a very rude wakening.

Second, on *execution*, China's macro policies must now be framed with a major emphasis on structural rebalancing. It is finally time to shift away from the export-led growth model to one that is more balanced and more supported by internal private consumption. The Chinese government has been talking about this for three years since the enactment of the 11th Five-Year Plan. But it simply hasn't happened. Like the rest of us, China appears to have been seduced by the boom of the past several years. Unfortunately, that boom has now gone bust—and the Chinese government has been caught without a back-up plan. As much as I am in great admiration of China's spectacular successes over the past 30 years, I have been very disappointed in the execution failure in this key aspect of the Plan.

It is now high time for China to get much more serious about promoting internal private consumption. I am not talking about more shopping vouchers. I think China needs to take major initiatives in reducing precautionary saving by finally making a commitment to build its long neglected social safety net. In particular, I urge the government to expand significantly the National Social Security Fund, which has an embarrassingly small amount of assets under deposit—only about $80 billion, or less than $100 for each Chinese worker in terms of lifetime social security benefits. I strongly encourage the government to announce an immediate doubling of the assets under management of the social security fund.

At the same time, I also urge the government to set an explicit target of taking the private consumption share of the Chinese economy from 36 percent at present to 50 percent of the GDP in five years. Only then can China speak with confidence about its rebalancing imperatives. I am fully confident that this nation can hit such a target—especially if it puts its mind to the task.

My third point is the issue of *credibility*. China is one of the world's most open economies. In 2007, exports and imports combined were 65 percent of China's economy. Given the nation's openness, it can hardly be expected to be an oasis of prosperity in an otherwise sharply contracting world. China most assuredly does not get special dispensation from an external demand shock. In that context, the government's steadfast insistence on hitting its official eight percent GDP growth target for 2009 is simply no longer credible in a sharply faltering global climate.

This is evident on careful examination of China's quarterly GDP growth pattern. On a quarterly basis, the +6.8 percent year-over-year growth rate as officially reported for the Chinese economy in the fourth quarter of 2008 turns out to be a number very close to zero if it is recalculated on a sequential basis compared with the third quarter of 2008. Moreover, given the sharp declines in exports in January and February, the economy remained quite weak in early 2009. As a result, it is almost mathematically impossible for China to grow by eight percent growth for the year as a whole. This needs to be recognized and communicated both within and outside of China.

Five to six percent is probably a more credible and realistic estimate of the growth outcome for this year. Although that would be a disappointment relative to the official target, such an outcome would still be an outstanding accomplishment for China in the midst of the worst slowdown of the world in eight decades. If China becomes more realistic and credible about its growth target, only then can it take bold steps on strategy and execution, the hallmarks of China's truly spectacular successes over the last 30 years.

The Chinese word for crisis, *weiji*, includes elements of both danger and opportunity. In my opinion, China needs to be more credible in recognizing its growth risks in order to seize the opportunity in the depths of this very serious global crisis. If any nation can turn danger into opportunity, China is best positioned to do just that. Strategy, execution, and credibility are all essential to China's ongoing reform and development in the midst of this major crisis.

*Postscript: After slowing further to a 6.1 percent year-over-year rate in the first quarter of 2009, the Chinese economy reaccelerated to a 7.9 percent pace in the second period—prompting many to reconsider the decoupling debate. Maybe China isn't so sensitive to the external climate after all, argued the optimists. Yet there can still be no mistaking the dramatic downshift of real GDP growth from 13 percent in 2007 to slightly less than half that pace by early 2009. Nor can a surge of 20 million layoffs in Guangdong Province be erased. Yet it's hardly a coincidence that both of these developments occurred at the same time that a massive shock in external demand unfolded. The decoupling debate is far from over.*

# Manchurian Paradox

## May 1, 2009

The Chinese word for crisis, *weiji*, includes elements of both danger and opportunity. This symbolic meaning has taken on especially great significance in recent years. The emergence of modern China as a global economic power can, in fact, be dated to the nation's willingness to seize critical moments of adversity. That was very much the case during the Asian financial crisis of 1997–1998, which marked a critical turning point in the ascendance of China as a major economic power. And it could also be the case today.

But there is an important catch: Unlike earlier crises, it is not altogether clear that China senses the gravity of the current danger. That leaves it caught in something much closer to denial, thereby making it difficult to seize the opportunity that danger can provide.

The world is in the midst of its most wrenching crisis since the 1930s. From subprime to no-prime, the once-proud icons of modern finance have all been turned inside out. An asset-dependent and increasingly integrated world has been quick to follow. The global economy is set for its first outright contraction since the end of World War II. Relative to a 40-year trend growth rate of 3.7 percent in world output, a likely decline on the order of 1.5 percent in the world's GDP in 2009 is all the more stunning. For a $64 trillion global economy, such a shortfall translates into $3.2 trillion of foregone world GDP. Never before has the modern global economy had to come to grips with such a severe and abrupt widening in the so-called global output gap.

The Chinese leadership needs to deepen its appreciation of the global shock that is now unfolding. Only then can Beijing truly comprehend the threat this recession poses to its long-successful outward-facing economic-growth model. And yet there are worrisome signs that China just doesn't get it—that it is clinging to antiquated policy and economic growth strategies that presuppose a classic snapback in global demand. That leaves China ill-prepared for what could well be the defining feature of the postcrisis world—a U.S.-led shortfall of external demand. China's export-led growth model is aimed right at the heart of what could well be the new weak link in the global growth chain.

Notwithstanding these worrisome imbalances, a newly assertive China has stepped up its efforts to shape the global policy debate—warning America of fiscal excesses that could erode the value of China's investments in U.S. Treasury securities and proposing a radically revamping of the global currency system. China's views and voice are important and need to be heard. The world has much to gain from a sounder and more stable international financial system. But if China pushes too hard in trying to reshape international policies and institutions without attending to its own imbalances, it could trigger further instability—possibly even a dollar crisis—that would only deepen the world's malaise. In the construct of *weiji*, that could tip the balance from opportunity to danger. Therein lies the paradox of Chinese economic power.

## Complacency Made in China

Relative to all the Asian economic-development efforts since the end of World War II, China stands alone in the massive bet it has made on externally led growth. According to calculations made by the research staff of the International Monetary Fund, China's share of world trade increased eight-fold in the 25 years following its economic takeoff in the early 1980s. That is more than two to three times the gains experienced by other Asian economies over comparable phases of their development journeys. Moreover, China upped the ante on this bet following its accession to the World Trade Organization, taking the export share of its GDP from 20 percent in 2001 to 36 percent in 2007. As the world's most open large developing economy—with exports and imports, combined, peaking at 65 percent of its GDP in 2007—China could hardly expect to get special dispensation from a global shock.

And it didn't. On the heels of a precipitous decline in exports, Chinese GDP growth slowed to 6.8 percent on a year-over-year basis in the fourth quarter of 2008, a major deceleration from the 13 percent increase in 2007. Significantly, the gain in the fourth quarter of 2008 turns out to be a number very close to zero if it is recalculated relative to activity in the third quarter. Moreover, with export growth turning sharply negative in early 2009—plunging 21 percent on a year-over-year basis during January and February—it is safe to say that the external-demand shock has brought the Chinese economy to a virtual standstill.

Chinese policy makers have been quick to respond to this extraordinary shortfall in economic activity. In November 2008, they adopted an RMB 4 trillion ($585 billion) two-year fiscal-stimulus package dominated by accelerated expenditures on infrastructure projects. Outlays on rural development, rail, highways, airports and the energy grid account for 47 percent of the total stimulus package and Sichuan earthquake-reconstruction efforts make up another 25 percent. This "proactive fiscal stimulus," as Chinese officials like to call such initiatives, borrows a page from China's response to two earlier external-demand shocks— the Asian financial crisis of 1997–1998 and the mild global recession of 2000–2001. In both of those instances, infrastructure-led fiscal support plugged the gap left by a temporary shortfall in external demand. When the global economy snapped back, China's export-led economy was perfectly positioned to capture the next upturn in global trade. It worked like a charm.

China seems to be betting on a similar outcome this time. In addition to its infrastructure-bolstering policies, Beijing is also providing support to export industries such as textiles, steel, equipment manufacturing, light industries and logistics as part of its recently announced 10-industry industrial-reinvigoration plan. And it has provided assistance to exporters by increasing their tax (VAT) rebates. The broad thrust of China's investment- and export-led policy focus is strikingly reminiscent of its earlier countercyclical stabilization efforts.

By contrast, the Chinese government is only paying lip service to measures aimed at supporting internal private consumption—long the lagging sector of this rapidly growing economy. Spending vouchers have been distributed to rural households and the government has enacted a relatively modest national-health-insurance scheme—costing just RMB 850 billion (about $125 billion) over the next three years. Although there is nothing wrong with these proconsumption initiatives, they are far too small, in my view, to turn around China's lagging consumption sector, which plunged to a record low of only 36 percent of GDP in 2007. China needs to get far more serious in funding a social safety net—especially social security and pensions—if it is to reduce the excesses of fear-driven precautionary saving and foster a more broadly based consumer culture.

By failing to embark on the heavy lifting of its own rebalancing, China is banking on the same export-led growth model that has worked so well in the past to take it out of the current downturn. In essence, that implies China is placing a big bet not just on its own proactive infrastructure-led fiscal stimulus, but also on the efficacy of policy actions being taken elsewhere in the world. That latter presumption underscores one of the biggest risks to this strategy. If, as I suspect, the American consumer has only just commenced a multiyear compression in the growth of private consumption, China could end up being very disappointed in the lingering sluggishness of its external-demand conditions. Like the circumstances of 1997–1998 and 2000–2001, the design of China's current stimulus strategy is very much dependent on an external-demand snapback scenario. Although that strategy worked well in the past, there is a distinct possibility that it is going to be very different in today's crisis-torn, postbubble world.

Unfortunately, the Chinese leadership strikes me as being overly complacent in assessing the risks of just such a possibility. By failing to move more aggressively to rebalance its unbalanced macrostructure, China runs the real risk of facing a more pronounced shortfall in economic growth. For a nation long fixated on the perils of social instability, the rising unemployment that would come from such a scenario could be exceedingly problematic. Chinese government officials have already voiced concerns over the mounting joblessness of its export-dependent migrant workforce— admitting that some 20 million unemployed migrant workers have recently returned to the countryside. In the external-demand snapback scenario, such distress would be relatively short lived. In a more protracted global slowdown, however, pressures on Chinese workers would only intensify, as would the risks of social instability.

## Political Disconnect

Economic forces, of course, don't operate in a vacuum. That's especially the case in financial crises and recessions, when intensifying economic pressures often beget powerful political responses. China is no different from any other nation in that regard. In the depths of this crisis, its political machinery has focused not only on internal problems, such as rising unemployment, but also on external concerns, such as its trade relationship with the United States.

In the context of China's mounting economic challenges, the geopolitical dimension of its export-led macro strategy is especially paradoxical. Recently, senior Chinese officials have singled out two key issues for special attention: their lack of confidence in U.S. Treasury securities and the role of the dollar as the world's major reserve currency. Premier Wen Jiabao has gone public—and loudly so—raising concerns about the safety of China's massive investments in dollar-denominated assets, some $700 billion in U.S. Treasury securities, alone. At the same time, Governor Zhou Xiaochuan of the People's Bank of China has joined the debate over the reform of the international monetary system—raising concerns about the stability of a dollar-based reserve system in an increasingly globalized and unbalanced world.

These concerns are both perfectly legitimate issues for China to raise. With the Obama administration warning of trillion-dollar U.S. budget deficits for years to come, the rapidly growing overhang of Treasury debt should not be taken lightly by America's largest foreign creditor. And with a saving-short U.S. economy likely to suffer from a persistent and large current-account deficit, the possibility of a further sharp depreciation of the dollar cannot be minimized. Such an outcome would have a major impact on the value of China's outsize holdings of dollar-denominated assets.

Yet the Chinese leadership is raising these concerns as if they are disconnected with their own macro imbalances. This is a critical aspect of the China power paradox. As underscored earlier, China remains heavily dependent on externally supported export-led growth. As in the past, it has set its counter-cyclical policy stance with an aim toward catching the wave of the next rebound in global growth. Its currency policy—a "managed float" that still keeps the RMB tightly aligned with the U.S. dollar—is a critical ingredient of this export-led growth dynamic. This currency regime effectively locks China into policies that require an ongoing recycling of its massive accumulation of foreign-exchange reserves into Treasuries. Without such dollar-based recycling of its foreign exchange reserves, the value of the RMB would skyrocket and China's products would be far less competitively priced in the global market. That, in turn, means China also has a vested interest in the stability of the U.S. dollar.

The bottom line for China: Until, or unless, it rebalances its economy away from export-led growth, Beijing can ill-afford to act on the concerns recently voiced by Premier Wen and Governor Zhou. Shifting its currency reserves out of Treasuries or other dollar-denominated assets would undermine Chinese export competitiveness at precisely the time the country's economy lacks support from internal demand. Consequently, notwithstanding the legitimacy of official China's concerns over the integrity of its dollar-centric international investment strategy, as an unbalanced export-led economy, it has few alternatives that would work well in its best interest. As such, Beijing's complaints about U.S. Treasuries and the role of the dollar ring hollow.

## The Wildcard

Because China is so heavily dependent on exports, the policies and economic conditions of other nations obviously have an important say in shaping the country's destiny. The impact of the Washington policy debate cannot be minimized in that regard. America's penchant for China bashing can hardly be taken lightly in the current climate. Over the 2005–2007 period, more than 45 separate pieces of anti-China trade legislation were introduced in Congress. The good news is that none of the bills passed. In large part, that's because they were introduced during a period of prosperity and low unemployment. The bad news is that both of those conditions have changed in the United States—prosperity has given way to a deep recession and unemployment is soaring. That means that long-standing pressures on American workers are intensifying—as are the related pressures on their elected representatives to act.

In times of adversity, the dark side of the American body politic tends to fixate on scapegoats. Wall Street is the domestic target *du jour* and China could well be the foreign focus. Washington's reasoning in going after China is based on three key considerations: that America's outsize trade deficit is a recipe for job destruction and real-wage pressures, that China accounts for the largest bilateral piece of the overall U.S. trade deficit, and that China manipulates its currency as a conscious element of its mercantilist policy strategy. Never mind that these arguments are all deeply flawed. First, a savings-short U.S. economy doesn't have a bilateral trade problem with China, but rather a multilateral trade problem that has led to deficits with one hundred of its trading partners. Second, the RMB has risen more than 20 percent against the dollar (in real terms) since China abandoned its currency peg over three years ago. And third, the plight of the U.S. workforce may also reflect America's chronic underinvestment in human capital and education reforms. Unfortunately, in times of distress and national angst, it is apparently easier for American politicians to point the finger at China rather than look in the mirror.

This raises the possibility of a most worrisome wildcard—that after three years of anti-China rhetoric and saber rattling, the U.S. Congress imposes some form of trade sanctions on China. Unfortunately, such a possibility can no longer be dismissed lightly. After all, the new U.S. Treasury Secretary, Timothy Geithner, raised the Chinese currency manipulation flag in his confirmation hearings. Moreover, Congress opted to insert a Buy-American clause into its recent stimulus package. And during his election campaign, the new U.S. president repeatedly made the distinction between free trade and fair trade when calling for the renegotiation of NAFTA.

Were the unthinkable to happen and the U.S. body politic acted on its anti-China concerns, then the Chinese response would be very different from the baseline strategy just outlined. In a U.S.-directed China-sanctions scenario, I am reasonably confident that Beijing would instruct its foreign-exchange-currency managers to boycott the next Treasury auction—triggering a full-blown crisis in the dollar and a related spike in real long-term U.S. interest rates that would exact a severe toll on a bruised and battered U.S. economy, to say nothing of the rest of the world. Yes, this would also impose considerable pain and hardship on the Chinese as America's largest holder of Treasury securities. But China would perceive trade sanctions as an all-out economic attack; Chinese national pride would then take precedence over investment considerations. In short, I have little doubt that Beijing would retaliate should Washington choose to vent its frustrations at China.

This wildcard is just that—a relatively low-probability outcome. Unfortunately, in a crisis and deepening recession, the probability of such a scenario is not as low as it should be. With the U.S. unemployment rate headed into the 10 percent zone over the next year, or sooner, I would place a 25 to 33 percent probability on the passage of anti-China trade legislation by Congress at some point this year or in early 2010. If such a bill were to pass, it would undoubtedly have broad bipartisan support—moving through both houses of Congress with potentially veto-proof margins in the unlikely event that President Obama chooses to resist a politically expedient groundswell of China bashing.

Wildcard scenarios are generally not worth emphasizing. But in this case, the consequences would be so grave—and so painfully reminiscent of a similar blunder that was made in the early 1930s with the Smoot-Hawley Tariff Act—that they bear special mention.

## A Riddle

On the surface, China seems to understand the flaws and potential vulnerabilities of its growth model. Two years ago, at the conclusion of the National People's Congress, Premier Wen warned of a Chinese economy that was "unstable, unbalanced, uncoordinated and unsustainable" (see p. 229–233). This warning did not come out of thin air. It was issued a year after the enactment of the 11th Five-Year Plan in early 2006, which was very much framed with an aim toward shifting the mix of Chinese economic growth away from excessive reliance on exports and investment toward a more balanced structure that would draw on private consumption for growth.

Despite its extraordinary successes over the past 30 years, China has failed to execute this key aspect of its own strategic plan. It's hard to know why, but I suspect the reason may lie in the same mindset that afflicted the rest of the world—the seduction of the great global boom of 2003 through mid-2007. The Chinese economy grew at an astonishing 12 percent pace over the three years ending in 2007 and, despite the perfectly legitimate concerns of Premier Wen, China's macro policy makers apparently are not willing to tamper with the formula that has created such extraordinary results. As the current growth slowdown indicates, that is too bad. Export-led China is paying a steep price for failing to heed the Premier's all-too-prescient warning.

Over the past three decades, China has repeatedly opted for reforms and the opening up of a once-closed system. This transformation has paid extraordinary dividends—spearheaded by a 10 percent aggregate GDP growth trend that led to a quadrupling of per capita incomes since the early 1990s. Notwithstanding this spectacular achievement, it was built on a foundation of an increasingly unbalanced Chinese economy. Like all macro imbalances, it is only a matter of time before they work at cross-purposes. Take a look at Japan in the 1990s—and at the United States in 2009.

Today's unbalanced Chinese economy faces a similar challenge. It is just a question of when—not if —the unbalanced system hits that proverbial wall. As its own premier said two years ago, the model that has served the world's most populous nation so well for the past 30 years is now in serious need of an overhaul. The same is true of the rest of Asia—an externally dependent region that has increasingly tied its fate to a China-centric export machine. Yet for whatever reason, Beijing seems unwilling—or unable—to embrace a new and more balanced growth model.

Ironically, China is expressing a new assertiveness on the global stage at just the moment when its own imbalances appear especially problematic. Its leaders speak with great pride about an economy that can still hit its precrisis 8 percent growth target. They speak about an economy that can be first in leading Asia and the world out of recession. Perceptions of resilience beget a new self-confidence that has also given rise to unusually explicit Chinese views on global currency reform and the lack of U.S. fiscal discipline.

There is nothing wrong with China's gathering sense of self-confidence and its concomitant contribution to the global debate. In fact, it is to be encouraged. China has earned its place at the table. Its views are well thought-out and need to be heard. For a nation steeped in five thousand years of inward-looking experience, China is looking outward as never before. The world can only benefit from this sea change. However, that underscores the biggest danger of all—the risk that China takes its newfound external dependence too far and ignores the lasting and serious pitfalls of a postcrisis world. If it fails to rebalance its unbalanced economy, China's power play could be surprisingly fleeting.

## Chapter 4

# Pan-Asian Challenges

## Introduction

Asia's vast collection of economies cannot be painted with one brush.
Yes, there are some striking similarities in terms of the region's large
population masses, export-led growth models, saving surpluses, and, most
recently, rapid accumulation of foreign exchange reserves. But there are
equally sharp differences—Japan's technological prowess, China's ownership transition driven by state-owned enterprise reforms, India's large
number of world-class competitive companies, Korea's still powerful
*chaebol* system, Vietnam's newly emerging manufacturing capabilities,
Indonesia's rich resource endowments, and so on. Most importantly, Asia
is a mosaic of different resource endowments, different human skill sets,
different approaches to economic development, and different market and
regulatory systems.

In this chapter, I explore the trade-off between the region's similarities and differences in the context of an important reality check—a

wrenching global crisis. This trade-off is not an ironclad relationship; it is, rather, an outgrowth of the interplay between the internal and external forces that bear down on any economy. For today's Asian economy, that balance is key in addressing the important distinction between the region's resilience and vulnerability to global forces. And the verdict in the current context is clear: Notwithstanding Asia's important intra-regional differences, powerful macro forces bearing down on the region's export markets have had an unmistakably serious impact on the region in late 2008 and early 2009. Every economy in Asia is either slowing very sharply or has moved into outright recession.

This outcome has come as a rude awakening to investors, policy makers, and Asian workers—the broad consensus of which had incorrectly come to believe that the region possessed newfound autonomy and resilience that would provide special dispensation from the impacts of an external shock elsewhere in the world. This view—the so-called decoupling thesis—was grounded in the positive actions taken in the aftermath of the wrenching Asian financial crisis of 1997–1998. Asia had learned its lessons well, went the argument—transforming current account deficits into surpluses, accumulating vast reservoirs of foreign exchange reserves, abandoning, for the most part, pegged currency regimes, and reducing its exposure to short-term international flight capital. At the onset of the subprime crisis in the summer of 2007—also the 10-year anniversary of the devaluation of the Thai Baht, the tipping point for the Asian financial crisis—the region's postcrisis healing was widely celebrated as testament to a much stronger and, therefore, better insulated economy. Yet there was an inherent contradiction in this logic. After all, decoupling is the antithesis of the cross-border linkages of globalization. You either believe in decoupling or globalization—but not both.

Despite these notable improvements over the past 10 years, decoupling never made sense as an operative framework to judge Asia's position in the broader global economy. As Asia upped the ante on its export-led impetus to economic growth, it did so in the midst of an extraordinary upsurge in global trade. That's been especially the case since the turn of the century—a seven-year period that may well go down in history as globalization's greatest boom. Over the 2000–2007 interval, the export share of Developing Asia's GDP went from 35 percent to 47 percent, whereas the export share of world GDP went from 25 percent to 31 percent. In one sense, Asia's timing was exquisite—an export tilt to panregional growth that coincided perfectly with a record burst of global trade. That put Asia in the enviable position as perhaps the greatest beneficiary of the new linkages of an increasingly robust globalization.

Yet there were many who believed that the greatest beneficiary of globalization could also decouple from an external shock. This gave rise to a dangerous complacency. In particular, it pushed Asian equity markets to unsustainably lofty levels in late 2007. The subsequent crash in these markets—with average Asian equity indexes down about 65 percent from their highs—reflected the growing realization that Asia's transformation was not as originally advertised. The shifting macro structure of the Asian economy said it all: Postcrisis Asia had, in fact, become far more dependent on external demand than was the case during the late 1990s. And so, when the external shock hit, driven by a rare synchronous contraction in the United States, Europe, and Japan, export-led Asia felt it with a vengeance. The lack of an offset from internal demand—with private consumption shares of panregional GDP having declined sharply throughout Developing Asia over the past decade—made the impacts of this external shock all the more severe.

Over the past decade, an increasingly China-centric Asia has masked many other important development stories in the region. India is a case in point. Long supported by solid micro fundamentals—namely, a large collection of world-class companies, a rapidly growing IT-enabled workforce, solid market institutions, relatively sound banks, democracy, and the rule of law—India has a major advantage over China. Where it suffered, however, was more in the macro comparisons, especially relatively low savings, inadequate foreign direct investment, and terrible infrastructure. In recent years, all these macro deficiencies have started to improve—having the potential to put India into the sweet spot of economic development by drawing support from both micro and macro factors. The Mumbai terrorist attacks of late 2008 underscore India's biggest remaining risk factor—instabilities in the politics of governance and control.

Asia's potential is not just an aggregation of country-specific growth stories. The region also has much to gain from moving further down the road of panregional integration. The establishment of a China-centric supply chain has been an important step in this regard, but it cuts both ways. As the Chinese economy slowed sharply in late 2008 and early 2009, China's main suppliers—especially Korea, Japan, and Taiwan— toppled into sharp recessions as their exports to China fell sharply. But the vulnerabilities of panregional integration need not outweigh the opportunities. Particularly promising in this regard is the potential offered by greater integration with Japan—still the largest economy in the region and a high-wage, labor-short nation that has much to gain from offshore efficiency solutions available elsewhere in Asia. At the same time, Japan has much to offer the rest of Asia in response—especially the clean technologies that a pollution-prone Asia so desperately needs. Greater Asian economic integration would be a major win–win for the region as a whole.

Asia has played an important leadership role in the global economy over the past decade. Many believe that this is just the beginning of the so-called Asian century. On the surface, the case is compelling. Asia's 37 percent share global GDP (on a purchasing power-parity basis) remains well below its 55 percent share of the world's population—underscoring significant further upside for this inherently high-productivity growth region. However, like China, the rest of Asia must rebalance its economy if it is to realize this upside; it must shift away from excessive reliance on exports and investment and draw greater support from private consumption. Without better balance—especially without a self-sustaining internal consumption dynamic—the hopes and dreams of the Asian century could well ring hollow.

# The Next Asia

*April 16, 2007*

Asia is on the cusp of a new phase of its spectacular growth story. An increasingly powerful panregional integration could be at hand. The first stage of this transformation saw the emergence of a China-centric Asian supply chain. The next stage could be driven by new linkages between the region's two powerhouses, China and Japan. If this occurs, Asia—to say nothing of the world economy and global competitiveness—may never again be the same.

The seeds of this dramatic transformation were sown in the depths of the Asian crisis of 1997–1998. Collectively, the region took this troubled period as a major wake-up call, and resolved never to let it happen again. Yet formidable structural impediments made this easier said than done. Lacking in solid support from private consumption, externally oriented Asian economies actually became more dependent on foreign trade. According to the Asian Development Bank, the export-to-GDP ratio for Developing Asia rose to nearly 45 percent in 2005, essentially double the world average. Ironically, that left the region still vulnerable to external shocks. Mindful of that potential chink in its armor, Asia moved aggressively on two fronts to insulate itself from external shocks—reducing its vulnerability to the vicissitudes of world financial markets as well as establishing new intraregional linkages through trade flows and cross-border investment.

This strategy has paid handsome dividends. By rebuilding foreign exchange reserves, reducing current-account deficits, limiting exposure to short-term capital inflows, and revamping foreign exchange regimes, Asia took several major steps toward tempering financial vulnerability. Similar progress was evident on the trade front, as the intraregional share of Developing Asia's exports went from 26 percent in 1985 to 37 percent in 2005. Particularly important was the emergence of a

China-centric Asian supply chain. That was especially the case within Greater China. According to IMF data, fully 22 percent of Taiwan's total exports went to China in 2005—nearly eight times the 2.8 percent share of 2000; at the same time, 45 percent of Hong Kong's exports went to the mainland in 2005—up significantly from the 34 percent share of 2000. The story is similar elsewhere in developing Asia—especially in Korea, where the Chinese share of exports went from 10.7 percent in 2000 to 21.8 percent in 2005, and even in India, where the portion of exports going to China surged from 1.8 percent in 2000 to 6.6 percent in 2005. Moreover, during the same five-year period, the Chinese export share for the Philippines rose more than five-fold, and it essentially doubled in Indonesia, Malaysia, Thailand, and Singapore. Nor do these figures probably capture the full extent of Asia's new China-centricity; in particular, there is good reason to believe that an increasing portion of third-party trade linkages, like those between Korea and Taiwan—ultimately flows into the Chinese assembly line.

Up until recently, Japan has been on the outside looking in insofar as pan-Asian trade integration is concerned. According to the Asian Development Bank, the Japanese share of Developing Asia's overall exports fell to 9.9 percent in 2005, almost half the 18 percent portion prevailing in 1985. Nevertheless, like the rest of the region, Japan has tilted significantly toward China. Japan's overall trade volume with China has doubled during the last five years (2002– 2007), with shipments from the Peoples Republic of China (PRC) and Hong Kong, combined, having surged from 5 percent of total Japanese imports in the early 1990s to close to 21 percent today. These trends, in my view, may well be an important precursor of the second stage of pan-Asian economic integration—growing linkages between China and Japan. Collectively, these two nations, the world's second and fourth largest economies, account for 82 percent of pan-Asian GDP as measured by the IMF's purchasing-power-parity (PPP) metrics. If they come together, as I suspect, the implications for Asia—as well as the rest of the world—would be enormous.

The possibility of such a new thrust to pan-Asian economic integration is more than just idle curiosity. In fact, that very potential was in the air during the discussions I had in mid April 2007 in Japan. My visit to Tokyo overlapped with that of China's Premier Wen Jiabao, the first such mission of a senior Chinese official in over six years. Premier Wen's visit followed shortly on the heels of last October's trip to China by then Japanese Prime Minister Shinzo Abe—the first foreign excursion of the then newly elected head of the Japanese government. Both leaders appear to be putting great personal stake in forging a new future for one of history's more volatile relationships. Premier Wen's speech to the Diet, the first time a Chinese leader has ever addressed the Japanese legislature, put the economic relationship between the two nations in an important context: By stressing complementarity and interdependence, Wen spoke of a China that appears willing to embrace Japan as a strategic economic partner rather than as an adversary. China and Japan now appear to be playing each other's music—not just on the economy and on their collective emphasis on North Korea-related security issues, but also with respect to overcoming the doubts and distrust that have long punctuated a rather painful shared history.

Japan has certainly come a long way in the past five years in rethinking its approach toward China. As recently as 2002, leading Japanese government officials were still casting China in the role of a major source of Asian instability—accusing the PRC of not only exporting deflation but also being responsible for a hollowing out of Corporate Japan.[1] The Koizumi government subsequently turned that attitude around—pushing proactive strategies of corporate restructuring that welcomed offshore efficiency solutions for high-cost Japanese manufacturers. China is now a prime beneficiary of this approach, as Japanese multinationals turn aggressive in pursuing offshore options. Japan's foreign direct investment into China hit $6.5 billion in 2005—greater than China-bound flows from all of Europe ($5.6 billion) and more than double those of the United States ($3.1 billion).

The significance of further momentum in economic cooperation between Japan and China cannot be minimized. These two economies—one a surplus-labor behemoth and the other a labor-short island—are highly complementary. As China now faces the imperatives of migrating from a long-standing fixation on the quantity of growth to a newfound focus on the quality of growth, what better partner could it ask for than Japan to provide technological assistance for energy conservation and pollution abatement? As a rapidly aging, high-cost Japanese economy faces increasingly intensive competitive pressures, who better could it turn to than China to offer offshore options with both the scale

---

1. See the December 12, 2002 op-ed piece in the *Financial Times,* "Time for a Switch to Global Reflation," jointly authored by Haruhiko Kuroda, then Vice Minister for International Affairs at Japan's Ministry of Finance, and his deputy, Masahiro Kawai.

and the quality control its production model needs? China needs Japan just as much as Japan needs China—precisely the complementarity that Wen Jiabao alluded to in his recent address to the Japanese Diet. Yet that same complementarity raises important questions for the rest of Asia—especially for those who worry about being marginalized by the growing integration of the region's two largest economies.

Asia's global potential is hard to minimize. Home to more than 55 percent of the world's population, the region collectively accounts for nearly 37 percent of PPP-based world GDP and almost 27 percent of global exports. Moreover, Developing Asia is leading the charge in the global productivity sweepstakes; recent IMF estimates place the latest three-year average for Chinese productivity growth at close to 9 percent and that for the rest of Emerging Asia at nearly 5 percent—both trends well in excess of the 2 percent productivity pace in the developed world. Adept in new technologies and endowed with increasingly modern infrastructure, the region's new synergies with Japan can only add to Asia's already impressive competitive prowess.

The asymmetries of the Asian growth model remain its greatest shortcoming. Its strengths have long been focused on the production side of the equation. Its weaknesses remain on the domestic demand side, dominated by a glaring deficiency of private consumption. By our estimates, the consumption share of Developing Asia has fallen from over 60 percent in the early 1980s to below 50 percent in 2007. China's consumption share is less than 38 percent of its GDP, and at 55 percent of GDP, Japan's private consumption share remains at the low end of the range in the developed world. Without greater support from internal consumption, a production-focused Asian growth model will always face sustainability questions. With protectionist pressures now bearing down on a consumption-deficient Chinese economy, the asymmetries of the Asian model loom all the more problematic.

New synergies between Japan and China don't eradicate the risks inherent in Asia's asymmetrical growth model. Asia still has an internal consumption problem that must be addressed, no matter what. The good news is that China is focused on precisely this challenge. The bad news is that it will take time to develop a thriving consumer culture in China, quite possibly a good deal more time than most suspect. In the meantime, Asia seems increasingly determined to reap the benefits of panregional economic integration. Not only are there new signs of progress in that direction between China and Japan, but there continue to be whispers of a new pan-Asian financial architecture, complete with the trappings of a common currency, integrated capital markets, collective management of a vast portfolio of foreign exchange reserves, and sharply reduced intra-regional trade barriers.

Asia is all about change. A key question for the rest of the world is how to cope with that change. The more the West resists the rise of Asia—precisely the risk as anti-China trade tensions continue to mount in the United States and Europe—the greater the chances the region will go its own way. In either case, whether the region draws support from within or from the rest of the world—or, hopefully, from both—the next Asia is a force to be reckoned with.

# Rebalancing Made in Japan?

## *February 13, 2006*

H ow quickly things change! Back in early 2006, investors described
Japan as being on fire. And on the surface, it certainly seemed
white hot—a stock market that had risen nearly 50 percent since
the spring of 2005 and an economy that surged by at least a 7 percent
annual rate in the final quarter of calendar year 2005, making Japan the
fastest-growing economy in the industrial world. That represented an
extraordinary reawakening for Asia's long-slumbering giant. Can the
world's second-largest economy play a meaningful role in the rebalancing of a still unbalanced global economy?

In answering that question, it helps to appreciate where Japan has
come from. For starters, the recent recovery did not materialize out of
thin air. After more than a dozen years of 1 percent real GDP growth,
the economy first moved into a 2.3 percent growth channel beginning
in 2003, and then accelerated to a 3.9 percent average annual pace in the
first three quarters of calendar 2005 (since revised down to 3.3 percent).
As momentum built over the course of 2005, the Japanese economy was
firing on all cylinders—external as well as internal demand, with the
latter driven by especially impressive gains in private consumption, residential construction, and business capital spending.

For my money, the most important element in this equation is Japanese
consumption. It would be one thing if Japan's re-acceleration were driven
largely by external demand or business fixed investment. But when the
consumer finally steps up, it's a different matter altogether insofar as mul-
tiplier effects to other sectors of the economy are concerned.

A sustained pickup in Japanese consumption could also be a very welcome development for the global economy. The key here is the import
side of the Japanese growth equation—the transmission of domestic
growth to a country's trading partners. Trends in import penetration tell

us whether Japan's revival of internal demand is sourced at home or through foreign production. And those trends have definitely changed. Historically, Japan has been a very closed economy. The import share of its GDP averaged only about 7 percent from the mid-1980s through the mid-1990s, about half the shares in the rest of the industrial world over this period. In recent years, however, Japan has done a dramatic about-face in embracing the efficiency solutions of low-cost offshore production. The import share of its economy has moved up appreciably in response, rising above 12 percent in late 2005.

Rising import penetration holds out the hope that a revival in Japanese internal demand spells heightened export impetus to the rest of the world—potentially moving Japan to center stage as a new engine of global growth. That does, indeed, seem like a fair assumption to make—but with an important twist: As can be seen in Figure 4.1, there has been a significant shift in the mix of Japanese imports in recent years that has altered the transmission mechanism between Japanese internal demand and its traditional trading partners.

As recently as 1999, the United States had the largest share of Japanese imports—implying that America would benefit the most from accelerating Japanese growth. That is no longer the case. The U.S. portion of total Japanese imports has fallen from close to 25 percent in 1999 to only about 13 percent in 2006. The reason: a stunning surge of Chinese imports. Japan's purchases of goods from Greater China (the PRC plus

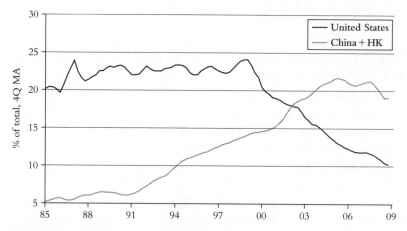

**Figure 4.1**  Shifting Mix of Japanese Imports

*Source:* Japan Ministry of Finance, Morgan Stanley Research.

Hong Kong) have risen from just 5 percent of its total imports in the early 1990s to about 22 percent in 2006. The share of Japanese imports coming from Europe (not shown in the chart) has also drifted down in recent years and currently stands at about 11 percent. But the erosion of Europe's share of the Japanese market has been relatively gentle when compared with the rapidly plunging U.S. portion.

The shifting character of Japan's imports—both their increased share in overall Japanese GDP as well as the rebalancing of the import mix away from the United States toward China—has important implications for the broader global economy. First of all, this mix shift is not going to be reversed overnight. A lot of effort goes into the establishment of supply chains, distribution networks, and service operations—underscoring the inertia of foreign sourcing patterns. It is hard and very costly for any nation to rip out one system (i.e., the low-cost China link) and replace it with another (i.e., the higher-cost American option). That means that the composition of Japan's import demand is likely to remain something quite close to its current configuration in the years immediately ahead. Consequently, to the extent that Japan is able to sustain its recovery in domestic demand—and that the import content of demand remains relatively stable—most of the incremental benefit would undoubtedly flow to China and Asia's increasingly China-centric supply chain. By contrast, that would leave U.S. and European exporters largely on the outside looking in with respect to sharing the spoils of Japan's economic recovery.

This has the potential to be a very important development for an unbalanced world. With the asset-dependent American consumer starting to fray around the edges as the U.S. housing market cools, a restarting of the growth engine of the world's second-largest economy is especially welcome. However, Japan's long-awaited economic recovery may do little to temper the world's largest and most serious imbalance—America's gaping current account deficit. In part, that's because the import content of recovering Japanese domestic demand seems likely to be made increasingly in China rather than in the United States.

This underscores what has long been one of the most worrisome aspect of America's current account imbalance—that there is little hope for a fix from the export side of the equation. With goods imports fully 89 percent larger than goods exports, even if exports grow at twice the rate of imports, the deficit on goods will remain essentially unchanged. In other words, just from an arithmetic point of view, it would be exceedingly difficult for the United States to export its way out of its trade deficit. The loss of market share in Japan by American exporters makes that even more of a stretch.

That underscores the essence of the U.S. current account problem— America's massive and ever-mounting import overhang. Consequently, barring a prompt reduction in U.S. imports, there is little immediate hope for any meaningful progress on the road to global rebalancing. Even a welcome and long-overdue recovery in the Japanese economy won't alter that verdict. Don't get me wrong—Japan's turnaround has been nothing short of stunning. As the momentum of its economic recovery builds, the world economy will benefit from the restarting of another growth engine. But don't count on Japan to fix the world's imbalances. That's a task that remains very much in the court of the most unbalanced economy of all—the United States.

# From Beijing to Dubai

## March 24, 2006

M y travel schedule is planned months in advance. It was only by happenstance that I found myself in both Beijing and Dubai in the second week of March 2006—two of the more recent flash-points in a U.S.-led pushback against globalization. What I found in both cities unsettled me—disappointment and frustration over America's attitude toward two of its major providers of foreign capital. The United States has been having a good deal of trouble with its overseas image in recent years. The feedback from Beijing and Dubai is that this image is going rapidly from bad to worse—something a savings-short U.S. economy can ill afford.

China is deeply troubled over the outright hostility from an increasingly xenophobic U.S. Congress. The senior officials I spoke with in mid March of 2006 in Beijing protested on two counts—China's fragility and America's penchant for scapegoating. On the first count, the Chinese don't believe that US politicians appreciate the potential risks that still lurk in this transitional economy. Instead, they are pressuring China as if it were operating from a position of much greater strength. China remains very much a tale of two economies—a booming coastal region and a lagging interior. Most in Washington view China from the lenses of Beijing and Shanghai, and conclude that these two thriving metropolises personify the emergence of a powerful and mighty nation. What they don't realize is that only 100 km away from either city lurks a China that has changed very little in the past thousand years. Yes, 560 million Chinese now live in urban centers around the country, although probably less than half these city dwellers have seen meaningful improvement in their standard of living over the past 30 years. Meanwhile, the rural population of some 745 million Chinese still tries to get by on one to two dollars per day.

At the same time, despite 25 years of 9.5 percent real GDP growth, serious vulnerabilities continue to plague the macro structure of the

Chinese economy. The financial system has only just begun the long march toward liberalization and development. Growth continues to draw the bulk of its support from external demand (i.e., exports) and fixed investments. Self-sustaining growth from the Chinese consumer is deficient, reflecting a pervasive sense of job and income insecurity that stems from ongoing reform-induced headcount reductions. Far from letting the invisible hand of market-based capitalism drive price-setting, the visible hand of administrative fiat still plays a major role in the determination of prices of goods and services in the real economy, as well as interest rates, the currency, and the prices of many other assets in the financial economy. All this speaks of a Chinese strain of market-based socialism that is still far too fragile to stand on its own.

China also feels that it is being victimized for America's structural problems. Premier Wen Jiabao was crystal clear on that point when he ended the recent China Development Forum by stating, "It is unfair to make China a scapegoat for structural problems facing the U.S. economy." There's no dark secret what he was referring to—China's important role as a provider of goods and financial capital to a saving-short U.S. economy. As long as America has a serious saving problem—and, of course, the U.S. net national saving rate plunged into negative territory for the first time in history in late 2005—trade deficits are a given in order to attract the foreign capital to fill the void. If the Schumer-Graham bill closes down U.S. trade with China through the imposition of steep tariffs, a saving-short U.S. economy will simply have to divert a significant portion of its multilateral trade deficit elsewhere. Undoubtedly, that means a higher-cost producer would have to take China's place as a low-cost provider of capital to the United States, thereby imposing the functional equivalent of a tax hike on the American consumer.

When I pointed this out to Senators Graham, Coburn and to Schumer, who were on a rare mission to Beijing, Senator Schumer said, "I understand the structural point, but China still has to give." The editorialist in me says, if Washington—or for that matter, beleaguered U.S. manufacturers—really wants China to give, then it needs to make that argument from a position of a macro strength and boost America's national saving rate. Until, or unless, that happens, U.S.-led China bashing is nothing short of political hypocrisy. In the meantime, Washington could well be about to compound one of America's most serious structural problems—at considerable expense both to the United States and Chinese economies. These are the lose-lose outcomes of globalization that can only end in tears.

In Dubai, I was met by a similar sense of consternation. Fresh from the wounds of the rejected Dubai Ports World transaction, several major private equity investors in the UAE were quite blunt in expressing their sudden loss of appetite for U.S. assets. As one seasoned investor in U.S. companies and properties put it to me, "As practitioners, as investors, we have become very shy of the U.S.—we just turned down a recent deal for that very reason." Another added, "For us, foreign direct investment into the U.S. has become far less palatable due to recent developments. The bulk of our dedicated offshore money is now going elsewhere." The comment that unnerved me the most took this exasperation to an even deeper level. One investor asked, "What can we do to push back, to send a signal?"

I certainly don't want to make too much out of an unscientific survey of a few private equity investors in Dubai. But up until recently, this was one of the Middle East's most pro-American investment communities. The individuals I met with in late March 2006 are seasoned participants of many a cross-border transaction into the United States. For them, the political shock wave from Washington has come from out of the blue, and they now see little reason to go back to the same well—especially given the wide menu of less contentious alternatives available elsewhere in the world. In the broad scheme of things, Dubai is a small player in the world of international finance. But to the extent that the Dubai backlash is emblematic of similar distaste from other Middle East investors—hardly idle conjecture, in my view—the repercussion cannot be minimized. Net foreign direct investment into the United States hit $128 billion in 2005, an increase of $22 billion from the inflows of 2004. If that trend now starts to reverse course, America's already daunting current-account financing problem will only get worse.

From Beijing to Dubai, there is a growing undercurrent of anti-American backlash. The irony of it all is truly extraordinary: The United States has the greatest external deficit in the history of the world, and is now sending increasingly negative signals to two of its most generous providers of foreign capital—China and the Middle East. The United States has been extraordinarily lucky to finance its massive current account deficit on extremely attractive terms. If its lenders now start to push back, those terms could change quickly—with adverse consequences for the dollar, real long-term U.S. interest rates, and overly indebted American consumers. The slope is getting slipperier, and Washington could care less.

# A Tale of Two Asias

## May 19, 2006

The China-India comparison is central to the Asia debate. It is also of great importance to the rest of the world. In the end, it may not be either/or. While the Chinese economy has outperformed India by a wide margin over the past 15 years, there are no guarantees that past performance is indicative of what lies ahead. Each of these dynamic economies is now at a critical juncture in its development challenge—facing the choice of whether to stay the course or alter the strategy. The outcome of these choices has profound implications—not just for the nearly 40 percent of the world's population residing in China and India, but also for future of Asia and the broader global economy.

As recently as 1991, China and India stood at similar levels of economic development. Some 15 years later, the Chinese standard of living was over twice that of India's, with China's GDP per capita hitting $1,700 in 2005 versus a little over $700 in India (see Figure 4.2). The two nations have approached the development challenge in very different ways. For China, it's been a manufacturing-led growth strategy, whereas for India, it has been much more of a services-based development model. While each approach has its advantages and disadvantages, China's outstanding performance in the development sweepstakes over the past 15 years makes it a very tempting model for the rest of Asia to emulate.

The contrast between the two approaches is dramatic. The industry share of Chinese GDP has gone from 42 percent to 47 percent over the past 15 years—maintaining a huge gap over India's generally stagnant 28 percent manufacturing portion over the same period (see Figure 4.3 on page 281). By contrast, the services share of Indian GDP has risen from 41 percent in 1990 to 54 percent in 2005—well in excess of the lagging performance in Chinese services, which has gone from 31 percent of GDP in 1990 to 40 percent in 2005. China's macro character fits

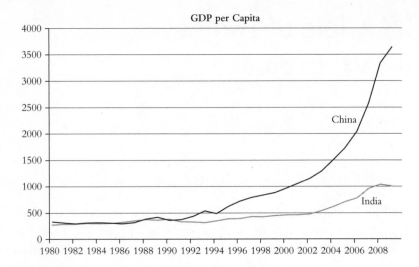

**Figure 4.2**   Two Asian Development Paths
*Source:* International Monetary Fund.

its manufacturing-led growth dynamic to a tee. Benefiting from a high domestic saving rate, huge inflows of foreign direct investment (FDI), and major efforts on the infrastructure front, Chinese economic growth has been increasingly fueled by exports and fixed investment. Collectively, these two sectors now account for over 75 percent of China's GDP—and are still growing at close to a 30 percent rate in 2006.

India's macro story is the mirror image of China's in many key respects. Constrained by a lower saving rate, limited inflows of FDI, and a sorely neglected infrastructure, India has turned to a fragmented services sector as the sustenance of economic growth. The labor-intensive character of services has provided support to India's newly emerging middle class—a key building block for India's consumption-led recovery. As a result, private consumption currently accounts for 61 percent of Indian GDP—far outstripping the 40 percent share in China. The growth contribution of India's export and investment sectors pales in comparison to that in China.

Interestingly enough, as both of developing Asia's largest economies look to the future, they do so with an eye toward emulating the other. China is now very focused on a rebalancing of its growth dynamic—moving away from exports and investment more toward an Indian-style consumer-led model. This is more by necessity than choice. A continuation of the export surge is a recipe for protectionism, while pushing an already excessive investment binge risks capacity overhangs and deflation. At the same time, China also aspires to match India's progress on corporate reforms. India currently has over 25 world-class companies, well-developed capital markets, a modern banking system, and a deeply entrenched rule of law. China is lacking in all of those key respects, and very much wants to move in those directions. China is also seeking to implement an Indian-style expansion of labor-intensive services in an effort to provide job and income support to its nascent consumer sector. However, given the high degree of precautionary saving sparked by massive layoffs arising from state-owned enterprise reforms, China may well encounter considerable difficulty in establishing a broad-based consumer culture.

At the same time, India very much aspires to match China's progress on the manufacturing front. India's political leadership is convinced that manufacturing is the answer to high unemployment in impoverished rural areas. Whenever I go to India, I always have the same debate with its politicians and policy makers. I take the side that the inherent labor-saving bias of capital-intensive global manufacturing platforms promises little hope for Indian employment. I have seen this first-hand on my visits to Indian manufacturing companies—factory floors more heavily populated by robots than by human workers.

India's leaders have a very different vision of manufacturing. They have seen what China can do and genuinely hope to achieve a similar outcome. In early 2006, at the World Economic Forum in Davos, I pressed senior Indian officials on the specifics of this strategy—asking them to identify the potential sources of manufacturing-led job creation. Their answer—food, textiles, and leather—potentially high-volume industries that could well offer gainful employment opportunities to relatively poor, undereducated, young rural workers. By contrast, unlike the Chinese, the Indian leadership is not all that enamored of the job-creating potential of labor-intensive services. In particular, they point out that IT-enabled services—the crown jewel of India's new economy—mainly offers employment to the elite graduates of India's prestigious institutions of higher education rather than providing opportunity for the rural poor.

What comes out of this debate is that both China and India are at important inflection points in their development experiences. They both are very focused on broadening out their bases of economic support. China wants to push more into services and establish a consumption-based growth dynamic. India wants to enlarge its manufacturing footprint by putting greater emphasis on infrastructure and FDI. In both cases, the growth objectives are focused on solving a very difficult rural unemployment and poverty problem. Moreover, in China's case, there is the added complication of its daunting ownership transition from a state- to a privately owned economy.

All this is not without rising political tensions. Reflecting understandable concerns over social stability that have arisen in both China and India, the interplay between politics and economics is clearly having an important influence on the execution of their respective broadening-out strategies. There are equally profound questions for the rest of the world: If India is to services as China is to manufacturing, what role does that leave for the high-cost developed world? Down the road, if India also succeeds in pushing into manufacturing while China makes successful forays into services, the same question becomes all the more challenging to the world's major industrial economies.

Protectionism is the biggest risk in all this. IT-enabled globalization is pushing economic development into both manufacturing and services at a breakneck pace. Moreover, IT-enabled connectivity has increasingly transformed once nontradable services into tradables—and has moved rapidly up the value chain and occupational hierarchy in doing so. The result is a mounting sense of economic insecurity in the developed world that has become a lightning rod for a politically inspired protectionist backlash.

This is not the response that orthodox economics was counting on. The win-win theory of globalization—workers in poor countries getting rich through trade but then turning around and buying things made by rich countries—just isn't working. That's because both the speed and scope of an IT-enabled globalization has broken the mold of the classic theory of comparative advantage. In days of yore, it was fine—albeit painful—for rich countries to give up market share in tradable manufactured products. That's because highly educated knowledge workers could seek refuge and shelter in nontradable services. However, with nontradables becoming tradable and with educational attainment and skill sets rising rapidly in the developing world, the security of the old way no longer exists. Sadly, that provides both the justification and the opening for protectionists.

China and India represent the future of Asia—and quite possibly the future for the global economy. Yet both economies now need to fine-tune their development strategies by expanding their economic power bases. If these mid-course corrections are well executed—and there is good reason to believe that will be the case—China and India should play an increasingly powerful role in driving the global growth dynamic for years to come. With that expanded role, however, come equally important consequences. IT-enabled globalization has introduced an unexpected complication into the process—a time compression of economic development that has caught the rich industrial world by surprise. Out of that surprise comes a heightened sense of economic security that has stoked an increasingly dangerous protectionist backlash. This could well pose yet another major challenge to China and India—learning how to live with the consequences of their successes.

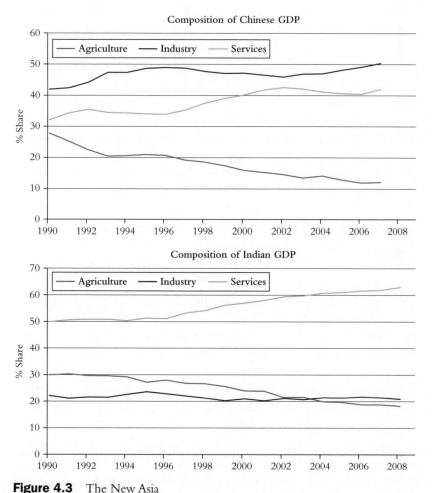

**Figure 4.3**   The New Asia

*Source:* China National Bureau of Statistics, Reserve Bank of India, CSO, Morgan Stanley Research.

# Kim's Boost to Globalization

## July 7, 2006

The North Korean missile crisis of mid 2006 is only the latest reminder of the fragilities that continue to beset a post-9/11 world. In less than five years since the terrorist attack on the United States, the world has been shaken by wars in Afghanistan and Iraq, saber rattling over Iran, and the ever-escalating Israeli-Palestinian conflict. At the same time, global imbalances have worsened, world trade frictions have intensified, oil and other commodity prices have soared, and the global liquidity cycle has gone to excess. The fate of globalization could well hang on the interplay between these geopolitical and economic risks. Could the events in North Korea be yet another a tipping point for globalization?

There are several channels by which this potential collision of forces could play out in both the real and financial sides of the global economy—namely, through oil prices, trade flows, inflation, and the liquidity cycle. The oil price has long been a proxy for geopolitical insecurity. Military hostilities that are perceived to threaten the secure supply of oil obviously tilt the price of crude higher. By way of reference, oil prices in mid-2006 are nearly three times the $27.77 quote (WTI basis) prevailing on September 11, 2001. With global oil consumption up just 8 percent from 2001–2005, there can be little doubt of the impacts stemming from the insecurities of a post-9/11 world. Military hostilities can also threaten the security of shipping lanes—underscoring the possibility of a disruption to the flow of global trade. Fears of such an outcome were a legitimate concern in the aftermath of 9/11—especially given the added pressures stemming from higher insurance rates and heightened security measures. So far, those fears have been unfounded—growth in global trade averaged 6.6 percent per year over the 2002–2005 period—actually faster than the 5.7 percent pace of the previous four years.

Globalization and the surging cross-border trade it has generated have led to increasingly powerful global arbitrages of labor costs and prices. This has provided a new and important impetus to disinflation in the world economy over the past 15 years. Should there be a serious setback to globalization for any reason—geopolitical or otherwise—disinflation could be dealt a tough blow. That would undoubtedly force a policy response from inflation-targeting central banks that could pose a formidable challenge to the liquidity-driven underpinnings of world financial markets.

Obviously, a lot is at stake here as an insecure world copes with yet another threat—this one made in North Korea. Globalization knits the markets and world economy together as never before. Yet one of the most painful lessons of modern history is the demise of an earlier wave of globalization that coincided with the outbreak of the First World War. A tipping point for geopolitical stability could well be a tipping point for globalization—and all the powerful economic, social, and political impacts it has spawned. This is the context in which the potential economic and financial market impacts of the North Korean missile crisis need to be assessed.

From my perch, the most critical aspect of this problem is containment—not just from a military point of view but also from an economic perspective. The risk of a potential shortfall in the North Korean economy is not the problem. Although the data on this economy are of dubious quality, at best, there is little to fear from the direct effects of any externally imposed curtailment of North Korean economic activity. The only reliable estimates (taken from the *CIA World Factbook*) place North Korean GDP at around $40 billion on a purchasing power parity basis—less than 5 percent the total output of South Korea. If the world unites in protest over North Korea's nuclear threat and imposes harsh economic sanctions, the economy is far too small to have any meaningful impact on the pan-Asian economy or the broader global economy.

That point is underscored by North Korea's limited external linkages. Three countries—China, South Korea, and Japan—account for over 80 percent of North Korea's foreign trade. As such, they are the only nations capable of applying any real economic pressure on this rogue state. However, given the small size of North Korea's external sector—exports and imports, combined, are only about 10 percent of its GDP—any such leverage is likely to be limited. In short, economic pressure is not likely to be effective if the international community wants to tame

North Korea's geopolitical belligerence. By default, that puts primary onus on the military option.

The real question, in my view, is whether the world unites or splinters in dealing with the North Korea problem. China, South Korea, and Japan are especially important in this regard. Not only does their proximity to North Korea put these nations on the first line of defense in the event of military aggression, but they have also invested significant political capital in the so-called six-party talks over North Korean nuclear weapon production and delivery capabilities. Yet in the aftermath of the July 4, 2006 missile launching, a wedge opened up in the international community. The United States and Japan were pushing hard for a UN resolution that would impose punitive sanctions on North Korea, whereas China, Russia, and even South Korea were expressing varying degrees of resistance to such an approach.

For Asia, this is where the rubber meets the road. It could well boil down to a trade-off between immediate threats to panregional security and longer-term benefits from the key alliances of globalization. China's role is critical in this regard. Through years of quiet diplomacy—especially over the past 10 years—China has forged important alliances within Asia, South America, and most recently, Africa. But perhaps the most important and oft-contentious relationship in this new era of globalization is that between the United States and China. It wasn't always this way. In fact, the motivation behind China's foreign relationships has changed dramatically over the past 27 years. Prior to the late 1970s, China formed alliances largely on the basis of its ideologically driven political ambitions. Since then, as China committed to opening up through aggressive reforms, its foreign relationships have been forged largely on an economic basis. There are two major exceptions to that rule—Iran and North Korea. In both of these cases, geopolitical security considerations have the upper hand. For North Korea, geographic proximity is an added complication.

The North Korean crisis could end up being an important milestone in China's emergence as a global power. It could well force the Chinese leadership to make a critical choice between a threat to regional security and the imperatives of economic prosperity. In a stable world, the choice would be an easy one—economics would trump military considerations in almost every instance, in my opinion.

From China's perspective, Taiwan is an obvious and important exception, but the destabilizing impact of Kim Jong Il's nuclear ambitions could possibly be another. Here, China needs to reach a judgment on the credibility of the North Korean threat. Needless to say, the aborted July 4, 2006 flight of the three-stage Taepodong-2 missile—the main delivery system for North Korea's long-range nuclear capability—raises serious questions in that regard. If China judges this threat to be over-blown or if it believes that U.S.-led pressure could lead to North Korean disarmament, then it has no reason to compromise its most important economic alliances of globalization. If, on the other hand, China places greater emphasis on the military threat, then it may weigh the trade-off very differently.

In the end, I suspect that China will side with the U.S. approach, thereby preserving and actively reinforcing its commitment to globalization. In the words of Zheng Bijian, Chairman of the China Reform Forum and one of official China's most highly regarded thought leaders, "China will play a part in everything that is conducive to stability and peace in the Asia-Pacific region, and strongly oppose everything detrimental to regional stability."[2] He goes on to add, "Beijing wants Washington to play a positive role in the region's security as well as economic affairs."[3] These comments put China's cards on the table: Despite its lukewarm initial reaction to Japan's draft UN resolution condemning North Korea, China is not about to side with Asia's major source of instability.

Globalization succeeds only if it works on economic, political, and military terms. Kim Jong Il poses yet another challenge to an already precarious post-9/11 world. If his threat is credible or if it succeeds in driving a wedge between the powerful alliances of globalization, the global economy and world financial markets could suffer considerable damage. I do not think that will be the case. The irony of the North Korean missile episode is that it forces China into a careful and more deliberate assessment of its own commitment to globalization. This is an awkward but ultimately constructive opportunity for the Chinese leadership to take another important step as a leading global power. I am hopeful that China will seize the moment. Unwittingly, that casts Kim in the role as a major booster for globalization.

---

2. From Zheng's April 2004 speech at the Boao Forum for Asia.
3. From Zheng Bijian's "China's 'Peaceful Rise' to Great-Power Status" in the September/October 2005 issue of *Foreign Affairs*.

# Japan's Missing Link

## October 20, 2006

The mood has shifted in Japan. When I was there in April 2006, a clear sense of euphoria was in the air. Conviction was deep that the long nightmare was over—deflation was coming to an end and economic recovery was finally viewed as sustainable. Now, six months later, the view is more granular and disconcerting. After extensive meetings with investors and business leaders, I detected two sets of concerns—one internal and other external: Worries were deepening over Japan's lack of a personal consumption dynamic, and its excessive dependence on China was increasingly viewed as a potential risk. No one feared the type of relapse that frequently punctuated the rolling recessions of Japan's 15-year deflationary nightmare, but there was certainly a more cautious assessment of the staying power of the growth miracle that was so widely celebrated just a few months ago.

The private consumption story has long been the most important missing link in the current Japanese recovery dynamic. Since the onset of the current economic upturn in the first quarter of 2002, private consumption has risen at just a 1.6 percent average annual rate—well below the 2.3 percent growth rate in overall GDP. As a result, the consumption share of Japanese GDP has fallen from 58 percent in early 2002 to 56 percent in mid-2006. Nor are there any signs in the recent data flow of any material improvement in the prospects for Japanese consumption. In July and August of 2006, our calculation of what can be called a synthetic gauge of Japanese consumption, which incorporates data from both the supply and demand side sides of the consumer equation, fell 0.8 percent below the April-June 2006 reading for retail sales and 1.1 percent below the three-month earlier reading for shipments of consumer goods. At the same time, the Cabinet Office's quarterly index of consumer confidence slipped for a second quarter in a row in the three months ending September 2006, a disappointing fallback after a hopeful rebound in late 2005 and early 2006.

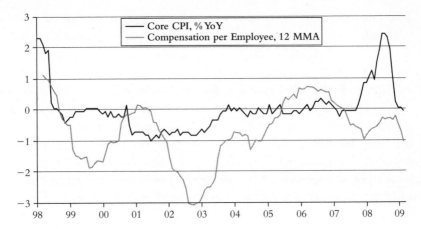

**Figure 4.4**  Japan's Real Wage Struggle

*Source:* Japan Cabinet Office, Morgan Stanley Research.

As a result, it probably pays to remain cautious on Japanese consumption prospects. Importantly, that reflects the likelihood that sluggish real wages will remain a persistent drag on household purchasing power. That dovetails with what has been a most disappointing performance on the Japanese wage front in 2006 (see Figure 4.4). After compensation per employee improved to a 1 percent year–over–year comparison during 2005, there has been a deceleration to just +0.5 percent growth over the course of 2006; moreover, this slowdown has occurred in the context of a long-awaited rebound in core inflation (i.e., consumer prices excluding fresh food have moved up to +0.6 percent year-over-year in recent months)—underscoring a meaningful compression of any expansion in real wages. Nor should this lingering stagnation in real wages be offset by developments elsewhere in the Japanese economy; in particular, it makes little sense to count on a spontaneous rebound in Japanese consumption driven by a declining personal saving rate, new-found wealth effects, or a shift in the distribution of income generation from capital to labor.

In my late October 2006 meetings in Tokyo, I got the distinct impression that concerns are mounting over this important missing piece to the Japanese economic recovery story. A Japan that is lacking in support from a self-sustaining internal consumption dynamic is, by definition, more dependent on capex and external demand. Significantly, external risk assessment suddenly looks a bit murkier as the Japanese peer into 2007 and worry about possible shortfalls in two of the most important foreign sources of its recovery—the American consumer and the Chinese producer. While U.S. consumption has held up quite well so far—providing ongoing support for Japan's largest export market—there is understandable concern that such support may diminish in a post-housing bubble climate. And now there are concerns that a China slowdown may finally come to pass—undermining support for what has now become Japan's second largest export market. Collectively, the United States and China currently account for fully 37 percent of total Japanese exports—by far, the largest and most concentrated piece of Japan's external demand. Moreover there has been a very important shift in the mix of Japanese exports to its two largest trading partners in recent years—a declining share to the United States (from 29.7 percent in 2000 to 22.5 percent in the first eight months of 2006) offset by a sharply increasing share to China (from 6.3 percent in 2000 to 14.1 percent thus far in 2006). Increasingly, China is the most powerful engine behind Japan's long important export machine.

Japan's tilt toward China is on everyone's mind in Tokyo these days. In the normal course of my visits here, I hold a series of roundtable discussions with corporate executives and senior institutional investors. I provide a brief macro overview and they then set the discussion agenda through their feedback. Over the past couple of years, the topic of China has become an increasingly important subject of exchange during these sessions. On this visit, the China focus was literally off the charts. Recent events certainly explain part of the increased interest: Newly elected Prime Minister Abe's first foreign mission was a quick trip to Beijing, underscoring the potential for a meaningful improvement in what had turned into a rather prickly relationship between these two Asian powerhouses in the Koizumi era. Moreover, the North Korean missile crisis has certainly heightened the attention on the strategic relationship between the two nations (see p. 282–285).

However, there is an important economic angle at work as well: Leading Chinese officials have recently refocused the debate on the off-again-on-again cooling off campaign for this overheated economy. The latest statements of Ma Kai, China's leading central planner and Chairman of the all-important National Development and Reform Commission are particularly important in that regard. And then there's China's just-released third quarter 2006 GDP report—a still very rapid 10.4 percent year-over-year increase but a downshift, nevertheless, from the blistering 11.3 percent pace of the second period. This could certainly be interpreted as the first installment on the road to a more meaningful slowdown—underscoring the potential for an important downshift in one of Japan's major external sources of economic growth. All in all, there can be little surprise in the heightened interest I detected in Japan with respect to the China factor.

The big puzzle in all this is Japan's lack of internal support for private consumption. I am struck by the similarities between the Japanese predicament and conditions in other major industrial economies. In my view, this is an unmistakable manifestation of one of the great paradoxes of globalization—a powerful global labor arbitrage that continues to put unrelenting pressure on the labor-income generating capacity of high-wage industrial economies. Japan is hardly alone in feeling this pressure—it's a serious constraint in Germany and even the United States. By our calculations for the G-7 plus, the real compensation share of national income fell to 53.7 percent of gross national income in early 2006, fully 2.3 percentage points below peak rates in early 2002. Until, or unless, the industrial economies figure out how to convert productivity improvements into enhanced labor income generating capacity, their private consumption dynamic should remain under pressure. That may be an uphill battle. To the extent that the fixation on intensified global competition and productivity enhancement rests on the tactics of increasingly aggressive corporate cost cutting—and that labor continues to account for the lion's share of business costs—it is hard to envision a spontaneous improvement in internally driven income generation.

Sure there are some unique aspects of the Japanese consumption experience that separate this economy from that of other industrial nations, namely, the ending of lifetime employment, a more urgent demographically-driven aging problem, and, of course, the very vivid recent memories of 15 years of rolling stagnation and deflation. But I don't think it is a coincidence that Japan is suffering from the same problem of labor income compression that afflicts the rest of industrial world. The initial euphoria of recovery tends to swamp those concerns, especially, since in Japan's case, it came after such a long nightmare. But as recovery matures and gives way to expansion, reality often sinks in and there is a perfectly natural refocusing of attention to any economy's lingering stresses and strains. That refocusing is now under way in Japan. The mood in Tokyo is very different than it was six months ago. With the American consumer and the Chinese producer now both in play, the missing link of the Japanese economy suddenly seems more problematic.

# India on the Move
## February 5, 2007

I am returning from India in early 2007 with great enthusiasm. Many serious problems remain, especially the ravages of poverty. But in the past several years, India has faced many of its macro imperatives head on, especially low savings, inadequate infrastructure, and lagging foreign direct investment. It is now making solid progress on two of those counts—savings and FDI—and infrastructure seems set to follow. These are just the breakthroughs that India needs—sufficient, in my view, to unshackle its great strengths in human capital and entrepreneurial talent. There is good reason to believe that India's macro and micro are finally coming together in a powerful combination. India is now on the move and could well be one of the world's most exceptional economic development stories over the next three to five years.

There's no dark secret about India's once seemingly chronic macro deficiencies. It is widely agreed that the key impediment has been an inadequate savings-investment equilibrium. The take-off phase of economic development has long been associated with saving and investment rates in excess of 30 percent of GDP. China's breakthrough came when its ratios pierced the 40 percent threshold. Yet for decades, those of India have lingered in the 20–25 percent range. Lacking in internal saving and maintaining a relatively restrictive stance toward foreign direct investment, India has been unable to achieve critical mass in infrastructure and capacity growth—the main drivers of any investment-led development strategy.

That is now changing. Official data now put national saving at 32.4 percent in the 12 months ending March 2006, up significantly from the 25 percent average of the 1990–2004 period (see Figure 4.5). At the same time, the aggregate investment ratio has moved up to 33.4 percent as of March 2006, a major breakout from the 26 percent average of the

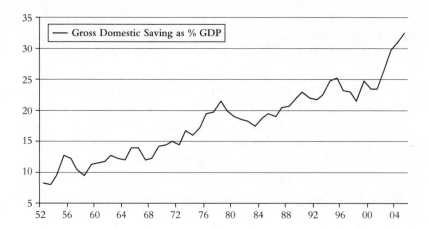

**Figure 4.5**  India's Saving Breakthrough

*Source:* Central Statistical Organization of India, Morgan Stanley Research.

preceding 15 years. And foreign direct investment is on target to hit $13 billion in the 12 months ending March 2007, more than double India's previous best of $5.5 billion hit in 2006. Infrastructure, however, remains a glaring laggard—likely to have held around 4.3 percent of Indian GDP in the 12 months ending March 2007 and little different from the range prevailing since the early 1990s.

No, these are not Chinese-style readings—saving and investment rates in the 40 to 50 percent range and annual foreign direct investment in the $50–60 billion vicinity. And the infrastructure contrasts are painfully obvious to anyone who travels in both India and China. But the real challenge for India is not the race with China but more the race with itself. The more important point for India is that it is now climbing out of the macro saving-investment quagmire of the past. That's what matters most insofar as the threshold effects of economic development are concerned.

With India's macro headwinds turning into tailwinds, it stands a much better chance of tapping its inherent strengths, namely, a high-quality stock of human capital, a large number of world-class companies, and a spectacular pool of entrepreneurial talent. In my earlier trips to India, I spent considerable time boring into the human capital story. My focus was on the dynamic IT services and business-process outsourcing companies—Infosys, Wipro, TCS, Accenture, and Genpact. Far from call centers and data processing, these organizations are all in the business of providing high value-added, increasingly complex systems solutions to local markets and multinational companies around the world.

Although I don't want to minimize India's human capital angle, in many respects, it's old news. What blew me away in February 2007 was the corporate and entrepreneurial angle. For all the buzz over China, one of the great paradoxes of the world's greatest development story is that it has only a handful of truly world-class companies. By contrast, India has a much deeper and broader stable of very powerful businesses. Moreover, it's not just IT services—it's also telecom, pharmaceuticals, energy, steel, and auto components. The just-announced Tata-Corus steel merger could well be a harbinger of the next wave of India's already impressive industrial prowess—the coming of age of the India-centric multinational corporation.

The real spark in India is a truly extraordinary entrepreneurial spirit. Mukesh Ambani, Chairman of Reliance Industries, is an excellent example. Not satisfied with the success of Reliance's core businesses in energy, petrochemicals, and textiles, Mr. Ambani is now pushing ahead on two of India's greatest challenges—retail and agriculture. India's highly fragmented retail sector—populated by over 12 million Mom-and-Pop-style establishments across the country—has long been ripe for a major efficiency campaign. And India's agricultural sector, home to over 60 percent of the nation's population, has been the biggest laggard in the nation's growth story. Mukesh Ambani's passion is to create a powerful synergy between these two opportunities—integrating what he calls the agro-input supply chain with a new network of large-scale retail establishments. His initial focus is on an IT-enabled agricultural distribution system, drawing on the scalable efficiencies of the Israeli kibbutz model while using new IT platforms and rapidly expanding rural connectivity. At the same time, he is forging ahead on the opening of new large-scale retail outlets—more than 50 stores have been opened in early 2006 with many more in the immediate pipeline. The concept and execution are fascinating, and the benefits for India in terms of lifting rural incomes and boosting consumer purchasing power fit the nation's macro imperatives to a tee.

India's entrepreneurs are also hard at work on the infrastructure story—tackling one of the most obvious of India's bottlenecks. While the aggregate numbers have yet to turn up, there's nothing but upside on the drawing boards. New Delhi highway construction is visible as soon as you leave the airport. The airport itself will be rebuilt by the GMR Group—the same organization that is pushing ahead on the new airport at Hyderabad. I had lunch with the Chairman and founder of this company, G.M. Rao, a self-made entrepreneur from very humble rural roots, who has an extraordinary vision of the future of Indian infrastructure. He spoke not just of new airports but of the "aerotropolis" concept that is now shaping the newest large airports of the world. GMR is also forging ahead on two other key aspects of Indian infrastructure—road construction and power generation. Mr. Rao's impressive track record, along with his drive, determination and vision, was contagious.

I had a similar impression after discussions with Dr. E. Sreedharan, Head of the Delhi Metro Rail Corporation and developer of a world-class subway in the Indian capital. I even took a ride on the new metro to see it for myself. As a veteran New York City straphanger, I instantly fell in love with the sleek, quiet, and ever-efficient Delhi subway. I also met with two key government officials charged with policy initiatives on the Indian infrastructure front—Praful Patel, Minister of Civil Aviation, and Sudhir Kumar, the number two official in the Ministry of Railways. They stressed a powerful common theme—a customer-centric, market-driven public-private sector partnership as the only option for Indian infrastructure. Many believe that the revival of Indian Railways is India's greatest corporate turnaround. Driven by reform-minded ministers who have remained steadfast in the face of political opposition, both India's rail system and the civilian aviation sector are likely to benefit significantly from a major acceleration of investment in the years ahead.

Finally, I spent some time with my old friend Rajiv Lall, Head of the Infrastructure Development Finance Corporation and a former member of our global economics team at Morgan Stanley in the 1990s. Rajiv is very focused on creative financing solutions that would enable India to achieve the intermediation capabilities to transform rising saving into accelerated infrastructure spending. He is confident in the macro end-game, an infrastructure investment share that rises from 4.3 percent of Indian GDP at present to 8 percent over the next three to five years. Based on what I learned on this trip from entrepreneurs, regulators, and financiers, it's hard to argue with that conclusion.

This was my fourth trip to India in the past three years (2004–2007). Each of these missions is like peeling away another layer of an onion—the story comes into sharper and sharper focus. This time, I was focused on three key themes—infrastructure, rural reform, and entrepreneurialism.

India impressed me as being on the move on all three counts. The China comparison is overdone. In my opinion, India suffers from excessive fixation in measuring itself against Chinese-style development metrics. We all know that China has opened up an extraordinary gap with India over the past 15 years, going from parity in per-capita GDP in 1991 to a tripling of India's standard of living today. I am a huge fan of the Chinese miracle, and the investment-saving dynamic that has driven its spectacular development story. But China has pushed this model to its limits and now faces rebalancing imperatives of its own. Meanwhile, India is making great progress on the macro saving-investment front, which better enables it to tap into its long-standing micro strengths.

In the end, the story is not China or India—but most likely China *and* India. And that poses what undoubtedly is the biggest challenge of all: Are the rich countries of the developed world prepared for the ultimate endgame of globalization? Right now, that is not the case (see "Unprepared for Globalization" on p. 155–159). Meanwhile, the developing world is not about to wait for the developed world to get its act together. I saw that firsthand early February 2007 in India.

# The Cranes of Dubai

*February 23, 2007*

I t has been almost three weeks since I returned from my latest trip to the Middle East, but I am still haunted by the sight of the cranes of Dubai. According to construction trade sources, somewhere between 15–25 percent of the 125,000 construction cranes currently operating in the world are located in Dubai. As a macro person, I am struck by two possible interpretations of this astonishing development: It could be a property bubble of epic proportions or it may be emblematic of a new Middle East that challenges its long-standing role as a financial recycling machine. Either outcome—or a combination of both—could have profound consequences for world financial markets and the global economy.

The comparison with Shanghai, Pudong—China's massive urban development project of the 1990s—is unavoidable. I saw Pudong rise from the rice fields and never thought anything could surpass it. I was wrong. The Dubai building boom is occurring on a scale that dwarfs the Chinese experience. Based on industry sources, 26.8 million square feet of office space is expected to come on line in Dubai in 2007, alone—more than six times the peak rate of completions in Pudong in 1999 and nearly equal to the total stock of some 30 million square feet of office space in downtown Minneapolis. Based on current projections, another 42 million square feet should come on line in Dubai in 2008. This is the equivalent of adding the office space of a downtown San Francisco. There is one obvious and critically important difference between Dubai and Shanghai: Pudong has an indigenous support base of 1.3 billion Chinese citizens. Dubai's current population is 1.3 million. Throw in the entire native population of the United Arab Emirates (UAE) and the support base is still only around 4 million domestic citizens. That's right, a region with less than 0.5 percent the population of China is out-building the biggest construction boom in modern Chinese history.

That doesn't necessarily spell trouble. After all, construction and economic development go hand in hand. The problems arise when building cycles go to extremes—fueled by speculation or funded by the easy money of state-directed lending. The jury is out on Dubai, although it's hard not to take note of the obvious excesses—ski domes in the desert, offshore cities in the shape of palm trees and the world, a massive eight-runway second airport under construction, the Tiger- and now Sergio-led golf-course bonanza, Venetian-like canals for the urban cruise in the desert, a world record 160-story skyscraper, and on and on. Dubai aspires to be the premier financial center and destination tourist resort for the Middle East. It may well get there. The problem is that other urban centers in the region are vying for the same title. Take a look at Doha, Bahrain, Riyadh, and even nearby Abu Dhabi. Far too many cities are in the same chase.

Bubble or not, the Dubai-led Gulf building boom is not an isolated development. Throughout the region, it has been accompanied by expanded infrastructure efforts, rapidly growing commitments to education and medicine, increased industrialization, and the growth of domestic capital market activity. These trends are emblematic of a new and important development in the Middle East that distinguishes the current period of elevated oil prices from the oil shocks of the past—a massive push toward internal development. The Dubai factor simply was not present in the two oil shocks of the 1970s or in the brief surge of oil prices in 1990.

Lacking in domestic spending commitments, the earlier inflow of elevated oil revenues spun quickly through a revolving door—reinvested in world financial markets, especially dollar-based assets. Such petro-dollar recycling quickly became synonymous for the oil shock. This shock is different. As noted above, internal absorption is now very much in focus for oil-producing countries in the Middle East. As oil prices have surged in recent years, imports of goods and services of the world's major oil producers more than doubled from around $170 billion in 1999 to $355 billion in 2005 (see Figure 4.6). At the same time, according to IMF estimates, primary government expenditures—a good proxy for publicly sponsored infrastructure and social spending initiatives—accounted for fully 15 percent of GDP growth in 2005 in the GCC (Gulf Cooperation Council, which includes Saudi Arabia, Kuwait, the UAE, Bahrain, Qatar, and Oman); by contrast, this share was basically zero in 2002 (see Figure 4.7). Moreover, the region's fiscal authorities are mindful of the policy

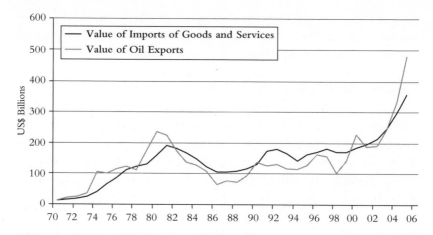

**Figure 4.6** OPEC Imports and Oil Exports

*Source:* International Monetary Fund, OECD, World Integrated Trade Solution.

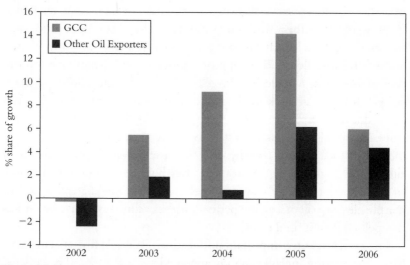

**Figure 4.7** Government Primary Expenditures: Oil Producers

*Source:* International Monetary Fund.

mistakes of the past, when mean-reverting oil prices led to substantial government budget deficits for those who had been too aggressive in opening up the spending spigot. For the developing economies of the Middle East, the IMF is estimating central government surpluses of a little more than 8 percent of GDP in 2007—about the same as in 2006 but a swing of around 11 percentage points of GDP from the 3 percent average deficits of 2002–2003. This more prudent fiscal response is a very encouraging development that could avoid the boom-bust cycles of the 1980s and thereby set the stage for more sustainable state-led spending initiatives in the years ahead.

Notwithstanding the push toward internal absorption, Middle East oil-producing states have not turned their backs on dollar-denominated assets. Due largely to dollar-pegged currencies, Gulf Cooperation Council (GCC) monetary authorities still need to invest a large portion of their outsize portfolio of official foreign exchange reserves in dollar-based assets. But the combination of new domestic spending programs and reserve diversification strategies challenges the time-honored conclusion that petro-dollar recycling is an automatic outgrowth of rising oil prices. There is an added and important twist in the current climate: America's post-9/11 Patriot Act now makes it much more difficult for Middle East portfolio investors to transfer funds into the United States. At the same time, the recent controversy over the purchase of U.S. assets by Dubai Ports World, together with congressional efforts currently underway to tighten up restrictions on foreign direct investment into the United States—the so-called CFIUS approval process—also discourages dollar-centric buying of Middle East investors. An offset comes from the sharp corrections in local stock markets since late 2005, underscoring the risks of the domestic capital markets option for non-dollar diversification strategies. But should these markets start to recover, I suspect local buying will intensify rather quickly, thereby diverting assets away from lower-return alternatives in the United States and elsewhere in the developed world. In short, there are many reasons to believe that in the current period of sharply elevated oil prices, the petro-dollar recycling story may be far less compelling than it used to be.

This conclusion has important implications for world financial markets. Most importantly, it challenges consensus views that high oil prices create a natural bid for dollar-denominated assets. In a climate where dollar risk remains an ongoing concern, that could be an especially important point for the currency debate. In light of recent dollar diversification concerns expressed by reserve managers in the Middle East—especially those in the UAE, Qatar, Iran, and Syria—that possibility should not be taken lightly.

The cranes of Dubai are emblematic of a much deeper point: We need to update our thinking about the Gulf economy—especially insofar as its internal development efforts are concerned but also with respect to its role in world financial markets. It was only a little over 33 years ago when rising oil prices first came into play. Since then, the economic development of Middle East oil producers has been staggering. Dubai underscores a critical difference between then and now. Even if it ends up being a bubble, I suspect there will be no turning back for the new Middle East. In a world where the globalization debate is dominated by China, it is high time to broaden our horizons.

# Asian Decoupling Unlikely

*March 26, 2007*

As the U.S. economy slows, most believe that Asia's growth machine will fill the void. Don't count on it. Policy makers in China and India are shifting toward restraint, tilting growth risks in the region's fastest-growing economies to the downside. Nor is an externally dependent Japanese economy likely to provide much compensation. To the extent the case for global decoupling is dependent on an Asian offset, prepare to be disappointed.

After years of doubt, convictions are deep that both China and India will stay the course of hypergrowth. There has been talk for years about the coming Chinese slowdown, but so far the downshift has failed to materialize. The 10.7 percent increase in Chinese GDP in 2007 (since revised upward to 13 percent) was the fastest since 1995, when the size of the economy was less than one-third what it is in March 2007. Moreover, with India now showing impressive improvement in its macro foundations of growth—especially saving, infrastructure, and foreign direct investment—there is good reason to believe that there may be considerable staying power to the recent acceleration in economic growth that averaged 9 percent during the 2005–2006 interval. Needless to say, if China and India hold to their recent elevated growth trajectories, the global economy would barely skip a beat in the face of a U.S. slowdown.

The case for global resilience is also an outgrowth of the mix of world GDP. Collectively, China and India account for about 21 percent of global output, as measured by the IMF's purchasing power parity framework—essentially equal to the 20 percent share the statisticians assign to the United States. Add in the recent acceleration in the Japanese economy—a 5.5 percent annualized increase in the final quarter of calendar year 2006 for an economy that accounts for another 6 percent of PPP-based world GDP—and it is understandable why so many believe that the impact of America's downshift could well be neutralized by the ongoing vigor of the Asian growth machine.

The Asian offset, in conjunction with a modest cyclical uplift in a long sluggish European economy, is the essence of the case for global decoupling—a world economy that has finally weaned itself from the great American growth engine. A key presumption of that conclusion is that Asia does, indeed, stay its present course. There are two flaws in that argument, in my view—the first being that internal pressures are now building in Asia's fastest-growing economies that could be sowing the seeds for slower growth ahead. In particular, both the Chinese and Indian economies are now displaying worrisome signs of overheating. In China, the symptoms have manifested themselves in the form of imbalances in the mix of the real economy, widening disparities in the income distribution, and a large and growing current-account surplus—to say nothing of the negative externalities of environmental degradation and excess energy and other resource consumption. In India, the overheating has surfaced in the form of a cyclical resurgence of inflation, with the CPI running at a 6.8 percent year-over-year rate in early 2007—a sharp acceleration from the 3.8 percent pace of 2002–2005.

In the early weeks of March 2007, I have met with senior policy makers in both China and India. It is clear to me that in both cases the authorities are in the process of shifting their policy arsenals toward meaningful restraint. In China, the direction comes from the top, in the form of growing concerns expressed by Premier Wen Jiabao about a Chinese economy that he has explicitly characterized as "unstable, unbalanced, uncoordinated, and unsustainable" (see p. 229–233). In my view, such a characterization has tightening written all over it.

Since the Premier first uttered those words at the end of the National People's Congress on March 15, 2007, Chinese authorities have been quick to respond. There was a monetary tightening the very next day and the securities regulators were quick to issue new rules that prevent companies from purchasing equities with proceeds from share sales. The former move is aimed at cooling off an overheated investment sector, while the latter action is addressed at dealing with a frothy domestic stock market that increased by 100 percent in the six months ending in late February 2007. I am more convinced than ever that Beijing is now deadly serious in attempting to regain control over its rapidly growing economy. This is good news for China but could be disappointing for the decoupling camp that expects rapid Chinese economic growth to remain resistant to any downside pressures.

India is similarly positioned. The Reserve Bank of India (RBI) does not take overheating and cyclical inflationary pressures lightly. I was actually in Mumbai the day the RBI tightened monetary policy last month (February 13, 2007), and it was clear to me in my discussions at the central bank that the bank was determined to alter the cyclical endgame. The RBI's official statement following that action said it all: "(A) determined and co-coordinated effort by all to contain inflation without unduly impacting the growth momentum is not only an economic necessity but also a moral compulsion." It doesn't get any clearer than that. At the same time, the Indian government's latest budget contained measures that would cut tariffs on food and other price-sensitive manufactured products. Indian authorities are fixated on a mounting cyclical inflation problem and appear more than willing to take a haircut on economic growth to achieve such an objective.

There is a second factor at work that is also likely to challenge the view that hyper growth is here to stay in Asia—the region's persistent reliance on external demand as a major driver of economic growth. A slowdown in the United States—the main engine on the demand side of the global economy—can't help but work its way through the export channel and reduce externally dependent Asian growth. This is less a story for India, with its relatively small trade sector, and more a story for the rest of Asia. China is at the top of the external vulnerability chain. Its export sector, which rose to nearly 37 percent of GDP in 2006, surged at a 41 percent year-over-year rate in the first two months of 2007. Moreover—and this is an absolutely critical point in the decoupling debate—the United States is China's largest export market, accounting for 21 percent of RMB-based exports. As the United States economy now slows, the biggest piece of China's out-size export dynamic is at risk. So, too, are the large external sectors of China's pan-Asian supply chain, especially Taiwan, Korea, and even Japan. Lacking in self-sustaining support from private consumption, the Asian growth dynamic remains highly vulnerable to an external shock. That's yet another important reason to be very suspicious of the case for global decoupling.

Decoupling and global rebalancing go hand-in-hand. A decoupled world is very much a rebalanced world and vice versa. On the surface, recent trends appear to lend some support to the decoupling thesis—especially a booming Asian economy but also a seemingly remarkable cyclical revival in Europe. Perspective is key here. The European upsurge is certainly a welcome development, but it is important to understand the global impact of this "strength." At most, it will add only 0.2–0.3 percentage point to a baseline view of world economic growth. Asia, especially China and India, is a very different story. This is a much larger segment of the global economy and it is growing at rates that are three times as fast as those in the developed world. An Asian economy that only barely widens its growth multiple relative to the rest of the world could well drive global decoupling on its own.

However, that's unlikely to be the case. Not only does Asia remain vulnerable to a U.S.-centric external shock, but the region's two most powerful growth stories—China and India—are now both very focused on matters of internal sustainability. The Premier of China has put his reputation on the line in attempting to bring an unstable, unbalanced, uncoordinated, and unsustainable Chinese economy under control. The Indian government is equally focused on an anti-inflationary policy tightening. Looking backward, both of these economies have been on an exceptionally strong growth path that, if left to its own devices, could play an increasingly important role in powering a decoupled world. Looking forward, however, it's likely to be a very different story. With growth prospects in China and India tipping to the downside at the same time the U.S. economy is slowing, a tightly coupled global economy is likely to be a good deal weaker than the decoupling crowd would lead you to believe.

# The Korea Test

*April 5, 2007*

A s the breathless negotiators staggered to a last-minute deal on the Korea-U.S. Free Trade Agreement (KORUS FTA), the political disconnect in the globalization debate came into ever-sharper focus. This is a good deal for the owners of capital, but workers—and their duly elected representatives—may have something else to say about it in both countries. And it may well be that this approach simply doesn't fly.

On the surface, KORUS FTA—as it is known in trade circles—goes a long way in tearing down trade barriers between the world's largest and 11th largest economies. The government-issued fact sheets celebrate an elimination of all duties on nearly 95 percent of the some $78 billion in bilateral trade between the United States and Korea within three years of enactment. And there are promises of relief for farmers, ranchers, service providers, investors, and knowledge workers. Who could ask for more?

The short answer is labor, especially a growing middle class that feels increasingly disenfranchised by the hype and esoteric theories of the win-win globalization mantra. Rightly or wrongly, labor sees itself very much on the outside looking in as the world rushes headlong down the road of trade liberalization. That's especially the case in the rich developed economies. For the G-7-plus—the United States, Japan, Canada, the UK, and the Euro-zone—the share of national income going to capital currently stands at a record high of 16 percent whereas the share going to labor stands at a record low of 54 percent.

But here's the rub: Courtesy of one trade deal after another, global trade is now closing in on a record 31 percent of world GDP—up 10 percentage points from the mid-1990s and double the preglobalization ratio of the mid-1970s. Surging trade and a falling share of labor income make for a nasty combination—something that has not escaped the attention of the body politic. That's especially the case in Washington, where a bipartisan backlash against globalization has never been stronger. In 2006, the United States ran a $13 billion trade deficit with Korea. Although that pales in comparison to the $230 billion shortfall with China, it was still America's fifth largest trade gap in Asia. With trade viewed by Washington politicians as the major source of pressure on beleaguered American workers, the risk is that KORUS FTA will be seen as just another in a long string of deals with countries that already have the upper hand on trade flows with the United States.

The new 110th U.S. Congress has put its cards squarely on the table in this debate. I saw this firsthand when I recently testified in front of both the House of Representatives and the Senate on the U.S.-China trade relationship. A deliberate and well-orchestrated process is now under way in the Congress that could culminate in a serious escalation of trade tensions between these two nations. It is absolutely key to understand that this is not a partisan development. To the contrary, the politics of a growing trade protectionism in Washington are distinctly bipartisan in character. Yes, congressional leadership has swung from Republicans to Democrats, but the GOP is every bit as strident on trade-related concerns as those on the other side of the aisle. I sat right behind Republican Senator Lindsey Graham as he put it quite bluntly to the Senate Finance Committee on March 28, 2007, "This is one issue where Republicans and Democrats are together, and we are going to act."

Moreover, borrowing a page from the Republican Revolution of 1994 and its subsequent "Contract with America," leading House Democrats recently unveiled "A New Trade Policy for America." Taking the place of Newt Gingrich—the fiery architect of the Republican contract—are Charles Rangel, Chairman of the all-powerful Ways and Means Committee and Sander Levin, Chairman of the Ways and Means Subcommittee on Trade. This New Trade Policy argues for principles-based trade negotiations to be driven by respect for international labor standards, environmental safeguards, and intellectual property rights; the agenda also stresses a host of China-specific concerns, assistance for trade-displaced workers, and heightened efforts at WTO compliance. But the new manifesto puts labor-related considerations right at the top of the agenda. In Rangel's words, "…we want trade that works for all Americans." Suddenly, the trade-off between labor and capital now has clear and important political consequences. The KORUS FTA trade deal will be scrutinized in that context.

There have already been some predictable criticisms of this deal, especially from Senator Max Baucus, Chairman of the Senate Finance Committee, over beef and from Congressman Levin over autos. Republican Senator Charles Grassley has also expressed some reservations, and several U.S. politicians expressed displeasure that protesting Korean farmers were able to get their way in staving off any concessions over rice. But sources close to the negotiations expect most of these concerns to be resolved in the weeks ahead. The potential dealbreaker is a much deeper issue that goes to the heart of the globalization debate—the tensions between capital and labor. That's where the rubber meets the road, in my view. I have a very hard time believing that the same overwhelming majority of U.S. politicians that seems dead set on taking action against China is suddenly going to reverse course and welcome a new trade deal with Korea. Quite simply, I don't see any room for a double standard in the current climate. For that reason, alone, and with the China debate likely to intensify over the balance of 2007, KORUS FTA could be in serious trouble in the U.S. Congress.

The proglobalization crowd has raised another criticism to the Korea-U.S. deal—that bilateralism is basically incompatible with the multilateralism that is needed to support a broadly based expansion of global trade. I am very sympathetic to this point. Not only can bilateral deals such as KORUS FTA deflect progress away from multilateral efforts such as the Doha Round, but they can also lead to distortions in cross-border trade patterns that are driven more by the height of country-specific trade barriers than by the inherent efficiencies of comparative advantage. Although this point may be technically correct, it misses the essence of the globalization critique: The politics of the prolabor backlash would be equally critical of bilateral and multilateral trade concessions. KORUS FTA certainly won't fail in the U.S. Congress because it undermines the case for Doha. Instead, it will most likely stumble on its own because it fails to deliver on Congress's main complaint—a globalization that has failed to alleviate the squeeze on American workers.

The upcoming debate over KORUS FTA could well provide an important litmus test of the new tough congressional mindset on trade policy. If the agreement sails through, my fears over a rising outbreak of protectionism will turn out to have been wrong. If, however, this deal stalls out in the Congress, the United States will have taken another step down a very slippery slope.

# Asia's Policy Trap

## May 29, 2007

Asia is brimming over with foreign exchange reserves. While that cushions the region from a replay of a 1997–1998 style crisis, it presents new and difficult challenges for Asian policy makers. Particularly worrisome are the excesses of a pan-regional liquidity cycle—complete with the risks of asset bubbles as exemplified by the current blow-out in domestic Chinese equities. A new policy framework is needed—before it's too late.

There is a striking twist to the current globalization. Unlike the globalization of the early 20th century when capital flowed from the rich countries of the developed world to settlement economies such as Argentina, Australia, and Canada, the opposite is true today in 2007. In the current globalization, incremental saving for the advanced economies of the developed world has come almost entirely from the developing world in the form of capital transfers from poor countries and oil producers. The United States, with its massive current account deficit, is the major beneficiary of this reverse Marshall Plan—absorbing about 70 percent of the world's surplus saving over the past three years (2004–2007). With that transfer has come a huge build-up in the foreign exchange reserves of the donor nations—especially those in Developing Asia. According to the IMF, foreign exchange reserves in Developing Asia are likely to exceed $1.8 trillion in 2007, a six-fold increase from 1999. Deeply scarred by the wrenching financial crisis of 1997-98 that was triggered by a paucity of reserves, the emerging economies of Asia are collectively saying "Never again." The risk is they may have gone too far in atoning for the mistakes of the past.

The problem comes with the recycling of this capital—especially from Asia to the United States. Lacking in well-developed domestic capital markets, it has been exceedingly difficult for countries like China to sterilize the massive purchases of Treasuries and other dollar-denominated assets that are required to maintain pegged or crawling pegged currency parities with the U.S. dollar. As a result, excess liquidity has seeped into Developing Asia's domestic financial systems, pushing broad money growth in this region up to a 17 percent annual rate in 2006. A similar overshoot has been evident in the expansion of bank credit, especially in China. Despite multiple tightening moves by the People's Bank of China during 2006, domestic bank lending was still surging at a 16.5 percent year-over-year rate through April 2007—more than three percentage points faster than the pace of credit extension in early 2005. Not only does the Chinese central bank have serious problems mopping up the excess liquidity from incomplete forex-related sterilization, but it continues to have great difficulty in achieving policy traction with a still highly fragmented network of branch banks.

At the same time, embryonic banking systems continue to play a highly disproportionate role in the intermediation of total credit flows in Developing Asia. Here again, that's especially the case in China, where the development of a domestic bond market has lagged and the banking sector still accounts for nearly 85 percent of total credit intermediation. In short, Asia, in general—and China, in particular—lacks the high-quality financial-market infrastructure that is commensurate with its linchpin role as the world's major provider of surplus saving. Senior leaders in Beijing concur on the urgency to address these shortcomings in the context of China's broader control problems. The recent surge of money and credit is indicative of the concerns that recently prompted China's Premier Wen Jiabao to characterize the Chinese economy as "unstable, unbalanced, uncoordinated, and unsustainable."

China's equity bubble—with the domestic A-share index up more than 160 percent over the course of 2006—is today's most visible manifestation of Asia's control problem. Nor is this an isolated occurrence. To the extent that China is now the engine of Developing Asia, its liquidity management problems are emblematic of broader control problems afflicting the entire region. India's Bombay Stock Exchange Sensitive Index (Sensex) Index has surged over 115 percent during the past two years, 2005 to 2007, and the Korean Composite Stock Price Index (KOSPI) is up more than 70 percent over the same period. Sharp gains are also evident in the region's smaller equity markets. With limited domestic absorption, quasi-pegged currencies, and rapid accumulation of foreign exchange reserves, most of these surplus-saving economies are awash in excess liquidity. Lacking in alternative assets and, especially in the case of China, with largely closed capital accounts, domestic equities have absorbed a disproportionate share of the Asian liquidity binge. The result is a classic asset bubble, in the end dominated by the same speculative forces that have taken markets to excess for hundreds of years.

China's equity bubble underscores a new and worrisome flaw in the Asian policy regime—a loss of control in setting currency expectations. By succumbing to the pressures of Washington-led China bashing, the renminbi is now a one-way bet versus the dollar. With the U.S. Congress now considering the enactment of WTO-compliant trade sanctions on China, most market participants have concluded that a large upward adjustment in the Chinese currency is the only way out. This stands in sharp contrast with the fixed-currency expectations that had been anchored by the once-solid RMB-dollar peg. The result has been a dramatic acceleration of hot-money inflows that have been aggressively channeled into domestic Chinese equities. What Stanford professor Ronald McKinnon once labeled "conflicted virtue"—high-saving economies acquiring dollar-based claims on their creditors—is now in danger of becoming increasingly vicious.[4]

So what should be done to enable China and the rest of developing Asia to get out of this policy trap? Three conditions must be satisfied: First, China needs to be more aggressive in reducing surplus saving. That can only occur through a significant increase in domestic private consumption—a clear objective of China's 11th Five-Year Plan unveiled over a year ago. The sooner the consumption share of Chinese GDP starts to rise, the import share of this open economy will follow—reducing China's trade surplus, a key component of its massive current-account surplus. China knows full well what it will take to boost domestic private consumption, namely, policies that establish and solidify a social safety net (i.e., pensions and social security) and thereby reduce the overhang of precautionary saving. Consumer cultures—especially for nations lacking in safety nets—don't spring to life overnight. The destabilizing financial signals currently coming out of China make it clear that the time path of this critical transition now needs to be shortened.

Second, the United States needs to own up to the role it is playing in triggering destabilizing conditions in China and elsewhere in Developing

---

4. See McKinnon's remarkably prescient 2005 book, *Exchange Rates Under the East Asian Dollar Standard: Living with Conflicted Virtue,* MIT Press.

Asia. The main problem here is America's unprecedented saving shortfall, a net national savings rate that averaged just 1 percent of national income over the 2004–2006 period. The more the U.S. relies on surplus savers from China and other Asian economies to fund its consumption-led growth, the more the destabilizing pressures of bilateral trade tensions will come into play. Relief from these tensions will also require the U.S. Congress to give up the ghost of promising a beleaguered American middle class that a bilateral RMB currency fix is the answer to all their problems. As I have stressed *ad nauseum*, it's hard to be optimistic on this count. Unfortunately, there is no escape from the Asian policy trap if Washington doesn't do its best to disarm it.

Third, Asia, in general, and China, in particular, needs to establish a new policy anchor. I don't think it is an accident that China's interplay between foreign exchange reserve accumulation and its equity market became increasingly destabilizing after the dismantling of the RMB-dollar currency peg in July 2005. This single action, in conjunction with intensified pressure from Washington on the currency front, is the genesis of the hot-money inflows that are driving China's forex reserves, domestic liquidity, and equity prices to excess. Chinese authorities need to be direct and firm in reestablishing a transparent policy anchor—whether it is a price target, a money or credit target, or even a new currency target. With over $1.2 trillion in official currency reserves—and rising—China clearly has the ammunition to punish those who want to bet against its willingness to hit a new policy target. With speculators eager to jump on the one-way RMB appreciation bandwagon, it will take vigorous two-way markets to unwind this bet. That won't happen without newfound Chinese policy credibility.

The rest of Developing Asia is very much beholden to the China fix. Linked to the real side of the Chinese economy through an increasingly integrated panregional supply chain, it is virtually impossible for other Asian economies to decouple from pressures that might affect the performance of China's trade engine. Similarly, the fate of the RMB could well hold the key to currencies elsewhere in Developing Asia. If the Chinese currency moves sharply to the upside, other Asian currencies—with the possible exception of the Japanese yen—should be quick to follow. Conversely, if China reverts to more of a quasi-stable RMB, currency adjustments elsewhere in the region are likely to be stymied, thereby putting the onus on U.S. saving as the main mechanism for a U.S. current account adjustment.

The perils of Asia's policy trap cannot be minimized. The Chinese equity bubble, in conjunction with mounting protectionist pressures in the U.S. Congress, hints at a potential flashpoint. Recent cooling-off actions by Chinese authorities aimed at an overheated economy are encouraging in this context. It is up to China and the rest of Developing Asia to put more robust policies and institutions in place that will insure stable and sustainable growth. Unfortunately, any such efforts could well be for naught if Washington-led China bashing doesn't back away from the brink.

# Complacency Asian Style

## January 8, 2008

T here is no looking back in Asia. Ten years later, with the region's economies and stock markets surging, memories of Asia's most wrenching crisis have faded. As the largest and most dynamic region in the world, many believe the century of the Asian boom has finally arrived.

If it were only that easy. Don't get me wrong. I am a long-standing optimist on Asia. In fact, I have bet my career on that optimism, having just relocated to the region as Chairman of Morgan Stanley's pan-Asian businesses. I believe strongly in this region's potential as the epicenter of the next powerful wave of global growth.

I am indeed heartened that Asia seems to have learned many a painful lesson from the devastating crisis of 1997–1998. In particular, foreign exchange reserves have been rebuilt; current account balances have gone from deficit to surplus; exposure to short-term foreign lending has been sharply reduced; and, for the most part, currency pegs have been replaced by floating foreign exchange regimes.

Alas, repairing the flaws that gave rise to the last crisis rarely prevents the next one. That's a lesson that spans centuries of economic history— for developed and developing nations, alike. It is a lesson rooted deeply in human nature—in backward-looking defense mechanisms that tempt us all into believing that lessons from the past guard against the perils from the future. However, time and again, we find that the future doesn't follow the autoregressive script that dictates safety through backward-looking remedies. For an all too complacent Asia, this is another one of those times.

A decade ago, global problems were made in Asia. This time, I suspect the tables will be turned. Global problems are likely to be made in America—driven by a stunning capitulation of the American consumer.

A bursting of the U.S. property bubble, in conjunction with subprime-related deleveraging and a downshift in labor income generation, point to the end of what has been a record spending binge for overextended American consumers. That could derail what has long been the major engine on the demand side of the global economy, triggering reverberations around the world that could deal an especially tough blow to Asia. Therein lie the seeds of the proverbial next crisis.

This conclusion is, of course, very much at odds with the notion of global decoupling—an increasingly popular belief that depicts a world economy that has finally weaned itself from the ups and downs of the U.S. economy. However, the global decoupling thesis is premised on a major contradiction. In an increasingly globalized world, cross border linkages have become even more important—making globalization and decoupling inherently inconsistent.

True, the recent data flow raises some questions about this contention. After all, the world seems to have held up reasonably well in the face of the slowing of U.S. GDP growth that has unfolded over the past year. But that's because the downshift in U.S. growth has been almost exclusively concentrated in residential building activity—one of the least global sectors of the U.S. economy. If I am right, and consumption now starts to slow, such a downshift will affect one of the most global sectors of the United States. And I fully suspect a downshift in America's most global sector will have considerably greater repercussions for the world at large than has been the case so far.

That's an especially likely outcome in Asia—the world's most rapidly growing region and one widely suspected to be a leading candidate for global decoupling. However, as Figure 4.8 indicates, the macrostructure of Developing Asia remains very much skewed toward an export-led growth dynamic. For the region as a whole, the export share has more than doubled over the past 25 years—surging from less than 20 percent in 1980 to more than 45 percent today. Similarly, the share going to internal private consumption—the sector that would have to drive an Asian decoupling—has fallen from 67 percent to less than 50 percent over the same period.

Nor can there be any mistake as to the dominant external market for export-led Asian economies. The United States wins the race hands down—underscored by a 21 percent share of Chinese exports currently going to America. Yes, there has been a sharp acceleration of intraregional trade in recent years, adding to the hopes and dreams of Asian decoupling.

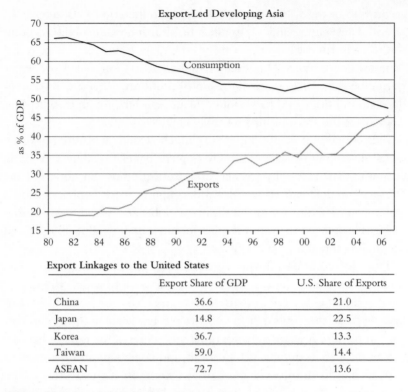

**Figure 4.8**   The Myth of Asian Decoupling

*Source:* International Monetary Fund, Morgan Stanley Research.

But a good portion of that integration reflects the development of a China-centric pan–Asian supply chain that continues to be focused on sourcing end-market demand for American consumers. That means that if the U.S. consumer now slows, as I suspect, Asia will be hit hard, with cross-border supply chain linkages exposing a long-standing vulnerability that will draw the global decoupling thesis into serious question.

A downshift of U.S. consumption growth will affect Asia unevenly. A rapidly growing Chinese economy has an ample cushion to withstand such a blow. Chinese GDP growth might slow from 12 percent to around 6 to 8 percent at some point in the 2008–2009 period—hardly a disaster for any economy and actually consistent with what Beijing has tried to accomplish with its cooling-off campaign of the past several years.

Other Asian economies, however, lack the hypergrowth cushion that China enjoys. As such, a U.S.-led slowdown of external demand could hurt them a good deal more. That's especially the case for Japan, whose 2 percent growth economy could be in serious trouble in the event of a U.S. demand shock that also takes a toll on Japanese exports into the Chinese supply chain. Although less vulnerable than Japan, Taiwan and South Korea could also be squeezed by the double whammy of U.S. and China slowdowns. For the rest of Asia, underlying growth appears strong enough to withstand a shortfall in U.S. consumer demand. But there can be no mistaking the endgame: Contrary to the widespread optimism of investors and policy makers, the Asian growth dynamic is quite vulnerable to a meaningful slowdown in U.S. consumption.

What can Asia do to prevent the next crisis—one that could be sparked by an external shock made in America? The answer lies is macro rebalancing—shifting the region's growth dynamic away from exports and investment toward one that rests more firmly on solid support from domestic demand, especially private consumption. This won't be easy, but in the end, it is Asia's only hope for the better balance that is essential for sustainable longer-term growth.

China will need to lead the way in that regard. The good news is that China is now pushing hard to instill more of a proconsumption growth dynamic. In particular, in accordance with the basic thrust of the 11th Five-Year Plan, it is increasingly focused on creating a safety net, especially a national social security system, pensions, and expanded medical care and education support; these are essential to overcome the bias toward precautionary saving brought about by the massive layoffs of state-owned enterprise reforms. The bad news is that this will all take time—quite possibly a lot more time than most believe. Yes, there are signs of a consumer culture starting to take hold in some of the urban pockets of coastal China. But with the nation's overall private consumption share tumbling to a record low of just 36 percent of GDP in 2006, these developments remain exceptions. China's proconsumption challenges are as daunting as ever.

Asia's optimism is both understandable and infectious. Yet I worry that this optimism is being distorted by the combination of frothy stock markets and seemingly unstoppable economic growth. As a surplus saving region, Asia has no compunction about recycling excess liquidity into its domestic financial markets. That's especially the case as the U.S. investment option starts to look dubious, as it does at the moment. Moreover, lacking in well-developed bond markets, domestic equity markets have become the asset class of choice, almost by default. For now, this all appears to be an increasingly virtuous circle—with more growth begetting stronger stock markets and with surging equity prices tempting investors to raise their long-term growth and earnings expectations. Yet if you are an optimist on Asia, the risk is that regional equity markets have more than discounted your upbeat scenario.

The biggest risk in all of this is complacency. Yes, Asia is booming. China mania is everywhere, especially with the Beijing Olympics just around the corner. Asia's stock markets have become a magnet for investors around the world, institutional and retail alike. The problems that led to a devastating financial crisis a decade ago seem to have been addressed. There is a sense that nothing can go wrong. Meanwhile, half way around the world, the American consumer is about to go into hibernation. An export-led Asia can't afford to take that possibility lightly. The heavy lifting of Asian rebalancing has never seemed more urgent. A down cycle is coming and Asia seems ominously unprepared.

# The End of the Beginning
## March 2008

The worst financial crisis since the 1930s poses great challenges to a globalized and increasingly interconnected world economy. It is tempting to focus on the virulent outbreak of cross-product contagion—from subprime mortgage debt and asset-backed commercial paper to the levered-loan market and auction-rate municipal securities—and conclude that the selling of distressed assets has exhausted most of its possibilities. Now that a major brokerage firm has failed, it is equally tempting to claim that the final wash-out has occurred, a classic sign of a crisis nearing its end. So, too, with the recent plunge in the U.S. dollar, a currency overshoot that belies what many believe are the still solid fundamentals of the ever flexible American economy.

If it were only that easy. At work is far more than a pure financial crisis. The U.S. economy, still the largest economy in the world, has, itself, become overly dependent on the very financial engineering that is now coming unhinged. And the rest of the global economy has ridden a powerful wave of U.S.-led global trade. As the financial underpinnings of this arrangement are now drawn into serious question, the fault lines of an increasingly integrated global economy have been exposed as never before.

The best we can hope for is that the first-order impacts of this crisis have largely run their course. Yet this financial market capitulation could well be followed by more to come on the real side of asset-dependent economies—generating feedback effects that could trigger another wave of cyclical pressures on already beleaguered financial intermediaries. Far from the beginning of the end, the global downturn may now be entering the end of the beginning.

Beneath the shifting sands is the increasingly shaky foundation of America's bubble-prone economy. As the United States lurched from bubble to bubble over the past eight years—first equities, then property and credit—a powerful transformation occurred. The U.S. consumer broke away from the fundamentals of an income-supported economy and became increasingly reliant on a new asset-dependent growth paradigm. The telltale signs of such a transformation were a plunging income-based saving rate, a massive current-account deficit, and a record household-sector borrowing binge.

The apologists celebrated these developments as visible manifestations of a new world order—the benign recycling of the so-called glut of global saving. Then Federal Reserve Governor Ben Bernanke provided the intellectual fodder for this assessment.[5] The naysayers, including yours truly, worried more about sustainability, warning that the longer the United States and the world lurched down this perilous course, the more difficult the moment of reckoning. But we were unable to call that moment with any precision. So the longer the unsustainable became sustainable, our voices became tired, fewer, and increasingly faint.

It all came to a head with the simultaneous bursting of America's housing and credit bubbles. Initially, pressures were concentrated in residential construction activity and housing-dependent consumption—two sectors that collectively peaked at about 78 percent of U.S. GDP. With not much else to stand on, the United States toppled into recession in early 2008—its second postbubble recession in seven years.

The rest of the world remains convinced that this is largely America's problem. The dollar's sharp decline in early 2008 against other major currencies says it all. Currencies are relative prices, and U.S.-based assets are being singled out for weakness relative to more resilient securities elsewhere in the world.

This is also likely to be wishful thinking. In an increasingly globalized and interdependent world, cross-border linkages into and from the world's largest economy can hardly be minimized. That's particularly the case for Developing Asia, the region of the world that has benefited the most from the upside of the globalization and world trade cycles of the past six years. As the global business cycle now turns down, the hopes and dreams of a

5. See Ben Bernanke, "The Global Savings Glut and the U.S. Current Account Deficit," March and April 2005. Available at www.federalreserve.gov.

miraculous decoupling—whereby Asia emerges unscathed—seem like an increasing stretch.

Asia's externally led economy can hardly afford to take lightly a pull-back of asset-dependent U.S. consumption. Americans consumed over $9.7 trillion in 2007—fully six times the combined private consumption of China and India. With Developing Asia's export share at a record 45 percent of panregional GDP in 2007, a demand shock to global consumption is a big deal for the world's fastest growing region.

Yes, Asia has learned important lessons from its own wrenching financial crisis of a decade ago. But it is about to learn yet another lesson: Asia will not get special dispensation from the world's most wrenching crisis of the modern era.

# Another Asian Wake-up Call

## November 27, 2008

It was the summer of 2007, and Asia was riding the crest of yet another boom—brimming with self-confidence and convinced that it had learned the painful lessons of the wrenching financial crisis of 10 years ago. Steeped in denial, the region actually entertained the ludicrous notion that it could decouple from all that ailed the rest of the world. An increasingly China-centric Asia truly believed that it had finally arrived as the world's most powerful growth engine.

That was then. Today, there is not a country in the region where economic growth is not either decelerating sharply or contracting. As always, learning the lessons of the last crisis rarely prepares one for the next crisis. And that is very much the case today throughout Developing Asia. It turns out that the region is far more dependent on exports than it was a decade ago. With the global economy in crisis—underscored by the first synchronous recession in the United States, Japan, and Europe of the post–World War II era—an externally dependent Asian economy is now being clobbered by the mother of all external demand shocks.

One number really says it all: In 2007, exports accounted for a record 47 percent of developing Asia's panregional GDP—fully 10 percentage points higher than the ratio prevailing in the financial crisis 10 years ago. An increasingly open Asian economy benefited hugely from a phenomenal expansion in global trade. With the world economy booming at nearly 5 percent in the four and a half years ending mid-2007, Asia quickly became a levered play on the strongest global boom since the early 1970s.

With that boom now having gone bust, Asia is paying a steep price for failing to address its structural imbalances. The flip side of the region's record export share of its GDP is an all-time low in the portion of regional output going to private consumption—also about 45 percent in 2007, or 10 percentage points lower than it was a decade earlier. A sharply declining private consumption share means that developing Asia lacks a major source of autonomous internal demand that could shield it from an external shock. Little wonder that regional growth is now slowing so sharply.

China's dilemma is emblematic of the risks that are now bearing down on Asia. With the export share of its economy having nearly doubled from 20 percent at the start of this decade to nearly 40 percent today, China is more exposed to external demand than ever before. And by failing to build out a social safety net—social security, pensions, unemployment and medical insurance—Chinese families remain predisposed toward precautionary savings and reluctant to step up as consumers.

The good news is that Beijing policy makers have moved aggressively toward stimulus. The bad news is that these actions will do little to rebalance the Chinese economy toward private consumption. Although the near-term downside to GDP growth could be contained at 6 to 8 percent, China is not well positioned to sustain more rapid growth in what could well be a multiyear slowdown in the broader global economy.

A decade ago, Asia's wake-up call was all about deficient foreign exchange reserves. Today, the wake-up call is all about structural imbalances and the need to shift away from excessive reliance on exports toward greater support from internal private consumption. Asia cannot afford to hit the snooze button. As the real side of the global economy continues to weaken, the imperatives of Asian rebalancing become all the more urgent.

# India's Virtuous Cycle

## June 2, 2009

I n recent years, the global view of India has been couched in terms of the daunting China comparison. It wasn't all that long ago—1991, to be precise—when Asia's two giants had similar levels of income per capita. That was then. Now, China's standard of living is more than three times that of India.

The China comparison has been India's wake-up call—a striking example of how economic development can be galvanized by proactive government policy. It's not that India has floundered. To the contrary, over the 2001–2007 timeframe, India's real GDP growth averaged close to 7.5 percent, an impressive pick-up from the 5.5 percent pace of the 1990s. Perhaps the most remarkable aspect of this accomplishment was that it occurred despite the government, in the face of stiff political headwinds.

Those headwinds could now quickly become tailwinds. Courtesy of the stunning victory of the Congress-led United Progressive Alliance (UPA) in the recently concluded mid-May 2009 elections, there is a distinct chance that India could now benefit from its own strain of proactive, development-friendly government policies. The same reformers that were so successful in opening up India in the early 1990s have been stymied by the politics of coalition management over the past five years. The massive win of the Congress Party all but removes that impediment, hinting at a new era of reforms that could well unshackle the increasingly robust potential of the Indian economy.

The dirty little secret of the Indian economy is that it has actually been performing much better beneath the surface than the China comparison might otherwise suggest. India has long had a much better *micro* story than China: a large population of world-class companies, outstanding entrepreneurs, a well-educated and IT-competent workforce, relatively sound financial markets and banks, a well-entrenched rule of law, and democracy.

By contrast, India has suffered more from its *macro* deficiencies—especially when compared with China. That's especially been true of saving, foreign direct investment, and infrastructure. Yet in the past three to four years, India has made impressive progress on at least two of those counts. Gross domestic savings rates have moved from the low 20s (as a percent of GDP) in the late 1990s to the high 30s in 2007–2008. Foreign direct investment accelerated to a $40 billion annual rate—still short of Chinese style numbers but a four-fold increase from the pace of India's inflows as recently as 2005. Even on the infrastructure front, where development constraints remain quite serious, the GDP share of such investments is up from the rock-bottom levels of the late 1990s.

Therein lies India's great potential—an increasingly virtuous cycle brought about the self-reinforcing interplay of its micro and macro drivers that now stands a real chance of being augmented by proactive government policy and reforms. The new government needs to seize this moment—moving aggressively on four fronts: public sector deficit reduction; infrastructure support; privatization; and deregulation of pension funds, retail, and banking. These are all tough battles for any politicians to wage. But if the government makes a down payment on these critical initiatives, the Indian economy is well positioned to benefit for years to come.

The world has fallen in love with the China miracle. India has slipped between the cracks in all this euphoria. Yet China now faces increasingly daunting challenges in coming to grips with long-simmering imbalances of its export- and investment-dominated macro structure. That could be a great opportunity for the sleeper. Shifting political winds now give a well-balanced Indian economy a real chance to emerge as Asia's biggest surprise in the years immediately ahead.

# Risks of an Asian Relapse

*June 8, 2009*

The spin game is on as the world tries to talk itself out of the worst recession since the end of World War II. The good news is that there is a slowing in the rate of deterioration in the global economy. The tougher news is that this is hardly surprising. In the aftermath of unprecedented annualized plunges in real global GDP on the order of 6 to 7 percent in the fourth quarter of 2008 and the first quarter of 2009, the pace of deterioration almost had to moderate.

With history books replete with tales of V-shaped recoveries following steep downturns, financial markets have become giddy, hoping that signs of bottoming beget the long awaited rebound. Nowhere is that more evident than in Asia—an increasingly China-centric region convinced it will be first to lead the world out of its long nightmare.

Not so fast. Contrary to the lore of the Asia Century, the region continues to suffer from a lack of internal support from its 3.5 billion consumers. The private consumption share of developing Asia's overall GDP fell to a record low of 47 percent in 2008, down from 55 percent as recently as 2001.

In other words, Asia remains an export machine. Developing Asia's export share has risen from 36 percent of panregional GDP during the financial crisis of 1997–1998 to a record 47 percent in 2007. And recent research by the IMF shows that Asian exports continue to be underpinned by consumers in the industrial world—especially from the United States. Despite a surge of trade within Asia, the bulk of these intraregional flows have been concentrated in parts and components that then go into finished goods eventually consumed by developed economies.

Little wonder that in the aftermath of a record contraction of U.S. consumer spending in late 2008—nearly 4 percent average annualized declines in the final two quarters of the year in real terms—every major economy in Asia either slowed sharply or tumbled into deep recession. More than ever, the region's fate remains made in America.

That is where hopes of an Asia-led rebound are most tenuous. After a dozen years of excess, the overextended American consumer is finally tapped out. The green-shoots crowd—those believing global recovery is nigh—drew special encouragement from a 0.6 percent rebound in real U.S. consumer expenditures in the first quarter of 2009. That encouragement is about to be dashed. Outright contractions in retail sales data in March and April point to a renewed decline of at least 1 percent in real consumption in the second quarter of 2009.

Hit by the triple whammy of collapsing property values, equity wealth destruction, and an ongoing unemployment shock, the American consumer is unlikely to spring back overnight. In fact, with asset-dependent U.S. households remaining income-short, overly indebted, and savings-deficient, subdued consumption growth is likely for years. This is because the U.S. consumption share of real GDP, which hit a new record of 72.4 percent in the first quarter of 2009, needs, at a minimum, to return to its prebubble norm of 67 percent. That spells a sharp downshift in real consumption growth from the nearly 4 percent average pace of 1995 to 2007 to around 1.5 percent over the next three to five years. There will be years when the consumer falls short of that pace. The contraction of more than 1.5 percent over the past four quarters is a case a point. And there will be years when consumption appears stronger. But the die is cast for a protracted weakening of the world's biggest spender.

Therein lies a critical challenge for Asia. Unless it comes up with a new consumer to support its export-led growth model, Asia will face stiff headwinds of its own. Nowhere is that more evident than in China, where the mood has turned particularly upbeat. Although I no longer doubt that China's performance will be better than expected in 2009, there is good reason to be wary of extrapolation. China's incipient rebound relies on a timeworn stimulus formula: upping the ante on infrastructure spending and stimulating the expert sector in anticipation of an eventual rebound of global demand for Chinese-made goods. It's the latter presumption that remains iffy as American consumers now opt for prudence over profligacy.

If export-led China doesn't get a kick from the American consumer, a relapse for China-dependent Asia is a distinct possibility next year. Don't be fooled by catchphrases such as "green-shoots" and the "Asian Century." In the aftermath of the modern world's worst financial crisis and recession, an Asian-led global healing remains a real stretch.

# Chapter 5

# U.S.-China Tensions

## Introduction

It is often said the relationship between the United States and China could well be the world's most important bilateral relationship of the twenty-first century. The argument seems compelling on economic, geopolitical, and military terms—a testament to the role of these two great powers in shaping what could well be a new bipolar global power structure. This raises the toughest question of all—whether this power structure leads to harmony or heightened tensions.

In economic terms, there can be no mistaking the natural symbiosis that currently exists between these two large economies—America, the consumer and low saver and China, the producer and high saver. But this co-dependence cannot be taken for granted as something that will forever cement the bilateral ties between these countries. In fact, it may well be that U.S.-Chinese symbiosis is nothing more than a passing phase—reflecting a coincidence of interests that will exist for only a relatively brief period of time. Yes, as long as a savings-short U.S. economy continues to run massive current-account deficits to support the excesses of personal consumption, it needs a lender like China to provide foreign capital. And as long as an excess-savings Chinese economy needs export-led employment growth to maintain social stability, it needs the world's largest consumer to absorb its output.

But what happens if those conditions change? If America starts to save more—a distinct possibility for its overextended postbubble consumers—the need to borrow surplus savings from China will diminish. Conversely, if China starts to spend more—an equally likely possibility in light of its excessive reliance on exports and investment—it will have less surplus savings to lend to the United States. If both of these adjustments are perfectly timed to occur at precisely the same moment, it is possible to envision a benign reduction of this symbiosis. However, the odds of such an exquisitely synchronized rebalancing of both economies are extremely low, in my view. That suggests the growing likelihood that symbiosis is likely to give way to disequilibrium—adding a new source of tension to the U.S.-China relationship.

Unfortunately, that's not the only source of economic tension between the United States and China. Over the 2005–2007 period, fully 45 pieces of anti-China trade legislation were introduced in the U.S. Congress. Although none of these bills passed, that may change. As U.S. unemployment now rises sharply in an ever-deepening recession, the politics of trade frictions may well gather greater support. The political case for China bashing is based largely on three factors—an outsize bilateral trade deficit between the two nations that hit a record $256 billion in 2007, long-standing claims of RMB currency manipulation, and a seemingly chronic stagnation of real wages for American middle class workers. Fix the China problem, goes the argument, and the unfair pressures on U.S. workers will be tempered.

That analysis is deeply flawed. The main reason: A savings-short U.S. economy needs to import surplus savings from abroad in order to keep growing. And it must run massive current-account and trade deficits to attract that capital. The U.S.-China trade deficit, along with deficits with 100 of America's other trading partners, is a direct outgrowth of that problem. America has a multilateral trade imbalance, not a bilateral problem driven by unfair Chinese competition. China has the largest bilateral piece of the multilateral deficit mainly because of conscious outsourcing decisions of U.S. multinationals, together with strong preferences of U.S. consumers for low-cost, high-quality goods made in China.

If, however, U.S.-China trade is closed down through tariffs or other means and America fails to address its savings problem—a distinct possibility in an era of trillion-dollar federal budget deficits—the United States will simply end up shifting the Chinese piece of its external imbalance to another trading partner. To the extent that shift is directed toward a higher-cost producer—most likely the case—the outcome will be the functional equivalent of a tax hike on the already beleaguered American middle class. Not only could China-bashing backfire at home but it could also prompt Chinese currency managers to retaliate and reduce their purchases of dollar-denominated assets, which would then lead to a sharp decline in the dollar and higher real long-term U.S. interest rates. And the world's two great powers will move all the closer to the slippery slope of trade protectionism.

Avoiding such an outcome—strikingly reminiscent of the trade wars of the 1930s triggered by America's Smoot-Hawley tariffs—poses a major challenge to the body politic of both nations. That's particularly true for U.S. President Barack Obama. Campaigning on a platform of support for middle-class American workers, Obama underscored his concerns about real-wage stagnation in an era of unfettered globalization. The real-wage issue is a serious issue. The challenge for Washington is to determine the linkage between this issue and trade policy. It may well be that real wage stagnation is related more to America's underinvestment in human capital—notably, the lack of educational reforms and reskilling in an era of rapid IT-enabled globalization—than it is to trade pressures. Resolving this dilemma will be an important and early leadership test for Barack Obama.

At the same time, China must also be sensitive to the impacts of its export-led growth model on its trading partners. Any subsidies—either to its own domestic wages or to its currency—take on heightened importance as China's stature in world trade grows. As now the second largest exporter in the world, China can hardly afford to take that responsibility lightly. Moreover, if China competes unfairly by ignoring environmental degradation and pollution, the world pays a much greater price for the cross-border labor arbitrage than a simple comparison of wages would suggest. To the extent that cost-effective outsourcing ignores environmental considerations, the real-wage squeeze in relatively greener economies may be all the more acute.

Resolving the complexities of the U.S.-China economic relationship is an urgent challenge for an unbalanced global economy. With a crisis-torn world having moved into a severe synchronous recession, the stakes can only grow larger. As both the U.S. and Chinese economies evolve and change, a fleeting state of symbiosis seems likely to give way to heightened tensions. The time to diffuse those tensions is now—before it's too late.

# A Slippery Slope

## *May 9, 2007*

I am pleased to appear before the U.S. House of Representatives. You in the Congress are now moving into a critical phase in the ongoing deliberations over America's international trade policies. These rare tripartite subcommittee hearings are a clear indication of the deep concerns that are shaping your efforts. Such angst is understandable. In a broad sense, this is a debate about America's commitment to globalization—the overarching force that is reshaping the United States and the global economy. In a narrow sense, the focus is unmistakably on China—the world's most extraordinary development story and yet the largest slice of America's gaping trade deficit. Much is at stake as you grapple with these weighty issues. You cannot afford to get it wrong.

But I worry that may be the case. There can be no mistaking the momentum in Congress to tighten the noose on China. My own experience underscores this point: This is the third time I have testified on U.S.-China trade policy in the past three months. You have framed the debate as a legislative response to America's outsize bilateral trade deficit with China. This point of view is seriously flawed—underscoring the risk of a policy blunder of monumental proportions. By going after China, you in the Congress are playing with fire.

## Playing with Fire

For starters, the legislative remedies currently under discussion are based on faulty macroeconomic analysis. China bashing doesn't address the real problem that Congress believes is bearing down on American workers—a massive trade deficit that hit a record $836 billion in 2006. Since the Chinese bilateral deficit of $232 billion amounted to the largest slice of

America's overall multilateral trade gap—28 percent for all of 2006 and fully 34 percent in the final period of the year—Congress has concluded that China is the major culprit behind the trade-related squeeze on middle-class U.S. workers.

That deduction overlooks one critical point: The United States runs trade deficits not because it is victimized by unfair competition from China or anyone else but because it suffers from a chronic shortfall of domestic savings. That's right, lacking in savings—as evidenced by a net national savings rate that plunged to a record low of 1 percent of national income over the 2004–2006 period—the United States has no choice other than to import surplus savings from abroad if it wants to keep growing. That means running current-account and trade deficits in order to attract foreign capital. China turns out to be the biggest piece in this equation not because it is unfairly undercutting American-made products but because it offers a menu of products that satisfies the tastes and preferences of a chronically savings-short U.S. economy. China bashers continually overlook the macro context of America's bilateral trade deficits at great peril.

Consider the consequences if a bipartisan coalition in Congress gets its way and U.S. trade with China is significantly curtailed: The immediate impact would be a tax on U.S. multinationals like Wal-Mart, which sourced some $18 billion of goods from China in 2006. That would either squeeze profit margins or, if passed through to retail prices, raise the cost of living for American consumers. Over time, if the sanctions were onerous enough, the impact would be to divert U.S. trade away from China. But here's where the problem gets especially thorny: Unless America increases its domestic savings, sanctions on Chinese products will do nothing to alleviate the overall trade deficit. The outcome would fit the water-balloon analogy to a tee—squeezing the Chinese piece would simply redirect the deficit elsewhere. And most likely that would reallocate savings-short America's multilateral trade deficit away from low-cost Chinese producers toward higher-cost foreign sourcing. That would be the functional equivalent of a tax increase on American consumers.

Unfortunately, by going after China, Congress is also biting the hand that feeds it. China is one of America's most important external lenders. To a large extent, this is an outgrowth of the same currency policy that has U.S. politicians so up in arms—a managed peg that has allowed the renminbi to increase by only about 7 percent versus the dollar from July 2005 to May 2007. To keep the RMB in this range, China must recycle a disproportionate share of its massive build-up of foreign exchange reserves into dollar-denominated assets. As of February 2007, China held $416 billion of U.S. Treasuries—second only to Japan and up nearly $100 billion from the level a year earlier. And there is good reason to believe that the Chinese hold another $300–400 billion in other dollar-based assets, such as agencies and corporate bonds. By continuing to allocate at least 60 percent of its ongoing reserve accumulation into dollar-denominated assets, China remains an important source of demand for American securities—thereby helping to keep U.S. interest rates lower than might otherwise be the case. In effect, Chinese currency policy is subsidizing the interest rate underpinnings of America's asset economy—long the driver of the wealth effects that support the income-short U.S. consumer.

Congressional pressure on China could put its bid for dollar-denominated assets at risk for two reasons: On the one hand, if China accedes to U.S. pressure and allows the RMB to appreciate a good deal more against the dollar, there would be less of a need to recycle FX reserve accumulation into dollar-based assets. Absent such buying, interest rates could rise for a savings-short U.S. economy that still needs massive capital inflows. On the other hand, if Washington enacts onerous trade sanctions on China, the Chinese might understandably have less of an appetite to maintain their overweight in dollar-based assets. In fact, there is a good chance that the Chinese government would simply instruct its reserve managers to diversify incremental reserve accumulation out of dollars. In that case, the dollar could plunge and longer-term U.S. real interest rates could rise sharply—a crisis-like scenario that could tip an already weakened U.S. economy quickly into a severe and lasting recession. Either way, by imposing sanctions on one of its major foreign lenders, Congress could be putting a savings-short U.S. economy in a very precarious situation.

Trade sanctions might also subject China to intense internal pressure that extends beyond the impact on its exporters. Despite its rapid growth and increasingly important role as one of America's major suppliers of goods and financial capital, China is still a very undeveloped economy. That's especially the case with respect to its financial system, dominated by four large banks that are only just starting to go public. Banks and China's other international borrowers need to be able to hedge their currency exposure, especially in the face of the large exchange-rate fluctuations that Washington lawmakers are seeking. Lacking in well-developed capital markets, such hedging strategies are very difficult to implement in China. A large RMB revaluation could, as a consequence, deal a potentially lethal blow to China's embryonic financial system.

There is also the distinct possibility that Washington-led China bashing could inflict major collateral damage on the rest of Asia. Contrary to popular folklore, China has not become the world's factory. Instead, it is functioning much more as the final destination of a huge pan-Asian supply chain, directly involving intermediate inputs and supplies from the region's other major economies like Korea, Taiwan, and Japan. China is, in fact, the largest export market for the first two of these externally led economies and is rapidly closing in on the US as Japan's largest export market.

Academic studies emphasize the pan-Asian linkages to the Chinese export machine. Professor Lawrence Lau of Stanford and the Chinese University of Hong Kong has estimated that domestic PRC-based content accounts for only about 20 percent of the total value of Chinese exports to the United States.[1] More recent research by economists at the central bank of Finland underscores how shifts in the RMB would reverberate throughout a vertically integrated pan-Asian production platform.[2] Congress is operating under the false presumption that trade sanctions would be a surgical strike solely on China. That is unlikely to be the case. Instead, there would undoubtedly be major cross-border spillovers that could quickly put pressure on the rest of a China-centric Asian supply chain.

There is a final misperception about the oft-feared Chinese exporter. It turns out that China has become an important efficiency solution for many of the world's multinational corporations. China's so-called foreign-invested enterprises—basically, Chinese subsidiaries of multinationals—have accounted for more than 60 percent of the explosive growth of overall Chinese exports over the past decade. That raises serious questions about the real identity of the all-powerful Chinese exporter. It may be less of a case of the indigenous Chinese company and more likely an outgrowth of conscious decisions being taken by Western companies. That poses the critical question: Who is the new China—is it them or us?

---

1. See Lawrence Lau's 2003 paper, "Is China Playing by the Rules?" presented as testimony in September 2003 before the US-China Economic and Security Review Commission.
2. See Alicia Garcia-Herrero and Tuuli Koivu, "Can the Chinese trade surplus be reduced through exchange rate policy?" Bank of Finland, BOFIT discussion paper no. 6, 2007.

With all due respect, I worry that you in the Congress are seeing the China problem from a very narrow perspective. At the root of this approach are understandable concerns about increasingly acute pressures bearing down on American middle-class workers. But the link between this painful problem and China is based on flawed macro analysis—mistakenly focusing on a large bilateral piece of a major multilateral trade imbalance of a savings-short U.S. economy. As is often the case, one error can beget another, and the real risk is that Washington-led China bashing could trigger a host of unintended consequences—not only taxing American consumers and U.S. multinational corporations but also triggering currency and real interest-rate pressures that could tip the U.S. economy into recession. But the biggest tragedy of all could come from a United States that squanders an historic chance to engage China as a strategic partner in an increasingly globalized world. If Washington pushes China away, I fear the rest of an increasingly China-centric Asia won't be too far behind.

## Protectionism and Inflation

At the same time, I also fear that disinflation could be at risk as Congress rushes headlong down the path of protectionism. The cross-border arbitrage of costs and pricing—one of the unmistakable hallmarks of globalization—could well turn unfavorable if China bashers get their way. This could be a recipe for the dreaded stagflation scenario—a perfectly awful outcome for financial markets and the functional equivalent of yet another tax hike on an already beleaguered American middle class.

The U.S. economy has benefited greatly from an outbreak of "imported disinflation" over the past decade. Researchers from the IMF have estimated that the so-called import-price effect has lowered the U.S. CPI inflation rate by an average of about one percentage point per year since 1997.[3] Such an externally driven reduction in domestic U.S. inflation is basically an outgrowth of rising import penetration from the low-cost developing world. Import penetration in the United States—purchases of foreign-made products as a share of domestic goods consumption—has risen from 22 percent in the early 1990s to about 38 percent in 2007. At the same time, low-cost developing economies have accounted for 58 percent of the

---

3. See "How Has Globalization Affected Inflation?" Chapter III in the IMF's *World Economic Outlook*, April 2006.

surge in total U.S. imports over the past decade. China and Mexico have led the way—making up nearly 60 percent of the cumulative increase of imports to the U.S. from developing economies since 1995.

Nor have currency swings or business cycles altered the disinflationary forces of globalization. Over the past 12 years, prices of nonpetroleum imports into the United States have been basically unchanged, punctuated by brief cyclical breakouts that never exceeded 4 percent that were, in turn, followed by periodic declines of approximately equal magnitude. This compares with a cumulative increase in the so-called core CPI of 31 percent over the 1995–2007 interval. Even during periods of modest cyclical acceleration in import prices, spillovers from foreign to domestic inflation have been limited. That's due in large part to the still-wide disparity between price levels of foreign and domestically produced goods—a disparity that has continued to open up in recent years. According to the U.S. Bureau of Labor Statistics, prices of nonagricultural U.S. exports, a good proxy for inflation of internationally competitive goods produced within the United States, have recorded a cumulative increase of about 10 percent since early 1995. Although that's hardly a major surge, it nevertheless stands in contrast with the stability of nonpetroleum import prices noted earlier. That only adds to the compelling arithmetic of imported disinflation for the United States.

I suspect there is an equally important productivity angle to this as well. Globalization and the record expansion of world trade it has engendered have played a new and important role in the execution of global efficiency solutions by U.S. businesses. This arises from increasingly powerful synergies of cross-border supply chains available to U.S. multinational corporations, as well as from the arbitrage between relatively antiquated high-cost facilities at home with newer vintages of low-cost production platforms abroad.[4] Similarly, there is compelling evidence of innovation-driven productivity spillovers from inward foreign direct investment.[5] To the extent that imported productivity growth dampens overall cost pressures in the domestic economy, globalization has created yet another powerful headwind holding back U.S. inflation.

---

4. See Federal Reserve Vice Chairman Donald L. Kohn, "The Effects of Globalization on Inflation and Their Implications for Monetary Policy," June 2006.

5. See Jonathan Haskel, Sonia Pereira, and Matthew Slaughter, "Does Inward Foreign Direct Investment Boost the Productivity of Domestic Firms?" CEPR Discussion Paper No. 3384, May 2002. Available at SSRN: http://ssrn.com/abstract=317681.

As a result of these trends, the sourcing of domestic consumption in the United States has shifted away from high-cost goods made at home to cheaper and increasingly high-quality products produced by low-cost developing economies. In one sense, these impacts are temporary—they reflect globalization-driven impacts on the U.S. economy that have taken it from one state of openness to another. Consequently, as import penetration eventually levels out, the impacts of imported disinflation could ebb. At the same time, should forces come into play that arrest globalization—namely an outbreak of trade protectionism—there could well be a reversal of the external pressures of disinflation, thereby boosting overall inflation.

Unfortunately, that is precisely the risk today. As you in Washington now move to contemplate policies that could lead to trade frictions and protectionism, America's global sources of disinflation would be very much at risk. Tariffs and nontariff duties are the functional equivalent of a tax on low-cost imports. Depending on pricing leverage, such taxes could be directly passed through to American consumers. At a minimum, they would boost cost pressures on U.S. multinationals, with the potential to interrupt the shifting of high-cost domestic production to cheaper offshore locations. Moreover, such frictions might also diminish the productivity dividend offered by global supply chains. This latter possibility could well be reinforced by ongoing efforts of the U.S. Congress to tighten up the so-called Committee on Foreign Investment in the United States (CFIUS) approval process for foreign direct investment into the United States—a development that has gathered considerable momentum in the aftermath of the aborted 2006 acquisition of U.S. port facilities by Dubai Ports World.

Nor is the cyclical timing of all these developments exactly ideal. The imposition of trade and investment barriers could lead to the return of the closed-economy inflation dynamic at just the time when slack has diminished in America's labor and product markets. And, of course, the dreaded dollar-crisis scenario—hardly a trivial consideration in a protectionist climate—could lead to a much sharper spike in import prices than has been evident in a long time. All in all, such an unfortunate confluence of circumstances could exacerbate domestically driven inflationary pressures at precisely the wrong point in the business cycle—in sharp contrast to a globalization that has acted increasingly to offset such cyclical pressures over the past 15 years.

There is great irony to congressional attempts to fix globalization: The odds are that the most extensive damage will be inflicted on the very constituency in the U.S. economy that the politicians are trying to assist—America's middle-class. One of the most important lessons of the 1970s is that inflation is the cruelest tax of all. And yet that lesson now seems all but lost on Capitol Hill today. There is no refuting the reality of pressures already bearing down on American labor. In the current economic upturn, the cumulative gains in private-sector worker compensation remain about $430 billion (in real terms) below the trajectory of the typical expansion. Moreover, according to the U.S. Bureau of Labor Statistics, the median wage—inflation-adjusted weekly pay for the worker in the middle of the wage distribution—has risen a cumulative total of just 0.9 percent over the seven years ending in the first quarter of 2007; that's an especially disturbing development in a period of accelerating productivity growth—very much at odds with the long-standing conclusions of economic theory and experience. As an outgrowth of these developments, the labor share of America's national income has fallen sharply in recent years and remains near its post-1970 low of 56 percent. Sadly, Congress now appears to be contemplating a response to these pressures that would impose the functional equivalent of an inflation tax on U.S. workers at precisely the time when they can least afford it.

America's beleaguered middle class deserves better. Due to underinvestment in education and human capital over the past 25 years, American labor is lacking in many of the skills required to face the new competitive challenges of an IT-enabled globalization that is bearing down on white- and blue-collar workers, alike (see "Unprepared for Globalization," p. 155–159). Moreover, by failing to save and being unwilling to embrace prosaving policies, the United States has set itself up for chronic current-account and trade deficits. This is a lethal political and economic combination that has injected a new sense of urgency into the globalization debate. And Washington politicians, rather than taking a hard look in the mirror, have embarked on a dangerous course of scapegoatism, that is, blaming China for all that ails the American worker. That has taken the Congress to the brink of moving beyond the rhetorical bluster of the past few years and enacting legislation that would impose severe trade sanctions on China.

In looking back over the past quarter century, few accomplishments in the economics sphere match the successes of the battle against inflation. Globalization and trade liberalization have become important in ensuring the post-inflation peace. Yes, for many, this has been a mixed blessing. There is no question that workers in the developed world have borne a disproportionate share of the cross-border arbitrage that lies at the heart of globalization. At the same time, I have little doubt that the ensuing disinflation has been key in fostering improvements in purchasing power that boost living standards of the same hard-pressed workers. Protectionism raises the risk of squandering this critically important disinflationary dividend—thereby eroding inflation-adjusted purchasing power. That is the very last thing America's middle class needs.

## Globalization at Risk

There are also important geopolitical consequences of the recent shift in U.S. trade policies. The more America resists the rise of Asia—precisely the risk in light of mounting protectionist pressures in Washington—the greater the chances the region will go its own way. Signs of such a development are already apparent—especially in the form of a new rapprochement between Asia's two economic powerhouses, Japan and China. That raises the worrisome possibility of disengagement between the United States and the world's most rapidly growing region. If that turns out to be the case, America will have squandered one of the greatest opportunities of globalization.

By embracing protectionist remedies and going after China, Congress is reacting to symptoms of much deeper problems—especially skill-set disadvantages of American workers and an extraordinary shortfall of domestic savings. Absolutely nothing is gained on either front by blaming China for problems such as these that originate at home. To the contrary, much could be lost—in the United States, the global economy, and world financial markets—if Congress makes a major blunder on U.S. trade policy. Wrong-footed macro analysis is a clear risk in this regard—especially holding a bilateral deficit with China accountable for what is truly a multilateral manifestation of America's chronic savings problem. At the same time, unwinding the disinflationary benefits of globalization would borrow a painfully familiar page from the stagflationary script of the 1970s. And the consequences of pushing Asia away from the U.S. sphere of influence cannot be minimized. All in all, the outcome of a protectionist tilt to U.S.-China trade policy could be treacherous—for both financial markets and the U.S. economy.

None of this is to say that there shouldn't be active and direct negotiations with the Chinese on more legitimate conflicts over trade policy—especially on those issues that bear directly on broad constituencies of the U.S. workforce. The area of intellectual property rights is especially important in that regard, particularly since it directly affects the core competencies of America's vast legions of knowledge workers—the professionals, managers, executives, sales workers, and office support staffs who collectively account for 61 percent of total U.S. employment. The U.S. Trade Representative's recent decision to initiate intellectual property rights (IPR) complaints against China with the WTO is a far more appropriate course of action than misdirected congressional scapegoating over the currency and bilateral trade deficit issues. Unfortunately, you in Washington are having a hard time making this critical distinction.

Globalization isn't easy. It puts pressure on developing and developed countries, alike. As the world's leading economic power, it falls to the United States to assume the special role as a steward of globalization. China bashing is tantamount to an abdication of that responsibility. It is not in America's best interest, and it could quickly take the world down a very slippery slope. Globalization, itself, may have an exceedingly difficult time recovering. You in the Congress must heed these risks—before it is too late.

# ■ Past the Point of No Return
## *May 14, 2007*

E ven the old timers in the Congress had never seen anything like it. On May 9, 2007, the U.S. House of Representatives held what was billed as a tripartite hearing of three subcommittees on "Currency Manipulation and Its Effects on U.S. Businesses and Workers." I was one of the expert witnesses at this hearing—invited to submit a written statement, present a brief summary to the assembled legislators, and then engage in an extensive question-and-answer session (see my written statement, "A Slippery Slope," on p. 331–340). It was an experience I will never forget. At the end of over three hours of intense give and take, I left Capitol Hill more convinced than ever that the protectionist train has left the station.

I suspect this hearing could mark a turning point in America's mounting resistance to trade liberalization and globalization. For starters, congressional historians offered the opinion that three committees had never before come together in one hearing to focus on a single issue. And yet present in one room were members of House subcommittees from Ways and Means, Energy and Commerce, and Financial Services—all having jurisdiction over matters of U.S. international trade policy. The unprecedented structure of this effort was carefully crafted to send the strongest message possible. As Sander Levin (Democrat from Michigan, who chaired this session) said, "This is an exceptional issue and an exceptional problem that hasn't been resolved. We need to consider the next steps. This is the real thing."

In terms of the substance of the debate, three things surprised me about this hearing: First, while the bulk of the discussion was about China, anti-Japan sentiment was formally brought into the current U.S. trade debate for the first time. The issue was the yen—characterized by the Congress as the world's most undervalued major currency. Second, the case against China

was framed mainly around the concept of treating Chinese currency policy as an "illegal subsidy," which is WTO-compliant jargon that frees up
Congress to impose sweeping countervailing duties on Chinese exporters. Third, the congressional representatives present at this hearing were
highly critical of the U.S. Treasury's bi-annual foreign exchange review
process and its failure to cite China for currency manipulation. This puts
the House on a similar track as the Senate—especially that espoused
by the leadership of the Senate Finance Committee, whose Chairman
(Max Baucus) and ranking minority member (Charles Grassley) endorsed
a similar approach in 2006. That was the first hint at a reconciliation
strategy on trade policy between the two chambers of Congress.

I didn't go to this hearing with the naïve expectation that I would be
able to change any minds. And there were no surprises on that count.
In particular, there was little sympathy on the part of the Congress for
linking trade deficits to domestic savings shortfalls. To the contrary, there
was a broad consensus that bilateral pieces of the massive multilateral
U.S. trade deficit are fair game—in essence, providing opportunities for
Washington to whittle away at the U.S. external gap one country at
a time. The consensus of congressional representatives at the hearing
was that China was the problem—even though the non-Chinese piece
of the overall U.S. trade deficit slightly exceeded $600 billion in 2006,
over two-and-a-half times the size of the Chinese bilateral deficit with
the United States. Many members of the House were especially upset
with being labeled "China bashers." At the same time, literally no one
responded to the concerns I voiced over the unintended consequences of
protectionism—namely that China bashing could backfire in the United
States, the rest of Asia, and the broader global economy. The bottom line:
The U.S. Congress just doesn't do macro.

All this underscores a striking disconnect with financial markets.
Congress is moving full steam ahead on anti-China protectionism, and
no one seems to care. Protectionist risks are not being taken seriously in
any major asset class—stocks, bonds, credit, or currencies. My discussions
with a broad global cross section of investors and business executives con-
firm this impression. Two reasons are most frequently cited: First, there
is a strong belief that the United States will eventually come to its senses
and do the right thing by living up to its role as the architect and leader
of the protrade, post–World War II global economic order. Second, the
boy-cries-wolf syndrome is very much alive and well in financial markets
today. The protectionist rumblings of the last couple of years have been
just that—more bluster than action. Investors stress that every time they

have tried to play this risk as an actionable outcome, they have lost money. The appetite to chase another protectionist scare is heavily influenced by the recent history of such misadventures in the markets.

So what makes me so smart? My answer is that this is not a case of the binary outcome—globalization or protectionism. Instead, it is much more about probabilistic risk assessments of a wide range of possible outcomes. The broad consensus of investor sentiment right now ascribes virtually no risk to a protectionist endgame. My experience in Washington over the months of February to May 2007—highlighted by three separate appearances in front of the Congress and considerable consultation with congressional and administration senior staffers—leads me to conclude that this risk assessment is far too sanguine. I continue to think that there is a 60 percent chance that a WTO-compliant bill aimed at curbing America's bilateral trade deficit with China will be passed by a veto-proof majority in both houses of Congress by the end of the year 2007.

Of course, there's never a sure thing when it comes to assessing the Washington risk factor. The recent compromise between the Bush Administration and congressional Democrats on labor standards and trade agreements is classic in that regard. Some view this as a sign that the Democrats are retreating to the high ground of the protectionist debate. Others claim this represents a White House capitulation that is aimed at tempering more extreme actions by the Congress. I am more sympathetic to the latter interpretation. In the end, my guess is that Congress is being careful to pick its spots. It does not want to be labeled as one-sided in the trade debate. The recent compromise on the labor standards issue underscores that point. At the same time, I see no let-up in efforts to single out China.

There's always a chance that I'm overreacting to an escalation of Congress's rhetorical assaults on China—that this will, indeed, be just another year of bluster. I wish that were the case. But on the basis of everything I have heard over the past several months, I remain more convinced than ever that Congress has finally thrown down the gauntlet. The May 9, 2007 tripartite hearing hammered that point home with disturbing clarity. As Barney Frank, Chairman of the House Financial Services Committee said, "This problem is not going away. We are going to have to act." If Congress changes its mind and backs away, I fear it will lose all credibility on this key issue with American workers. With respect to China, I am afraid that means the U.S. Congress has now gone past the point of no return.

# Debating U.S.-China Trade Policy

*October 13, 2006*

The U.S.-China trade debate could well be one of the most important and contentious issues in the current era of globalization. It not only has far-reaching implications for both nations but also for world financial markets and many of the pressures bearing down on the global economy. Recently, on the invitation of the Council on Foreign Relations, Desmond Lachman of the American Enterprise Institute and formerly of the IMF and I engaged in an online debate on the topic: Is China Growing at the United States' Expense? A transcript of our exchange follows:

## Don't Scapegoat China

Stephen Roach | October 9, 2006

China has become the scapegoat for one of America's toughest economic problems. Workers and their elected representatives are understandably concerned about the persistence of subpar job growth and a decade of nearly stagnant real wages. With these pressures occurring in the midst of a record foreign trade deficit and with China accounting for fully 25 percent of that imbalance, the blame game is on. In the year and a half since the beginning of 2005, fully 27 pieces of legislation have been introduced in the U.S. Congress that would impose punitive actions on China for engaging in unfair trading practices with the United States.

Although I certainly think Washington needs to be tough in its trade negotiations with China—especially in the area of intellectual-property rights—I fear the politicians don't get it. The U.S. trade deficit—to say nothing of the Chinese piece of this deficit—has not come out of thin air. It is a reflection of our inability to face one of our biggest economic shortcomings as a nation—a dearth of domestic savings. In 2005, America's net national savings—the combined savings of individuals, the government, and the business sector net of depreciation—fell to a record low of just 0.1 percent of national income. Lacking in domestic savings, the United States must import surplus savings from abroad in order to grow—and run massive current-account and foreign-trade deficits to attract the capital.

With the current-account deficit running at an $870 billion annual rate in the second quarter of 2006, the United States needs about $3.5 billion of foreign capital each business day to fund its external shortfall. The fact that the biggest portion of our trade deficit is with China is actually a good thing—it provides Americans with low-cost, high-quality products. If Washington were to get its way and raise the cost of doing business with China, then that would be the functional equivalent of a tax on the American consumer. Barring an increase in national savings—namely, a cut in the government budget deficit and/or a boost to personal savings—the trade deficit would not go away. Instead, it would simply be directed toward a higher-cost producer elsewhere in the world. And China, for its part, would probably rethink its strategy of buying Treasuries and other dollar assets—putting pressure on the dollar and U.S. interest rates.

It's time to stop blaming China for what ails us and look in the mirror. If the United States doesn't get its own house in order and start saving more as a nation, the scapegoating of China could end up being a policy blunder of monumental proportions.

## China Must Play by the Rules of the Game
Desmond Lachman | October 10, 2006

Stephen Roach is certainly right in drawing attention to the important role that improved U.S. savings performance must play in addressing today's record payment imbalances and in improving U.S. labor market performance. However, he is very wide of the mark in turning a blind eye to China's pursuit of flagrantly mercantilist policies and to its deliberate manipulation of its currency to gain an unfair competitive advantage.

Today's unprecedented large global payment imbalances raise the very real risk of intensifying protectionist pressures that could, in time, undermine the world's trading system. This calls for the orderly correction of the large U.S. current account imbalance, which in turn will require both a reduction of U.S. domestic expenditures as well as a switching of global expenditures toward the U.S. traded goods sector.

In proposing that the United States substantially improve its savings performance, Stephen Roach is focusing on only the expenditure reduction part of the solution to the U.S. external deficit problem. However, if the United States is to correct its external deficit, while avoiding a deep recession, it will need not only a higher level of domestic savings, but it will also need a much cheaper dollar to promote its exports and to discourage its imports.

China now pays lip service to the need for a more appreciated Chinese renminbi as part of the solution to the global payment imbalance problem. In July 2005, China did appreciate its currency by 2 percent and it committed itself to a more flexible currency policy. Over the past 15 months, however, nothing much has changed. China has only allowed a further 2 percent appreciation in its currency and it still, in effect, pegs to a depreciating dollar, which keeps its currency grossly undervalued by any reasonable measure.

The net upshot of China's currency manipulation is that China has now become the world's largest surplus country and the world's largest holder of foreign exchange reserves. China's current account surplus has already surpassed that of Japan, and it is on the way to exceeding $250 billion (in U.S. dollars), or 9 percent of its GDP in 2007.

In short, I fully agree with Stephen Roach that the United States should not simply scapegoat China and should address its own serious savings problem. However, if we are to avoid a train wreck in the global trading system, China should start playing by the international rules of the game and stop manipulating its currency. It should do so in both its own long-run interest and in that of the global economy.

## Beijing Not Ready for Reform
Stephen Roach | October 10, 2006

Like all disputes, there are two sides to the U.S.-China trade debate. What concerns me is the one-sided nature of this dispute. Desmond Lachman's argument is classic in that regard—as is that of the Washington consensus. To paraphrase: Sure, we in America need to fix our deficits—and maybe someday we will—but China needs to get its act together now.

A stronger RMB may seem to be in our interest—although I have my doubts, as noted later. But it may well be that a currency revaluation is simply not in China's best interest at this point in time. The reason: China has an undeveloped financial system. Its banks are only just starting to go public and its capital markets are tiny by our standards. Currency fluctuations could, as a result, place great strain on the Chinese financial system at a critical juncture in its economic development. We may not accept that logic, but at least we need to consider the possibility that China may know a good deal more about the inherent risks in its financial system than we do.

This may be nothing more than a sequencing problem. Financial reforms may not have gone far enough in China to allow it to cope with the stresses and strains that might arise from sharp currency fluctuations. China is committed to the long-run objective of a flexible currency, and as Desmond notes, has taken some small steps in that direction. It has been very frank in admitting that it needs to go much further. Linking the timetable to a broader financial market reform agenda seems like a very prudent course of action.

Even if Washington were to get its way, it might end up being very disappointed over what little would be accomplished by a sharp revaluation of the Chinese currency. America's gaping trade deficit is, first and foremost, an excess import problem. In the second quarter of 2006, U.S. merchandise imports were fully 84 percent larger than exports. This voracious appetite for foreign-made products is an outgrowth of an unsustainable consumer-buying binge—personal consumption has surged to a record 71 percent of GDP while personal savings has fallen into negative territory for the first time since 1933. A revaluation of the RMB—unless it was of a draconian magnitude—would do next to nothing to curtail excess consumption and reduce America's import-led trade deficit.

None of this is to argue that China shouldn't work harder to reduce its large trade surplus. As I noted in my opening comment, it needs to do much more in preventing the piracy of intellectual property. And China also must stimulate its own consumer in order to boost purchases of foreign-made goods, which, actually, was a goal that was underscored in its recently enacted 11th Five-Year Plan. But just as America needs time to get its deficits under control, China needs time on the reform front. Sadly, that's the other side of the story that Washington doesn't want to hear.

## Current Deal Delays United States' "Day of Reckoning"
Desmond Lachman | October 11, 2006

Stephen mischaracterizes my view as condoning U.S. inaction on its budget deficit problem while pressing China for immediate currency action. To be clear, my view is that resolution of today's global payment imbalances will require both (a) an early and credible medium-term U.S. deficit reduction program and (b) significant and early movement in China's exchange rate. More substantive Chinese currency action is required not simply to address China's extraordinarily large current account surplus, but it is also needed to facilitate a more generalized appreciation of other Asian currencies.

Stephen condones China's paltry 2 percent currency appreciation since July 2005 at a time when China's very large basic balance of payment surplus would suggest that its currency is undervalued by around 20 percent. He rationalizes China's currency inaction on the grounds that China's fragile banking system could not tolerate a greater degree of currency movement. He makes this argument even though the Chinese banking system does not have any significant currency mismatch between its assets and liabilities. He also does so knowing full well that if meaningful currency movement awaits the restoration to health of China's chronically undercapitalized banking system, we will be waiting for many years to come.

To question, as Stephen does, whether a greater degree of currency movement is in China's best long-term interest is misguided for at least three reasons: First, without a greater degree of currency movement, together with measures to encourage domestic consumption, China will continue to run unacceptably large external current account surpluses. This will almost certainly invite damaging protectionist pressures against China in both Europe and the United States, especially in the event of a global economic downturn. Second, in the absence of greater currency flexibility, China's central bank's scope to use interest-rate policy to regulate the economy will continue to be highly limited by the unwanted capital inflows that higher interest rates would attract. This will make it difficult for China to avoid the type of overinvestment cycles and speculative excesses that it is presently experiencing, which, in the end, will further weaken China's rickety banking sector. Third, China's *de facto* pegging of its exchange rate requires that the Chinese central bank engage in costly foreign exchange intervention to the tune of a staggering $250 billion (in U.S. dollars) a year. The dollars the central bank buys at an overvalued dollar rate could end up costing China as much as 2 percentage points of GDP each year.

Stephen is, of course, right in suggesting that the United States presently has a good deal going for itself by having China send goods to the United States in exchange for dollar pieces of paper. The trouble with this deal, however, is that it dangerously increases China's financial leverage over the United States and it only delays the United States' day of reckoning for presently living well beyond its means.

## Currency Fix Is the Wrong Medicine
Stephen Roach | October 12, 2006

Desmond's recommendation for "significant and early movement in China's exchange rate" is a classic textbook prescription for fixing a large current account imbalance. Unfortunately, China is far from a classic textbook economy, making the currency fix the wrong medicine at the wrong point in time.

Despite 27 years of extraordinary reforms, China is still very much a blended economy. Notwithstanding the emergence of a thriving market-based sector, State-owned enterprises account for only about 35 percent of Chinese GDP. Moreover, China is not a centralized, well-integrated macro system. Power still resides mainly in provincial, city, and village governments, making it very difficult for Beijing to steer the nation as a whole. The banking system is equally fragmented. As recently as late 2004, the four biggest banks collectively had over 75,000 branches—most of which have autonomous deposit-gathering and lending capabilities.

A blended and fragmented Chinese economy cannot be effectively controlled by conventional macro stabilization policies. Beijing can pull the fiscal and monetary levers but there's no telling what the response will be. Unfortunately, what Desmond misses is that the same is true of currency policy.

Over the past decade, China's exports have increased by six-fold. Yet fully 63 percent of that increase can be accounted for by "foreign-invested enterprises"—Chinese subsidiaries of foreign multinational corporations and joint ventures. In other words, the power of the Chinese export machine is mainly an outgrowth of a Western penchant for offshore efficiency solutions.

Moreover, since the mid-1990s, China's imports have quintupled—driven increasingly by demand for manufactured components from its Asian neighbors. This reflects China's role as the world's assembly line—a very different function than that of the manufacturing behemoth the protectionists believe is gaining unfair advantage because of a cheap currency. In short, courtesy of globalization, China has experienced explosive growth on both sides of the foreign trade ledger. Can we truly expect a currency fix to stop cross-border economic integration dead in its tracks?

This debate touches many of America's economic hot buttons—subpar job growth, near stagnation in real wages, deficit financing, and the hollowing out of smokestack industries. These are critically important issues that the U.S. can no longer duck. Historically, our greatest strength as a nation has been to look inside ourselves and rise to the competitive challenge. The scapegoating of China is antithetical to that greatness.

I am deeply troubled that discussions of U.S.-China trade issues always come back to what we in America think China is doing wrong. China is far from perfect and must accept greater responsibility for its role in trade disputes, especially with respect to intellectual property rights. But, in the end, there's a limit to what can be expected from China and a lot more we can ask of ourselves.

## China Does Have the Means to Balance Its Economy
Desmond Lachman | October 13, 2006

Stephen Roach appears to be very much more pessimistic than I am about China's ability to reduce its unusually large current account surplus in a timely manner. He takes the view that China's particular circumstances as a blended economy render ineffective both conventional macro-stabilization policies and the use of the exchange rate.

If Stephen were right on this count, a train wreck in China's trade relations with Europe and the United States would only be a matter of time. Meaningful protectionist measures against China have already surfaced in the U.S. Congress in response both to China's very large trade surplus and to the downward pressures on wage growth stemming from the integration of China's large labor force into the global economy. Protectionist pressures can only be expected to intensify should China's payment surplus persist, especially were there to be a global economic slowdown. China is presently making a grave mistake in underestimating the risk of a protectionist backlash and in ignoring earlier sad historical precedents with the integration of large countries in the global economy.

Fortunately, there is little evidence to support the view that China does not have the means to reduce the level of its domestic savings and to wean its economy from its overdependence on a widening trade surplus. Experience in many countries would suggest that, over time, China could appreciably reduce its unusually high savings rate, which now is around a staggering 50 percent of household income. It could do so by supplementing the use of conventional monetary and fiscal policy with the elimination of the many underlying market imperfections that presently result in China's very high rate of precautionary savings. To that end, China might introduce a more robust retirement system, provide better health insurance, strengthen property rights that would lead banks to lend less on collateral and more on projects, and develop private insurance.

Although China is indeed a mixed economy, a large part of its economy engaged in external trade is responsive to price signals. As such, there is little reason to doubt that meaningfully moving the exchange rate would, over time, have the desired effect of discouraging exports and encouraging imports in much the same way as it has done in many other transitional economies.

Where I do fully agree with Stephen is that the United States must refrain from using China as an excuse not to get its own house in order. Any orderly resolution of today's global payment imbalance problem must require that the U.S. takes early measures to improve its dismal savings performance. It should do so at the same time that China takes measures to redirect its economy away from the export sector and toward domestic demand.

# Who's Subsidizing Whom?

*December 18, 2006*

F ederal Reserve Chairman Ben Bernanke offered the Chinese much in the way of good advice in a speech he recently gave in Beijing as part of the newly instituted Strategic Economic Dialog discussions that were just held between the United States and China.[6] Unfortunately, he also offered some very bad advice in assessing the ramifications and risks of Chinese currency policy. In essence, the Bernanke critique was a one-sided interpretation of a key issue that could backfire and lead to a worrisome deterioration in the economic relationship between the United States and China.

The offensive passage in the written version of the Bernanke speech posted on the Fed's web site was the assertion that the current value of the Chinese renminbi is an ". . . effective subsidy that an underval-ued currency provides for Chinese firms that focus on exporting rather than producing for the domestic market." The use of the word *subsidy* is a highly inflammatory accusation—in effect, putting the Chinese on notice that America's most important macro policy maker believes that RMB currency policy provides the Chinese with an unfair advantage in the world trade arena that fosters distortions in China's economy, the U.S. economy, and the broader global economy. In my view, this is a very biased assessment of the state of Chinese currency policy and reforms. It pays little attention to the context in which RMB policies are being formulated and, ironically, fails to provide any appreciation for the ben-efits that accrue to America as a result of this so-called subsidy. Moreover, Bernanke's spin continues to downplay the role that the United States is playing in creating its bilateral imbalance with China—to say nothing

---

6. See Ben Bernanke, "The Chinese Economy: Progress and Challenges," December 15, 2006. Available at www.federalreserve.gov.

of the role the United States is playing in fostering broader imbalances in the global economy.

The real question in all this is, who's subsidizing whom? Conveniently overlooked in the Bernanke critique is the important flip side to the managed float that continues to drive RMB policy—China's massive purchases of dollar-denominated assets. The exact numbers are closely held, but there is general agreement that between 60 to 70 percent of China's current $1 trillion in official foreign exchange reserves are split between some $345 billion invested in U.S. Treasuries (as of October 2006, according to the U.S. government's Treasury International Capital [TIC] reporting system) and a comparable amount held in the form of other dollar-based fixed-income instruments. With Chinese reserve accumulation now running at over a $200 billion annual rate, that implies new purchases of dollar-denominated assets of at least $120 billion per year. Such foreign demand for American financial assets is absolutely critical in plugging the funding gap brought about by an unprecedented shortfall of domestic U.S. savings—a net national saving rate that fell to a record low of just 0.1 percent of national income in 2005. Without China's purchases of dollar-based assets—a key element of its efforts to manage the RMB in accordance with its financial stability objectives—the dollar would undoubtedly be lower and U.S. interest rates would be higher. In effect, that means China is subsidizing U.S. interest rates—providing American borrowers and investors with cut-rate financing and rich asset valuations that otherwise would not exist were it not for the dollar recycling aspects of Chinese currency policy.

There is an added element of China's subsidy to the United States. As a low-cost and increasingly high-quality producer, China is, in effect, also providing a subsidy to the purchasing power of U.S. households. Close down trade with China—as many in the U.S. Congress wish to do—and the trade deficit for savings-short America would show up somewhere else, undoubtedly with a higher-cost producer. That would be the functional equivalent of a tax hike on the American consumer—also cutting into the subsidy the United States currently enjoys by trading with China. The Fed chairman is making a similar suggestion: By allowing the RMB to strengthen, China's dollar buying would diminish—effectively eroding the interest rate and purchasing power subsidies that a savings-short and increasingly asset-dependent U.S. economy has come to rely on.

We can debate endlessly the appropriate valuation of the Chinese currency. Economic theory strongly suggests that economies with large current account surpluses typically have undervalued currencies. China would obviously qualify in that regard—as would, of course, Japan, Germany, and many Middle East oil producers. The fact that China is being singled out for special attention is, in and of itself, an interesting comment on the biases in the international community. Nevertheless, it is quite clear that China understands this aspect of the problem. By shifting to a new currency regime in July 2005, Chinese policy makers explicitly acknowledged the need for more of a market-based foreign exchange mechanism. The RMB has since risen about 6 percent against the dollar—not nearly as much as many U.S. politicians are clamoring for, but at least a move in the right direction. Risk-averse Chinese policy makers feel strongly about managing any currency appreciation carefully—understandable, in my view, given the still relatively undeveloped state of China's highly fragmented banking system and capital markets. The potential currency volatility that a fully flexible foreign exchange mechanism might produce could have a very destabilizing impact on an undeveloped Chinese financial system. That's the very last thing China wants or needs.

Chairman Bernanke's criticism of the Chinese for subsidizing their export competitiveness by maintaining an undervalued RMB completely ignores the benefits being enjoyed in the United States through equally important subsidies to domestic interest rates and purchasing power. Sure, a careful reading of Bernanke's China speech finds it laced with the typical caveats of Fed speak that, in this instance, acknowledge America's role as a deficit nation in contributing to this problem, as well as special considerations China deserves as a developing economy. But the tone and emphasis are clear: The Fed chairman is paying no more than lip-service to the other side of the coin through his emphasis on a sharp critique of China's monetary and currency policies. Particularly striking in this regard is Bernanke's failure to acknowledge the extraordinary fragmentation of a highly regionalized Chinese banking system—dominated by four large banks that still have well over 50,000 autonomous branches between them. How a central bank gets policy traction with such a decentralized banking system is beyond me. Moreover, he basically overlooks another critical reason for China's irrational investment process—the lack of well-developed capital markets and the continued reliance on policy-directed lending by China's large banks. Instead, Bernanke suggests that a flexible currency is the best means to foster an efficient allocation of investment projects. In short, the flaw in the Bernanke critique is his failure to appreciate the very special transitional needs of a still blended

Chinese economy—currently straddling both state and private owner-ship systems, as well as centrally planned and market-directed allocation mechanisms. The Fed chairman is offering advice as if China was a fully functioning market-based system—perfectly capable of achieving policy traction with the traditional instruments of monetary and currency poli-cies. Nothing could be further from the truth.

This is not the first time Ben Bernanke has assessed an international financial problem with such one-handed analysis. In his earlier capacity as a governor of the Federal Reserve Board and then as the chairman of President Bush's Council of Economic Advisers, he led the charge in pin-ning the problem of mounting global imbalances on the so-called saving-glut thesis—in effect, arguing that the United States was doing the rest of the world a huge favor by consuming an inordinate surplus of saving.[7] Although this is a most convenient argument from the administration's standpoint, it downplayed America's role in fostering the problem—unchecked structural budget deficits, a plunge in the income-based sav-ings rate of U.S. households, and a record consumer debt binge. Lacking in domestic saving, the United States must import surplus savings from abroad in order to grow—and run massive current account and trade deficits in order to attract the capital. This is quite germane to the debate over China. As noted earlier, the Chinese have emerged as important pro-viders of savings for a savings-short, overly indebted U.S. economy.

The scapegoating of China remains a most unfortunate feature of the global climate. United States politicians want to pin the blame on China for America's trade deficits and pressures bearing down on U.S. workers. Now Ben Bernanke piles on more blame by accusing China of using its macro policies as de facto export subsidies. Sure, China could do better on trade policy, especially in the all-important area of protecting intel-lectual property rights. But I think the world can also expect more of the global leader—like facing up to a very serious and potentially desta-bilizing savings shortfall of its own that requires the rest of the world, including China, to subsidize its profligate ways. The longer the United States frames this debate in such a biased and one-sided fashion, the more difficult it will be for others in the world, like China, to accept a face-saving compromise.

---

7. See Bernanke's March 10, 2005 speech, "The Global Saving Glut and the US Current Account Deficit," *op cit*.

There are some interesting footnotes to the Bernanke speech. Significantly, the Fed chairman actually flinched when it came to the oral version of his speech—offering a last-minute substitution of the word *distortion* for *subsidy*. That may have saved him from an embarrassing moment or two on the stage in Beijing, but it did nothing to diminish the subsequent flap that has since arisen over this accusation. Meanwhile, U.S. politicians were quick to take the cue from Bernanke. Sander Levin, Democrat Congressman from Michigan and soon-to-be Chairman of the House Subcommittee on Trade, immediately threatened to reintroduce legislation that would require the U.S. Commerce Department to cite Chinese currency manipulation as a violation of U.S. *antisubsidy* laws—thereby allowing U.S. companies to seek the remedy of offsetting, or countervailing, tariffs. Moreover, while Bernanke may have stumbled on the word *subsidy* in public, it remains the operative concept on record in the official version of the speech on the Fed's web site. Sadly, as evidenced by the predictable reactions of Washington protectionists, the damage has already been done.

I have long argued that the U.S.-China relationship could well be the most important bilateral underpinning of a successful globalization. I worry increasingly that the economic tensions between these two nations are in danger of being politicized, with the nation-specific considerations of localization increasingly taking precedence over globalization. I am encouraged by U.S. Treasury Secretary Hank Paulson's attempts to put the China debate in a much broader context. Unfortunately, the Bernanke speech is a major step backward.

# Protectionist Threats— Then and Now

*January 29, 2007*

A merica has been down this road before. In many respects, the Japan bashing of the late 1980s has an eerie similarity to the China bashing of today. Ironically, most observers find that ultimately encouraging. The hope is that the outcome of nearly 20 years ago is emblematic of what can be expected today—a lot of bluster, but trade frictions that stopped far short of protectionism. Unfortunately, some important complicating factors may draw this optimistic conclusion into serious question.

For starters, there can be no mistaking the red flag for the protectionists. As of the third quarter 2006, the U.S. current-account deficit stood at −6.8 percent of GDP—double the −3.5 percent shortfall hit in the fourth quarter of 1986 when the external imbalance was at its worst in the Japan bashing days. In both cases, the trade deficits were dominated by large bilateral imbalances with two major trading partners; Japan accounted for 37 percent of the peak US merchandise trade deficit in 1987 whereas the Chinese share is about 29 percent in early 2007. While the concentration factor was actually worse for Japan back in the 1980s, the scale implications of today's massive external deficit paint a very different picture. China's bilateral imbalance is currently about −1.9 percent of US GDP—more than 50 percent larger than the peak −1.2 percent share of Japan back in the late 1980s.

With the China factor considerably bigger than the Japan factor, many claim there is much more to fear from one trading partner today than was the case nearly 20 years ago. Yet that turns out to be a very superficial and dangerous conclusion—especially when it gets in the hands of xenophobic politicians. Fixating on China as the culprit behind America's trade deficit—the imbalance that is widely identified in political circles as the major source of pressures bearing down on American workers—misses two key points: First, a savings-short U.S. economy must import surplus saving from abroad in order to grow—and run massive current account and trade deficits in order to attract the foreign capital. By sourcing the largest piece of this deficit with China, a savings-short U.S. economy has access to low-cost, high-quality products. If Congress were to close down trade with China, America's savings shortfall wouldn't be altered, nor would the concomitant multilateral trade deficit. Instead, the Chinese piece would just be sourced by higher-cost producers—resulting in the functional equivalent of a tax on the U.S. consumer.

A second reason the China concentration ratio overstates the source of America's trade problem is that a surprisingly small proportion of the goods shipped from China to the United States reflect value added inside China. Academic research by Stanford Professor Laurence Lau has, in fact, shown that only about 20 percent of the value of Chinese exports to the United States reflect domestic Chinese content; the rest consists of components and parts from China's trading partners—predominantly those elsewhere in Asia.[8] It turns out that China is more of an assembler than a manufacturer. Although it may send a disproportionate share of its finished goods exports to the United States, that's more a reflection of China being the final point in the assembly line than anything else. Yet the bilateral trade data make no allowance for the distinction between domestic content and linkages to China's supply's chain. In effect, it's all or nothing in America's point-of-sale data system—fully 100 percent of the value of a good shipped out of China is credited as an American purchase of a product made in China.

Notwithstanding a more careful assessment of the China factor that puts its share of the U.S. deficit in a very different perspective, there can be no mistaking the intensity of the angst bearing down on the American workforce. I suspect something else may be at work here. As I have already noted, an extraordinary disparity has opened up between the capital and labor shares of U.S. national income. The profits share currently stands at a 50-year high of 12.4 percent, whereas the labor compensation share is just 56.3 percent—back to levels last seen on a

---

8. See Lau's testimony before the U.S. Congressional Executive Commission on China, "Is China Playing by the Rules?" September 2003.

sustained basis in the late 1960s. It turns out that's a very different juxta-position of economic power than the one that prevailed during the Japan bashing of the late 1980s. Back then, the shares of both capital and labor were under pressure: The profits share of about 7 percent was well below the 10 percent reading hit a decade earlier, whereas the labor compensation share of about 58 percent was down markedly from the 60 percent reading hit in the early 1980s.

In my view, this underscores a key element of tension in America's current backlash against globalization that was not evident in the late 1980s. Today, in 2007, the pressures are being borne disproportionately by labor, whereas 20 years ago, capital and labor were both under pressure. In the late 1980s, many of the once-proud icons of corporate America were fighting for competitive survival at the same time that U.S. workers were feeling the heat of global competition. The pain was, in effect, balanced. Today, U.S. companies, as seen through the lens of corporate profitability, are thriving as never before while the American workforce is increasingly isolated in its competitive squeeze. In essence, capital and labor are work-ing very much at cross purposes in the current climate, whereas back in the late 1980s they were united in feeling that they were both stuck in the same boat.

There is an added and important dimension of the current angst of American labor—a perception of growing inequalities within the wage, compensation, and wealth distribution. By almost all measures, inequal-ity is worse in the United States today than it was 20 years ago. This can be seen in the so-called Gini coefficient—a statistical measure of the dispersion of income shares within a country (see Figure 5.1). A Gini Index reading of 0 represents perfect equality, with each segment of the income distribution accounting for a proportionate share of total income. Conversely, a reading of 100 represents perfect inequality, with a nation's overall personal income concentrated at the upper end of the distribution spectrum. In other words, the higher the Gini coefficient, the more unequal the income distribution. For the United States, the verdict is clear: Based on income distribution data collated by the U.S. Census Bureau, America's Gini coefficient has deteriorated markedly from the days of Japan bashing—moving up over 12 percent from about 39 in 1986 to 44 in 2005.

What is particularly disturbing is that America's income distribution has become more unequal in a period of rapidly rising productivity growth. The best academic research I have seen on this topic is by Robert

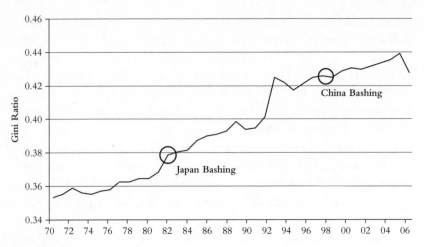

**Figure 5.1**  Rising U.S. Income Inequality

*Note:* 1 indicates perfect inequality; 0 indicates perfect equality.

*Source:* U.S. Census bureau, Morgan Stanley Research.

Gordon and Ian Dew-Becker of Northwestern University.[9] They found that only the top 10 percent of the U.S. income distribution have experienced growth in labor income equal to or above aggregate productivity growth since 1997. This is a stunning result. Basic economic theory teaches us that, over time, workers are rewarded in accordance with their marginal product. For 90 percent of the U.S. workforce that does not appear to have been the case. Nor has there been any meaningful cyclical improvement in recent years. Over the five-year, 2001–2005 period, real compensation per hour in the nonfarm business sector expanded at just a 1.4 percent average annual rate—less than half the 3.1 percent pace of trend productivity over this same period. Consequently, no matter how you cut it—labor versus capital or high-income versus low-and middle-income workers—most of the American labor force has been on the outside looking in during the current period of mounting trade tensions.

There are other differences between then and now that could also be intensifying the antiglobalization angst of the American worker today, in 2007. Back in the late 1980s, the perceived adversary, Japan, was a

9. See "Where Did the Productivity Growth Go?" *Brookings Papers on Economic Activity,* 2005.

wealthy developed country that paid its workers wage rates comparable to those in the United States. Today, in 2007, the fixation is over a poor developing country, China, where manufacturing workers are paid at about 3 percent the hourly rate of those in America. In the case of Japan, the competitive threat came from like-rewarded workers. In the case of China, the threat comes at a wage level that most American workers can't even begin to contemplate. Moreover, the competitive pressures of the 1980s were the slow-moving variety bearing down mainly on the manufacturing sector. Today, in 2007, courtesy of IT-enabled outsourcing, the threat is intensifying at hyperspeed, while spreading rapidly from manufacturing to once nontradable services. All in all, it is really not that difficult to understand why the fear factor of U.S. workers is far more exaggerated today, in 2007, than it was during the late 1980s.

All this, of course, feeds into the political backlash that is now bubbling over in the newly elected U.S. Congress. Prolabor Democrats have heard the message loud and clear. Middle-class American workers feel isolated as never before—not only threatened by a rapidly changing competitive dynamic but also left far behind by high returns accruing to the owners of capital. Consequently, I have reluctantly come to the conclusion that in this climate, it pays to take the threat of protectionism far more seriously than was the case during the late 1980s. That's good reason to worry that the politics of China bashing could end up being a good deal worse than the Japan bashing of some 20 years ago. For those with a keen sense of the lessons of history, protectionism seems almost unimaginable. Think again.

# The Ghost of Reed Smoot

## April 2, 2007

The label on the photograph sent a chill down my spine: "Reed Smoot, Republican of Utah, Senate Finance Committee Chairman, 1923–1933." Along with photos of other past chairmen, it was hung on the wall in the anteroom to the U.S. Senate Finance Committee hearing chamber on Capitol Hill. The formal high-collared pose of the dapper senator was the last thing I saw before I entered the hearing room on March 28, 2007 to testify on U.S.-China currency policy before the Senate Finance Committee. The legislator from Utah was, of course, the co-sponsor of the notorious Smoot-Hawley Tariff Act of 1930—a policy blunder of monumental proportions that played a key role in sparking a global trade war and the Great Depression. Some 77 years later, his spirit was very much in evidence as the Senate Finance Committee gathered to debate the China threat.

Over the years, I have participated in several congressional hearings on U.S.-China economic relationships. Around the end of February 2007, I testified on this same issue in executive session in front of the Subcommittee on Trade of the U.S. House Ways and Means Committee. This latest hearing in front of the all-powerful Senate Finance Committee was different. I left the Dirksen Senate Office Building convinced that U.S.-initiated trade sanctions against China are now inevitable. Support is deep and bipartisan. And the experts tell me that the margin of support appears broad enough to be veto-proof in the event that President Bush objects. After years of talk and bluster, protectionism no longer seems like an empty threat. This time, it looks like the real thing. I now suspect an anti-China trade or currency bill could actually become law by year-end 2007.

This conclusion quickly became evident in the opening minutes of the hearing. An ominous and well-coordinated warning was delivered by two of America's leading trade activists—Senators Chuck Schumer

(Democrat from New York) and Lindsey Graham (Republican from South Carolina). Their bipartisan teamwork over the past five years (2002–2007) has been key in elevating the China debate in the U.S. Congress. They were the co-sponsors of the infamous bill that would have imposed a 27.5 percent tariff on China as a penalty for maintaining a currency that they believe was undervalued by a like amount. Senator Schumer now admits this proposal was nothing more than a stalking horse to galvanize support from his fellow senators. That tactic succeeded well beyond his wildest expectations.

Chuck Schumer and Lindsey Graham have now embarked on a far more serious course of action. They have joined forces with two other heavyweights—Senators Max Baucus (Democrat from Montana and Chairman of the Senate Finance Committee) and Charles Grassley (Republican from Iowa and ranking minority member on Senate Finance), with a pledge to present a new China currency bill by midyear. Unlike the tariff bill, which the senators now admit was not WTO compliant, they have promised to make their new proposal fully compliant with WTO rules and provisions. That means relief will undoubtedly be sought through countervailing tariffs and/or antidumping subsidies—both of which are officially sanctioned WTO remedies.

Over the past two years (2005–2006), 27 separate pieces of anti-China legislation were introduced in the 109th Congress. None of them passed. In 2007, it could well be different. In just the first three months of the 110th Congress, at least another dozen such actions have been introduced. But the big one has yet to come. That's the real significance of the Baucus, Grassley, Schumer, and Graham coalition—it is emblematic of what could well be a major shift in U.S. trade policy. Despite the political acrimony that pervades Washington these days, these four senators are staunchly united on this one issue—as are most of their colleagues in the upper chamber of the U.S. legislature. Chairman Baucus closed the hearing with a very clear statement about where the four-senator coalition is headed on the China currency bill over the next couple of months. In his words, "We want to do it right. We want to be effective. We want to be firm. And we want to act."

Two days later, another shoe fell in the ever-quickening march toward protectionism. In a stunning about-face for U.S. trade policy and in an effort to appease the anti-China sentiment in the Congress, the U.S. Department of Commerce imposed countervailing duties on the imports of coated free sheet paper from China. On the surface, the Commerce Department action is a targeted initiative on a tiny piece of America's foreign trade. The United States imported $224 million of coated free sheet paper from China in 2006—10 times the pace of 2004 but only 0.02 percent of total U.S. merchandise imports. The action is significant less for its direct quantitative impact and more for the precedent it sets in revamping U.S. trade policy toward developing economies.

For the past 23 years, Washington has operated under the principle that countervailing duties should not be applied to nonmarket economies such as China. The argument rested on the notion that it was very difficult to assess the economic impacts of government-sponsored trade subsidies of centrally planned economies, such as the then-dominant Soviet Union. Largely for that reason, the United States has long relied on less onerous antidumping duties to deal with trade issues from nonmarket economies such as China. The Commerce Department is now arguing that these Soviet-era principles have been rendered obsolete by the emergence of a new and powerful force in global trade—China. In his statement that accompanied the March 30, 2007 action, U.S. Commerce Secretary Carlos Gutierrez was very direct in insisting that China's evolution into a strong economy justifies a new approach to trade policy. Many believe that this shift in the U.S. stance toward developing countries—adding countervailing duties to antidumping tariffs—could open the door to a floodgate of further actions on U.S.-China trade, especially on items such as steel and textiles.

Unfortunately, I don't think the Commerce Department's policy shift will be enough to stem the congressional backlash on trade. I am convinced it will take a lot more than the imposition of a single tariff on one product line to turn around the congressional juggernaut on China. There is even the possibility that such an approach may backfire. Congress is seeking firm and broad-based remedies in tackling the China problem. A surgical strike along the lines of the Commerce Department's action hardly fits that bill—especially since it could face a lengthy appeal process in the courts. Moreover, Congress was incensed by the lack of deliverables from the Treasury-sponsored Strategic Economic Dialog (SED) that took place in Beijing, December 2006. More talk accompanied by little progress on U.S.-China trade policy—precisely the risk in the next SED slated for May 2007 in Washington, DC—could push this action-oriented Congress over the edge.

Nor does China take these developments lightly. Its Ministry of Commerce was quick to respond to the March 30, 2007 initiatives of the U.S. Commerce Department by noting it ". . . reserve(s) the right to take any necessary action." Where China goes in that vein is anyone's guess, but I don't expect a major response to the single-product tariff that was just announced. The more worrisome *quid pro quo* would come in the event of more broadly based U.S. actions that might stem from further applications of countervailing duties or from currency-related legislation.

In these more extreme scenarios, any number of possible Chinese actions might be expected—ranging from retaliatory tariffs of its own to restrictions on foreign direct investment to limits placed on over-seas portfolio inflows. Then, of course, there is China's ultimate trump card—the asset allocation decisions that shape the currency mix of its massive reservoir of over $1 trillion in foreign exchange reserves. In the event of major trade sanctions imposed on China by the United States, I think this option could well come into play—not in the form of out-right sales of existing positions of China's dollar-based holdings but more from the diversification of new inflows of foreign exchange reserves into non-dollar-based assets. In that event, America would undoubtedly feel the full force of China's wrath in the form of a sharp decline in the value of the dollar and a concomitant increase in real long-term U.S. interest rates.

Sadly, I am not all that surprised by this turn of events. I have been warning of a rising backlash against globalization for the past couple of years, and now the moment of truth finally seems to be close at hand. Ironically, this is all playing out when the U.S. unemployment rate is hovering near its cycle low of 4.5 percent. Yet with downside risks to an already sluggish U.S. economy building by the day, the jobless rate has nowhere to go but up—a development that will only further inflame the bipartisan politics of trade protectionism.

One thing is now certain: America's anti-China brinksmanship is esca-lating. At the same time, China, after 300 years of feeling maligned by the West, is not likely to take these actions sitting down. I suspect that the Chinese will respond in some form or another—a reaction that could then only further inflame the Washington consensus. All this underscores the painful possibility that increased trade frictions can quickly take the world down a very slippery slope.

Rising protectionist risks could well be the biggest macro shock in many a year. Yet for their part, the overwhelming majority of investors remain steeped in denial with respect to such an outcome. The ghost of Reed Smoot is a haunting image of an increasingly treacherous endgame for both the global economy and world financial markets. I could have sworn that I saw a wink of his eye as I staggered out of the Senate Finance Committee hearing room in March 2007.

# China's Pace, America's Angst

*May 25, 2007*

Round II of the Strategic Economic Dialog (SED) has come and gone. In just eight months' time, this carefully orchestrated consultation between senior officials from the United States and China has established a robust framework of engagement between the world's first and fourth largest economies. The good news is there is progress to report. The bad news is that the progress has been incremental, at best—insufficient to defuse the political angst now bubbling over in the U.S. Congress.

There were no major surprises coming out of the May 2007 SED. The Chinese announced market-opening measures in air transportation and financial services, and joint initiatives were established in the areas of environmental protection and energy security. The all-important issue of intellectual property rights was singled out for special attention in future negotiations. This is unequivocally good news. These actions underscore China's ongoing commitment to market-based reforms and offer yet another demonstration of the open-economy model of Chinese economic development—an approach that provides its trading partners with steadily increasing access to the world's most populous domestic markets. China's open development model stands in sharp contrast to the closed-economy strategy used by Japan during its development, which kept the rest of the world on the outside looking in. In an era of accelerating globalization, the Chinese strain of open development offers the world considerably greater opportunity than the closed approach long advocated by Japan.

The U.S. Congress could care less. The political pressures bearing down on Washington come straight from the American middle class. And with understandable reason: According to the U.S. Bureau of Labor Statistics, the median real wage—inflation-adjusted wages for the worker in the middle of the pay distribution—has risen a cumulative total of just 0.9 percent over the seven years ending in the first quarter of 2007. This is a particularly disturbing development for a U.S. economy that is in the midst of a powerful productivity revival—an outcome that would normally lead to proportionate gains in real wages. This disconnect between the contribution and the reward of American workers is, in my view, at the heart of Washington's political dilemma. The easy answer is to blame someone else—in this case, scapegoating China because it accounts for the largest bilateral piece of America's record multilateral trade deficit. The tougher answer is to get to the bottom of the real wage stagnation problem—and put policies in place that could rectify this situation. Lacking in good answers and unable to muster patience in this era of the quick fix, Congress has opted for the former option—putting China in the cross-hairs of a classic blame game.

I've droned on enough over the past several months about what I believe are serious flaws to the Washington response to this problem (see my congressional testimony, "A Slippery Slope" on p. 331–340). My critique can be summed up in three words—trade, saving, and globalization. First of all, Congress is operating under the dangerous presumption that there is cause and effect between median real-wage stagnation and a record trade deficit. On both theoretical and empirical counts, the jury is very much out on this key issue. In addition, U.S. politicians have failed to put America's trade deficit in the broader context of an unprecedented shortfall of domestic saving—refusing to accept the algebraic logic of a multilateral trade deficit as an outgrowth of subpar saving and incorrectly fixating on a bilateral resolution of the Chinese piece of this equation. Finally, Washington has little or no appreciation of how the IT-enabled hyperspeed of the current globalization has unleashed extraordinary pressures on a broad cross-section of American workers—blue and white collar, alike. In short, the China fix does an enormous disservice to these critical macro considerations and, since it also opens the door to retaliatory actions, risks a policy blunder of monumental proportions.

Not surprisingly, the China perspective is all but lost in the shuffle in the halls of Congress. China is viewed on Capitol Hill as America's major economic adversary—a threat to middle-class workers and an affront to the rules and principles of global trade. Overlooked in this perception is the enormous progress China has made on the road to development over the past 29 years—and the opportunities that presents for the United States, the rest of Asia, and the broader global economy. Equally ignored is the still very delicate nature of China's astonishing transition—underscored by Premier Wen Jiabao's recent characterization of the Chinese economy as being "unstable, unbalanced, uncoordinated, and unsustainable." (See p. 229–233.) Congress, by contrast, makes little allowance for the serious development challenges China still faces—in effect, treating China like a much more economically advanced trading partner from the developed world. Such is the classic illogic of politics.

Nor does the Congress seem to have much appreciation of the distance China has traveled in the short span of three decades. China's unprecedented development successes are largely an outgrowth of its unwavering commitment to reform—not just the transition from a state-owned toward a privately controlled system but also the shift from a centrally planned toward a market-based system of resource allocation. These reforms are far from complete, and the outcome of the just-completed SED promises further movement in that direction. Over the past 30 years, China has been exceedingly careful to balance the pace of reforms against the risks of instability. At no point did it follow the shock-therapy approach embraced by states of the former Soviet Union. "Determined incrementalism" is the best way I would describe the character of three decades of Chinese reforms—no backtracking but steady and unrelenting progress toward private ownership and markets. This approach is very much at odds with the search for the magic potion that always seems to dominate the short-term problem-solving mentality of Washington politicians. The radical currency-fix option that is now on the table in Washington is very much at odds with the gradualism that has served China so well over the past 30 years.

I had the opportunity to participate in the closing event of SED II—a reception for the 15-minister Chinese delegation followed by a dinner speech from the leader of the China negotiating team, Vice Premier Wu Yi. Both the Vice Premier, as well as U.S. Treasury Secretary Hank Paulson, who also spoke at the dinner, made the same point: The Strategic Economic Dialog is a framework of engagement on longer-term issues shaping the economic relationship between the United States and China. By definition, that implies it is designed to achieve incremental results rather than come up with grand solutions to short-term concerns such as those currently playing out on Capitol Hill. This underscores a major mismatch between two sets of forces driving the bilateral U.S.-China relationship: the incrementalism of the SED approach and the more draconian quick-fix mindset of the Congress. Nevertheless, unlike the first meetings of last December, which did not involve the U.S. Congress in any way whatsoever, the just concluded summit included four meetings between the Chinese delegation and key U.S. legislators—one with the House leadership, another with the Senate leadership, and then separate meetings with the House Ways and Means and Senate Finance Committees.

When asked how the sessions with Congress went, Vice Premier Wu said in perfect English, "Very difficult." That reinforced concerns she expressed in her prepared remarks when she warned of the perils of a large RMB adjustment, especially with respect to its potential impact on the Chinese economy. She also underscored her previously stated concerns that the recent WTO complaints filed by the United States on intellectual property rights issues ". . . runs counter to the understanding between our two leaders and could have a serious impact on our bilateral trade relationship." To me, that is a clear and worrisome sign of what to expect in the way of a retaliatory response, should the U.S. Congress actually throw down the gauntlet and impose trade sanctions on China.

China's incremental approach to reform has served a stability-fixated nation quite well over the past three decades. However, the gradual pace of Chinese transition is very much at odds with the quick fix mentality of a large currency adjustment that is now dominating the political debate in the U.S. Congress. Therein lies what could potentially be a fatal flaw of the SED: Judging the outcome of this meeting of the largest group of senior United States and Chinese policy makers ever assembled, America's protectionist politicians could well characterize a predictable incremental result as a negotiating failure of the highest order. That could well establish even firmer political grounds for U.S. legislators to take matters into their own hands. SED II did not dissuade me of these concerns.

# The Politics of Trade Frictions

*October 24, 2007*

C hina is the scapegoat *du jour* for all that ails the American middle class. At least, that's certainly the conclusion that can be drawn from spending any time these days in Washington.

Unfortunately, the U.S. body politic has long had a penchant for such scapegoatism when it comes to trade policy. Remember the Japan bashing of the late 1980s? And of course, just three years ago there was an outcry of concern over India as the lightning rod of the new threat of white-collar offshoring. Meanwhile, the Doha Round is dead, bilateral free trade agreements are going nowhere, Congress has allowed fast-track presidential negotiating authority to lapse, and public opinion polls show an American public with a serious distaste for trade liberalization and globalization.

The politics of congressional-led China bashing fit all too neatly into this inflammatory climate. Although there is always a certain amount of bluster evident in Washington, this time the threats seem serious and worrisome. By my count, over 18 pieces of antitrade legislation have been introduced in the first nine months of the 110th Congress. And in almost all cases, the target—either explicit or implicit—is China. Nor has this outbreak of China bashing appeared out of thin air. In the previous two years, the 109th Congress floated some 27 anti-China proposals. The difference between the two sessions of the U.S. Congress is troubling. In the end, the 109th Congress was all talk and no action. By contrast, the 110th Congress seems highly likely to pass one of the measures currently in the legislative hopper—and with a large enough bipartisan margin to withstand the threat of a presidential veto.

There are three leading anti-China approaches currently under consideration by the U.S. Congress—two very similar efforts in the Senate and a somewhat different approach in the House. At present, it appears that Congress has deferred immediate consideration of these initiatives, although the two Senate versions have both been cleared by overwhelming bipartisan mark-ups in both the Finance and Banking Committees. The probability of passage by veto-proof margins—either in late 2007 or in early 2008—remains over 60 percent, in my view. It's hard to say which version will prevail in the end or what type of hybrid might emerge from a Conference Committee. But it's important to lay bare the assumptions embodied in Congress's penchant for China bashing in order to understand where this approach is coming from—and what unintended consequences it may well trigger.

First and foremost, the debate is grounded in very legitimate concerns over the increased economic insecurity of middle-class American workers. Real wage stagnation is at the top of the list. In the second quarter of 2007, inflation-adjusted median weekly earnings for full-time U.S. workers were unchanged from levels prevailing seven years ago in the second quarter of 2000. Yet over that same period, productivity in the nonfarm business sector recorded a cumulative 18 percent increase. Contrary to one of the basic axioms of economics, American workers have not been paid their just reward as measured by their productivity contribution.

As voters, workers are holding their elected representatives accountable for this extraordinary macro disconnect. And politicians are scrambling to come up with both reasons and solutions. At the top of the political answer column is trade and globalization. Congress is presuming that America's record foreign trade gap, namely an −$838 billion deficit on merchandise trade in 2006, has been a decisive factor in squeezing both jobs and real wages of middle-class American workers. And that supposition has dictated the politically expedient solution—attacking the external imbalance by going after the so-called bad citizens among America's trading partners.

That's, of course, where China enters the equation. America's bilateral trade deficit with China accounts for, by far, the largest slice of the overall imbalance: 28 percent of the total U.S. merchandise trade deficit in 2006 and about 31 percent of the cumulative shortfall in the first eight months of 2007. Carrying the label of the "Great Currency Manipulator" seals China's fate in the eyes of Congress and in the view of many economists and politicians. End of story—at least, in the eyes of the Washington Consensus.

Not quite so fast, I'm afraid. It doesn't take a rocket scientist to figure out that America has a multilateral trade problem. Just count up the countries in deficit with the United States in 2006, and you'll come up with a list of about 100 of them. Yes, China has the biggest of America's bilateral trade deficits. But is that because of its currency policy? Or is it an outgrowth of a China-centric supply chain constructed by America's multinationals desperately in search of efficiency solutions in an increasingly competitive world? Or is it a reflection of the simple—and possibly related—fact that China happens to produce (or assemble, to be more accurate) a broad cross-section of products that satisfy the tastes, pricing, and aspirational wants of American consumers?

Either way, the congressional math of the blame game is fatally flawed. Stripping out the China gap still leaves a U.S. trade deficit of over $600 billion in 2006—a number nearly three times as large as the shortfall with China. So assume for the moment that Congress fixes the Chinese piece of the U.S. trade deficit—a dubious assumption, as I note later. But even if that were the case, that still leaves a rather large remainder for the U.S. trade gap. What is the policy to address that? Is Congress telling us that China is merely first in line—that, one by one, they will go down the list of U.S. trading partners, imposing trade sanctions until the deficit has been eliminated?

It follows that the so-called currency fix now being contemplated by the U.S. Congress is equally preposterous—presuming that pressure on a bilateral cross-rate will solve a multilateral deficit. All that will do will be to send a relative price signal that will shift the mix of the deficit elsewhere—and most likely to a higher-cost producer. That's like rearranging the deck chairs on the Titanic. And, of course, it is also the functional equivalent of a tax hike on middle-class America—the aggrieved victims in all this.

The multilateral characteristics of the U.S. trade deficit are the smoking guns to this problem. And it is painfully clear what the root cause is—an extraordinary lack of U.S. domestic savings. America's net national savings rate—the combined savings of individuals, businesses, and governmental units adjusted for depreciation—averaged a mere 1.5 percent of national income over the five years ending in 2006. That's the lowest national saving rate for a five-year period in modern U.S. history and apparently the lowest saving rate for the hegemonic power in world history. Lacking in domestic saving, the U.S. must then import surplus saving in order to grow—and run massive current account and trade deficit in order to attract the capital.

That, I am afraid, is the real end of this story. If America wants to fix its trade deficit and relieve the concomitant pressures that are bearing down on middle-class workers, it must address its seemingly chronic savings deficit. I am highly critical of the overwhelming majority of my U.S.-based macro peers who only pay lip service to this critical aspect of the problem when appearing alongside me as expert witnesses in offering congressional testimony on these key issues.

Of course, in Washington, it has long been easy to duck the facts and weave a good yarn. China bashing, I am afraid, is largely a by-product of that predilection. But it's actually far worse than that. Who is really to blame for inadequate saving—the root cause of the U.S. trade deficit? Washington is at the top of that list, in my opinion, with its penchant for budget deficits, consumption incentives, and an asset-based saving mind-set that has been underwritten by the Federal Reserve. But the same Washington is utterly incapable of taking a deep look in the mirror and accepting responsibility for problems such as these. It is much easier to indulge in scapegoating and point the finger elsewhere. China is but the latest in a long line of such targets. Just ask Japan what it was like some 20 years ago—or India just a few years ago.

China bashing is also emblematic of a deeper problem that grips the U.S. body politic—an unwillingness to embark on the heavy lifting of education reform and other investments in human capital that are required to equip American workers to compete and prosper in a Brave New World. Instead of investing in a hard-pressed work force, Washington apparently believes in shielding U.S. workers from low-wage talent pools in the developing world. The doubling of the world's labor supply that has occurred in the past two decades has evoked a response of fear and protectionism.

Sadly, that puts America at grave risk of becoming more insular and inward looking. Yet over the long sweep of U.S. economic history, our workers have actually done best when they are pushed to their limits by a risk-taking, entrepreneurial, and innovative society. By blaming others for our own shortcomings—especially on the saving and human capital fronts—America runs the very real risk of losing its most special edge of all, an indomitable economic spirit. By shirking its responsibility for putting U.S. savings policy on a sound path, Congress is, instead, now veering toward the slippery slope of protectionism.

Finally, just a word about China, where I spend an awful lot of my time these days. China is a living miracle of economic development. The world has never seen anything like the transformation of the Chinese economy that has occurred over the past 25-plus years. This extraordinary development trajectory is based primarily on a steadfast commitment to market-based reforms—something that Washington as the bastion of capitalism should applaud, not criticize.

But China also has a new strength—one that takes a page right out of our own experience in the United States. Dynamic private companies are now springing up all over China; of the 16 new Chinese companies that Morgan Stanley has brought public in the first nine months of 2007, 15 of them are private. For China, the newfound spirit of its privately employed workers and businesspeople is contagious and very reminiscent of what has long been central to the American dream.

Yes, like any economy, China has its share of problems and risks, especially structural imbalances, environmental degradation, and income disparities. Currency policy has long been a topic of discussion in official Chinese policy circles as well. But, despite its remarkable progress, China is still a very poor country with many other important things on its plate.

Therein lies a critical difference between the two perspectives: Washington's penchant for the quick fix singles out the Chinese currency as a lightning rod in the great middle-class globalization debate. China, by contrast, views the currency issue not as an end in and of itself but as one of many pieces in the broad mosaic of financial reforms. That leads to a completely different perspective from both sides, which has now boiled over in the form of trade frictions.

Ironically, in contrast to American intransigence on the savings issue and the multilateral trade deficit it has spawned, China is making important progress in relieving this source of tension. As China puts its financial system increasingly on a market-based footing, its leaders have given every indication that the currency regime will follow. The shift to a managed float in July 2005 was an important first step in that direction. At the same time, China is taking dead aim on the imperatives of a consumer-led growth dynamic—a very different economic structure that will boost imports and thereby reduce its destabilizing trade surplus.

For China, the timing and sequencing of these moves are being considered with due deliberation—but mainly with an eye toward keeping its embryonic financial system stable. There are clear risks in this approach—excess liquidity and asset bubbles are most obvious in this regard. But these are China's risks to accept and manage, rather than our place to dictate the terms of engagement. China's pace may not fit America's political imperatives, but whose fault is that?

Globalization isn't easy. The win-win mantra long offered by the economics profession does this megatrend a great disservice. It oversimplifies the problems and overlooks the inherent tensions of an IT-enabled globalization that is now proceeding at hyperspeed. Globalization is full of opportunity and challenge, as well as fear and risk. But in the end, globalization is nothing more than trust—that is, trust in economic partners to act out of collective interests in making the world a more prosperous place. I fear that a China-bashing U.S. Congress has lost sight of this noble objective at great peril.

# A Wake-Up Call for the United States and China: Stress Testing a Symbiotic Relationship

*February 15, 2009*

S ince the turn of the century, no two nations have been more important in driving the global economy than the United States and China. The American consumer has been the dominant force on the demand side of the global economy, whereas the Chinese producer has been the most powerful force on the supply side. Few argued with the payback. Over the four-and-a-half years leading up to the onset of the so-called subprime crisis in mid-2007, world GDP growth averaged nearly 5 percent—the strongest and most sustained boom in the global economy since the early 1970s.

But now both engines are sputtering, with ominous consequences for a world in its worst crisis since the 1930s. This poses great challenges for each nation, as well as to the bilateral relationship between them. There is hope but it comes with a big "if"—if China and the United States pull together in forging common solutions. However, if these two nations end up at odds with one another, they will both suffer—with dire consequences for the rest of a crisis-torn global economy. The stakes are enormous. There is no margin for error.

## A World in Crisis

No nation has been spared the impacts of this wrenching financial crisis and recession. Although America's so-called subprime crisis may have been the spark that ignited the inferno, every region in this globalized

world is now faltering in lock-step fashion. That includes China—long
the most resilient economy in an otherwise weakened world. And it
includes the rest of an increasingly China-centric Asia, where all economies either have tumbled into outright recession or are slowing sharply.
Ten years after the Asian financial crisis wreaked havoc in the region, a
new crisis is at hand.

Far from having decoupled from the rest of the world, Asia's problems—
and China's in particular—are tightly linked to the crisis and recession
that started in America and have since spread like wildfire throughout
the developed world. These problems have arisen, in large part, because
of the unbalanced state of both economies. America's excess consumption model is in serious trouble because the asset bubbles that have long
supported it—property and credit—have both burst. China's export-led
growth model is in trouble because it is being adversely impacted by
a massive external demand shock that is very much an outgrowth of
America's postbubble compression of consumer demand. The rest of
Asia—export-dependent economies that have become tightly integrated
into a China-centric supply chain—has nowhere to hide. Ten years after
the wrenching upheaval of 1997–1998, Asia is in serious trouble again.

Significantly, these imbalances did not occur in isolation from each
other. America's consumption bubble was, in effect, sourced by an equally
destabilizing Asian export bubble, and now both sets of bubbles have
burst—on the demand side as well as on the supply side of the global
economy. It had to happen at some point: Long-simmering global imbalances have finally come to a head in a postbubble world (see Figure 5.2).

## China: Unbalanced and Unstable

During the boom, China's imbalances actually worked in its favor. Over
the 2001–2007 period, the export share of Chinese GDP nearly doubled
from 20 percent to 36 percent while the global export share of world
GDP went from 24 percent to 31 percent (see Figures 5.3 and 5.4). In
other words, China's timing was perfect. It upped the ante on its export
dependence at precisely the moment when global trade enjoyed its most
spectacular growth. That effectively turbocharged China's benefits from
the strongest global boom since the early 1970s, powering GDP growth
at a 10.4 percent average rate in the seven years ending in 2007.

That was then. Reflecting the impacts of a rare synchronous recession in the United States, Europe, and Japan, the world trade boom

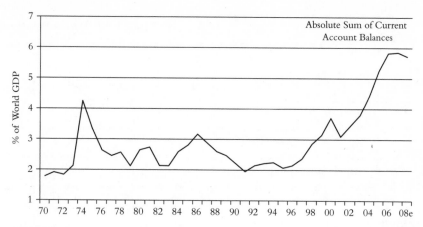

**Figure 5.2**  Global Imbalances

*Source:* IMF, Morgan Stanley Research.

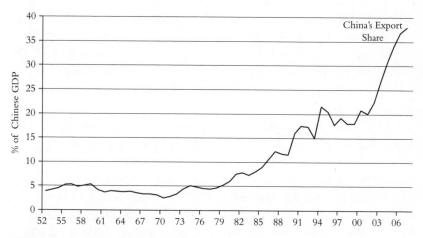

**Figure 5.3**  Chinese Export Surge

*Source:* China National Bureau of Statistics and Morgan Stanley Research.

has now gone bust. And Chinese exports, which had been surging at a 25 percent year-over-year rate as recently as mid-2008, reversed course with a vengeance—ending the year in a mode of outright contraction, falling by 2.8 percent in December, before plunging to a -17.5 percent comparison in January 2009.

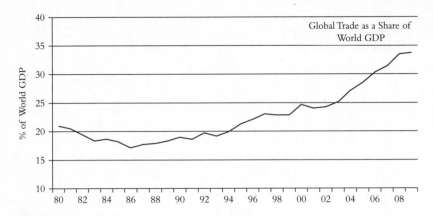

**Figure 5.4**   The Great Boom in Global Trade
*Source:* International Monetary Fund, Morgan Stanley Research.

With exports such a large and rapidly expanding slice of the Chinese economy, little wonder measures of aggregate activity slowed in an equally dramatic fashion. Industrial output increased only 5.7 percent in December—one-third the average 16.5 percent growth pace of the preceding five years. And real GDP growth ended the year at just 6.8 percent—in sharp contrast to the nearly 12 percent pace of the preceding three years.

China's growth compression as reported on a year-over-year basis masks the severity of its recent downshift. A translation of these figures into sequential quarterly changes, such as those reported by the United States, suggests that Chinese GDP and industrial output growth had slowed to a virtual standstill as 2008 came to an end. As seen from this real-time perspective, the Chinese economy hit a wall late last year. Such an abrupt downshift implies it will be extremely difficult for China to achieve the government's 8 percent GDP growth target for 2009. An outcome closer to 6 percent is a distinct possibility. China is hardly an oasis of prosperity in a crisis-torn world.

For a nation long focused on social stability, this growth shortfall is a worrisome development. It has already taken a serious toll on Chinese employment. The government has now acknowledged job losses in coastal export manufacturing businesses of over 15 percent—or 20 million workers—of the nation's pool of some 120 million migrant workers. If the export and GDP shortfall persists, more slack would open up in the Chinese labor market—raising long dreaded risks of worker unrest. I remain convinced that the Chinese leadership will do everything in its power to avoid such an outcome. But in this global recession, the challenge is daunting, to say the least.

## Asia: China-Centric and In Peril

It has become conventional wisdom to proclaim that the 21st century would be the Asian Century. China's miraculous development story is central to this vision—a transformation that many believe would inevitably push the pendulum of global power from West to East. It's hardly an exaggeration to claim that such a tectonic shift would turn the world inside out. The Asia Dream is an exciting and powerful story—a magnet to financial and human capital from all over the world.

It may be premature to crack out the champagne. The Asian century is hardly as preordained as most seem to believe. The main reason, in my view, is that the region continues to rely far too much on exports and external demand. Developing Asia's export share hit a record high of 47 percent last year—up 10 full percentage points from levels prevailing in the late 1990s (see Figure 5.5). That hardly speaks of a true economic power that has become capable of standing on its own.

At the same time, there can be no mistaking the increasingly China-centric character of the Asian economy—another dimension of the region's search for growth. As China boomed, the rest of Asia tethered

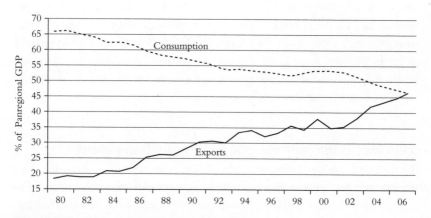

**Figure 5.5**  Export-Led Developing Asia

*Source:* International Monetary Fund, Morgan Stanley Research.

itself to the regional powerhouse. A China-centric supply chain led to increasingly tighter panregional integration, with assembly lines in China drawing freely on inputs and components from Japan, Korea, Taiwan, Malaysia, Singapore, Indonesia, and elsewhere in the region. Yet that dependence cuts both ways—a two-way causality that is now complicating the here and now of the Asian century. As noted earlier, the China boom was itself very much tied to the record surge in global trade. But now, with global trade contracting for the first time since 1982, China's export-led impetus has been quick to follow.

This has hit China-centric Asia extremely hard. The December 2008 export comparisons were nothing short of disastrous for the other major economies in the region: For example, Taiwan's exports were down an astonishing 42 percent year-over-year, with the Chinese piece off 56 percent; Japan's exports plunged 35 percent, with the Chinese piece off 35 percent; and Korean exports fell 17 percent, with the Chinese piece also off 35 percent. In all three of these cases, China had become each country's largest trading partner in recent years—accounting for 28 percent of total Taiwanese exports, 23 percent of Korean exports, and 16 percent of Japanese exports. But now that the Chinese export machine has screeched to a standstill, the rest of the region has weakened even more. This puts an Asian spin on an old adage: When China sneezes, the rest of Asia catches a bad cold.

I am convinced that the Asian century is coming. But the risk is that it may take a lot longer than widely presumed. All this underscores the biggest test to the Asian century—the ability of the region to stand more on its own in the event of an external shock. In the late 1990s, it was an external funding shock. Today, it is an external demand shock. These developments should put the region on notice that its leadership agenda is far from complete. Until export-led growth gives way to increased support from private consumption, the dream of the Asian century is likely to remain just that.

## America: Bubble-Prone and Externally Dependent

There can be little doubt that this global crisis started in America. The ever-deepening recession in the U.S. economy is very much an outgrowth of a massive postbubble shakeout. It began with housing but has now spread to the biggest sector of all—the American consumer. At its peak in early 2007, U.S. consumption accounted for fully 72 percent of real GDP—a record for the United States, and for that matter, a record for any major economy in the modern history of the world (see Figure 5.6).

The problem with this consumption binge is that it was not supported by the U.S. economy's underlying income generating capacity. In the now-ended expansion, private sector labor compensation expanded at an unusually sluggish pace—falling over $800 billion (in real terms) below the trajectory of the previous four business cycles (see Figure 5.7).

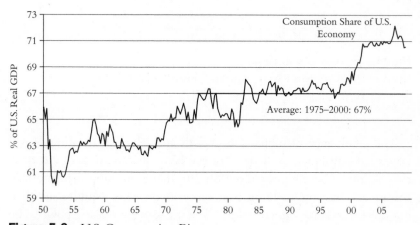

**Figure 5.6**   U.S. Consumption Binge

*Source:* Haver Analytics, Morgan Stanley Research.

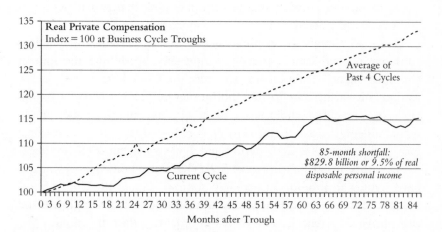

**Figure 5.7**   U.S. Labor Income Shortfall

*Source:* U.S. Bureau of Economic Analysis, Morgan Stanley Research.

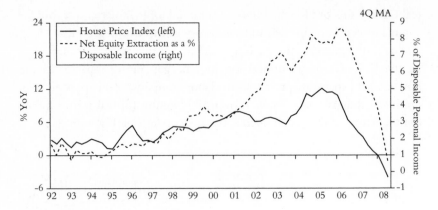

**Figure 5.8**  U.S. Wealth Shock

*Source:*   OFHEO, Federal Reserve, Morgan Stanley Research.

The confluence of subpar job growth and relative stagnation of real wages left consumers well short of the labor income that would typically support booming consumption. But that didn't stop the American consumer. Drawing freely on asset appreciation—first equities and then housing—consumers uncovered new sources of purchasing power. The credit bubble was icing on the cake—enabling homeowners to extract equity at little cost from ever-rising home values and then use the proceeds to fund current consumption and build savings for the future. Net equity extraction soared from 3 percent of disposable personal income in 2000 to nearly 9 percent in 2006 (see Figure 5.8).

There are important consequences of such a bubble-dependent consumption and saving strategy. Significantly, by shifting the mix of consumer support from income to assets, the United States drew down its domestic savings rate to rock-bottom levels. The net national savings rate—the sum of household, business, and government savings after adjustment for depreciation—plunged to a record low of 1.8 percent of national income over the 2002–2007 period, and then actually tumbled into negative territory in 2008 (see Figure 5.9). The global consequences of this development are profound: Lacking in domestic savings, the United States was forced to import surplus savings from abroad in order to grow—and run a massive current-account deficit in order to attract the capital.

The saving shortfall of a bubble-prone U.S. economy is a major source of vulnerability. During good times, it made America increasingly

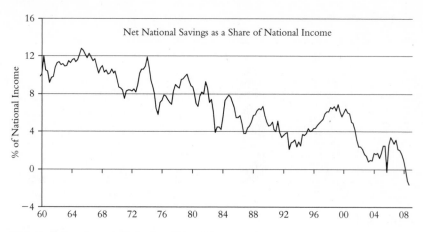

**Figure 5.9** America's Saving Shortfall

*Source:* U.S. Bureau of Economic Analysis, Morgan Stanley Research.

dependent on foreign lenders, such as China, to fund economic growth. During bad times—especially in the aftermath of the bursting of the property and credit bubbles—it triggered a massive consolidation of asset-dependent U.S. consumption. Real consumption expenditures fell at close to a 4 percent average annual rate in the final two quarters of 2008—the first time in the post–World War II era when consumer demand fell by more than 3 percent for two consecutive quarters.

Despite the unprecedented contraction of consumption in late 2008, there is good reason to believe the capitulation of the American consumer has only just begun. The consumption share of U.S. GDP has fallen only about one percentage point from its 72 percent peak to 71 percent in late 2008—still leaving this gauge four full percentage points above the prebubble norm of 67 percent that prevailed from 1975–2000. On this basis, only about 20 percent of the consumer's mean reversion to pre-bubble norms has been completed. Notwithstanding the extraordinary monetary and fiscal stimulus measures that have recently been put in place by U.S. authorities, the postbubble deleveraging of the American consumer is likely to be an enduring feature of America's macro land-scape over the next three to five years.

Therein lies the essence of a massive and sustained global demand shock. The American consumer is the biggest consumer in the world (see Figure 5.10). United States consumption growth has long outstripped far

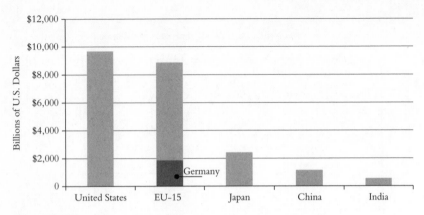

**Figure 5.10**   The Global Consumer
*Source:*   National Sources, UN, Morgan Stanley Research.

more sluggish gains elsewhere in the developed world. Little wonder the
postbubble capitulation of the American consumer proved so decisive
in undermining the external demand underpinnings for China and for
the rest of export-dependent Asia. Nor is it likely to be over quickly.
A multiyear headwind imparted by a sustained weakening in the growth
of U.S. consumption could well be the most powerful force shaping the
demand side of the global economy for years to come.

## Mounting Bilateral Tensions

The current global crisis poses new challenges to the relationship
between the United States and China—quite conceivably the world's
most important bilateral relationship of the twenty-first century. Those
challenges were underscored in the recent Senate confirmation hearings
of America's new Treasury Secretary, Timothy Geithner, when he accused
the Chinese of currency manipulation. Moreover, with the United States
in recession and unemployment high and rising, there is good reason to
fear that Geithner's comments were just a warning shot of more China-
bashing on the horizon.

This is an unfortunate outgrowth of the blame-game mentality that
has long been prevalent in Washington. During tough times, U.S. politicians apparently need scapegoats to deflect attention away from the
role they have played in creating serious problems. Wall Street is being

singled out for causing the financial crisis—despite regulatory and central bank complicity—and China, with its large bilateral trade deficit with the United States, is being blamed for the pressures bearing down on American workers.

Washington's logic for turning tough on China trade policy is based largely on three factors—an outsize bilateral trade deficit between the two nations that hit a record $256 billion in 2007, long-standing claims of RMB currency manipulation, and a seemingly chronic stagnation of real wages for American middle-class workers. Fix the China problem, goes the argument, and unfair pressures on U.S. workers will be relieved.

This argument is deeply flawed. The main reason is that the U.S.-China trade deficit did not arise in a vacuum. As noted earlier, a bubble-prone, savings-short U.S. economy needs to import surplus savings from abroad in order to keep growing. That also means it must run massive current-account and trade deficits to attract that capital. The U.S.-China trade deficit, along with deficits with 100 of America's other trading partners is, in fact, an important outgrowth of that problem. America has a multilateral trade imbalance—not a bilateral problem driven by unfair Chinese competition. China has the largest bilateral piece of America's multilateral deficit—not because of the value of its currency but mainly because of conscious outsourcing decisions of U.S. multinationals.

Nor is the evidence on the so-called undervaluation of the Chinese renminbi nearly as conclusive as many U.S. experts seem to believe. For starters, the RMB is up nearly 21 percent against the U.S. dollar (in real terms) since China abandoned its currency peg in mid-2005. Moreover, recent academic research puts the RMB's multilateral under-valuation on the order of only 10 percent—hardly a major advantage for China.[10] Significantly, these same researchers go on to demonstrate that China's bilateral and multilateral trade flows are not nearly as sensitive to movements in its currency as the RMB bashers would want to believe.

Nevertheless, if U.S.-China trade is diminished or closed down through forced RMB revaluation, tariffs, or other means, and America fails to address its savings problem, a savings-short U.S. economy will still need to run a large multi-lateral trade deficit. That means it will simply end up shifting the Chinese piece of its external imbalance to another

10. See Yin-Wong Cheung, Menzie D. Chinn, and Eiji Fujii, "China's Current Account and Exchange Rate," a January 2009 working paper of the U.S. National Bureau of Economic Research.

trading partner. To the extent that shift is directed toward a higher-cost producer—most likely the case—the outcome will be the functional equivalent of a tax hike on the already beleaguered American middle class. But it won't stop there. Undoubtedly, Chinese currency managers would retaliate by reducing their purchases of dollar-denominated assets. And that would push the world's two great powers all the closer to the slippery slope of trade protectionism.

Avoiding such an outcome—strikingly reminiscent of the trade wars of the 1930s triggered by America's infamous Smoot-Hawley tariffs—poses a major challenge to the body politic of both nations. That's particularly true for America's new president. Campaigning on a platform of support for beleaguered middle-class American workers, Barack Obama underscored his concerns about real wage stagnation in an era of unfettered globalization. The real wage issue is a serious issue. However, the challenge for Washington is to determine the linkage between this issue and trade policy. It may well be that real wage stagnation is related more to America's underinvestment in human capital—especially, lagging educational reforms and reskilling programs in an era of rapid IT-enabled globalization—than it is to cross-border trade pressures. It may also be that trade deficits are far more a function of flawed policies that discourage saving—a problem that is now going from bad to worse in what now appears to be a protracted era of trillion dollar budget deficits. Resolving this dilemma, without derailing globalization, will be an early and important leadership test for President Obama.

## Don't Count on Symbiosis

In economic terms, there can be no mistaking the natural symbiosis that has long existed between America, the consumer and low saver, and China, the producer and high saver. But this complementarity cannot be taken for granted as a co-dependence that will forever cement the bilateral ties between these countries. In fact, it may well be that U.S.-Chinese symbiosis is nothing more than a passing phase—reflecting a coincidence of mutual interests that will exist for only a relatively brief period of time. Yes, as long as a savings-short U.S. economy continues to run massive current-account deficits to support the excesses of personal consumption, it needs a lender like China to provide foreign capital. And as long as an excess-savings Chinese economy needs export-led employment growth to maintain social stability, it needs the world's largest consumer to absorb its output.

But what happens if those conditions change? If America starts to save more—a distinct possibility for its overextended postbubble consumers—the need to borrow surplus saving from China will diminish. Conversely, if China starts to spend more—an equally likely possibility in light of its excessive reliance on exports and investment—it will have less surplus saving to lend to the United States. If both of these adjustments are perfectly timed to occur at precisely the same moment, it is possible to envision a benign reduction of this symbiosis. The odds of such an exquisitely synchronized rebalancing of both economies are extremely low, in my view. That suggests the growing likelihood that symbiosis is likely to give way to disequilibrium—adding a new source of tension to the U.S.-China relationship.

Unfortunately, that's not the only source of economic tension between the United States and China. Over the 2005–2007 period, fully 45 pieces of anti-China trade legislation were introduced in the U.S. Congress. Although none of these bills passed, that may change. As U.S. unemployment now soars in an ever-deepening recession, the politics of trade frictions may well gather greater support. Treasury Secretary Geithner's warning on Chinese currency manipulation is especially worrisome in that regard. The same can be said of the Buy-America provisions that have slipped into America's recently enacted stimulus package.

At the same time, China must also be sensitive to the impacts of its export-led growth model on its trading partners. Any subsidies—either to its own domestic wages or to its currency—take on heightened importance as China's stature in world trade grows. As now the second largest exporter in the world, China can hardly afford to take that responsibility lightly. Moreover, if China competes unfairly by ignoring environmental degradation and pollution, the world pays a much greater price for the cross-border labor arbitrage than a simple comparison of wages would suggest. To the extent that cost-effective outsourcing ignores environmental considerations, the real wage squeeze in relatively greener economies may be all the more acute.

Resolving the complexities of the U.S.-China economic relationship is an urgent challenge for an unbalanced global economy. As a crisis-torn world now moves into a severe recession, the stakes can only grow larger. As both the U.S. and Chinese economies evolve and change, a fleeting state of symbiosis could well give way to heightened tensions. The time to diffuse those tensions is now—before it's too late.

## China's Policy Imperatives

Ironically, China saw many of these problems coming. As noted above, Premier Wen Jiabao warned that the Chinese economy was "unstable, unbalanced, uncoordinated, and unsustainable." Similar vulnerabilities were anticipated in the 11th Five-Year Plan enacted in 2006, which stressed China's need to embark on a major structural transformation from export- to consumer-led growth.

But the government's execution of this aspect of its plan was lacking. In particular, it failed to build out an institutionalized social safety net—the support system necessary to temper the fear-driven precautionary saving that inhibits the development of a more dynamic consumer culture. As a result, the consumption share of Chinese GDP fell to a record low of 36 percent in 2007—underscoring the dark side of China's macro imbalances that is now so problematic in this global crisis (see Figure 5.11). A severe external demand shock found an unbalanced Chinese economy without a back-up plan.

A proconsumption rebalancing is the only sustainable answer for China. Proactive fiscal stimulus measures, such as the recently announced RMB4 trillion infrastructure-led investment initiative, can help temporarily.

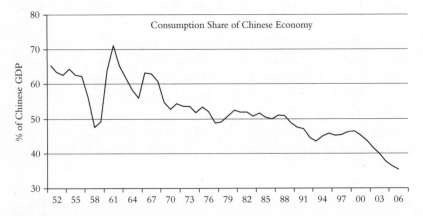

**Figure 5.11**   Chinese Consumption Shortfall

*Source:*   China National Bureau of Statistics and Morgan Stanley Research.

Such efforts borrow a page from China's counter-cyclical script deployed in the Asian financial crisis in the late 1990s and again in the mild global recession of 2000–2001. But these actions are not enough to compensate for the structural vulnerabilities that China's externally dependent growth model now faces as American consumers begin a multiyear retrenchment.

China needs to be bold and aggressive in framing proconsumption policies. It should start by announcing major initiatives on the safety net front. Specifically, China should sharply expand the funding of its National Social Security Fund, which currently has only a little over $80 billion in assets under management—not even enough to provide $100 of per capita lifetime retirement income for an aging Chinese population. China also needs to move quickly in establishing a comprehensive private pensions scheme, as well as in broadening its support to nationwide health and unemployment insurance. Recent passage of an RMB850 billion three-year medical reform plan is an encouraging, but small, step in that direction.

The bottom line for China: Its unbalanced economy must be rebalanced. The export-led growth formula, which served the nation well for three decades, must now give way to the internal impetus of consumer-led growth. For China, the imperatives of such a rebalancing have never been greater. For the rest of Asia—to say nothing of an unbalanced global economy—China's post-crisis economic leadership role hinges importantly on this critical rebalancing.

## Policy Risks

Needless to say, a weakened economy usually doesn't take kindly to suggestions that it ought to increase the value of its currency. That's especially the case for an export-led Chinese economy, where sequential growth slowed to a virtual standstill in late 2008. With overall economic growth remaining weak in early 2009 and currently falling short of the 6 to 8 percent zone that China requires to absorb surplus labor and maintain social stability, the procyclical implications of a tighter currency policy would only add to mounting downside risks.

Little wonder that U.S. Treasury Secretary Geithner's recent remarks on currency manipulation were met with an incredulous response in Beijing. Although such strident rhetoric hardly implies action, it is worth considering the consequences if the war of words leads to outright trade sanctions. The impacts would be felt immediately in financial markets. Given America's reliance on China's funding of its external deficit—a reliance that can only grow in an era of open-ended trillion dollar budget deficits—the United States is in no position to risk reduced Chinese buying of dollar-denominated assets. Yet that is exactly what might occur if a proud but wounded China retaliates to currency-induced trade sanctions imposed by Washington.

Such retaliation could take the form of a China that simply doesn't show up at an upcoming U.S. Treasury auction. That's hardly a trivial consideration for a United States that needs about $3 billion of capital inflows each business day to fund its current account deficit. If China fails to provide its share of America's external funding, the dollar could plunge and real long-term interest rates could rise. A dollar crisis is the very last thing a United States in recession needs. But it could happen if the United States turns rhetoric into action in the form of imposing sanctions on Chinese trade. In short, Washington is treading on increasingly thin ice in blaming the Chinese currency for America's woes. A postbubble U.S. economy is suffering from a major shortfall in domestic demand that is unlikely to be remedied by China bashing. Saber rattling in this climate is both ill-advised and dangerous.

At the same time, it is equally important to underscore what China should not do. First and foremost, Chinese policy makers must not be overly optimistic in counting on the old external demand model to start working again. A multiyear weakening of the U.S. consumer is tantamount to a global consumption shock that will impart a protracted drag on any export-led economy. As such, the imperatives of Chinese rebalancing have never been greater. It is increasingly urgent that China shift its growth model from one that has been overly reliant on exports to one that draws increased support from private consumption.

Nor should China be tempted to use the currency lever or other subsidies to boost its export sector. In an era of rising unemployment and mounting concerns in the developed world over the benefits of globalization, such efforts could be a recipe for anti-China trade sanctions. As previously noted, those actions might then prompt China to reconsider its role as one of America's most important overseas lenders. And then, as was the case in the 1930s, the race to the bottom could be on.

## Wake-Up Call

There has long been a dispute over the English language translation of the Chinese word for crisis. One popular view is that *weiji* roughly translates into the compound phenomenon of both *danger* and *opportunity*. Unfortunately, that meaning—correct or not—has been lost on a world in crisis. Today, more than ever, a world in crisis and recession needs to pull together—not push itself apart. Globalization and its cross-border connectivity through trade and capital flows leave us with no other choice.

The blame game is completely counterproductive in this environment. Those blaming surplus-savings economies such as China for America's unsustainable spending binge ought to be embarrassed. This is a U.S. problem and one that must be addressed at home with a new and disciplined approach to monetary policy, tough regulatory oversight, and more responsible behavior on the part of consumers and businesses, alike. A bubble-dependent economy that lived beyond its means for a dozen years must now accept the reality of having to live within its means—and not holding others accountable for this painful yet necessary adjustment.

Similarly, China needs to accept that the export-led growth formula always had its limits. An unprecedented external demand shock, driven by rare synchronous recessions throughout the developed world, drives this point home with painful clarity. Economic development is not just about producing for others—especially if those others are living beyond their means. In the end, export-led growth must eventually give way to the internal demand of a nation's private consumers. China is ready for this transition and must begin the process as soon as possible.

In short, it is high time for an unbalanced world to begin the heavy lifting of global rebalancing. By framing such an adjustment in the context of the United States and China, the verdict is clear: America needs to save more and consume less, while China needs to save less and consume more.

Easier said than done. But a world in crisis can no longer afford to perpetuate an unstable *status quo*. Global rebalancing is not a quick fix—and therefore, is not all that appealing to myopic politicians. But in the end, it is the only way to put the world back on a sustainable growth track. If there is a silver lining to this crisis, it must be in the wake-up call that it sends to politicians and policy makers throughout this unbalanced world.

# ■ *Afterword* ■

Macroeconomics has its limits and, as any long-standing practitioner would claim, its virtues.

The dismal science is at its best in offering the rigor of an analytical framework—identifying a set of forces or tensions that depict key transitional adjustments for economies in disequilibrium. The business cycle call is classic in that regard—nailing the forecast of a recession or recovery. Closer to home, global rebalancing is a similar analytically driven prognosis—depicting the requisite adjustments of an unbalanced world, as, for example, Asian savers become spenders and American consumers become savers.

The dismal science is at its worst in predicting the timing of such adjustments. Tensions in economies can exist for a long time until they hit their breaking point. Examples are America's seemingly chronic current account deficit, China's surplus saving, and Europe's structural malaise. In each of these cases, there can be little doubt of the endgame—a weaker U.S. dollar, the emergence of the Chinese consumer, or chronically high European unemployment. The questions boil down to when—not if. I know full well from my own experience that, more often than not, the macro practitioner tends to be early in calling for major economic adjustments.

With these caveats in mind, I think it is important to try and tie the loose ends of the *Next Asia* together. In what follows, I attempt to provide a frank assessment of how this story has played out relative to the script I have written over the past three years—three of the most tumultuous years in modern economic history. Rest assured, this is not just an attempt at closure—always an illusion for us macro types. It is mainly an effort to glean insights or lessons from what went right or wrong in the saga of the *Next Asia*—and to draw the implications of what such a post mortem might offer for the future.

## A World in Crisis

My macro framework told me something had to give—and, when it did, that it was probably going to be a very serious problem. I had long focused on the U.S. economy as the potential epicenter of the coming shakeout. I argued that the savings-short, bubble-dependent, overly indebted, income-constrained American consumer was the weak link in the macro chain—not just for the United States but for a still U.S.-centric global economy. I also had long suspected that the bursting of the American housing bubble would probably trigger this implosion—culminating not just in a postbubble U.S. recession but also in a surprisingly synchronous downturn in an increasingly interdependent global economy. I will certainly admit to being early in making this call—writing and speaking of the growing risks of something close to an economic Armageddon as far back as late 2004.

As bearish as I was on the real side of the U.S. and global economy, never in my wildest dreams did I anticipate the full extent of the crisis that was about to embroil financial markets and the financial services industry. The cross-product contagion that was sparked by the bursting of America's subprime bubble in the summer of 2007 went far beyond anything I had ever feared. In retrospect, I should have seen that coming as well. As I look back on my analysis and writings in the final days of the boom, my pieces were laced with a strong sense of foreboding over the looming perils of the bursting of the credit bubble—and the cross-border transmission of the coming shakeout through the "originate and distribute" mechanism of the derivatives explosion. Yet I honestly thought that modern risk management practices—at the micro as well as the macro level—were far more robust than they ended up being. *Mea culpa.*

*Implications:* There is no quick fix for this crisis—nor for a crisis-torn world. The major impacts of this crisis are now in the process of shifting from battered capital markets and the financial services industry to the real side of the global economy. The postbubble shakeout stands to be dominated by a protracted adjustment of the American consumer— providing powerful and lasting headwinds on the demand side of the global economy for years to come. This points to a very subdued postcrisis recovery in the global business cycle—closer to an L-shaped outcome than a classic "V." I worry that myopic and quick-fix-oriented politicians and policy makers have a strong bias toward going back to the old ways of an unbalanced world—led by overextended U.S. consumers and funded by surplus savers in Asia. If that turns out to be the case, I fear another crisis will be in the offing in the not-so-distant future.

## The Globalization Debate

The main thrust of my analysis of globalization is that we tend to take this megatrend for granted. And in doing so, many of the stresses and strains of globalization have been minimized or just plain ignored. For example, the global labor arbitrage—a key aspect of the efficiency solutions for high-cost producers in the developed world—has led to a near stagnation of real wages in high-productivity economies like the United States. At the same time, the speed of a new IT-enabled connectivity between once nontradable service industries has put unprecedented pressure on the job security and wages of long sheltered knowledge workers, triggering a heretofore unique strain of white-collar shock. These powerful and lasting developments have become fodder for an increasingly politicized backlash against globalization.

Reflecting these new and uncomfortable twists in the competitive landscape, I underscored the emergence of important tensions in the globalization debate. These reflect not only the struggle between capital and labor in the developed world but also increasingly contentious frictions between industrial and developing economies. These tensions have not been lost on the world at large. They have played a key role in the ascendancy of prolabor politicians in the West and have been decisive in the apparent demise of the Doha Round of multilateral trade negotiations. Thanks to the enduring insights of British political economist David Ricardo in the mid-nineteenth century, the case for globalization is compelling in theory. But that theory is now in serious need of an update in the twenty-first century.

*Implications:* Far be it for me or anyone else to predict the demise of globalization. However, there is an alternative future that needs to be given more serious consideration in the years ahead—something much closer to a "localization" scenario. In that world, the rising tide of economic nationalism tempts nations to look inward—driven more by self interest rather than by the outward-looking aspirations of collective interest that shape a deeper commitment to globalization. A tough business cycle, exacerbated by sharply rising unemployment and a muted recovery, could well reinforce the tendencies of the localization alternative. At a minimum, that points to an era of heightened trade frictions and far less virtuous cycles for inflation, interest rates, currency adjustments, and economic development.

## Chinese Rebalancing

I have been constructive on the Chinese economy for over a dozen years. I still am. Back in the depths of the Asian financial crisis of 1997–1998, I saw firsthand a China that was cut from a different cloth than the rest of Asia—a China that remained steadfast in its commitment to reforms and financial stability. I argued at the time that this powerful commitment would separate China from the rest of the pack as a new leader of the postcrisis Asian economy. That conclusion has withstood the test of time. I am still struck by China's fierce determination to stay this same course. I remain quite confident that the Chinese economy will continue to play a key role in shaping Asia and the broader global economy for years to come.

At the same time, I must confess to a growing sense of unease over the medium-term prospects for the Chinese economy. China's Premier, Wen Jiabao, had it right when he worried in early 2007 of a China that was "unbalanced, unstable, uncoordinated, and unsustainable." The only sustainable answer to the Premier's complaint lies in the rebalancing imperatives of the Chinese economy, namely, shifting away from an export- and investment-led growth model to one that increasingly draws support from internal private consumption. Yet contrary to my analysis of the past couple of years, the Chinese consumer has failed to deliver in driving this rebalancing—at least, so far. This is a classic example of what it's like to be early on an important macro call.

*Implications:* The longer China defers the heavy lifting of its macro rebalancing, the more I remain convinced that it has to happen. The current crisis in the global economy may serve as an important catalyst to this transformation. China has elected to respond to this crisis by deploying its standard arsenal of what it calls the proactive fiscal stimulus—using infrastructure-led investment to buy time until a snapback in external demand prompts a vigorous rebound in export-led Chinese growth. To the extent that external demand remains weak—very much my conclusion for a postcrisis world—then China will have no choice other than to accelerate its efforts toward a long-overdue rebalancing. I remain confident that China will deliver on that count but concede that the risk remains that I will continue to be early in anticipating this key shift.

## Pan-Asian Challenges

My fascination with Asia has long been with the region's willingness to cope with change. In keeping with this extraordinary attribute, Asia has been quick to reinvent itself in the years following the panregional crisis of the late 1990s. For most of the post–World War II era, Japan was the unmistakable leader of Asia. Now the baton of economic leadership has passed to China. Asia's China-centric supply chain has become a new and important source of panregional growth for most of its major economies, especially Japan, Korea, and Taiwan.

Panregional economic integration has also provided Asia with a new identity. This development cuts both ways: As long as China stays the course on the upside, Asia is fine. But as soon as China faces tougher times—very much the case today—its problems are compounded for the rest of the region. That's pretty much the way it has played out, with every major economy in the region currently either in outright recession or in the midst of a sharp slowdown. A key premise of my Asia view is that it makes no sense to look at this externally dependent region through the lens of decoupling. It is more integrated than ever before and equally more connected to the rest of the world. With export shares of Developing Asian GDP having soared from 36 percent in the late 1990s to 47 percent in 2007, Asia still remains a levered play on global growth.

*Implications:* Asia's unbalanced macro structure could prove especially problematic in the anemic recovery scenario that seems likely for a post-crisis world. Asia will be forced, as a result, to look for new sources of growth. Two candidates are especially promising—internal private consumption and increased panregional economic integration, especially between China and Japan. Meanwhile, India, which has long drawn support from the micro side of its development equation, could well start to close the gap with the rest of the region—benefiting from macro improvements on the savings, foreign direct investment, and infrastructure fronts. Much has been written about this century being the Asian century. If Asia stays the course as a change agent, I very much endorse the prospects of this conclusion. If, on the other hand, Asia gets stuck in the old way and fails to uncover new sources of growth, that verdict may end up ringing hollow.

## U.S.-China Tensions

I have long maintained that the bilateral relationship between the United States and China could well be the most important economic relationship in today's world. At the same time, I have been increasingly worried about mounting tensions on the trade front between these two nations. I got the tension part right; more than 45 anti-China trade bills were introduced in the U.S. Congress over the three-year period, 2005–2007. However, I was wrong to expect those tensions to come to a boil in the form of the enactment of one of those bills. There turned out to be more bark than bite on this key issue.

Once again, it may simply be a matter of being early. As the U.S. recession lingers and the unemployment rate climbs toward 10 percent in the second half of 2009, pressures on already beleaguered American workers will only intensify. Their elected representatives have singled out China—incorrectly, in my view—as the scapegoat in this tough turn of events. It remains to be seen whether Washington will take explicit action in using trade policy as a mechanism of relief. If that turns out to be the case, then I remain convinced China would retaliate by shifting its currency reserve allocation away from dollar-denominated assets. Senior Chinese leaders hinted of such actions by raising concerns in early 2009 about the safety of dollar-based assets and the integrity of a dollar-centric international reserve system. These tensions are clearly a two-way street, with the United States needing China to fund its deficits and China needing the United States to buy its exports. A trade war and the related risk of a dollar-crisis scenario would be a lose-lose scenario for both nations as well as for the world economy.

*Implications:* I must confess that I am now increasingly wary of having cried wolf on this particular concern for too long. Recent developments give me greater pause for thought in believing that Washington would throw down the gauntlet and impose trade sanctions on China. U.S. Secretary of Treasury Timothy Geithner has changed his position recently, backing away from the view expressed during his confirmation hearing when he warned the Chinese of currency manipulation, and the Congress seems to have developed a deeper appreciation of the painful lessons of the trade wars of the 1930s. While I don't want to minimize the risks of mounting trade tensions between these two powerful nations, I am now more hopeful than I have been in a long time that sanity has returned to the U.S.-China trade policy debate and that reason and the lessons of history will ultimately prevail. Still, if I had to put my finger on the biggest potential wildcard in the post-crisis world, an escalation of U.S.-China trade tensions would be at the top of my list.

The *Next Asia* is already coming into focus. Consistent with the region's penchant for change, it looks to be very different from the Asia of the past 30 years. The transition from old to new will need to be driven by a major rebalancing of its economy—with export- and investment-led growth giving way to a more balanced macro structure, increasingly supported by internal private consumption.

This transition will also help Asia come to grips with many of the negative externalities that have arisen from the open-ended industrialization requirements of the region's export machine. Environmental degradation and widening income disparities are two of the most egregious externalities that could be tempered by a rebalancing. Significantly, the coming structural transformation of Asia will require an important refocusing of growth imperatives away from a fixation on quantity, or sheer speed, toward a deeper appreciation of the quality dimension of the growth experience. As such, the long awaited emergence of the Asian consumer is the soul of the *Next Asia*.

Yet there are no guarantees in such a daunting transition. The mounting tensions of a new globalization pose a major challenge for Asia. Fears of a zero-sum globalization loom particularly worrisome in that regard, especially through their impacts on the all-important U.S.-China trade relationship. Those concerns take us full circle to Asia's rebalancing imperatives. Rebalancing is Asia's most effective way to release the tensions—both external and internal—that might otherwise derail the world's most exciting and powerful growth story. The *Next Asia* will be a rebalanced Asia, providing enormous opportunities for the world's largest population mass, as well as for the rest of us in an increasingly globalized world.

# ■ *Sources* ■

## Chapter 1   A World in Crisis

*A Subprime Outlook for the Global Economy*:   Based on a speech delivered at the *World Knowledge Forum* in Seoul, South Korea on October 17, 2007.

*Save the Day*:   Copyright © 2007, *The New York Times*. Reprinted by permission.

*Double Bubble Trouble*:   Copyright © 2008, *The New York Times*. Reprinted by permission.

*Even When the Worst Is Over—Watch Out for After-Shocks*:   This essay was first published as an op-ed article in the *Financial Times* on April 15, 2008.

*Panic of '08: Enough Scapegoating*:   This essay was first published as a column in *The International Herald Tribune* on October 1, 2008.

*Global Fix for a Global Crisis:*   This essay was first published as an op-ed article in the *Financial Times* under the title "Time ripe to go for overkill and forget about underkill" on October 9, 2008.

*Changing the Fed's Policy Mandate:*   This essay was first published as an op-ed article in the *Financial Times* under the title "Add 'Financial Stability' to the Fed's Mandate" on October 27, 2008.

*An Early Leadership Opportunity for Barack Obama:*   This essay was first published as a column in *The International Herald Tribune* on November 6, 2008.

*Dying of Consumption:* Copyright © 2008, *The New York Times.* Reprinted by permission.

*Uncomfortable Truths about Our World after the Bubble:* This essay was first published as an op–ed article in the *Financial Times* on December 3, 2008.

*A Post-Bubble Global Business Cycle:* This essay is based on "Die lange Schwäche der Weltwirtschaft" originally published on January 4, 2009 in Germany's *Handelsblatt.*

*America's Japan Syndrome:* This essay was first published as an op–ed article in the *Financial Times* under the title "US not certain of avoiding Japan-style 'lost decade'" on January 13, 2009.

*Whither Capitalism?:* This essay is based on "Dem Kapitalismus eine zweite Chance" originally published on February 23, 2009 in Germany's *Handelsblatt.*

*After the Era of Excess:* This essay first appeared in "What Matters." Copyright © 2009 McKinsey & Company. All rights reserved. Reprinted with permission.

*Same Old, Same Old:* This essay was first published as an op–ed article in the *Financial Times* on March 10, 2009.

*Depression Foil:* This essay was first published as a BLOOMBERG NEWS® story under the title "Averting Depression as Consumer in U.S. Fades: Stephen Roach" on April 13, 2009. Copyright © 2009 Bloomberg Finance L.P. All rights reserved. Used with permission.

## Chapter 3 Chinese Rebalancing

*China's Rebalancing Challenge:* This essay is based on a speech given on April 22, 2006 at the *Boao Forum for Asia* in Hainan, PRC.

*China's Global Challenge:* This essay is based on a presentation at *The Academic Summit* of the *China Development Forum* on March 22, 2008 in Beijing, PRC.

*Consumer-Led Growth for China:* This essay was first published as an op–ed article in the February 16, 2009 edition of the *Asahi Shimbun GLOBE.*

*China's Macro Imperatives:*   This essay was first published as an op-ed article in the March 27, 2009 issue of *China Daily* and is based on a speech at the 10th *China Development Forum* held March 21-23, 2009 in Beijing, PRC. Reprinted with permission.

*Manchurian Paradox:*   This essay was first published in the May–June 2009 issue of *The National Interest.*

## Chapter 4   Pan-Asian Challenges

*Complacency Asian Style:*   This essay is based on an article published in *Caijing Magazine*'s Annual Outlook 2008.

*The End of the Beginning:*   This essay was originally published in the April 2008 issue of *FinanceAsia.*

*Another Asian Wake-Up Call:*   This essay was originally published in the December 2008-January 2009 issue of *FinanceAsia.*

*India's Virtuous Cycle:*   This essay was first published in *The Economic Times* of India under the title "India can now emerge as Asian superpower" on June 2, 2009.

*Risks of an Asian Relapse:*   This essay was first published in the June 8, 2009 Vol.173 No. 22/*Time Asia* edition of *Time* magazine under the title "No Sail: Why rising hopes for an Asia-led recovery are bound to fail." Copyright © 2009 Time Inc. Reprinted by permission.

## Chapter 5   U.S.-China Tensions

*A Slippery Slope:*   Testimony before the U.S. House of Representatives Sub-committees from Ways and Means, Energy and Commerce, and Financial Services; May 9, 2007.

*The Politics of Trade Frictions:*   This essay was prepared for a conference on "China's Exchange Rate Policies" in Washington DC, sponsored by the Peterson Institute for International Economics, on October 19, 2007.

*A Wake-Up Call for the US and China: Stress Testing a Symbiotic Relationship:* Testimony before the U.S.-China Economic and Security Review Commission of the U.S. Congress; February 17, 2009.

# ■ *About the Author* ■

**Stephen Roach** has been a thought leader on Wall Street for over 30 years. Currently the Hong Kong-based Chairman of Morgan Stanley Asia, for the bulk of his career he served as the firm's chief economist, heading up a highly regarded team of economists around the world. His recent research on globalization, the emergence of China and India, and the capital market implications of global imbalances has appeared widely in the international media and in testimony before the U.S. Congress. Prior to joining Morgan Stanley in 1982, he worked in senior capacities at Morgan Guaranty Trust Company and the Federal Reserve Board in Washington D.C. He holds a Ph.D. in economics from New York University and was a research fellow at the Brookings Institution. He is a jet-lagged resident of multiple time zones, splitting his time between eight Asian countries and his family home in Connecticut.

# ■ *Index* ■